THE SCOTS & THE TURF

THE SCOTS
& THE TURF

RACING AND BREEDING –
THE SCOTTISH INFLUENCE

ALAN YUILL WALKER

BLACK & WHITE PUBLISHING

First published 2010
This edition first published 2017
by Black & White Publishing Ltd
Nautical House, 104 Commercial Street
Edinburgh EH6 6NF

1 3 5 7 9 10 8 6 4 2   17 18 19 20

ISBN: 978 1 78530 141 4
Copyright © Alan Yuill Walker 2010, 2017

Cover Images: One for Arthur (front) © REUTERS/Alamy Stock Photo;
Lucy Alexander (back/left) © Allstar Picture Library/Alamy Stock Photo;
Derek Fox and Lucinda Russell (back/centre) © David Davies/PA Archive/PA Images;
Keith Dalgleish (back/right) © Grossick Racing Photography

The publisher has made every reasonable effort to contact copyright
holders of images in the picture section. Any errors are inadvertent and
anyone who, for any reason, has not been contacted is invited to
write to the publisher so that a full acknowledgement can be made
in subsequent editions of this work.

A CIP catalogue record for this book is available
from the British Library.

Typeset by Iolaire, Newtonmore
Printed and bound by Nørhaven, Denmark

To Sarah, William and Freddie

CONTENTS

AUTHOR'S ACKNOWLEDGEMENTS

When it comes to the recording of both racing and breeding in the British Isles down the years the twin towers have been Weatherbys' two publications, *The Racing Calendar* and *The General Stud Book*.

While the *GSB* remains the standard work of reference, the annual *Form Book* (Flat and National Hunt) published by *Raceform* now represents the official returns for all racing results. *Raceform* comes under the umbrella of the *Racing Post*, which superceded the *Sporting Life* as the sport's daily newspaper.

These titles, together with the *Biographical Encyclopedia of British Flat Racing* and *Timeform's Annual Racehorses*, have been the principal sources of reference in the writing of *The Scots & the Turf*. Additional information has been gleaned from many and varied sources, both published and unpublished, much of it gleaned from personal encounters down the years.

So far as individual books are concerned special mention should be made of *The Tartan Turf* (by the late Tom McConnell: Mainstream Publishing, 1988), while obituaries from *The Bloodstock Breeders' Annual Review* (1912–81) have, as always, proved invaluable.

Many people featured in *The Scots & the Turf* helped as did an assortment of friends and colleagues. While they are too numerous to mention individually a very special word of thanks is due to Jonathan Garratt, formerly of Scottish Racing, without whom I would probably have never found a publisher!

I am also much indebted to Sandy Kilpatrick, who was a

tremendous help regarding photographs, my brother-in-law, Sandy Taylor, who kept me well-briefed about the Borders, together with the team at Black & White Publishing, and Susan Cameron for her proofreading expertise.

It should also be emphasised that the raison d'etre of the book was to highlight the contribution made by Scots and people of Scots' descent to racing and breeding within the British Isles – it does not include those who have done so overseas. That would be to open a whole new can of worms!

Just for the record the cut-off point for this revised edition of *The Scots & the Turf* was Glorious Goodwood in August 2017 so any eventualities after that stage of the season missed the proverbial boat.

To everyone who helped and lent encouragement I am extremely grateful. I just hope there are not too many people who think they should have been included, but have been omitted for whatever reason – to them I can only apologise.

FOREWORD

by The Duke of Roxburghe

When Alan Yuill Walker asked me to write the foreword to *The Scots & the Turf*, my first reaction was to feel very flattered to have been asked, something which has never happened to me before! My second thought was that the book would be fairly short, what could there be to justify writing a whole book on this subject?

How wrong I was, as this fascinating book travels through time from the 1800s to the present day with an intriguing insight into the many ways the Scots have played a major role in British racing. No aspect of racing has been untouched by Scottish influence; there have been owners such as the Earls of Rosebery and the Queen Mother, trainers led by that wonderful character Kenneth Oliver, and the indomitable Mark Johnston, a great jockey in Willie Carson with his seventeen classic victories, and successful breeders like Reg Tweedie and Sandy Struthers.

The racehorses owned or trained by Scots play their part too with famous names from the world of National Hunt racing like The Benign Bishop, Wyndburgh, Merryman and Freddie. I was staggered to discover that in the 1800s Scotland had more than fifty racecourses, which dropped to eleven in the twentieth century, and down to just five now. It should be no surprise that so many participants, both human and equine, started in the hunting field, but that so many had their roots in the Borders both surprised and delighted me!

In the last few years the Scots have come to the fore ever more prominently. With Lucinda Russell rising up the training ranks with

One For Arthur winning the Grand National for the redoubtable Two Golf Widows, not to mention the successful exploits of Lucy Alexander and Keith Dalgleish, all of these merit a chapter in their own right.

Alan has pulled together all the strands and links involving Scottish people and the Turf into a most illuminating and interesting insight of the sport we all love so dearly. I learnt an enormous amount, as I am sure will all who read it.

Floors Castle
Roxburghshire

PREFACE

My own fascination regarding the Scottish connection with the Turf came purely by chance.

A son of the manse from Innerleithen in Peeblesshire, my father practised as a GP for many years – he had studied agriculture and medicine at Edinburgh University. However, his first love was farming and after the Second World War, in which he served in the Cameron Highlanders, he bought a farm near Bishop's Waltham, between Winchester and Southampton.

This was next door to the Upham trainer, Bill Wightman. Bill allowed me to ride my pony on his Stephen's Castle Down gallops and I remember being taken round evening stables aged twelve or thirteen and being totally enthralled by the whole set-up.

Subsequently my father returned to his native Scotland to farm in East Lothian, outside Haddington, where Wilfrid Crawford trained in those days. In the opposite direction a few miles down the A1 at Dunbar was George Boyd's very successful stable, Tilton House at Westbarns.

As a schoolboy during the 1950s I was fortunate enough to visit Tilton House and I also went racing at George Boyd's local course, Edinburgh (now Musselburgh), where he saddled so many winners. I can vividly remember the excitement of meeting George Boyd (I always thought he looked like James Cagney) and being taken round evening stables by him.

Some of the stables as I recall were laid out like a traditional cow byre with an internal passageway running in front. My lasting impression on a wet and windy evening was just how snug all the horses seemed in the fading light, with an intoxicating smell of horses, bran mash and tack. In a previous incarnation Westbarns had been a brewery and doubtless these stalls with their cobbled floors had been utilised by the dray horses – Clydesdales to be sure.

Looking back it's fair to say that my passion for racing was initiated inadvertently by these two trainers and thereafter keeping tabs on their runners became a daily routine. Few would have recognised Bill, who was born and brought up in England, as a fellow Scot, but that is how he regarded himself – his father came from Edinburgh and his mother's family from the Shetland Islands.

George Boyd and Bill Wightman represent the parameters in terms of the personalities that make up the contents of this book. Of course many others fall between these two extremes, most of them actually born in Scotland but, like so many of their brethren, migrants across the border that separates the two countries.

Alan Yuill Walker
Kintbury
Berkshire

1

THE BACKGROUND TO RACING
IN SCOTLAND

The title of this book, *The Scots & the Turf*, sounds ominously like an oxymoron. Surely the monumental contribution that those from north of the border have made in most spheres of human endeavour does not embrace to any marked extent the altogether frivolous world of racing?

While the Scots and the Irish, surely the number one nation when it comes to the Thoroughbred (there are appreciably more foals born in Ireland than Great Britain every year), may share intellectual and artistic talents, they have an entirely different ethos to work and play. The Catholic Church always seemed to encourage the mass invasion by priests to the annual National Hunt Meeting at Cheltenham as it always used to be known – there is no knowing how often their prayers were answered, but there never seemed to be any shortage of cash to back the next Irish good thing. Such conduct would never be condoned by the Church of Scotland – it's not that long ago that the puritanical members of the Kirk would have had apoplexy at the suggestion of a harmless game of tennis on the Sabbath.

Fortunately, Scotland has had a plentiful supply of aristocrats with sporting tastes. There are three dukes living within a twenty-mile stretch of the Tweed Valley, with the Duke of Roxburghe at Floors Castle, outside Kelso, and further upstream the Duke of Buccleuch at Bowhill, close to Selkirk, and the Duke of Sutherland at Mertoun, near St Boswells.

In their different ways these dynasties have all made a valuable contribution either directly or indirectly to the world of racing and breeding. The present Duke of Roxburghe is a major breeder, trading

1

as Floors Farming, as well as owning Kelso racecourse. The Buccleuch family's contribution has revolved largely around the Buccleuch Hunt which they have sustained over a prolonged period, a pack of foxhounds that played such an integral part in the education of many good chasers.

Still substantial landowners, the Sutherlands made part of their Newmarket estates available for the creation of the Equine Fertility Unit, which was named Mertoun Paddocks after their Borders home, but unfortunately closed down in 2007 through lack of funding.

However, the Sutherland family has another significant involvement in the veterinary world. On another part of their Stetchworth Estate, close to the National Stud, is the new Newmarket Equine Hospital, the brainchild of Greenwood Ellis and Partners, formerly based off Newmarket High Street. Ten years in the planning and eleven months in the building, it stands on a fifteen-acre site and cost £10m. The largest and most up-to-date facility of its kind in Europe, the NEH opened for business in the autumn of 2008.

The fact that Guy Roxburghe owns Kelso, one of only five racecourses north of the border, should be sufficient to guarantee that the course has an assured future, although his personal priority when it comes to racing is the Flat rather than jumping. Perth is in a similar situation. Another jumping-only course, it is in the lovely grounds of Scone Palace, home to the Earls of Mansfield, while Hamilton Park, a green oasis outside Glasgow, owes much historically to the patronage of the Dukes of Hamilton as well as Lord Hamilton of Dalzell.

As home of the Scottish Grand National and the Ayr Gold Cup, Ayr is Scotland's premier racecourse, in a beautiful location looking across the Firth of Clyde to the Isle of Arran. It was transferred there from its previous location at Craigie in 1907. The first stewards to preside at the new venue were the Scottish grandees, the Duke of Montrose, the Earl of Eglinton and Winton, and the Marquess of Bute. And 'Fine Scotch Whisky was 2s/6d a bottle, carriage paid'.

During the second half of the twentieth century no one gained more pleasure from having winners at the annual Ayr Western Meeting in September than the 6th Earl of Rosebery. He and his trainer, Jack Jarvis, would be represented by a strong raiding party from Newmarket for the Scottish fortnight. In those days the Jockey Club allocated a generous travel allowance to raiders from the south and, although they would stay in Scotland for the duration, that financial inducement was paid every time a horse ran, so multiple appearances were nothing untoward. It was an arrangement which Lord Rosebery was quick to exploit.

Every year the Western Meeting or Ayr Gold Cup Festival, as it is referred to nowadays, stages the Harry Rosebery Stakes. Without Rosebery's undoubted influence his local course of Musselburgh would have been lost like Lanark and Bogside. Since those precarious times, a flourishing jumping course has been added.

Between them Harry Rosebery and his father owned and bred five Derby winners. The family's Scottish home, Dalmeny House, is at South Queensferry. How many racegoers travelling from Edinburgh to Perth, either by rail or by road, as they prepare to cross the Firth of Forth, realise the significance of this location in racing terms? Dalmeny House is three miles to the east of the great Forth Railway Bridge, while three miles to the west is Hopetoun House, home to the 2nd Marquess of Linlithgow, breeder of the 1960 Grand National hero, Merryman II.

No two trainers in Scotland did more to promote jumping in Scotland than Stewart Wight at Grantshouse in Berwickshire, and Kenneth Oliver at Hawick in Roxburghshire. Stewart Wight dominated proceedings in the 1950s and 1960s with a string of talented chasers headed by that gallant mare, Bramble Tudor, and that iconic grey hunter-chaser, The Callant. No sooner had Stewart Wight retired than Ken Oliver maintained the impetus, inheriting the gallant Wyndburgh upon his marriage to that horse's owner-breeder, Rhona Wilkinson.

While stalking deer and grouse shooting are primarily Highland pursuits, sport in the Lowlands has long been typified by hunting and fishing, and nowhere is this more in evidence than along the fertile Tweed Valley. Here are to be found the old mill towns of Innerleithen, Hawick and Galashiels, which flourished until the outbreak of the Second World War thanks to the indigenous blackface sheep that grazed the steep, heather-clad hillsides of Peeblesshire with their trickling burns, as well as the bleak expanse of the Cheviots and the Lammermuirs. But by the middle of the twentieth century these woollen mills were in terminal decline.

With sheep farmers facing particularly hard times, there came an increasing emphasis on arable and alternative livestock farming. There are as good stockmen in the Lowlands of Scotland as are to be found anywhere in the British Isles and inevitably many of them are sporting farmers. Small wonder then that hunts in the area, like the Jedforest, the Duke of Buccleuch's, the Lauderdale and the Berwickshire, flourished as did the North Northumberland pack just across the River Tweed.

The area around Selkirk and Hawick across to Berwick-upon-Tweed on the east coast has proved a wonderful source of talented horsemen. In the old days the upper classes and the more prosperous members of the farming community always had a stud groom to look after their hunters. Just as many an English household employed a Scottish housekeeper, a Scottish cook or a Scottish nanny, so the outside staff of a substantial English country house might well include a Scotsman looking after their horses.

In modern times this trend for Scots migrating to England to seek employment in the bloodstock world is exemplified by the Cowe brothers from Berwickshire. In 2005 Footstepsinthesand and Motivator won the Two Thousand Guineas and the Derby respectively. Both colts were bred in Newmarket, the former by Anthony Oppenheimer of Hascombe Stud, and the latter by Salah Fustok of Deerfield Farm.

Hascombe was managed by Walter Cowe and Deerfield by Bill Cowe and just for good measure their eldest brother, Jim, was manager to Prince Khalid Abdullah at his Estcourt Estate, near Tetbury in Gloucestershire. Before crossing the border Walter had looked after New Brig, one of Scotland's most successful ever jumping stallions, at the Forth Stud, near North Berwick.

Jim, Walter and Bill were born and bred near Duns where their father was the long-serving stud groom to Charles Baillie, nephew of Sir James Miller, the second baronet. As a subaltern in the 14th Hussars, James Miller bought Sainfoin just before his Derby victory in 1890 and then established the Hamilton Stud at Newmarket where the horse

4

sired his 1903 Triple Crown winner, Rock Sand. Hamilton Stud is now part of Tattersalls' extensive sales complex.

The Pritchard-Gordons, who hail originally from Aberdeenshire, are three more brothers closely involved in racing and breeding – tanker-owner Giles owned Slaugham Park Stud in West Sussex; former Newmarket trainer Gavin was executive director of the Thoroughbred Breeders' Association before taking up a new appointment in 2008 as executive chairman of British Bloodstock Marketing; and Grant, formerly racing manager to Prince Khalid Abdullah of Juddmonte Farms, now runs his own agency, Badgers Bloodstock.

No owner-breeder has a bigger stake in bloodstock breeding in Great Britain and Ireland than Sheikh Mohammed, also owner of Inverinate, a magnificent sporting estate of over 50,000 acres in the West Highlands at Kyle of Lochalsh. The Highlands have proved a rich source of racehorse names over the years, highlighted by the greatest steeplechaser of all time. Arkle was named after a mountain on the Westminsters' estate in Sutherland, as was the sensational 1967 Grand National hero, Foinavon (who now has a fence at Aintree named after him); so too was another fine chaser in Ben Stack.

In the autumn of 1981, Sheikh Mohammed bought Dalham Hall Stud, Newmarket, now the centre of his worldwide bloodstock empire. The problem of finding a suitable stud manager was resolved by promoting Alec Notman, the existing stud groom. And when the time came to appoint a senior stallion man, the position was filled by another native of Roxburghshire, Ken Crozier, who had previously worked at Floors Stud.

Alec Notman left school aged fifteen to assist his father, who was stud groom to Marjorie Robson-Scott at Newton Stud, between Jedburgh and Hawick. Apart from three years of National Service in the Argyll and Sutherland Highlanders, Alec spent his working life with Thoroughbreds. Newmarket became his adopted home and for many years he was at Lord Derby's Woodlands Stud where he remembers the great Hyperion in his dotage.

Another key figure is John Ferguson, whose success in buying yearlings for Mollers Bloodstock inevitably brought him to the attention of Sheikh Mohammed, for whom he became the big white chief at Dalham Hall. John Ferguson, whose grandfather hailed from Aberdeen, followed his father into the Scots Guards. Surely no one in the history of bloodstock sales worldwide has signed more sales dockets for more money than John Ferguson!

However, in June 2017 the bloodstock world was shocked when John Ferguson resigned after a quarter of a century's involvement. It was a most unexpected development as he had not long given up his own string of jumpers comprising ex Sheikh Mohammed horses, to concentrate on his exclusive role as chief executive of the Godolphin/Darley organisation.

Thanks to vastly increased media coverage, particularly on television, there is a new awareness of just how vital members of staff are in any successful racing stable. Sir Michael Stoute, John Dunlop, Mark Johnston and John Gosden are just four top trainers who have relied heavily on Scots staff over the years – Stoute with head lad Jock Brown; Dunlop with travelling head lad Rob Hamilton; and Johnston with assistant Brian 'Jock' Bennett.

One of John Gosden's key personnel is Robert Havlin. An invaluable work rider, this Scot had been riding an increasing amount in public for the stable, but he failed a drug test at Saint-Cloud in October 2016 and an appeal against the subsequent six-month ban by the French authorities was dismissed.

If anyone is deserving of a long-service medal it is Eddie Watt, who was born at Ecclefechan, near Lockerbie. He retired aged seventy-six in 2009 having worked at Castle Stables, Arundel since the early 1950s for Willie Smyth and his son, Gordon, before John Dunlop took charge. During that extended period he was travelling head lad for twenty-four years and head lad for the last twenty-four years. His favourite horse was Ragstone, who realised a lifetime's ambition for the Duke of Norfolk, then Her Majesty's Representative at Ascot, by winning the Gold Cup.

The name Lockerbie calls to mind Graham Lockerbie, who was travelling head lad to Peter Easterby during the golden years of Sea Pigeon, Night Nurse and Alverton; he also had a spell as head lad to John Hammond at Chantilly. Having ridden successfully for Denys

Smith and Arthur Stephenson, Graham himself trained for a short period in Yorkshire, before retiring to his native Dumfries.

Another Scot, Larry Poland, who was a key figure at the late Gordon Richards' Greystoke stables in Cumbria for over thirty years, was associated with his two Grand National winners in Lucius (1978) and Hallo Dandy (1984). Few trainers turn out more winners than Sussex-based Gary Moore (father of Ryan and Jamie) who took on as his assistant the former Epsom trainer, David Wilson, an old Harrovian from Troon. And Dave Goodwin came down from Roxburghshire to do two Derby winners for Henry Cecil in Slip Anchor (1985) and Commander in Chief (1993).

For a prolonged period George Foster, who hails from Kelso, was an indispensable cog in the wheel at the historic Manton training establishment then owned by the Sangster family outside Marlborough in Wiltshire. During his time there he assisted Michael Dickinson, Barry Hills, Peter Chapple-Hyam, John Gosden and Brian Meehan. For an interim period he trained himself in Lambourn and he also held the fort at Manton for a brief period in 1999 when bridging the gap between Chapple-Hyam and Gosden. In 2007 he returned to train in Scotland before retiring.

Of course countless others beaver away in the background with scant recognition. Representing just the tip of the iceberg are Robert Forbes, who was stud groom to the Hue-Williamses of Woolton House Stud, breeders of the great Altesse Royale before retiring to Inverness-shire; Ken Oliver's former head lad, Robert Irvine from Galashiels, who became stud groom to Bold Edge's breeder, Lady Whent; and Sandra Morton, a native of the Isle of Bute, who found employment with West Country breeder, Rosemary Pease, mother of former leading Chantilly trainer, Jonathan Pease.

If asked to name the one Scotsman who has made the biggest contribution to racing in recent times, most people would surely nominate Mark Johnston, who has been the driving force in putting Middleham in North Yorkshire firmly back on the map as a training centre. He restored Middleham's classic credentials by winning the 1994 Two Thousand Guineas with Mister Baileys, and in 2004 he won the One

Thousand Guineas with the Scottish-bred Attraction. Every year he features near the top of the list of leading trainers and in 2009 he became the first trainer to saddle 200 domestic winners during a calendar year.

Mark Johnston concentrates on Flat horses, but one of his compatriots, Alan King, is making a great name for himself as a trainer of jumpers at his Wiltshire base, near Marlborough. The son of a farmer from Lanarkshire, he is now rated as one of the outstanding National Hunt trainers in the country and just for good measure he also maintains a very good ratio of winners to runners on the Flat.

Back in the nineteenth century the great trainer, Mathew Dawson, and his compatriot, James Waugh, left Gullane in East Lothian, eventually setting up their stalls in Newmarket where they made their names not only with the horses in their charge, but also as patriarchs of families destined to produce generations of successful trainers. One of the last prominent Scottish-born trainers in Newmarket was the late Alec Stewart from Kinross-shire, but sadly the trainer of champion Mtoto died all too young.

Metaphorically speaking, Willie Carson is head and shoulders above any of his compatriots when it comes to Scottish jockeys. In a career spanning forty years, Willie was five times champion and rode the winners of seventeen English classics, including the Derby four times. He also has the unique distinction of riding an English classic winner of his own breeding – Minster Son in the 1988 St Leger. That is a monumental achievement and one which has never received the credit it deserves. He also bred the 2015 Derby runner-up, Jack Hobbs.

Three more distinguished Scots-born Flat jockeys since the war are Duncan Keith, Sandy Barclay and Richard Quinn, all of whom have ridden classic winners and are or were in the very top class. The most prominent Scottish jump jockey of recent vintage is Peter Niven. Now training at Barton-Le-Street, outside Malton, he partnered the great majority of his thousand-plus winners for Cleveland-based Mary Reveley.

So far, a handful of Scottish owners have been involved with Group 1 winners during the twenty-first century. They are headed by Manchester United supremo, Sir Alex Ferguson, part-owner of Rock of

Gibraltar. Raced in partnership with Sue Magnier, but carrying his red and white colours, 'The Rock' became the first horse to win seven consecutive Group 1 races and was voted Europe's 'Horse of the Year' as a three-year-old in 2002.

This outstanding racehorse duly retired to Coolmore Stud. However, a very acrimonious and public dispute ensued regarding Alex Ferguson's entitlement to stud fees before the impasse was finally settled out of court. The Scot also has jumpers in training with Paul Nicholls, and was part-owner of What A Friend, winner during the 2009–10 season of the Lexus Chase at Leopardstown and the Totesport Bowl at Aintree, both Grade 1 events.

Another Scot involved in professional football, as a players' agent, is Willie McKay. Previously owner of a private stable at Bawtry, near Doncaster, he raced Les Arcs, winner of two Group 1 sprints in 2006, the Golden Jubilee Stakes (formerly Cork & Orrery Stakes) and July Cup – not bad for a six-year-old gelding who had previously been beaten almost seventy lengths in a maiden hurdle at Cartmel!

Another aged gelding trained in Yorkshire was Borderlescott, hero of the 2008 and 2009 Nunthorpe Stakes for fellow Scots, Jimmy Edgar (an education officer for the Scottish Football Association) and Les Donaldson. Borderlescott was named after Donaldson's company, Border Rail & Plant Limited. When he won the 2008 all-aged sprint championship at Newmarket (York was abandoned due to waterlogging), he established a new course record for five furlongs on the July Course. Borderlescott has a race named after him at Musselburgh.

If you cannot beat them, join them, is an old maxim. Jim Hay, a native of Glasgow and a graduate of Strathclyde University, together with his oriental wife Fitriani, have made their mark as owners in the second decade of the twenty-first century. At one time they owned the famous Uplands Sables in Upper Lambourn where Fred Winter trained and were substantial investors in yearlings. But they then focused their attention across the Irish Sea with funds accrued from his JMH Group of companies which have been heavily involved in the enormous building programme in Dubai masterminded by Sheikh Mohammed.

Around 2010–11, the Hays acquired a substantial interest in three star racehorses from Aidan O'Brien's omnipotent Ballydoyle stable: the Derby runner-up, Fame and Glory, who proceeded to win the Ascot Gold Cup, along with two Galileo colts, Cape Blanco and Treasure Beach, successful in the two previous runnings of the Irish Derby. In 2011, Treasure Beach carried Fitri Hay's colours to victory in three Grade 1 events in the USA.

The Hays' sizeable string of horses is managed by Alex Cole, son of the Whatcombe trainer and their association with Aidan O'Brien and his leading patrons continues. Amongst their current horses in training at Ballydoyle is the homebred Deauville. Yet another son of Galileo, he won the 2016 Grade 1 Belmont Derby in the USA. In 2017 the Hays had the surprise winner of the Group 1 Sussex Stakes with the seven-year-old gelding Here Comes When.

From a Scottish viewpoint, one of the most gratifying developments when it comes to trainers north of the border is the relentless climb up the ladder enjoyed by Keith Dalgleish (see Chapter 34). 2017 was only his seventh season since setting up at Carluke in Lanarkshire, but the former jockey with Mark Johnston has not only taken over from Jim Goldie as the country's leading Flat trainer, but he must also be the first trainer north of the border to have a mixed string well in excess of one hundred horses. It really has been an instant success story.

The Scots & the Turf is an attempt to place on record the surprising, yet considerable, contribution that Scots have made to racing and breeding within the British Isles. The main text of the book concentrates on major players in differing roles, while the appendix is an alphabetical list of additional people who have also made a significant impact. Needless to say the selection is arbitrary, but hopefully it provides a fair cross-section of worthy individuals.

2

'TO BE BORN IN CHINA DOES NOT NECESSARILY MAKE ONE CHINESE'

Ascertaining whether someone is Scottish or not can be problematical. Of course it is not a prerequisite to be born in Scotland, although this alone may be a sufficient qualification to represent Scotland in sport or even join a Scottish regiment. Traditionally one of the country's greatest exports has been people, so it is irrational to exclude someone of Scottish ancestry simply because they were born elsewhere – if one is born in China it does not necessarily make one Chinese.

Indeed, that is to treat people in the same way as racehorses. Officially they have a suffix, be it IRE, FR, USA or whatever, indicating their place of birth rather than their true country of origin. For example, a foal born in Ireland from a mare in British ownership and normally resident in Great Britain will automatically be classified IRE rather than GB. With broodmares travelling regularly between the two countries to be covered by a stallion, this is a common occurrence, as some mare owners prefer the foal to be in utero in transit rather than newly born, but it gives a totally misleading picture so far as nationality is concerned.

It goes without saying that all the people who feature in this book are intrinsically Scots or, at least, have very strong Scottish lineage in the male line and all of them have made an invaluable contribution to the Turf in one way or another. In fact, there is one person who, while Scottish blood ran in his veins, never regarded himself as Scottish and consequently was never thought to be Scottish. To the casual observer John Hislop (see Chapter 24) appeared the quintessential Englishman. A distinguished author and journalist, one could safely say that his preference would have been for Rupert Brooke rather than Robert Burns!

The problem of determining who qualifies as Scottish is exemplified to an extreme degree by the McCalmont family. To the racing world at large they are regarded as Irish, but in fact they migrated to the north of Ireland from Scotland early in the seventeenth century.

Two equally Scottish names are Dunlop and Henderson. John Dunlop, who presided over Castle Stables, Arundel, considers himself to be Northern Irish (he completed his National Service in the Royal Ulster Rifles), but with a name like Dunlop he probably qualifies as an Ulster Scot. Nicky Henderson of Seven Barrows, outside Lambourn, is none too conversant with his forebears, but he confirms that they did originate north of the border; indeed, he once possessed a kilt!

Such is the predominance of Irish jump jockeys that most people presume that Sir Tony McCoy (with twenty consecutive championships to his name, the greatest ever rider over obstacles) is one of them, but he was born in Co. Antrim in Northern Ireland. Conversely Donald 'Ginger' McCain, who, with four Grand National victories to his credit shares top honours with Fred Rimell, says in his autobiography that his family might well come from Ireland, but that he himself was born in Lancashire.

Some might argue that attributing nationality to the male line at the exclusion of the female line is akin to the laws of primogeniture, in other words decidedly unfair and somewhat old-fashioned. Be that as it may, the system has stood the test of time as has the custom of a woman adopting her husband's name upon marriage. Consequently there must be many prominent figures in racing as in other walks of life who have Scottish distaff relations, but are not perceived as Scottish.

An historical illustration of just such a situation occurs with Sir Abraham Bailey (1864–1940). He was born in South Africa, where he accumulated a vast fortune through mining in the Transvaal and property in what was then Rhodesia. His mother was born Ann Drummond McEwan and she was Scottish, as her name clearly indicates. Created a baronet in 1919 for his services to the British Empire, of which he was a staunch supporter, Abe Bailey became one of the most prominent owners in England before and after the First World War.

Abe Bailey's bloodstock interests were indelibly linked with his great friend, Donald Fraser. Also of Scots descent, Donald owned Tickford Park Stud, Newport Pagnell, Buckinghamshire. Dark Ronald, the first good horse owned by Abe Bailey, stood at Tickford Park where he sired his homebred celebrity, Son-in-Law. Son-in-Law sired Foxlaw (bred by Donald Fraser), who in turn sired Tiberius, both of whom won the Ascot Gold Cup in Sir Abe Bailey's colours. He also won the 1936 Oaks with Lovely Rosa.

Of course, it is impossible to ascertain how many people fall into a similar category to this South African 'Randlord', but there is always the temptation of 'making the foot fit the shoe'. However, one thing is certain – any book of this nature is certain to run into difficulties concerning nationality.

Turning to the present, one of the more glaring anomalies concerns a prominent father and son combination. Harry Beeby, chairman of Goffs UK (formerly Doncaster Bloodstock Sales based in Hawick) is an Englishman, who adopted Scotland as his home; whereas Henry, the managing director of Goffs UK, was born and bred in the Borders. He certainly regards himself as Scottish and is a tremendous Scottish rugby fan. The anomaly will be perpetuated for, as chief executive of the new Goffs/Doncaster merger, he and his American wife and their children now reside in Ireland.

Henry Cecil, the outstanding trainer of his generation, was extremely proud of his Scottish ancestry. Not only were he and his twin brother, David, born in Aberdeen, but also their mother, Rohays, was the only daughter of Sir James Burnett of Leys and her family home was sixteenth-century Crathes Castle, near Banchory, in Kincardineshire, by the River Dee. (Crathes is famous for its magnificent Jacobean painted ceilings.) It became the custom for Henry Cecil to fly the flag, literally, at Warren Place on the occasion of a Group 1 victory – the standard depicts the Horn of Leys, a historic heirloom gifted in 1323 by Robert the Bruce.

Henry was knighted in 2011 not long after Frankel provided him with a twenty-fifth English classic victory. By the time the colt retired as a four-year-old, he was unbeaten in fourteen starts and on ten occasions it was necessary to hoist Henry's personal standard to the top of the flagpole. Many aficionados considered the son of Galileo to be the outstanding racehorse within living memory and the ten-times champion trainer regarded him as 'the best I've seen in my lifetime'.

There was a great outpouring of emotion when Henry Cecil died from cancer in June 2013. In becoming a Knight of the Realm for services to racing, he was following in the footsteps of both his step-father Cecil Boyd-Rochfort and his former father-in-law Noel Murless, both of whom trained for Queen Elizabth II. Surprisingly perhaps, Henry never emulated them in that regard, despite his ancestor William Cecil being Queen Elizabeth I's right-hand man.

Another leading trainer with strong Scottish connections is East Ilsley-based Hughie Morrison, responsible for the July Cup winners, Pastoral Pursuits and Sakhee's Secret. His elder brother, Alastair, is the 3rd Lord Margadale, a name taken from their estate on the northern part of the Isle of Islay in the Inner Hebrides, which was acquired in 1851 from the Campbells of Islay. It is an idyllic spot, synonymous with the finest of malt whiskies and shooting driven woodcock. Islay was also a regular port of call in the days when the Royal Yacht cruised annually around the Western Isles.

At their Tisbury home, near Salisbury, the Margadale family own Fonthill Stud, which has a very special claim to fame. Within the space of four years from 1975 to 1979 their homebred mare, Set Free, produced Juliette Marny and Scintillate, both of whom won the Oaks carrying the colours of James Morrison (father of Alastair and Hughie), and Julio Mariner, victorious in the St Leger. In so doing Set Free became the first mare to be accredited with three individual English classic winners for 100 years. Juliette Marny, incidentally, is the third dam of the Hughie Morrison trained Group winner, Intrepid Jack, who was bred by the family stud.

It was one of Hughie Morrison's forebears, a nineteenth-century draper's assistant, who proceeded to establish an enormous warehouse business in London. He cornered the market in black crepe, much in demand for funerals and the interminable periods of mourning during the Victorian era, which must have made an appreciable difference to the Morrison family coffers. The apocryphal story goes that towards the close of the previous century another of Hughie's ancestors hiked from the Highlands to the Wallops on the border of Hampshire and Wiltshire to seek his fortune.

Another Old Etonian, Hugo Palmer was assistant to Hughie Morrison for a brief period. Then following fifteen months in Australia, Hugo took out a licence for the 2011 season at Newmarket's Kremlin Cottage Stables with a handful of horses, many of them acquired on spec and duly syndicated.

Within the space of six seasons Hugo's stables had become one of the most fashionable in town, his string having expanded to 170 with a long list of high profile owners. Topping his ever expanding role of honour are classic winners Covert Love (2015 Irish Oaks) and Galileo Gold (2016 Two Thousand Guineas).

In 2017 Hughie Morrison was the subject of a BHA investigation when one of his runners was found to have contravened the rules with regard to a prohibited substance, a charge which could cost him his licence – the trainer promptly offered a £10,000 reward to help apprehend the perpetrator. Hugo Palmer earned different headlines by helping the cause of lady jockeys, Josephine Gordon rewarding him with success at Group level.

Whether one counts Hugo as a Scot is debatable. A scion of the family associated with Huntley & Palmers, the famous biscuit manufacturers from Reading, he was brought up on the Scottish Borders at Manderston, a very substantial Edwardian mansion at Duns in Berwickshire, where he learned to ride at an early age. This is the home of his father the fourth Lord Palmer (whom he will succeed one day); he featured prominently in a television documentary on the House of Lords.

Another large house in the Borders, Henderside, near Kelso, is also the home of former trainer, Peter Harris. One time father-in-law of the late Walter Swinburn, who partnered three Derby winners, he retired to Scotland when Walter took over the running of his stables in Hertfordshire.

One of the biggest and most successful supporters of National Hunt racing has been Andy Stewart. The majority of his jumpers are trained by Paul Nicholls in Somerset and they race in the collective ownership of the Stewart family, which also includes his wife, Judy, and grown-up sons, Mark and Paul – Andy's great-great-grandfather was born and lived in Glasgow.

The Stewarts, who have homes in London (Mayfair), Sussex and Barbados, have raced a string of distinguished French-breds. The very first horse they owned outright was Cenkos. A brilliant two-mile chaser, Cenkos was held in such high esteem that his owner named the stock-broking arm of his business Cenkos Securities. It is another of his financial services companies, Collins–Stewart, which provided the choice of racing colours, red, white and black – and his business offices include a branch in Edinburgh.

After some near misses, the Stewarts had to wait the best part of a decade before achieving a first victory at the Cheltenham Festival when Celestial Halo prevailed in the 2008 Triumph Hurdle. Since then they have owned a multitude of top performers, but none more so than Big Buck's, who won four consecutive World Hurdles from 2009–12.

Andy Stewart has also put a toe in the water on the Flat and in 2007, in partnership with Paul Roy, then chairman of the British Horseracing Authority, he shared a sensational Group double at Glorious Good-wood with the juveniles Strike The Deal and Fleeting Spirit, running in the name of 'The Searchers'. Fleeting Spirit proceeded to gain a famous victory in the 2009 July Cup.

Two more leading patrons of Paul Nicholls' West Country stable have been Margaret and Harry Findlay. Mrs Findlay, the joint owner of 2008 Cheltenham Gold Cup winner, Denman, lives at Bourne End, near Marlow, but was born in Perth, whereas her son, Harry, was born in Paisley. Harry's parents moved to Essex when he was five. His father belonged to a family of fishermen from Cullen on the Banffshire coast. This picturesque seaside town with its brightly painted cottages is synonymous with Cullen skink, a nutritious soup made from smoked haddock.

A professional gambler living near Bath, Harry Findlay somehow managed to master the seemingly impossible Scoop6 challenge which formed an intrinsic part of Channel 4's racing coverage on a Saturday afternoon. He also had a considerable number of horses in training, mostly in partnership, with a variety of trainers under both Rules. However, in June 2010 this colourful character was warned off by the British Horseracing Authority for six months for laying one of his own horses to lose.

Arbroath is another fishing port on Scotland's east coast famed for its smoked haddock (known as Arbroath smokies). It was home to Walter Buick, the father of William Buick. William, an exceptionally talented young rider, who was joint champion apprentice for the 2008 season, was actually born in Norway, where his father was eight-times champion jockey. In January 2010 William Buick, twenty-one, was appointed stable jockey to the powerful John Gosden stable before switching his allegiance to Godolphin.

No owner in the north has spent more money on jumpers than Graham Wylie. Founder of Technology Services Group and formerly involved with the software giant, Sage, he and his wife Anthea used to own the vast majority of the 180 or so horses trained by Howard Johnson until the Co Durham trainer lost his licence due to an infringement of the rules regarding medication.

The outstanding performer trained by Howard Johnson for the Wylies was Inglis Driver, who scored three times in the Grade 1 World Hurdle at the Cheltenham Festival – retired to his owners' Chesters Stud, adjacent to Hadrian's Wall, he died in 2009. Following his trainer's enforced absence, the Wylies reduced their involvement and one of the new trainers they patronised was Willie Mullins in Ireland. The new partnership has enjoyed conspicuous success, highlighted by a Grade 1 double on the same day of the 2017 Cheltenham Festival with Nicholas Canyon in the Stayers' Hurdle (the former World Hurdle) and Yorkhill in what used to be called the Golden Miller Chase.

As he was born in Hawick, Graham Wylie has frequently been referred to as Scottish, but this was merely coincidence as his parents just happened to be living in the Borders at the time.

First cousins and leading bloodstock agents, Charlie Gordon-Watson and James Wigan share a common Scottish ancestor with the late David Morley, the former Newmarket trainer – their maternal grandfather,

Charles Gordon. A successful racehorse owner himself, he belonged to that coterie of Glaswegians whose fortune was derived from the world of shipping on the Clyde. James Wigan's mother, Dawn Wigan of West Blagdon in Dorset, was the most successful foal vendor of her day thanks to descendants of the grey foundation mare, Pelting, whom she inherited from her father.

Dawn Wigan's late brother-in-law, Michael Gordon-Watson, was at one time manager at William Hill's Whitsbury Manor Stud outside Fordingbridge in Hampshire. Formerly owned by the celebrated book-maker, William Hill, and now by his nephew, Christopher Harper, Whitsbury is probably the most important public stud outside New-market. Two of Gordon-Watson's successors have Scottish antecedents – Bob Urquhart, who went on to run his own Hunsley House Stud in East Yorkshire, and Charles Oakshott.

Charlie Oakshott exemplifies just how confusing nationality can be. He was actually born in Kenya, where his father was a tea and coffee planter, and was under two years of age when the family returned home, taking up residence in Kirkcudbrightshire, first outside Castle Douglas, and then Barwhinnock. Brought up on a livestock farm, Charlie was educated at Merchiston Castle in Edinburgh. Although Charlie's father is not Scottish, his mother's family come from Perth-shire – although she herself was born in Rhodesia. Not surprisingly, Charlie identifies with Scotland rather than England.

For a long time, Bob McCreery, who died in 2016, was a leading figure in the racing and bloodstock world and he is another who can claim Scottish blood on the distaff side. Twice leading amateur rider in the 1950s and the breeder of two classic winners, High Top and Old Vic (a champion sire of jumpers), his grandmother was a descendant of eighteenth-century road builder John Loudon McAdam, who was born in Ayr. It was just after the First World War that she built the family home, Stowell Hill, on the border of Somerset and Dorset. However, the McCreerys consider themselves Northern Irish by origin.

It would be all too easy to overlook the present Lady Halifax as a successful Scottish breeder. From Melrose in Roxburghshire and a member of the Younger brewing family, the former Camilla Parker

Bowles (confusingly!) owned the occasional mare in her own name at her husband's Garrowby Stud in East Yorkshire. It was Camilla Halifax who bred the 1997 Irish One Thousand Guineas winner, Classic Park, dam of the 2005 Derby runner-up, Walk in The Park. Incidentally Hardiemma, the dam of the Halifaxes' homebred 1978 Derby winner, Shirley Heights, gained her only two successes in modest company at Lanark and Ayr carrying the primrose and light green sleeves of Edinburgh owner, Mrs Ian Miller.

Another member of the 'beerage' was Sir John Rutherford, owner of the great Solario, winner of the Ascot Gold Cup and the most expensive stallion ever sold at public auction, realising 47,000 guineas in July 1932. Today some of his relatives live at Rutherford Lodge, Kelso, but that is misleading. John Rutherford, a bachelor whose title lapsed upon his death, was a native of Blackburn in Lancashire, home to the family's Salford New Brewery.

The proximity of Northumberland and Cumbria to the Scottish Borders also presents complications, particularly with regard to Penrith. Bob Armstrong, father of Gerald (Willie Carson's original mentor) and Sam, themselves leading trainers in Middleham and Newmarket respectively, all have surnames readily identifiable as 'north country'.

Bob Armstrong was actually born in Penrith, whereas Tommy Robson, whose own mentor was the great Scottish trainer Stewart Wight, was born on one of the Duke of Northumberland's farms and was a graduate of the Edinburgh veterinary school. Tommy made a particular contribution to the Scottish Grand National – he rode the winner, Queen's Taste, in 1953; rode and trained the 1962 winner, Sham Fight; and trained Brasher to score in 1965, the last time the race was run at Bogside. The previous year he had saddled Magic Court to win the Champion Hurdle for Jimmy McGhie, one of the biggest milk retailers in Dumfriesshire.

Tommy Robson was succeeded at Penrith by Gordon W. Richards (the initial W was used to differentiate from the great Flat jockey Gordon Richards, before he was knighted), who was succeeded in turn by his son, Nicky. Later Gordon Richards' former head lad, Dick Allan, trained Pat's Jester to win the 1988 Scottish Champion Hurdle for R.P. Adams Ltd, a Selkirk-based chemicals company. Pat's Jester accompanied Dick when he moved from St Boswells in Roxburghshire to Cornhill-on-Tweed in Northumberland. Pat's Jester also won the Bula Hurdle, Cheltenham, and was runner-up in the King George VI Chase.

Although Gordon Richards was not Scottish himself, some of his owners were, amongst them Fiona Whitaker, for whom he saddled the Grand National winner, Lucius, and David Stevenson, formerly of Edinburgh Woollen Mills Ltd, one of the biggest supporters of National Hunt racing in Scotland at one time.

Considering that Hector Christie served in the Gordon Highlanders during the Second World War before becoming private trainer to Countess of Lindsay at Kilconquhar in Fife, one might have thought that this one-time prisoner of war was a Scotsman, but not so. Later the Old Etonian moved to Lambourn, training Fortina to win the 1947 Cheltenham Gold Cup for Lord Grimthorpe, whose son, Teddy, who succeeded his father, is Prince Khalid Abdullah's racing manager. The only entire to win the Gold Cup, Fortina became one of the most successful sires of chasers of all time. Although Lady Lindsay's colours incorporated the Lindsay tartan, she was a member of the Shaw family, colliery owners in the West Riding of Yorkshire.

Just as backgrounds can be misleading, so too can names. Bruce Robertson Hobbs, who became the youngest rider ever to win the Grand National when prevailing at the age of seventeen on Battleship (trained by his father, Reg) in 1938, may sound Scottish, but in fact his family came from the Shires, where they were steeped in the world of hunting and dealing.

Amongst the leading trainers in Newmarket is Michael Bell who saddled Motivator to win the 2005 Derby. Bell may be a name synonymous with the invention of the telephone and a well-known proprietary brand of whisky, but Michael's connection with Scotland is through his maternal grandfather, Sir Stewart Menzies, a legendary figure in the annals of the British Secret Service – he gave Scottish author, Ian Fleming, the inspiration for the James Bond character 'M'.

One of the most influential names in *The General Stud Book* is Perdita II, dam of the celebrated own-brothers, Persimmon and Diamond Jubilee, for the future King Edward VII. She was bred by the 2nd Earl of Cawdor, owner of Cawdor Castle, Nairn, the only private castle in Scotland to have a drawbridge. Perdita raced for David Falconer, for whom she won the Ayr Gold Cup in 1884. David Falconer left Scotland to establish a thriving jute business in London. His nephew, Hugh Falconer, who was chairman of the British Wool Marketing Board, farmed at Reston, near Eyemouth, in Berwickshire and rode as an amateur between the wars.

Conversely there is a handful of Englishmen who made their names in Scotland. For an intermediate period in the 1830s William I'Anson became private trainer at Gullane in East Lothian to William Ramsay, an Edinburgh landowner, for whom he trained the remarkable Lanercost. The pride of Scottish racing enthusiasts, this versatile horse won the inaugural Cambridgeshire in 1839, the 340-mile trip from Gullane to Newmarket being undertaken in a three-wheeled horse-drawn van. Two years later Lanercost won the Gold Cup at Royal Ascot.

Subsequently William I'Anson returned to Malton, where he bred many of his own horses. These included Blink Bonny (1857 Derby and Oaks), and her son Blair Athol (1864 Derby and St Leger). Unbelievably he had reacquired Blink Bonny's dam, Queen Mary, from a Forfarshire farmer in foal to a Clydesdale stallion. Blair Athol was four times champion sire in the 1870s.

William I'Anson's son of the same name, who was born in Gullane, also became a trainer in Malton, while another son, Robert, was considered the best jump jockey of his day. Taking up training at Epsom, Robert saddled the entire, Austerlitz, to win the 1877 Grand National as a five-year-old ridden by his eccentric owner, Freddy Hobson – his riding technique over jumps involved holding onto the cantle of his saddle! William I'Anson Snr's great-grandson, Tom I'Anson Gates, trained at Lewes after the Second World War.

Both Harry Whiteman and Gerry Laurence trained in their native England until taking up residence at the famous Cree Lodge stable in Ayr (see Chapter 10). However, the man who succeeded where all other Scots had failed was John Leadbetter from the West Midlands. He saddled Rubstic to win the 1979 Grand National, and this horse was the solitary National winner to be trained in Scotland until One For Arthur in 2017 (see Chapters 21 and 32). How ironic that he should be trained by an Englishman!

Then there is the case of Lockerbie-based Andrew Parker, trainer of the 2010 and 2012 Scottish Grand National hero, Merigo. He may have been the first Scottish-trained winner of Scotland's premier chase since Cockle Strand prevailed for Ken Oliver in 1982, but Andrew was born in Hexham and he succeeded his father, Colin, who was born in Cumbria. And just for the record, Andrew's brother, David, who is assistant to Pauline Robson at Capheaton, outside Newcastle, was born in Hawick.

Because it is so difficult to ascertain who qualifies as Scottish and who does not, some deserving personalities will, inadvertently, have been omitted from this book. Of course, there has to be some limit on who can reasonably be perceived as Scottish. Neither the Morrisons nor the Stewart family, for example, feature in the main text, as they are deemed to be just too far removed from their Scottish roots. While they are certainly more Celtic than Anglo-Saxon, one has to draw the line somewhere.

Some will say that if one must differentiate between United Kingdom citizens, the only people who should be regarded as Scottish are those who were actually born in Scotland. Those who subscribe to that view would have to include Henry Cecil in *The Scots & the Turf*, but exclude the late Queen Mother. So that is obviously nonsensical! One just has to use one's discretion and admittedly that can all too easily be misinterpreted.

3

HISTORY HAS EXERTED A
SINGULAR INFLUENCE

The Stuart kings played a pivotal role in the development of racing and breeding in Great Britain. Although Queen Elizabeth I had made it a penal offence to 'make over a horse to the use of any Scottishman', her successor was King James VI of Scotland and I of England. This monarch was responsible for establishing the small market town of Newmarket on the border of Suffolk and Cambridgeshire as a fashionable centre for field sports, most notably hunting, hawking and coursing.

In 1660, following the Cromwellian era, the House of Stuart was restored to the throne with James VI's grandson, King Charles II (1630–85), who built a royal palace at Newmarket, a seal of approval that soon earned it the reputation as the headquarters of racing in England, the open expanse of heath land being ideal for the purpose. He founded the Royal Plates and rode in races himself. In 1665 he initiated the Newmarket Town Plate which is still in existence, albeit his decree that it should be run on the first Thursday in October *ad infinitum* has fallen by the wayside. Not only was the king nicknamed 'Old Rowley' after his favourite hack – it also gives its name to the course over which the two Newmarket classics are run.

It is remarkable that Ascot, probably England's other greatest racecourse along with Epsom, also owes its origin to the House of Stuart. It was King Charles II's niece, Queen Anne, who founded the home of the Royal Meeting. The daughter of King James II (who succeeded his brother, Charles II), Anne inherited the Stuarts' love of the chase, albeit as a spectator only, as her outsize physique precluded any active participation. Traditionally the Royal Ascot Meeting always opens with the Queen Anne Stakes, a convention that was reinstated in 2008 after a temporary lapse.

Newmarket and Ascot are two of the great pillars supporting the very existence of the Turf as we know it today. Racing without them would be akin to cricket without Lords or The Oval, or golf with no St Andrews or Muirfield. Although Newmarket and Ascot are two of the most famous racecourses in the world, few racegoers would be familiar with their origins. The simple truth is that, like so many enduring institutions, their existence was fortuitous rather than planned, resulting from the passing fancy of two related British monarchs whose nationality in this instance was unequivocally Scottish.

King Charles II was also inadvertently responsible for another of England's great racecourses, Goodwood. Situated some 175 feet above sea level on the Sussex Downs, overlooking the Solent and Chichester harbour, it is regarded as the most picturesque racecourse in the country. Its owner is the present Duke of Richmond and Gordon and it was the 3rd Duke who started racing on his country estate in 1801. The title had been created in 1675 for one of Charles II's illegitimate sons, born to a mistress, Louise de Keroualle.

In 2007, the tercentenary of the Act of Union between England and Scotland, the Duke of Richmond felt it an appropriate moment to publicise his own Scottish connections. From August through to October, Goodwood House displayed 'Scotland in Sussex' and 'The Gordons at Goodwood' with a host of artefacts, portraits and prints, furniture and silver, letters and books, celebrating the Scottish ancestry of the Royal House of Stuart – together with the Duke's own Scottish connection through the Lennox and Gordon families. The original family home, Gordon House, was located north of Aberdeen.

Nowhere in the United Kingdom is the horse more revered than on the Scottish Borders, with its long history of vicious tribal feuding, both cross-border and inter-family. This is manifested down to the present day by the so-called common riding. This unique tradition takes place annually in the towns and villages on the Scottish side of the Borders that were constantly under attack from the English in medieval times – the peel towers in this part of Scotland and the north of England were built specifically to guard against such invasion.

In those days, the land on both sides of the border was divided into marches, with wardens appointed to try and keep the peace between the warring factions. At the heart of the troubles were the border towns of Hawick, Jedburgh and Kelso, which were situated in the Scottish middle marches. The feuding started in the late thirteenth century and lasted for over 300 years, reaching a peak in the mid-1500s. It was not until King James VI acceded to the English throne in 1603 that the troubles finally receded.

The Scots had the reputation as a hard race and the border reivers (robbers, marauders or plunderers) probably did as much as anyone to foster that popular concept, but these were fraught times. Life depended on survival of the fittest, so murder, theft, kidnapping, arson, extortion and rape were everyday occurrences. No one was safe and no livestock could be left unguarded. Mounted raiding parties could number 300 or more and they encompassed everyone across the social divide. Their apparel – white leather jackets and steel helmets – gave no indication of their individual standing in the community.

Such men had to be proficient riders and it is only to be expected that horses would play a major role when it came to recreation, so inevitably they indulged in racing their horses. The Stuart kings were the first to import good stock from Hungary, Poland and Spain, and they helped to improve the native breed – the Borders horses of the time tended to be small. The prizes were usually bells and a reminder of these medieval trophies dating from the 1580s occurs every June with the running of the Carlisle Bell which is on the same card at Carlisle as another historic event, the Cumberland Plate. In 2017 the Carlisle Bell was transferred from the local Tullie House Museum for permanent exhibition at the new National Heritage Centre for Horseracing and Sporting Art in Newmarket.

Until the closure of Lanark racecourse in 1977 (up to the late 1990s it staged trotting races and point-to-points), the Lanark Silver Bell was reputed to be not only the oldest established race in Great Britain, but also the oldest race still staged at its original venue. When the charismatic Richard Coeur de Lion presided over the throne of England, his counterpart in Scotland was King William the Lion. He was frequently in residence at Lanark Castle, in order to hunt and watch horses competing on the muir. It is reputed that sometime during his reign (1165–1214) he inaugurated the race for a 'siller tanker and bell'.

Racing became well established in Scotland in the sixteenth and seventeenth centuries, when meetings invariably formed part of a town's annual celebrations. By 1621 the sport was so popular that the Scottish Parliament passed an Act introducing an early form of betting tax. Anyone winning '. . . the summe of an hundredth merks within the space of twenty four houres . . .' should give the surplus to the church.

During the nineteenth century, Scotland even had a locality known as the 'Newmarket of Scotland'. Nowadays Gullane (pronounced 'Gillun' by some, much to the chagrin of the locals), north of Haddington and east of North Berwick, is a golfer's paradise, but in those bygone days what must now be fairways were gallops. Gullane continued as a training centre until 1891 when the Court of Session in Edinburgh declared that generations of trainers has been utilising part of the Dirleton Estate illegally. All this coincided with Gullane Golf Club building a new clubhouse and the Honourable Company of Edinburgh Golfers moving to Muirfield.

At one time Scotland had more than fifty racecourses, but that number had dwindled to just eleven in the twentieth century. The decrease was not due to lack of support, but rather the prerequisite for improved facilities. The courses to disappear during the 1900s were Oatridge (last meeting 1901), Dunbar (1906), Paisley (1907), Dumfries (1914), Bogside (1965) and Lanark.

As was the case in other parts of the country, Scottish racecourses were severely disrupted for the duration of the Second World War. Only Edinburgh and Lanark staged meetings in 1940 and 1941. Lanark resumed in 1945 with Ayr, Edinburgh and Hamilton Park back in business the following year. It was not until 1947 that the jumpers returned to action at Bogside, Perth and Kelso.

The traditional home of the Scottish Grand National, Bogside played an important role during hostilities as an air defence site protecting the adjoining Ardeer explosives factory; Perth was next door to RAF Scone Park; and Kelso was an army camp for British and Polish troops. Ayr, Hamilton, Edinburgh and Lanark were all utilised by the army in one capacity or another. Edinburgh also had a Home Guard detachment, while Lanark had a joint RAF involvement.

Nowadays there are just five racecourses in Scotland: Ayr, Mussel- burgh, Hamilton, Perth and Kelso. Ayr and Musselburgh stage both Flat racing and jumping; Hamilton is restricted to the Flat; and Perth and Kelso are jumps-only courses. Significantly, perhaps, all are inde- pendently owned, but since 2000 they have come under the promotional umbrella of Scottish Racing. Its annual report for 2016 showed that racing in Scotland generated more than £300 million to the economy, creating over 3,400 full-time jobs and was second only to football as a spectator sport.

As the solitary Grade 1 venue north of the border, Ayr is Scotland's premier racecourse under both Rules. The Ayr Gold Cup Festival in September, formerly known as the Western Meeting, is Scotland's pre- mier Flat fixture. Since the closure of Bogside, Ayr has also been the home of the Scottish Grand National in April – on the same card is the Scottish Champion Hurdle. The first running of the 'West of Scotland Grand National' with a prize of £197 was at Bogside in 1867.

Ayr, which benefits from the relatively mild weather enjoyed on that section of the west coast thanks to the Gulf Stream, is close to two of Scotland's world famous golf courses, Turnberry and Royal Troon. It has a long and distinguished heritage. Official records date back to 1777, but racing of some description was taking place in the vicinity as far back as the sixteenth century. In 1907 the venue was transferred to its present location at Craigie, no distance from Alloway, Robert Burns' birthplace.

The Scottish Government celebrated the 250th anniversary of the national bard with Homecoming Scotland 2009, and William Hill, spon- sors of the £150,000 (Ayr) Gold Cup, commissioned a special gold trophy hand-crafted by Graham Stewart from Dunblane, whose handiwork is to be seen in the Scottish Parliament building. There is also a corre- sponding silver trophy for the Silver Cup and each bears an inscription from Burns' poem, 'The Auld Farmer's New Year Morning Salutation to his Auld Mare, Maggie'.

The Gold Cup, which dates from 1804 and became a handicap in 1855, was always promoted as the most valuable sprint handicap in Europe. Also staged on the Saturday of this two-day autumnal highlight are two other old established contests, the Doonside Cup, a Listed race over 10 furlongs, and the Firth of Clyde Stakes – the latter is for two-year-old fillies and is the only Group race run at Ayr. Another juvenile event is the Listed Harry Rosebery Stakes on the previous day. Two more Listed races are the Rothesay Stakes in May and the Land O'Burns Stakes in June – one of the stands at Ayr is called Rothesay after the Duke of Rothesay, aka Prince Charles.

From 1988 to 2005, Ayr was also home to the Scottish Classic, which metamorphosed into the Scottish Derby – originally a Listed race founded in 1979, it was promoted from Group 3 to Group 2 status in its new guise. The first Group race in Scotland, it had an extremely misleading title, being run over a mile and a quarter, and was open to older horses. Unfortunately the race never attracted many runners and was invariably farmed by fashionable stables from the south – Michael Stoute won four of the last five runnings.

In 1989 Ayr staged a bona fide classic when the St Leger was transferred there after the ground at Doncaster had been declared unsafe the previous Saturday. The winner was the Henry Cecil-trained Michelozzo. The only time that the oldest classic was lost altogether since its inception in 1776 was when Lord Rosebery's Blue Peter was denied the opportunity of landing the Triple Crown, the race being cancelled due to the outbreak of the Second World War. Ironically ground conditions on the Flat course at Ayr have brought their own problems, culminating with a seven-horse pile-up on the home bend in July 2009.

Ayr has also had to survive a management crisis in recent times and its precarious finances were only ever going to be resolved with commercial ownership. In May 2003 the Western Club sold the course for £9.3m to two partners, the Dawn Group, a Glasgow-based construction company, and Thorntoun Limited, a firm specialising in health care. Their combined resources succeeded in attracting the necessary investment, enabling the racecourse to embark on a £35m face-lift with Coral bookmakers lending support as major race sponsors.

However, shortly before the Ayr Gold Cup festival in 2008, at a time when advance bookings and corporate hospitality were at record levels and the season's attendances were at their highest for fifty years, the new owners unexpectedly put the racecourse back on the open market. At that stage more than £14m had been spent on improvements, but the downturn in the overall economy in general, and its effect on building in particular, meant that the necessary funding to complete the master-plan could not be sustained – the balance of the money was to have come from residential and commercial developments on surplus land for which planning permission had taken much longer than anticipated.

The possibility existed that the racecourse (held on a ninety-nine-year ground lease) and the Western House Hotel might be sold separately. Ironically, with racing in Scotland apparently booming as never before, the prospects for Ayr's continued involvement has never looked more precarious, a state of affairs underlined by the vacancy created at the historic Cree Lodge training stables following Linda Perratt's departure. It transpired that the only prospective purchasers were the Reuben brothers on behalf of Northern Racing, but in early 2010 they withdrew their tentative offer.

There has been racing at Hamilton Park, Scotland's only designated Flat course, since the late eighteenth century, but the present course opened in 1926. Always innovative, it became the first racecourse in Britain to stage not only the first evening meeting (18 July 1947), but also the first morning meeting (8 May 1971). A valuable new race was introduced in 2017, the £30,000 Almada Mile in July, named after a street in the town.

Since 1973 Hamilton has been owned by a trust with all profits being ploughed back into the business. With prize money for 2017 topping the £1m mark for the first time, the course benefits from its proximity to Glasgow and the M74. Evening fixtures from May through to September combined with a pop concert are well supported. Two main attractions are the Saints & Sinners meeting in June, and the Scottish Stewards' Cup run over 6 furlongs in July.

From 2009 to 2011, Hamilton actually lost its prestigious Saints & Sinners charity meeting to Ayr. However, when the authorities decided to resurrect the historic Lanark Silver Bell, which had been in mothballs since the closure of Lanark, Hamilton was given preference over Ayr so this iconic symbol of Scotland's historic racing heritage returned to its rightful home in Lanarkshire.

Another race to have acquired a permanent home at Hamilton is the Glasgow Stakes, which is the same race that used to be run at the York Ebor Meeting. This Listed event is run on the same Friday evening as the Scottish Stewards' Cup. One race that has lost its Listed status is the Braveheart Stakes in May, while the winner of the Scottish Trophy in August receives the Lord Hamilton of Dalzell Memorial Challenge Cup.

Despite its proximity to Scotland's industrial and commercial heartland, Hamilton Park, within the high-walled grounds of the old palace, is a green oasis with its manicured lawns, well-maintained flower beds and colourful hanging baskets. With a profusion of mature trees and Tinto Hill clearly visible on the horizon (at over 2,200ft the highest point in Lanarkshire), this qualifies as one of the best-run small racecourses in the country. In 2007 it became the first racecourse in Scotland to receive the Racehorse Owners' Association's (ROA) gold standard, signifying overall excellence in the race-day experience for owners and their runners, an accolade it has sustained ever since.

In 1816, Edinburgh races were transferred from Leith Sands, where they were dependent on the tidal surges in the Firth of Forth, to their current location nearby on the meadows at Musselburgh. Apart from the Second World War and an outbreak of cholera in Edinburgh in 1832 (when sport was transferred to Gullane), racing has continued unabated at Musselburgh down to the present time – the 6th Lord Rosebery saved the course from closure during the cutbacks of the 1960s. Today the buildings have a sense of uniformity in design and layout that sets Musselburgh apart from most racecourses, all of which blends admirably with the 'honest toun' itself. In 2007 it was awarded five-star status by the tourism body, VisitScotland.

As part of Holyrood Week, the Queen visited Musselburgh racecourse on 8 July 2016, for a double celebration, the bicentenary of the racecourse and her own ninetieth birthday. This was promoted as a family day and the band of the Royal Regiment of Scotland and the pipes and drums of the Royal Scots Borderers were on hand to mark the occasion. On a previous visit twenty-one years earlier Her Majesty had opened the Queen's Stand.

On Easter Saturday 2017 Musselburgh staged two valuable handicaps to commemorate the Queen's visit, the £100,000 Queen's Cup (1 mile 6 furlongs) and the £50,000 Royal Mile. The Musselburgh executive have a sense of occasion as on Derby Day the entire card is sponsored by Edinburgh distillers, Ian Macleod & Co, which also incorporates Edinburgh Gin. This includes the £80,000 Edinburgh Cup (1 mile 6 furlongs) and a Listed race for fillies over 7 furlongs. On the Saturday before Royal Ascot, there is the £100,000 Scottish Sprint Cup over 5 furlongs.

Old-timers at Musselburgh will also appreciate the Le Garçon d'Or Handicap which recalls the winner of thirty-four races from 1960 to 1972. One of the many racecourse bars is named after this stalwart and two more commemorate the Scottish-trained celebrities, Rockavon and Freddie.

Since jump racing was introduced in January 1987, Musselburgh, in conjunction with East Lothian Council, has implemented a ten-year plan of phased improvements, making it one of the best appointed small courses in Great Britain. The final stage was the construction of a state-of-the-art stables complex with accommodation for over 100 horses, which was opened officially by Alex Salmond, First Minister for Scotland, in June 2010. Unfortunately, a £12m blueprint to create Scotland's first all-weather track, which was to be floodlit, had been scuppered by the Scottish Executive three years earlier.

In July Musselburgh stages two days (Saturday and Sunday) of harness racing. The Musselburgh Fair Day Races, which have been in existence since 1893, are considered by the British Harness Racing Club to be the most prestigious of the year and they include the Famous Musselburgh Pace Cup – the Derby of the trotting world, this is the culmination of a series of heats at the meeting. The Famous Musselburgh Pacer itself is run on the Sunday, which is designated as a family race day for the Heart of Midlothian Football Club.

Diversity has long been the keyword at Musselburgh, where the links of the historic Old Course are regarded as the oldest surviving golf course in the world, dating back to 1672 – six Open Championships were staged here between 1872 and 1892. Another major attraction is an athletics competition over 110 metres, dating back to 1870, which coincides with the New Year Meeting (this claims to be the oldest professional athletics race in the world). There is also the Musselburgh Silver Arrow, an annual archery competition originating in the mid-seventeenth century.

The Saturday following One For Arthur's 2017 Grand National victory he was paraded at Musselburgh on a day featuring the inaugural Queen's Cup. However, the euphoria soon evaporated. It transpired that the management team at Musselburgh had for some time been at loggerheads with East Lothian Council, which owns the course, and was operating under a restricted temporary licence. Furthermore the British Horseracing Authority declared that should their differences not be resolved by June 2017 the licence would be revoked. A temporary truce was negotiated just in time, but the future of Musselburgh as a racecourse remained far from certain.

Racing at Perth on Tayside takes place in the grounds of historic Scone Palace, home to the Earls of Mansfield. Once the capital of the Picts, it has great historic significance from the crowning ceremonies for kings of Scotland and as a seat of parliament. Once home to the Stone of Scone (or Stone of Destiny), which was recovered from its temporary home at Westminster Abbey, the palace has the longest room in Scotland, a gallery stretching 142ft, along which Charles II walked to his coronation.

The earliest reports of racing in the vicinity of Perth date back to 1613 when competition took place on the South Inch for one of those ubiquitous bells. Myth or folklore, but Bonnie Prince Charlie was reputed to have mingled amongst the spectators at one race meeting prior to the Jacobite Rebellion. The final meeting on the North Inch took place in 1892 and it was not until 1908 that it was resurrected at Scone as a jumping only venue. Prize money at the festival meeting held to celebrate Perth' centenary was £250,000, with a £40,000 three mile chase, the most valuable race ever run at Britain's most northerly course.

With only fifteen days' racing a year, sport at Perth is off the radar for the winter months, their restricted season lasting from April through to September. The highlight of the year is the three-day April gathering of the clans culminating with the Highland National over an extended three and three quarter miles. The River Tay Handicap Chase and the Gold Class Novices' Hurdle (Listed) feature on the two previous afternoons. In addition there are four two-day meetings with the City of Perth Gold Cup staged on a solitary day in June. A new Listed race is being introduced at Perth's April fixture in 2018 with a mares-only chase over three miles.

As is the case with Cartmel in Cumbria, the unique parkland atmosphere at Perth draws disproportionately large crowds and is supported by an ever-increasing number of trainers from all over the UK, including such distant locations as Wales and the West Country, not to mention the north and south of Ireland. The leading English-based trainer in recent years has been Nigel Twiston-Davies, although his Cotswold yard is a nine-hour drive by horsebox. Another colleague to regularly tackle the 380-mile journey from Gloucestershire to Perth is Tom George.

Irish raiders have become a particular feature of racing in Scotland in recent times, with Co. Meath-based Gordon Elliot enjoying particular success on his regular forays across the water. Gordon has been a great supporter of Perth since saddling his first winner there as a professional trainer in May 2006. Trainer of the 2007 Grand National winner, Silver Birch, his tally of winners at Perth is well over 100.

Situated in the Borders, where so many famous jumpers have originated, Kelso has a unique reputation with the hunting and farming fraternity thereabouts – where else is every winner rewarded with a bag of carrots? This very testing course at Berrymoss, owned by the Duke of Roxburghe and located mid-way between Newcastle and Edinburgh, has been attracting National Hunt enthusiasts from both sides of the border since 1867. The historic main stand, which was erected when Kelso catered only for the Flat, is very close to the course itself, affording spectators an unrivalled view of the action. And there are homely log fires and mulled wine to help keep the cold at bay.

The Tweedie Stand, opened in 2000 in memory of Freddie's popular owner-trainer and long-serving chairman and steward at Kelso, Reg Tweedie, provides a number of well-appointed first-floor boxes. In the distance, a pointed obelisk can be seen which has connections with the poet James Thomson, who is credited with the words for 'Rule Britannia'.

The Kelso management is extremely proud of the fact that for many years every race has been sponsored, one of the main beneficiaries being the £45,000 Scottish Borders National in December backed by Persimmon Homes, whose principal Duncan Davidson lives nearby on the other side of the Tweed.

In February there is the Morebattle Hurdle. Nicky Henderson is a good supporter of this Champion Hurdle trial when he likes to get in a bit of fishing as well, but he was in for a bit of a shock in 2010 when his previous year's Triumph Hurdle victor Zaynar was beaten at odds of 1–14, the shortest-priced loser in the history of jump racing. Not as big a shock, however, as when Equinoctial won the Grants Whisky Novices' Handicap Hurdle at Kelso on 21 November 1990 at 250–1, the longest priced winner in British racing history.

Another event at the February fixture is the Ivan Straker Memorial Chase, commemorating the man who did so much to save the Grand National (he died in 2013), while one of the March fixtures features a Grade 2 novices' hurdle and a Listed chase – the Premier Chase has been won by Grand National heroes Ballabriggs and Many Clouds. In January Kelso also stages a chase commemorating the historic Royal Caledonian Hunt.

Hunter chases have always been popular at Kelso and the (Royal Caledonian Hunt) Buccleuch Cup takes part of its name from the historic society formed by members of the local aristocracy and part from the Duke of Buccleuch, whose principal residence, Bowhill, is no distance away, outside Selkirk.

The Royal Caledonian Hunt is Scotland's most ancient and elite racing club. It is restricted to seventy elected members, who must either be born in Scotland or be Scottish landowners. Historically it was confined to 'the great gentlemen of Scotland' – indeed Robert Burns dedicated the second edition of his poems to the 'noblemen and gentlemen of the Caledonian Hunt'. For many years the Caledonian Hunt Cup was a feature of the prestigious Western Meeting at Ayr in September.

Instigated at Hamilton in 1777 as the Hunters' Club, this long-standing institution became the Caledonian Hunt the following year. The royal tag was assumed following the visit by King George IV to Scotland in 1822, when members held a ball in Edinburgh in his honour and the sovereign reciprocated by becoming patron of the hunt. The reigning monarch continued as patron until 2002, when Queen Elizabeth II was succeeded in the role by her daughter, the Princess Royal. Princess Anne had previously been honorary president, a role subsequently filled by the Duke of Kent.

The Royal Caledonian Hunt meets just once every year at one of the five Scottish racecourses. Traditionally, members were required to wear their striking scarlet tailcoats, buff waistcoats, dark green ties and black silk top hats, but nowadays wearing the club tie suffices. However, formal attire is still *de rigueur* for the annual dinner held at the New Club in Edinburgh on the second Monday in November, and fines are imposed on those who fail to comply with the rules. Other annual activities may include a day's hunting, a point-to-point race or a cross–country race.

South-west of Kelso, Hawick remains one of the centres for common riding. For centuries the border between Scotland and England was a source of conflict and lawlessness and this ancient tradition re-enacts the necessity of protecting the town's boundaries. Over a period of eight weeks in the summer, hundreds of riders trek over the surrounding countryside. The custom celebrates a momentous occasion in Scottish history. In 1514 a group of young Scots killed a number of the 'Auld Enemy' (i.e. the English) in retribution for the mass slaughter the previous year of their monarch, King James IV, and many of their fellow countrymen at the Battle of Flodden Field, just across the border in Northumberland.

Every day of the common riding is different, but the route is well defined and the procession is led by the cornet, adorned in a red sash and top hat. Always a bachelor, he is elected for a year and carries the blue and gold pennant. It's all highly entertaining and attracts horses and ponies of every description and just as big a cross-section of riders and enthusiastic followers. The ceremony involves some extraordinary customs, from 'snuffin' (envelopes full of snuff are dropped from first-floor windows) to drinking a unique rum-and-milk cocktail.

The common riding is a major gathering of the clans, with speeches and songs, and ribbons, flags and pennants in abundance. A celebration of guts and glory, it is very much a male-orientated occasion and when the participants ride around the reservoir the married men take the high road and the unmarried ones take the low road. The proceedings start early in the morning with a drum and pipe band and conclude when the cornet, after a relentless gallop, lowers his staff into the waters of the River Tweed, its flag unsullied and unclaimed for another year.

The common riding is only part of the attraction, however, as there is also unofficial racing – or 'flapping', as it is called – on the site of the old racecourse at Hawick, reputed to be one of the oldest in Great Britain. A slightly undulating course about six furlongs in circumference with a one-and-a-half-furlong straight, it is a permanent venue south of the town. Competitors come from all over the country and the main attraction is the Tradesmen's Handicap, funded by local tradespeople. Nowadays every race meeting seems to be labelled a festival, but Hawick and other flapping meetings are indeed real festivals for the local community.

So far as the British Horseracing Authority and the Jockey Club are concerned, such racing is illegal. Any horse that participates is automatically banned for life from running under their jurisdiction, while any owner, trainer, rider or official involved is subject to suspension. A recent incident concerned two owners from Northern Ireland who ran their gelded Milton Star at Hawick in the summer of 2007 under the assumed name of Fergies Boy. One of the owners was warned off for three years, together with a fine of £2,000, and the other was disqualified for a total of two years.

In the circumstances it is rather surprising that flapping persists, but in that respect it has something in common with the survival of hunting and point-to-points – foxhunting was banned officially in Scotland before it was in England, but this has proved an ineffectual piece of legislation.

Nowadays Scottish hunts stage nine point-to-point meetings, spread between five locations. Three of these fixtures – the Jedforest, the Buccleuch and the Berwickshire – are held at Friars Haugh on the Duke of Roxburghe's Floors Estate, outside Kelso. The remainder comprise the Dumfriesshire/Stewartry at Netherby Park, near Carlisle; the Lanarkshire, the Renfrewshire and the Eglinton at Overtown Farm at Carluke; the Fife at Balcormo Mains, north of Leven; and the Lauderdale at Mosshouses, near Galashiels.

4

THE OUTSTANDING TRAINER OF THE VICTORIAN ERA

The Dawsons were a remarkable Scottish family of racehorse trainers in the second half of the nineteenth century. The patriarchal figure was George Dawson, who trained from stables at his home, Stamford Hall, Gullane, in Haddingtonshire (now East Lothian). He had four sons, all of whom became trainers, three of them at Newmarket, and one at Middleham in North Yorkshire. Between them they saddled a veritable galaxy of English classic winners during the Victorian era.

In the best Scottish tradition, the brothers stood out from the crowd as innovators. It was customary in those days to subject racehorses to sweating. This involved working them at distances up to two miles in heavy rugs. The theory was that this prevented horses carrying any surplus flesh. In reality it increased the risk that they would break down and tended to make them bad-tempered and intractable. George Dawson's eldest son, Thomas, who was based at Middleham, was the first trainer to eliminate such Draconian methods from his training regime.

Mathew, the second son, was also an innovator in so far as he was one of the first trainers to open a public stable, into which he accepted only the horses belonging to owners of his own choosing, as opposed to being a private trainer to one particular patron. Up till then trainers were little more than glorified grooms, their status being that of a servant answerable to his employer. Indeed, Mat Dawson changed the status quo to such a marked extent that the owners at Heath House tended to defer to him rather than vice versa, an extraordinary situation for those bygone days. With Sir Mark Prescott, Bart, in charge, probably not too much has changed at Heath House since then!

Following his brother's example, George Dawson's third son, Joseph, became the first trainer in Newmarket not to sweat his horses. Based at Bedford Lodge (now an hotel) in the Bury Road, Joe pioneered a fresh approach to the way in which foals and yearlings were reared. Realising that it must be advantageous to feed young stock properly in their formative years, he ensured that his youngsters in the paddocks behind his house received only top-quality oats, sent down from the Carse O'Gowrie in his native Scotland, and drank the richest of milk from Channel Island cows.

The fourth son, John, took up residence in Newmarket via Middleham, where he worked for a time as head lad to his eldest brother, and Roden House, Compton, in Berkshire, where Peter Cundell succeeded his father, Ken. After an interim period, spent as a replacement for his brother Mat at Heath House, John finally moved to Warren House, where in due course his own son, George, took over. Up till then, George had been a prosperous brewer in Burton-on-Trent.

Although all four brothers made their mark as trainers, it was Mat who earned the highest accolades. Born on 9 January 1820, he was apprenticed to his father at Gullane, and like his brother John was head lad to their eldest brother, Thomas, at Middleham, before returning to Scotland to train on his own account.

Following the death of their father in November 1846, Mat crossed the border once more to take up an appointment with the Duke of Buccleuch's brother, Lord (John) Scott, and his partner, Sir John Don-Wauchope. He trained for them at Yew Tree Cottage, Compton, as well as supervising their stud at Cawston Lodge, near Rugby. In 1853 he gained a first classic success when John Scott's Catherine Hayes, bred by Don-Wauchope, triumphed in the Oaks.

By the late 1850s, both partners had given up racing and breeding, whereupon the Scottish ironmaster, James Merry, bought the remaining horses, an arrangement which was incumbent on Mat training them at Merry's own stables, Russley Park, above Lambourn. An unsavoury character, his priorities in life were cock-fighting and gambling. He had the necessary funds to pursue his interests as he had inherited a fortune from his father, a wealthy ironmaster from Ayrshire.

The short-lived association at Russley Park yielded two classic winners for Mat Dawson: Sunbeam, the first of his seven St Leger winners, and Thormanby, the first of his six Derby winners. Thormanby proceeded to win the following year's Ascot Gold Cup and was champion sire of 1869. At the time of his Derby victory his owner was MP for Falkirk Burghs, and thereafter Prime Minister Benjamin Disraeli referred to him as 'The member for Thormanby'.

In 1866 Mat moved to Newmarket, where he rented Heath House. Situated in the elbow between the Bury and Moulton Roads, opposite The Severals, Heath House is one of the oldest training establishments still in existence. One of Newmarket's great characters, Tregonwell Frampton had taken up residence there in 1689 and his close involvement with various monarchs earned him the soubriquet 'The Father of the Turf'.

Initially Mat Dawson's two principal patrons at Heath House were the Duke of Newcastle and the Duke of Hamilton. Unfortunately this aristocratic duo had something in common with the infamous James Merry – they liked a tilt at the ring. Despite their trainer's best efforts to recommend a little restraint over their extravagant betting, both were forced to withdraw from racing, having incurred substantial and unsustainable losses.

Fortunately for Mat Dawson his next major patron had no interest in gambling, his involvement in racing being the pursuit of classic winners as an owner-breeder. Because of his abstinence from betting, the 6th Lord Falmouth was one of the most respected figures on the Turf and he was so successful that the 5th Lord Rosebery had a special form printed on which to convey his congratulations. In fact Lord Falmouth, Mat Dawson and Fred Archer became such an invincible combination as owner, trainer and jockey, that they were invariably referred to as the triumvirate. The twelve domestic English classic winners they shared constituted a record.

It is indicative of Fred Archer's standing in the world beyond the racecourse that in Victorian times cab drivers would greet one another with the salutation 'Archer's Up', to convey that all was right with the world, such was his reputation in the saddle. Born in Cheltenham in

1857 – the year before his father, William, a professional jump jockey, won the Grand National on Little Charley – Fred Archer joined Mat Dawson as an apprentice in 1868, at the age of eleven.

As Mat Dawson and his wife, Mary Rose, from Kilwinning in Ayrshire, had no children, they more or less adopted Fred Archer. He exhibited a number of Scottish traits which doubtless met with their approval – he was ambitious, hard-working and thrifty. But more importantly, he exhibited an amazing talent from a very early age. Unbelievably, he rode his first winner, a pony named Maid of Trent, in a steeplechase at Bangor aged twelve, weighing just 4st 11lb.

Much to the surprise of most racing professionals, Mat Dawson promoted his protégé as stable jockey from 1875. It was a controversial appointment, not only because of Fred Archer's relative inexperience, but also because it necessitated putting up a tremendous amount of dead-weight in weight-for-age and condition races. Ironically it was depression, brought on by persistent wasting to keep his weight under control, that contributed to his suicide aged only thirty in 1886. Another factor must have been the death of his young wife, Helen Rose (John Dawson's daughter), after giving birth to a daughter.

Thanks to the patronage of the dukes of Newcastle, Hamilton, St Albans and Portland, as well as Lords Falmouth, Stamford, Cawdor and Lascelles, the Heath House stable became known as the 'aristocratic stable'. Of all these grandees, none contributed more to the escalating reputation of Heath House than the 6th Lord Falmouth.

From the time Lord Falmouth's horses arrived at Heath House until his dispersal sale more than fifteen years later, Mat Dawson saddled the winners of fourteen classics in his magpie colours: the Derby with Kingcraft and Silvio, and the other four classics three times apiece – the Two Thousand Guineas with Atlantic, Charibert and Galliard; the One Thousand Guineas with Cecilia, Spinaway and Wheel of Fortune; the Oaks with Spinaway, Jannette and Wheel of Fortune; and the St Leger with Silvio, Jannette and Dutch Oven. All were homebred and all bar Kingcraft and Cecilia were partnered by Fred Archer.

Champion jockey for thirteen consecutive seasons, Fred Archer was known affectionately as 'The Tinman'. Evelyn Falmouth was a native of Cornwall, a renowned tin-mining area, where he owned the Tregothnan Estate on the banks of the river Fal. Here he bred pedigree sheep and cattle. The son of a clergyman and trained as a barrister, he had inherited the title unexpectedly from a cousin.

However, it was his marriage to Baroness Le Despenser, a peeress in her own right, which brought him Mereworth Castle, near Maidstone in Kent, where he established his highly successful stud. Incidentally, the stud at Mereworth remained operational after the Second World War, when owned jointly by the Beckhampton trainer, Jeremy Tree, and his brother. During the 1980s that part of the estate, including a Palladian mansion, was sold to an associate of the Maktoums.

The unqualified success of the triumvirate reflected their mutual trust and understanding and only two isolated instances seem to have sullied their relationship, and then only temporarily. Early on, Mat Dawson requested that Lord Falmouth remove his horses after some misunderstanding over contradictory riding instructions, an impasse that was resolved by the diplomatic intervention of Joe Dawson. Then, the year before he retired from racing, Falmouth questioned the tactics Archer had adopted in the Derby on his Two Thousand Guineas winner, Galliard, only to retract his criticism unreservedly.

Mindful of the enormous contribution that the Falmouth horses had made to his career, and the help that His Lordship had given him over his financial affairs, Fred Archer named his Newmarket home Falmouth House. Previously he had lived in modest accommodation at Heath House. Despite Archer's spiralling fame as a jockey, Mat Dawson, a strong disciplinarian, ensured that he kept his feet firmly on the ground. He was forced to attend Mrs Dawson's evening and Sunday classes and slipshod or disrespectful behaviour was never tolerated.

The 6th Duke of Portland described Mat Dawson as 'full of Scottish humour and Scottish caution'. By all accounts he was kind, generous and loyal. A devout church-goer, he was extremely well read and appreciated poetry and painting. His manners were impeccable, whether addressing one of his owners or one of his staff, and he was always immaculately turned out. He patronised the best London tailors and boot-makers and invariably wore a black silk top hat. And these high standards were reflected in every aspect of his attitude to training racehorses.

As one might expect he had very strong views about training. One of his priorities was that racing was first and foremost a sport to be enjoyed. If owners wanted their horses to run somewhere, then their wishes should be given due consideration. He also had a particular foible about galloping horses at home. He insisted that good horses should always be led by inferior ones as otherwise they quickly become bored and discouraged. That was not a view shared by many of his colleagues and it may go some way to explaining his extraordinary success.

Lord Falmouth's withdrawal from the scene in 1884 was a watershed for Mat Dawson. After winning the following year's Derby and St Leger with Lord Hastings' Melton, he handed over Heath House to his nephew, George Dawson. He acted as a private trainer to a consortium headed by the Duke of Portland, on whose behalf he was to train the winners of ten classics in seven seasons. In 1898, the lease on Heath House expired, the consortium was dissolved, and George Dawson succeeded his father, John Dawson, at Warren House.

Meanwhile Mat Dawson had also been hitting the classic trail again. On vacating Heath House he had gone into semi-retirement on the outskirts of Newmarket at Exning, where he renamed the establishment Melton House after his dual classic winner. There he prepared Minting to win the 1886 Grand Prix de Paris followed by three more classic successes with Minthe in the One Thousand Guineas and Mimi in the One Thousand Guineas and Oaks.

By this stage Mat was in his seventies, yet Lord Rosebery, a fellow Scot, persuaded the veteran trainer to take on his string. So it was that he added four more classic victories to his tally within the space of two years, the Two Thousand Guineas and Derby with Ladas in 1894 and the Derby and St Leger with Sir Visto in 1895.

These victories provided the Dawson family with an unprecedented classic tally. From 1842 to 1898, the four brothers, Thomas, Mathew, Joseph and John, together with John's son, George, saddled the winners of a phenomenal fifty-two English classic races, including eleven Derby winners.

The winners of no fewer than twenty-eight of these classics were attributable to Mathew Dawson, yet at the end of his career he declared, 'I have trained only one good horse in my life – St Simon,' and Fred Archer, who rode both St Simon and Ormonde, was adamant that St Simon was the better of the pair. The horse, whom he rode only as a two-year-old, was never entered for either the Derby or the St Leger and had to miss his solitary classic engagement in the Two Thousand Guineas as the entry became automatically void upon the death of his owner-breeder, Gustavus Batthyany.

St Simon was purchased as an unraced two-year-old at the dispersal of Batthyany's bloodstock by the young Duke of Portland for 1,600 guineas in 1883, just a year before Lord Falmouth sold off all bloodstock due to advancing years. Never extended in nine outings at two and three years, he won the Gold Cup and the Doncaster Cup by twenty lengths and was just as good over shorter distances. Champion sire nine times, he spent the duration of his stallion career at his owner's Welbeck Stud, where he died aged twenty-seven.

Fred Archer and St Simon are two magical names when it comes to the history of the Turf. How remarkable it is that the careers of two such iconic figures should revolve around a Scotsman, who, together with three of his brothers, made such an inordinate contribution to racing in the second half of the nineteenth century.

In old age, the Jockey Club gave Mat Dawson permission to go on to Newmarket Heath in a brougham, as severe gout prevented him from walking without the aid of sticks. Evidently the Prince of Wales (later King Edward VII) rode over to talk to him one summer's morning. Rather than turn his back in order to close a window through which a severe draught was blowing, the old trainer caught a chill and he died soon afterwards on 18 August 1898, aged seventy-eight.

5

WAUGHS AND RUMOURS OF WAUGHS

Alec Waugh has worked on studs in two of the world's great Thoroughbred breeding centres. The first is Kentucky, in the famous 'bluegrass' country of the USA, where these pristine showplaces with their miles of white-boarded paddocks are always referred to as farms. The other is Normandy, the very embodiment of France's bloodstock culture. Here a picturesque château may well have a name prefaced by the word Haras, indicating its role as a Thoroughbred stud.

That is with the notable exception of the establishment that Alec Waugh owns and manages at Mandeville en Bessin, not far from Deauville, which he calls Jedburgh Stud. Jedburgh was the codename given to the most covert of operations involved with the D-Day landings in Normandy in 1944, but Alec Waugh chose the name for an altogether different reason – after the county town of Roxburghshire in Scotland, the home of his forebears.

Jedburgh, which is famous for its ruined Romanesque abbey, has additional medieval associations. The Borders' Justiciary Court dispensed 'Jeddart Justice', which seemed to entail hanging the miscreant before trying him at a later date, and a game called 'Jeddart hand-ba', which involved wielding a long pole with the severed head of an Englishman – a re-enactment of this macabre game is still played every Shrove Tuesday, albeit with footballs!

Alec Waugh started Jedburgh Stud, which extends to seventy acres with an additional fifty rented acres for yearlings, in January 1997. He had gained valuable experience with Marc de Chambure at Haras d'Etreham and then at Hagyard Farm, an American property owned by the Head family who themselves originated in Scotland. The Heads provide an ongoing link to the time when there was a coterie of British trainers in residence at Chantilly. Nowadays there are usually about thirty boarding mares at Jedburgh which is only a few miles from Etreham, with an annual draft of yearlings sent to the prestigious Deauville sales.

Two high-profile winners bred there are Chineur, winner of the King's Stand Stakes in 2005 (when this Royal Ascot feature was run at York due to rebuilding at Ascot), and All Is Vanity. Bred by Jedburgh Stud (rather than from a boarding mare), All Is Vanity was successful in the 2007 Prix de Sandringham at Chantilly. She belongs to a female family associated with Sir Harold and Lady Zia Wernhers' Someries Stud, managed in latter years by Alec's father, John Waugh.

In addition Alec also managed the Wildenstein mares based in Normandy at their Haras du Bois-Roussel. Previously these mares, which traded as Dayton Ltd, had been based for a four-year period at Jedburgh, where a number of Wildenstein celebrities were bred and reared, including such mega stars as Aquarelliste, Bright Sky and Westerner. It's a bit of an anomaly that in the old days, despite being one of the world's top breeders, the Wildensteins never owned a stud of their own.

Alec's great-great-grandfather, James Waugh (1832–1905), was born and spent his early working life in Jedburgh in the Scottish Borders, only to become the patriarch of a remarkable family of racehorse trainers at Newmarket from the second half of the nineteenth century up to the last couple of decades of the twentieth century. While there are no Waughs training at Headquarters now, there is still a descendant in William Jarvis, who lives at Phantom House in the Fordham Road – he is a great-grandson of James' daughter, Janet.

James Waugh, who claimed the outlaw Rob Roy MacGregor as an ancestor, was the seventh son of Richard Waugh, who worked at various times as a ploughman and a carrier/carter before becoming coachman to Dr Hume, a GP in Jedburgh. Throughout the nineteenth century, horses of all descriptions, be they for work or pleasure, were an integral part of daily life and this locality was famous for the common riding that still persists down to the present time. Richard had a natural talent not only with horses but also with dogs; evidently at one stage he was looking after thirty greyhounds.

Like his father, James followed the plough on leaving school, but he soon had a stroke of good fortune. Aged just twenty, he was asked by a Mr Grainger, a Scottish banker, to become his private trainer (a position which corresponded to a present-day head lad) at Cessford Manor, just outside Jedburgh, and he combined those duties with riding as a steeplechase jockey. With a growing reputation as a horseman, he was approached by Sir David Baird and Sir J. Boswell to train at Stamford Hall on Goose Green at Gullane.

At this juncture, the Waugh family became interlinked with another famous Scottish racing family, the Dawsons, who also trained on the racecourse at Gullane, now the Gullane Links; adjacent is the celebrated Muirfield golf course. Stamford Hall was the home of the Dawson family, and it was upon Mat Dawson's suggestion that James Waugh moved south in 1867. At first he went as private trainer to the Australian Wybrow Robinson in Berkshire before moving across the border into Wiltshire to succeed Mathew Dawson himself as James Merry's private trainer at Russley Park.

It soon became evident why Mat Dawson had vacated Russley Park to start a public stable in Newmarket, where he established himself as one of the greatest trainers of all time. Their patron was a singularly unsavoury character. A fellow Scot, whose father had made a fortune as an ironmaster in Ayrshire, James Merry was mean (albeit he did raise his trainer's annual salary from £250 to £300), and suspicious. He was convinced that foul play was afoot when his homebred Macgregor was unplaced in the 1870 Derby as an odds-on favourite after winning the Two Thousand Guineas. The truth was that Macgregor, never a sound horse, had broken down.

A few weeks later James Waugh handed in his resignation and he was soon on his travels again, this time overseas. He took the post as private trainer at Count Henschel's Carlburg stables at Naclo in Poland, before crossing the border into Hungary to train for Count Esterhazy and Prince Festitics at Kesthely, beside Lake Balaton, the country's largest lake. Altogether he spent ten years in Europe. One season he won forty-five races including the Grosser Preis von Baden and the Derby at Hamburg. However, the failing health of his wife, Isabella, obliged him to return to England in 1880.

Isabella Waugh died the following year aged forty-seven. Not altogether surprisingly, the birth of eleven children in the space of two decades, not to mention the strain of coping with such an extended family in foreign climes, had taken its toll. The logistics of the situation are exemplified by their journey home, when they brought along a goat to provide milk for the children, only for the itinerant nanny to be refused entry at the German border. The deprivations continued, for on arrival at Middleton Cottage in Newmarket's Exning Road, space was at such a premium that the family was obliged to sleep five to a bed.

During his European sojourn, James Waugh had made a large number of valuable contacts, enabling him to set up as a public trainer for the first time. He retained the patronage of Count Esterhazy, while other foreign nobility for whom he trained were Prince Lobomirski, counts Caroli, Kinsky, Lehndorff and Modrouski, and barons Oppenheim and Nathaniel de Rothschild. A noted socialite seen at all the best parties, Charles Kinsky rode his own horse, Zoedone, to win the 1883 Grand National. Additional owners included John Hammond, a former Newmarket stable lad and one of the most astute gamblers of his time, and Sir Robert Jardine, a Scottish businessman.

Although Macgregor was to remain his solitary English classic winner, James Waugh inherited St Gatien, who had dead-heated for the 1884 Derby for his trainer, Robert Sherwood. James saddled St Gatien to win his third consecutive Jockey Club Cup. Whilst still at Middleton Cottage, he also dispatched Eurasian to win the staying double of the Gold Vase and Alexandra Stakes at Royal Ascot in 1887. Two years later he won the Cambridgeshire with Laureate. St Gatien, Eurasian and Laureate were all owned by John Hammond. The trainer's leading winners during the 1890s, when based at Meynell House (now Hurworth House) in the Fordham Road, were the handicappers The Rush (Chester Cup), Piety (Manchester Cup) and Refractor (Royal Hunt Cup).

James Waugh was described as 'a tall, upright figure, smart, vigorous and charming, with an unblemished reputation; genial, hospitable with courtly manners'. When he died in 1905, he left behind a truly remarkable legacy, as six of his eight sons became trainers, and two of his three daughters married trainers. As a consequence, with the passing of the years, the Waugh descendants were related to just about every influential racing family in Newmarket and beyond.

Richard, the eldest brother, preceded his father to Russley Park, and then went to Germany via Newmarket (Albert House). He spent twenty-seven successful years training Kaiser Wilhelm's horses at the Imperial stables at Graditz. His successor there was Reg Day. One of Newmarket's great characters, the veteran trainer was in his midseventies when saddling Sweet Solera to win the 1961 One Thousand Guineas and Oaks, thirty-six years after he had saddled Solario to win the St Leger.

Richard's four sons, Percy, Jim, Alec and Frank, all became trainers abroad. However, it was the wrong time to be training in Germany. For four years during the First World War, both Percy and Alec were interned in Ruhleben prison camp, where the conditions were appalling. The inmates were housed in twenty-three barracks, accommodating about 200 men apiece. The food was basic in the extreme, mostly bread and vegetable soup, and they had to pay for whatever clothes were provided by the British Prisoners' Fund.

After the war, Percy made a name for himself training in Denmark and he won numerous classics in Scandinavia; Jim trained all his life at Hoppegarten in Germany; and their youngest brother, Frank, left Germany after the war to pursue a successful training career in Sweden.

It was in Germany that Alec Waugh made his home for the best part of thirty years spanning the First World War, first in Dusseldorf and then in Cologne as private trainer to Baron Alphonse de Rothschild. Unlike his brothers, when they set up their stall in Newmarket, he did not benefit from the support of rich foreign patrons – his first owner was Emanuel Dee, who had extensive chemical interests in the Middle East.

A few of Alec's owners liked a bet. Twice successful in the Beeswing Stakes at Newcastle, Kesrullah was owned by the professional backer,

Alex Bird. He won the Scarbrough Stakes at the Cesarewitch Meeting, having disappointed when joint-favourite at Ascot just four days earlier. Summonsed to explain the disparity in running, both trainer and owner were exonerated when Alex submitted evidence of a £7,000 wager on Kesrullah at Ascot with no financial interest at Newmarket! Another patron of the stable was Chris Jarvis, who liked to back his horses whenever they ran. A greengrocer from North London, his most memorable victory came when Kelling landed a substantial ante-post gamble in the 1950 Cambridgeshire.

During the 1950s John Waugh, who had assisted his father, became assistant to fellow Newmarket colleagues George Colling, trainer of the 1949 Derby winner, Nimbus, and Reg Day. Later John signed on as private trainer at Fitzroy House to Sir Robin McAlpine (see Chapter 23), a member of the celebrated Scottish family of civil engineering contractors. When Sir Robin decided to have a significant proportion of his horses trained in France, John switched to running his patron's Wyck Hall Stud in Newmarket, which was leased from the Jockey Club.

From the 1960s through to the 1980s, John and his brother, Dick, were two of the most prominent stud managers in Newmarket. Towards the end of his career John managed four major studs simultaneously: Lord Derby's Stanley House and Woodlands Studs, Someries Stud for Nicholas Phillips and Wyck Hall Stud. At one time Dick managed Jim Philipps' Dalham Hall and Derisley Studs (renamed Gazeley and Dalham Hall respectively), Dick Perryman's Aislabie Stud (for an interim period when owned by Neil Adam, a Scot, it was known as Collin Stud), and Marcos Lemos' Ashley Heath and Warren Hill Studs, which now come under the umbrella of Cheveley Park Stud.

One of the last highlights for John Waugh came in 1993 when Sir Robin's tartan colours achieved a posthumous homebred double at Royal Ascot with Jeune (Hardwicke Stakes), subsequent winner of the Melbourne Cup, and his half-brother, Beneficial (King Edward VII Stakes), who became a leading sire of jumpers based in Ireland. Now living in retirement in Newmarket, where he has lived all his life, John has the satisfaction of following the burgeoning stud interests of his son, Alec, in France.

By far the most successful of Richard Waugh's five younger brothers to train was Willie. Born at Gullane, he took over from their father when he left Hungary, only to follow him home to Newmarket, where he became private trainer at Falmouth House to furniture magnate Sir John Blundell Maple. For the owner of Childwick Bury Stud in Hertfordshire, he trained the 1898 One Thousand Guineas heroine, Nun Nicer.

Upon John Porter's retirement, Willie then took over the powerful Kingsclere stable on the Hampshire/Berkshire border, where he trained three more classic winners, Troutbeck (St Leger), Winkipop (One Thousand Guineas) and Clarissimus (Two Thousand Guineas). Finally, he returned to Newmarket, promptly renaming Zetland House as Balaton Lodge, after Lake Balaton in Hungary. From 1942 to 1998 Balaton Lodge served as the world-famous Equine Research Station.

The next brother, Alec, qualified as a veterinary surgeon at the Royal (Dick) Veterinary College in Edinburgh. He married Polly Jennings and followed the family tradition by training for Count Esterhazy in Hungary. The first official starter to be appointed by the Hungarian Jockey Club, Alec earned a considerable reputation as an international equine vet. He travelled all over Europe and on one memorable occasion whilst sleighing in Russia his shooting skills proved invaluable when he was pursued by a pack of wolves. In later life he was to be the manager at Childwick Bury Stud.

Polly Jennings was a member of another famous racing family which – like the Carters and Cunningtons, all of whom were related by marriage – established a tribe of expatriate trainers based at Chantilly. Tom Jennings will always be associated with the French-bred Gladiateur, known as the 'Avenger of Waterloo' after winning the 1865 Triple Crown. By that time his trainer was based at Newmarket's Phantom House, the yard now occupied by Willie Jarvis.

Due to the ill health of his brother Richard, Charlie Waugh spent a brief period as a stand-in at the Imperial stables at Graditz. He won the German Derby twice for the Kaiser, before moving to Newmarket where his foreign benefactor, Prince Soltykoff, has a race named after him. From Kremlin House, Charlie moved to Park Lodge and then in

1900 he built Carlburg Stables on the Bury Road. Up to the First World War, his more notable successes were in the Lincolnshire with Over Norton and Sansovino, the Cambridgeshire with Marcovil, the Great Metropolitan Handicap with Kilbroney and the Chesterfield Cup with Kiltoi.

Although Sir Victor Sassoon became a patron of the stable in the period between the two World Wars, Charlie Waugh's career never really got going again and he retired from training in 1939. An easily recognisable figure on Newmarket Heath, he dressed in clothes that were last fashionable in the Victorian era. He sold Carlburg in 1947 to Manton trainer Joe Lawson, who proceeded to win the Derby and St Leger with Never Say Die. In due course Joe Lawson handed over the reins to Scotsman, Fergie Sutherland.

Just as Charlie Waugh had come to the rescue on brother Richard's behalf at Graditz, so Mathew Dawson Waugh did likewise for brother Willie, then training for Prince Festitics in Hungary, when he became ill. In fact he proved an admirable replacement, winning all the top races there over a three-year period. He then followed the siblings' traditional path to Newmarket and was soon appointed private trainer to Walter Raphael at Somerville Lodge.

Mathew Dawson Waugh (always known as Dawson), who was the seventh son of a seventh son and christened after his godfather, did well for Walter Raphael, a Jewish financier of Dutch extraction. Although the combination had few horses to start with, they were responsible for the 1912 Derby winner, Tagalie, who is the only grey filly ever to win the Blue Riband. Homebred Tagalie had previously given Dawson Waugh a first classic victory in the One Thousand Guineas.

In 1909, the same owner-trainer combination had provided the runner-up at Epsom, when Louviers was beaten a short head by King Edward VII's Minoru. In common with many spectators that day, his trainer was convinced that the judge had placed the two principals in the wrong order. Four years later Two Thousand Guineas hero Louvois, an own-brother to Louviers, was placed second in another sensational Derby when the first home, Craganour, was disqualified in favour of

Aboyeur. This was the occasion when the suffragette Emily Davison was killed under the heels of His Majesty's colt, Anmer, on the approach to Tattenham Corner.

Between the wars Dawson Waugh trained principally for the 8th Lord Howard de Walden (Thomas) and newspaper proprietor, Sir Edward Hulton. Prior to becoming a famous foundation mare, Sir Edward's Straitlace won the 1924 Oaks, Coronation Stakes and Nassau Stakes.

Initially St Louvaine, the dam of Louviers and Louvois, was a poor feeder, a problem which her trainer resolved by putting a goat in her box. Similar understanding tactics were employed with the highly strung Straitlace. She had a gelding as a constant companion and he always accompanied her to the races.

Dawson Waugh was a much-loved character in Newmarket, where he was a church warden for many years. He did much to encourage young people who exhibited an interest in racing and took particular trouble with his apprentices. His daughter, Marjory Hemphill, bred and trained her own horses in Kenya, including two winners of the Derby.

The youngest of James Waugh's six trainer sons was Tom, who took over Meynell House upon the death of his father in 1905 to become one of four Waugh brothers training in Newmarket simultaneously, the others being Willie, Charlie and Dawson. For his principal owner, Scotsman Sir Robert Jardine, Tom saddled Cinna to win the 1920 One Thousand Guineas and Coronation Stakes. Tom's interests also extended to other livestock and he kept Red Poll cattle on a plot of land between the Fordham and Snailwell Roads. He also had White Wyandotte chickens and racing pigeons.

Tom's wife, Eleanor, was the daughter of Alfred Hayhoe, who succeeded his father, Joseph Hayhoe, as virtually private trainer to Baron Meyer de Rothschild and his nephew, Leopold de Rothschild, at the historic Palace House Stables at Newmarket. From 1853 to 1904 the Hayhoes trained the winners of thirteen classic races – 1871 was labelled 'The Baron's Year' when Joseph saddled Favonius to win the Derby and Hannah took the fillies' Triple Crown. Hannah was named by Baron Meyer after his daughter who married the 5th Earl of Rosebery (see Chapter 7).

53

Tom's three sons all served in the Second World War and two of them became trainers in Newmarket – Jack (J.A.J.) and Tom Jnr. Jack had suffered the indignity of arriving at Victoria Station on his return from Dunkirk in his underpants (his rain-soaked trousers had blown away when he hung them out to dry from the carriage window). He was injured in the raid on Dieppe and invalided out of the Royal Artillery. He then took over from his uncle, Dawson Waugh, at Somerville Lodge – initially he had been assistant to his father, Tom Snr, before joining Basil Jarvis.

For a quarter of a century Jack Waugh trained with considerable success from Heath House, synonymous with the great Scottish trainer, Mat Dawson, with the support of many of the country's leading owner-breeders. They included John Howard de Walden (the 9th Baron), the owner of Plantation Stud, the Fairhaven family (Barton Stud), the Macdonald-Buchanans (Lavington, Lordship and Egerton Studs), Bernard Hornung (West Grinstead Stud) and Stanhope Joel (Snailwell Stud).

It was through Stanhope Joel that Jack Waugh came to train for John Ferguson, who had won the 1946 Derby with Airborne, the last grey to prevail in the Blue Riband. John Ferguson nearly brought off the double when Arabian Night finished runner-up in the 1956 Derby, the nearest his trainer came to a classic winner. It was for John Ferguson's widow that top sprinter Matador triumphed in the 1956 July Cup, her husband having died the previous month.

Jack Waugh's principal patron was John Howard de Walden, for whom he trained such celebrities as Amerigo, Panjandrum, Almiranta, Ostrya and Oncidium. Another of his owners was John U. Baillie of Crimbourne Stud, later owned by Sir Eric Parker, joint owner of the 1991 Grand National hero, Seagram. The breeder of two champion sprinters in So Blessed and Lucasland, John U. Baillie had ridden as an amateur when his horses were trained by Dawson Waugh, who was not too impressed by his owner's riding skills!

Jack retired in 1970 and sold Heath House to his former assistant, Sir Mark Prescott, the present incumbent, whereupon he took over the management of the Macdonald-Buchanans' two Newmarket studs.

Tom Waugh Jnr commenced training at Wroughton House after the Second World War, but he had had a thorough grounding in the game, first with his cousins, Frank and Fred Butters, Janet Waugh's two sons, and then with Harvey Leader, a relative by marriage. From Wroughton House (a name derived from Alan King's training base on the Wiltshire Downs north of Marlborough), Tom trained Privy Councillor to win the 1962 Two Thousand Guineas before moving to Sefton Lodge, then owned by Jim Joel, for whom he trained a top filly in Rose Dubarry.

Through marriage, Janet, the first of James Waugh's three daughters, and her sister, Grace, provided an entirely new dimension to the Waughs' extended family of leading Newmarket trainers.

Janet's husband, Joe Butters, had served his apprenticeship with his future father-in-law, James Waugh, before joining Mat Dawson at Heath House. He accepted an offer to ride in Austria for Emperor Franz Josef in 1873. Successful in many of the most important races in Austria, Hungary and Germany, as both a jockey and a trainer, he then returned to Newmarket in 1903 to preside over Kremlin House. Joe's best horse was Nassovian, who was beaten a neck and a head for the 1916 Derby won by the filly, Fifinella.

Joe's elder son, Frank, was destined to become one of the great trainers of his generation, winning no fewer than fifteen English classics. Born near Vienna, he followed in his father's footsteps by becoming a successful trainer in Austria. It was at the British Embassy chapel in Vienna that he married Cossie Marsh, sister of the royal trainer, Richard Marsh, the father of Marcus Marsh. The extraordinary aspect of Frank's career is that he only started training in Newmarket when he was nearly fifty years of age and yet he proved by far the most successful of all his many relatives.

After the war Frank moved to Italy before returning to fulfil a four-year contract to train for the 17th Earl of Derby at Stanley House (upon the retirement of George Lambton) – his father had been born on the Derby family's Knowsley Estate, near Liverpool. At the end of that period, which coincided with the Wall Street crash, Lord Derby decided to cut back and momentarily Frank Butters found himself out of a job. But no sooner had he moved into Fitzroy House than he was asked to take charge of the Aga Khan's powerful string, the Aga having fallen out with the Irishman, Dick Dawson, at Whatcombe.

Frank Butters was leading trainer no fewer than eight times. The most influential horse he trained for Lord Derby was Fairway (St Leger), destined to be champion sire on four occasions. He also trained two of the Aga Khan's four Derby winners, Bahram and the grey Mahmoud, the former winning the Triple Crown in 1935, a feat not repeated until Nijinsky in 1970. There was a sad postscript as Frank Butters suffered a severe head injury when knocked off his bicycle by a passing lorry as he was leaving the yard, an incident that terminated his career.

Although overshadowed by his elder brother, Frank, Fred Butters also achieved classic glory when Mid-day Sun triumphed in the 1937 Derby. Owned in partnership by Mrs G.B. Miller and her mother, Mrs J.A.W. Talbot, Mid-day Sun was the first Epsom Derby winner to be owned by a woman – Lady James Douglas' homebred Gainsborough had won a substitute Derby at Newmarket in 1918.

Joe's daughter, Isabel, married Willie Jarvis, a link which had extraordinary repercussions. Willie was the elder brother to Basil and Jack (later Sir Jack). Willie and Isabel Jarvis had two children, Ryan and Bridget. Ryan married Jean Hall and their son is Willie Jarvis. Named after his grandfather, Willie is the solitary descendant of James Waugh currently training in Newmarket. The best horse trained by the master of Phantom House is Lord Howard de Walden's homebred Grand Lodge.

Willie's aunt, Bridget, married Bill Rickaby, son of Fred, both distinguished jockeys – indeed Bill enjoyed a very successful association with Sir Jack Jarvis's Park Lodge stable. Marriage to Bill Rickaby brought the ultra-distinguished Day, Cannon, Armstrong and Piggott families into the genealogical mix.

Jean Jarvis was the daughter of Tom Hall, a brother of Sam and Charlie Hall, all successful Yorkshire trainers. To complete the jigsaw, yet another leading family of trainers is added through the marriage of Sir Jack Jarvis to Ethel Leader. The latter's father, Tom Leader, was a leading trainer as were Ethel's brothers Tom Jnr (father of Ted Leader), Colledge, Fred and Harvey.

The inter-relationship that existed between the Waugh, Butters, Jarvis, Hall and Leader families is without precedent and yet another highly esteemed name occurs through the marriage of Janet Waugh's sister, Grace, to Jack Dawson, a member of the Dawson clan whose ancestry is discussed in the previous chapter.

When Alec Notman, who was born and bred in Roxburghshire, retired as the first manager at Dalham Hall Stud, Newmarket, for Sheikh Mohammed, the runner-up for this most prestigious job was Alec Waugh. He was educated at Framlingham College in Suffolk, as were scores of his relations, but it is somewhat ironic that he should find himself domiciled in France, as he explains: 'French was definitely my least favourite subject at school!'

*Simplified family tree of James Waugh's racing descendants
down to the present time*

JAMES WAUGH (1832–1905)

RICHARD (1855)

> PERCY
>
> JIM
>
> ALEC
>
> > JOHN
> >
> > > ALEC
> >
> > DICK
>
> FRANK

JANET (1856) = Joe Butters

> Frank Butters
>
> Fred Butters
>
> Isabel Butters = Willie Jarvis
>
> > Ryan Jarvis = Jean Hall
> >
> > Willie Jarvis
> >
> > Bridget Jarvis = Bill Rickaby

GRACE (1858) = Jack Dawson

WILLIE (1860)

ALEC (1862) = Polly Jennings

CHARLIE (1870)

DAWSON (1873)

TOM (1874) = Eleanor Hayhoe

> JACK
>
> TOM

6

WHISKY GALORE

Escorting visitors around his bonded warehouse in Leith Docks on the outskirts of Edinburgh, Eric Macdonald, chairman and managing director of Highland Queen whisky, confided that the cost to him of the glass bottle and the label exceeded the cost of the contents, which he described as 'a few pickles of barley mixed with some peaty water'. Despite the excessive excise duty levied on a bottle of whisky, there was obviously a fortune to be made if one had the necessary business acumen – it was no coincidence that this particular firm of whisky producers had one of its representatives in America in 1932 when Prohibition was abolished.

Eric Macdonald was too much of a canny Scot to be tempted into the unpredictable and costly world of racing and breeding top-quality bloodstock, but two of his business competitors most certainly were and they and their families were to make a considerable contribution in both spheres. The first was Thomas Robert Dewar (1864–1930), from Perth, always known to his family as Tom or T.R., who became Lord Dewar. The other was James Buchanan (1849–1935), later Lord Wool-avington. By the time of Lord Dewar's death the respective firms of Dewar and Buchanan were amalgamated and in due course they became part of the giant Distillers Company. But their original rivalry in business spilled over onto the racecourse.

It was Thomas Dewar's father, John Dewar, who had started the family business in Perth where he had previously worked in a wine shop. He had sold his whisky in glass bottles instead of the traditional jars or wooden casks. In 1885 Tom and his brother, John (later Lord Forteviot), opened a branch of the business in London which expanded rapidly. When it came to promoting their wares, they cleverly exploited the association between whisky and the romance of the Highlands. More than half a century later, advertising for White Label whisky, one of Dewar's most popular brands, always depicted a Highland piper in full ceremonial regalia.

However, the scotch was a blended variety rather than the traditional malts preferred in Scotland, as somehow this appealed more to the English palate. By the 1890s whisky and soda had become the quintessential drink of the English gentleman in his London club and the Dewars, like so many of their business rivals, became multi-millionaires. Tom Dewar led the way. He became the first whisky lord in the Upper House and only the third man in Great Britain to own a motor car. The first was the Scottish tea magnate, Thomas Lipton, and the second was King Edward VII, then Prince of Wales. On one memorable occasion the German emperor, Kaiser Bill, on being asked whether he had seen his friend, King Edward, replied, 'No, not lately, I expect he is out boating with his grocer!' Today the Caledonian Club in London still stocks some 150 different varieties of whisky.

A bachelor, Tom Dewar first registered his colours, 'white, tartan cross back and front', in 1897 and soon they were carried to victory by runners with such eminently Scottish, but rather unimaginative, names as Perthshire and Forfarshire. But it was not until 1911 that he had his first notable success with Forfarshire's son, Braxted, in the Stewards' Cup. That Goodwood victory on the Sussex Downs more or less coincided with the foundation of his Homestall Stud, on the edge of Ashdown Forest, near East Grinstead, also in Sussex.

One racehorse and one broodmare proved the twin pillars on which Homestall Stud's reputation was established. The first was homebred Abbot's Trace, who was tried in the highest company, but was only really a handicapper. It was his misfortune to be brought down towards the finish of the 1920 Derby ridden by Steve Donoghue, but later that season he did manage to defeat the Derby winner, Spion Kop, in a match at Derby. The racecourse closed on the advent of war never to open again – it is now the county cricket ground. Abbot's Trace stood at Homestall until being exported to France. It is a measure of Abbot's

Trace's stud success that his fee rose from just nine guineas to 300 guineas.

In the long term, the most significant acquisition for Homestall was Lady Juror, who became a great foundation mare albeit Lord Dewar died before her true worth became manifest. Winner of the Jockey Club Stakes, she was bought as a four-year-old in 1923 for 8,600 guineas at the dispersal of Lord Manton's bloodstock. It was the soap manufacturer, Joseph Watson, who acquired the famous Manton training establishment in Wiltshire. The inevitable mating with Abbot's Trace produced The Black Abbot (Gimcrack Stakes), but Lord Dewar's demise preceded her outstanding offspring, Fair Trial, by two years.

Tom Dewar was only sixty-six when he died quite unexpectedly at Homestall in April 1930. In May of the preceding year the Jockey Club had revoked the rule whereby classic entries (made in the autumn when the animal was a yearling) became void upon the death of the nominator. This was to have serious repercussions regarding two colts owned by Lord Dewar – Challenger, foaled in 1927, remained ineligible for the classics whereas Cameronian, foaled in 1928, became eligible under the new ruling and as matters turned out that was just as well!

Challenger was a colt for whom Lord Dewar had paid 5,000 guineas as a yearling from the National Stud. Third top-rated on the Two-Year-Old Free Handicap, when he had won his only two starts, the Richmond Stakes at Goodwood and the Clearwell Stakes at Newmarket, the son of Swynford was sold to America not long after his owner's death. Known there as Challenger II, he was to make an indelible contribution to American racing as the sire of Gallorette, one of the truly great matriarchs in the *American Stud Book*.

Meanwhile, Homestall Stud, together with all Lord Dewar's bloodstock, was inherited by his nephew, John Arthur Dewar (1891–1954), the only son of Charles Dewar of King's Lynn in Norfolk. Arthur Dewar (as he was always known to his friends) had served in the Argyll and Sutherland Highlanders in France and Salonika during the First World War. Before inheriting Homestall Stud, he had not shown much interest in racing, but he persevered with the horses in the care of Fred Darling at Beckhampton, the yard now occupied by Roger Charlton. As his fortunes prospered so too did his enthusiasm and he soon acquired the soubriquet 'Lucky' Dewar.

Amongst the horses Arthur Dewar inherited was Cameronian, then a two-year-old. As was the custom with all his father's homebreds, he had been sent from Homestall as a weanling to his breeder's subsidiary Newchapel Stud, near Lingfield, before going into training. During the Second World War the Dewar breeding stock were based in Ireland at Dollanstown Stud, Co. Kildare, which Dewar had also bought. Meantime the stud in Surrey was occupied by greyhounds – in June 1955 it was sold to Winston Churchill, who used it to breed such celebrities as High Hat and Vienna. Eventually Newchapel was renamed Churchill Stud in honour of the great man.

Cameronian proceeded to win the Two Thousand Guineas and the Derby and hopes were high that he might win the Triple Crown. In his only other start before the St Leger he was an impressive winner of the St James's Palace Stakes at Royal Ascot. Usually a very placid individual, Cameronian was uncharacteristically on edge at Doncaster and he finished last. He exhibited all the symptoms of having been doped, but his trainer strongly refuted any such suggestions. It took Cameronian time to recover, but he bowed out as a four-year-old by winning the Champion Stakes. Ironically he sired a St Leger winner in Scottish Union, before leaving Homestall Stud for export to Argentina.

Meanwhile the Dewar colours had been carried prominently by Fair Trial. Like Cameronian he was blessed with an equable temperament, but he did have physical problems. His knees were a constant source of anxiety as were his very shelly feet – to keep his soles off the ground Fred Darling had him fitted with especially wide aluminium plates. In the end a sprained tendon ended his racing career, but not before he had proved a top-class miler, scoring twice at Royal Ascot, in the Queen Anne Stakes at three years and the Rous Memorial Stakes at four years.

It was as a stallion based at Homestall Stud that Fair Trial really made his mark. The champion sire of 1950, he had only once finished out of the top half-dozen in his previous ten seasons with runners. Predictably his progeny excelled at distances up to a mile. Most important of his sons proved to be Court Martial, who was twice champion sire, Petition, another champion sire (his son Pitcairn was also champion sire), and Palestine, another notable sire of sires. Fair Trial was also a champion broodmare sire and one of his daughters bred the fillies' Triple Crown winner, Meld.

Two of Fair Trial's half-sisters, Riot and Sansonnet, bred classic winners for Arthur Dewar, the former with Commotion (1941 New Oaks), and the latter with Tudor Minstrel (1947 Two Thousand Guineas). Tudor Minstrel justified favouritism by eight lengths at Newmarket, but ironically one of his chief rivals, Fair Trial's son Petition, did not give his true running, having injured himself after rearing over backwards at the start. A ridiculously short-priced favourite for the Derby ridden by Gordon Richards, Tudor Minstrel failed to stay. Initially retired to Homestall Stud before moving to Harwood Stud (now Gainsborough Stud), he established a highly influential male line both in Europe and in the USA, his adopted home.

When Fred Darling retired in 1947, Arthur Dewar purchased the Beckhampton training establishment lock, stock and barrel for £60,000 and installed Noel Murless as the resident trainer. In 1952 Murless moved to Newmarket and Dewar transferred his horses to Noel Cannon (trainer of Cameronian's son, Scottish Union) at Druid's Lodge on Salisbury Plain. The new partnership was rewarded when Festoon, a homebred daughter of Fair Trial, triumphed in the 1954 One Thousand Guineas.

A few months later Arthur Dewar died at Montecatini in Italy and at his record-breaking dispersal sale at Newmarket, Anthony Askew bought Festoon for 36,000 guineas and Gerald Askew paid 30,000 guineas for her half-sister Refreshed, both record prices for a broodmare at auction. The purchasers were nephews of James Vose Rank, the flour miller and owner of Druid's Lodge.

It was something of a coincidence that two Scottish whisky magnates should not only become patrons of the same stable, but also stud owners in Sussex. There was more to follow. Fair Trial, the outstanding horse bred by Arthur Dewar, was a grandson of Lady Josephine, and Abernant, the outstanding horse bred by Lord Woolavington's daughter, Lady Macdonald-Buchanan, was a great-grandson of Lady Josephine; Abernant's granddam, Mumtaz Mahal, was the most influential of all the old Aga Khan's foundation mares. Furthermore Abernant was trained by Noel Murless at Beckhampton at a time when Arthur Dewar owned the stable.

The surname Macdonald-Buchanan was created when Catherine Buchanan married Reginald Macdonald, a captain in the Scots Guards, in 1922. She duly inherited all the bloodstock upon the death of her father in 1935. Completely disregarding his advice to take up blood-stock breeding on only a very limited scale, Catherine soon had three studs and one of the biggest broodmare bands in the country. She kept the family's Lavington Stud at Graffham, near Petworth, in Sussex, and added two more studs on the periphery of Newmarket, Lordship and Egerton, adjacent properties on opposite sides of the Cambridge Road.

Catherine Macdonald-Buchanan inherited a great classic tradition from her father, the one and only Lord Woolavington. He took his title from Woolavington Down overlooking the park at Lavington – during the Second World War the house was requisitioned as an army hospital. James Buchanan was actually born in Canada, but a year later his father, Alexander, decided to leave Ontario and return to his native Glasgow.

Aged thirty, James ventured to London to act as agent for a firm of whisky distillers, only to branch out in business on his own, trading as James Buchanan and Company. Expansion was rapid and soon he needed larger premises. With a reputation for sound business sense and complete integrity, he had no difficulty in raising the necessary £90,000 in the City to buy the Old Swan distillery in Holborn.

James Buchanan's enterprise provided an unorthodox entrée on to the Turf. Periodically he took long sea voyages for the benefit of his health and on a trip to the Argentine in 1898 he was introduced to Flat racing (he had already owned a few jumpers) by Alec Kincaid, a cousin. It all made such a favourable impression that on his return from Buenos Aires, the Scotsman brought with him a trainer called Alvarez and a jockey named Gomez. He installed them at Queensberry Lodge stables at the top of Newmarket High Street (many years later the house became the headquarters of the British Bloodstock Agency). His blood-stock adviser was Mr Livock, a well-known Newmarket veterinary surgeon, who had practised in the Argentine.

Racing under the *nom de course* 'Mr Kincaid', the future Lord Woolavington and his employees at Queensberry Lodge were an unconventional team, but they enjoyed some major successes. These included Epsom Lad – who won the Eclipse Stakes despite a slipped saddle, when Gomez performed miracles to maintain the partnership, riding virtually bareback – and the former selling plater, Black Sand, winner of the Cesarewitch and Jockey Club Cup. The previous owners of Epsom Lad and Black Sand were Lord Rosebery and Sir James Miller respectively, both Scotsmen.

Alvarez's contract expired after three years and James Buchanan spread his horses between various public trainers, most notably Sam Darling at Beckhampton. When the latter retired in 1913 the long and rewarding association began with his son and successor, Fred Darling. The following year the new master of Beckhampton, a martinet if ever there was one, bought a yearling colt by Marcovil from a National Hunt breeder for 500 guineas, who was destined to bring classic success to his owner both on the racecourse and at stud. James Buchanan had struck gold for a minimal outlay.

Named Hurry On, this chesnut was so large and backward that he never ran as a two-year-old, yet he was described by Darling, who saddled nineteen English classic winners, as 'the best horse I have ever trained; the best I am ever likely to train'. Never entered in the Derby on account of his size (he stood seventeen and half hands), Hurry On contributed to that impressive classic tally in the St Leger (a substitute affair run as the September Stakes at Newmarket because of the war). Undefeated in six starts that season, he also won the Newmarket St Leger and Jockey Club Cup. It was a shame that the war curtailed Hurry On's racing career as many considered him superior to Pommern, Gay Crusader and Gainsborough, all Triple Crown winners during that traumatic period, but there was due compensation at stud.

Hurry On spent the duration of his stallion career at James Bucha-nan's Lavington Stud, where he died in 1936 aged twenty-three. Initially he proved very difficult to handle and he saw off eight different stallion men in the space of eighteen months. Eventually a diminutive man from the east end of London was engaged to look after him and against all the odds he struck up an amazing rapport with this giant of a horse, aided by a plentiful supply of bullseyes, a very popular sweet at the time!

The champion sire of 1926 and three times the leading sire of brood-mares, Hurry On revived the flagging fortunes of the Matchem male line single-handedly. In the long term his greatest single influence came through his son, Precipitation (sired when Hurry On was twenty years old), who made a worldwide contribution. On the home front Hurry On sired three winners of the Derby, two winners of the Oaks and two winners of the One Thousand Guineas.

His three Derby winners were Captain Cuttle, Coronach and Call Boy. The first pair were homebred at Lavington and remarkably Captain Cuttle resulted from the very first mare that the war-time St Leger hero ever covered. He won the Derby in 1922, running in the name of Lord Woolavington who had only just become a peer. There was consternation before the start at Epsom when Captain Cuttle was found to be lame after spreading a plate, but all was well and he and Steve Donoghue came home in record time. Also successful at Royal Ascot in the St James's Palace Stakes, he then strained a tendon which forced him to miss the St Leger as well as the Gold Cup, his long-term objective as a four-year-old.

Coronach, who was much more precocious than Captain Cuttle, was rated the leading two-year-old of 1925. The following season he emulated Captain Cuttle by winning the Derby and St James's Palace Stakes, prior to winning the Eclipse Stakes and the St Leger in record time. As a four-year-old he went in the wind, but not before he had won the Coronation Cup and Hardwicke Stakes. As illness prevented Woolavington from leading in his Derby winner, his wife did the honours in the pouring rain with the victorious jockey, Joe Childs, explaining how he had been forced to make all the running as his mount had refused to settle and nearly pulled his arms off!

Coronach might well have won the Two Thousand Guineas instead of finishing runner-up. In the early 1920s his owner bought a yard at Newmarket, where those famous veterinary surgeons, Brayley Reynolds and Fred Day, used to practise, and here the Beckhampton runners would be stabled overnight. Beside the yard was a line of trees with a rookery and evidently the commotion caused thoroughly upset Coronach and consequently he never settled. Not the easiest of horses to handle, the Derby winner once cornered Fred Darling in his box and endeavoured to savage him – the trainer managed to extricate himself and the miscreant was administered a severe thrashing.

In due course Coronach, always his owner-breeder's personal favourite, joined Captain Cuttle at Lavington and, although both got their share of winners, they were only successful to a limited extent. Eventually both were dispatched overseas – Captain Cuttle to Italy and Coronach to New Zealand, where he was a resounding success. Coronach's best offspring in Europe was Corrida. The first filly to win the Prix de l'Arc de Triomphe twice, Corrida was purloined by the Germans during the war and disappeared without trace.

Lord Woolavington's classic winners carried his distinctive colours, 'white, one black hoop, red cap with gold tassel', which were inspired by a very special brand of whisky manufactured by James Buchanan and Company for the House of Lords and the House of Commons – the bottles had a distinctive white label, black lettering and a red cap with gold lettering. His daughter, Catherine Macdonald-Buchanan, inherited these colours, but most of their horses ran in the name of her husband, Reginald, whose 'black, white hoop and armlets' reflected the company's most famous brand of whisky, Black & White.

Just as the 1922 Derby winner, Captain Cuttle, resulted from the very first mare that Hurry On ever covered, so the 1941 substitute Derby winner, Owen Tudor, became the very first foal born at Catherine Macdonald-Buchanan's newly acquired Lordship Stud at Newmarket. Furthermore he was a son of Mary Tudor II, winner of the French One Thousand Guineas and the very last mare that her father ever purchased.

A good horse on his day but inconsistent, Owen Tudor disappointed more often than not for no apparent reason, but he also gained a memorable victory as a four-year-old in a substitute Gold Cup run over two-and-a-quarter miles at Newmarket. For a horse who stayed so well, Owen Tudor had a remarkable stud career, divided between New England Stud and neighbouring Egerton Stud. Two of his outstanding progeny were the very close relatives trained at Beckhampton, Tudor Minstrel and Abernant. These two horses have a particular significance to this story as the former was a Dewar flagbearer while the latter put Reginald Macdonald-Buchanan's colours firmly on the map.

Two knights of the Turf regarded Abernant as the fastest horse with whom they were associated – champion trainer Noel Murless and champion jockey Gordon Richards. Top of the Free Handicap as a juvenile, the grey was beaten a short head in the 1949 Two Thousand Guineas, the first time the result of an English classic had been determined by the photo-finish camera, and then proved virtually invincible over sprint distances, winning the July Cup, Nunthorpe Stakes and King George Stakes at both three and four years. As a sire he did exceptionally well with his fillies so it was no surprise that he was a successful broodmare sire, but disappointingly he failed to establish a male line of any lasting importance.

Sir Reginald and Lady Macdonald-Buchanan, as they became, raced on a very extensive scale with a host of stallions based at Lavington Stud in Sussex and Egerton Stud at Newmarket, while the majority of the mares were maintained at Lordship. Between them they bred and raced numerous top-class horses, but the halcyon days of Owen Tudor and his son, Abernant, were never repeated. Indeed, of all the mares subsequently recruited to the stud, none surpassed Mary Tudor. Apart from producing Owen Tudor and the unraced King Hal, who became a champion sire of jumpers, she was also the granddam of Royal Forest.

This high-class colt started favourite for the 1949 Derby in which he finished fourth. An exact contemporary of Abernant, Royal Forest was also a brilliant two-year-old, winning the Coventry Stakes and Dewhurst Stakes, but in the interim he caused a major sensation. Back at Ascot, in a field of four runners, he was beaten a half length by Burpham, a colt making his debut. Royal Forest was returned at 1–25, then the shortest-priced loser in British racing history. It was rumoured that Royal Forest had been stung by a wasp down at the start. Perhaps more to the point, he had been sweating uncharacteristically in the paddock preliminaries, but no dope test was ever undertaken.

Keen followers to hounds, the Macdonald-Buchanans lived at Cottesbrooke Hall in the heart of the Pytchley country. A magnificent Queen Anne house thought to have been the inspiration for Jane Austen's *Mansfield Park*, it is home to one of the finest collections of sporting art in private hands. It was the custom for any member of the Jockey Club, who had the good fortune to own a Derby winner, to present a portrait of the horse to the club and paintings by Lynwood Palmer of Captain Cuttle and Coronach are amongst the prized collection of pictures hanging in the Jockey Club Rooms in Newmarket.

Reginald predeceased his wife, Catherine, who died in 1987 aged ninety-two. By then the family's racing interests were much reduced, and their son, John, who died in 2014, made further substantial cutbacks. Both Newmarket studs were sold, and their long-serving stud manager in Newmarket, Michael Oswald, switched his allegiance to the Royal Studs at Sandringham. A nucleus of mares, shared between John and his son, Alastair, has since been maintained under manager Tim Read at Lavington, which ceased standing stallions after the 2007 covering season.

Meanwhile Egerton had a succession of unsatisfactory owners, before reverting to its original role as a training stable with David Elsworth, Lordship having been bought by Trevor Harris, breeder of the 2000 Oaks winner Love Divine and her 2006 St Leger winning son, Sixties Icon.

While the names of Dewar and Woolavington convey nothing to the present generation of racegoers, their descendants have not disappeared without trace. The 1978 Grand National winner, Lucius, was owned by Fiona Whitaker, a great-granddaughter of the 1st Lord Forteviot. Successful in the 1990 Irish One Thousand Guineas, International Stakes and Champion Stakes, as well as the Coronation Cup,

In The Groove was bred by John Macdonald-Buchanan, a grandson of the founder of Buchanan's whisky and trained by David Elsworth, then based at Whitsbury in Hampshire.

Whisky distillers have been staunch supporters of racing and Glenfarclas of Ballindalloch on Speyside, purveyors of the finest malts, sponsor the series of cross country races at Cheltenham staged in November, December and at the Festival Meeting in March. Run over a convoluted course it presents a unique challenge with thirty-two obstacles to be negotiated, two more than the Grand National. The Festival race was initiated in 2005 and Glenfarclas have been involved since 2009. It is a particular favourite with the Irish and John P. McManus has won it six times, five of those winners trained by Enda Bolger and four of them ridden by the leading lady amateur, Nina Carberry.

7

POLITICS AND THE TURF

David Cameron, whose father was joint owner of a Cheltenham winner trained by Alec Kilpatrick, belongs to a landowning family from Inverness-shire, and his great-great-great-uncle was Duke of Fife. He never dwelt upon his Scottish ancestry unlike his political predecessor Gordon Brown, a son of the manse. However, both followed a well trodden path at Westminster as during the thirty turbulent years from 1894 to 1924, no fewer than four Scotsmen served as prime minister: Lord Rosebery, Arthur Balfour, Sir Henry Campbell Bannerman and Ramsay MacDonald.

When it came to lineage, the 5th Earl of Rosebery, who only survived as Liberal prime minister for two years, could not quite compete with Arthur Balfour, a Conservative claiming descent from Robert the Bruce. The Rosebery family name is Primrose and they came from the Kingdom of Fife. In the seventeenth century Archibald Primrose, one of Charles II's loyal supporters, was rewarded with the lands of Dalmeny on the opposite side of the Firth of Forth, and Dalmeny House at South Queensferry remains the family home to this day. Lord Dalmeny is also the courtesy title of the Rosebery heirs.

Whenever anyone recalls the 5th Earl of Rosebery, another Archibald, reference is always made to a wager he was alleged to have made whilst an undergraduate at Christ Church, Oxford: that he would become prime minister, marry the richest woman in England and win the Derby. When he was a leading politician these heady aspirations permeated into the public domain, but he never denied the story. Against all the odds his prediction came to fruition as he married Hannah de Rothschild and won the Blue Riband of the Turf, not once, but three times, on the first two occasions during his short premiership.

When the 8th Lord Howard de Walden, another leading owner-breeder of his day, chose plain apricot for his racing colours it was at the suggestion of the artist, Augustus John, who advised that this would stand out best against the green background of the turf. There were obviously no such visual considerations when it came to choosing the Rosebery family silks, as the 'primrose and rose hoops' were derived from two of the family names. The colours were destined to become as famous in their time as those of the Arab sheikhs of today.

The machinations of primogeniture were unusual in the case of Archibald Primrose. His father died when he was a boy, but he had to wait until the death of his grandfather, the 4th Earl, in 1868 before inheriting the title. Just twenty-three years old when elected to the Jockey Club, he was already a racehorse owner of some years' standing – though not a particularly successful one – when in 1878 he married the heiress, Hannah de Rothschild, the only daughter and principal beneficiary of Baron Meyer de Rothschild, who had died four years earlier.

An extremely wealthy man in his own right, Archibald Rosebery was now an even richer one. Only the previous year he had bought The Durdans, a country house with stud land close to Epsom race-course. This was where the previous owner, Sir Gilbert Heathcote, had bred and reared the once-raced Amato, who in 1838 became the first Epsom-trained winner of the Derby. Originally a hunting box owned by Charles II, Rosebery's benefactor all those years ago, The Durdans was owned by Lord Halifax, but it had been allowed to fall into a state of disrepair. It was Rosebery who built the striking Grade II listed indoor school with its spectacular timber ceiling and raised dais from which he could watch his horses at exercise.

Rosebery also inherited Mentmore, a neo-Gothic edifice near Leighton Buzzard, boasting an established Rothschild stud (where a statue of Baron Meyer's dual champion sire, King Tom, presided). Together with The Durdans, this provided him with two breeding establishments which were to be run in close conjunction over the next half century. The Durdans was on chalk, which suited the young stock, while Mentmore's heavy Buckinghamshire clay soil ensured plenty of grass for his own mares during those dry summer months.

From 1883 to 1924 Lord Rosebery won eleven English classic races with nine individual horses, all of them homebred at Mentmore. They comprised Ladas, Sir Visto and Cicero in the Derby; Bonny Jean in the Oaks; Sir Visto in the St Leger; Ladas, Neil Gow and Ellangowan in the Two Thousand Guineas; and Chelandry, Vaucluse and Plack in the One Thousand Guineas. Astonishingly, in all those years Lord Rosebery was never once leading owner, but he was three times leading breeder.

Just as remarkable, five of these classic winners trace back to the homebred broodmare, Illuminata, the dam of Ladas and Chelandry; the second dam of Cicero and Neil Gow (ex Chelandry); and the third dam of Vaucluse. Illuminata herself was a daughter of Archibald Rosebery's great foundation mare, Paraffin. She was procured in unusual circumstances. Initially, Lord Rosebery was a patron of James Dover's East Ilsley stables in Berkshire where he took a liking to the filly, Chevisaunce. Her owner, General Pearson, agreed to sell her to Rosebery, forgetting that she was already spoken for. So in the end Rosebery bought her half-sister, Paraffin, instead.

Ladas won the Two Thousand Guineas and the Derby in 1894 and Sir Visto won the Derby and St Leger in 1895. They were the last of twenty-eight classic winners trained by fellow Scot, Mathew Dawson, then in his seventies, whom their owner-breeder had prevailed upon to come out of semi-retirement. Ladas had the same name as the very first winner that Rosebery ever owned when up at Oxford – he was responsible for his young owner leaving the university prematurely as the dean was not prepared to countenance racehorse ownership by an undergraduate. Sir Visto was out of Vista (1879), one of the very first Mentmore-bred foals to be registered in Rosebery's name.

Ladas, Sir Visto and Cicero, Rosebery's third Derby winner, all returned to Mentmore for stallion duty (all three were buried at The Durdans), but they were not particularly successful. Ladas sired Troutbeck (St Leger), and Cicero sired Friar Marcus, a champion broodmare sire, whose daughter, Feola, proved a great foundation mare for the Royal Studs; Sir Visto was a failure at stud. The Two Thousand Guineas winners, Neil Gow (named after a Scottish violinist) and Ellangowan, also retired to stud, the former at Mentmore and the latter at Scaltback Stud, Newmarket, in the ownership of his trainer, Jack (later Sir Jack) Jarvis. He also trained Archibald Rosebery's final classic winner, Plack.

During his lifetime, Archibald Rosebery had nearly as many trainers as he had horses. Latterly he transferred his string of thirty-five to Jack Jarvis's Park Lodge stables, Newmarket. Immediately the Rosebery colours were back in classic winning mode with the relatives Ellangowan (1923 Two Thousand Guineas) and Plack (1924 One Thousand Guineas). That move was at the instigation of Harry Rosebery, who was forty-seven when his father died in 1929. This marked the beginning of a long and successful partnership based on mutual trust and friendship which lasted until Jack Jarvis died in 1968.

As a young man Harry had followed his father into politics, but first he earned a considerable sporting reputation. At Eton he excelled at all games, but cricket was his particular forte. In the era of gentlemen and players, he was a forceful batsman and, as Lord Dalmeny, a conspicuously successful captain of Surrey from 1905 to 1907. It was his privilege to award Jack (later Sir Jack) Hobbs his county cap. In later life as master of the Whaddon Chase, the pack of hounds that hunted the demanding country round Mentmore, he proved a masterful heavyweight MFH.

He was also an excellent shot, up to international standard at polo, and a proficient golfer. He spent a great deal of time on a grouse moor, but on one occasion in Dalmeny Park his shooting expertise was faced with an unexpected challenge. A bull got loose when disembarking from the train at Ratho Station. After attempting to gore anyone who got in his way, the animal escaped into the park. Harry Dalmeny, who had been out rabbit shooting, quickly substituted his shotgun for a rifle and after a memorable chase felled the enraged bull with a shot through the heart.

Commissioned into the Grenadier Guards after Sandhurst, he left the army within a few years at his father's behest to stand as the Liberal candidate for Edinburghshire (Midlothian) in the general election of 1906. It was a two-edged sword. Returned with a handsome majority in this the safest of Liberal seats, he became the youngest MP aged just twenty-four. However, he felt duty-bound to support his father's radical views, and as things turned out that rather scuppered whatever long-term political aspirations he may have had.

In fact Harry Rosebery had never wanted to leave the army, but he had the opportunity to serve his country in two World Wars. He was severely wounded during the First World War, when three of the top brass in the British Army were Scotsmen: Lord Robertson, Sir Ian Hamilton and Field Marshal Douglas Haig. He served on Lord Allenby's staff, and was awarded the DSO, MC and Légion d'Honneur. In the 1939–45 conflict he was regional commissioner for civil defence in Scotland. Also secretary of state for Scotland for a period, he was lord lieutenant for Midlothian from 1929 to 1964.

The period spanning the Second World War was a difficult time on a personal level as he obtained an acrimonious divorce from his first wife, Lady Dorothy Grosvenor, sister of the 3rd Duke of Westminster, while his younger brother, Neil Primrose, was killed in action in Palestine. Although there were far more important issues at stake, it was nonetheless a frustrating period so far as Harry Rosebery's racing interests were concerned. In 1943 his luckless filly, Ribbon, was beaten a neck for the One Thousand Guineas, a neck for the Oaks and a short head for the St Leger, all substitute races run on the July Course at Newmarket.

Neil Primrose's daughter, Ruth, had a great racing pedigree which she further enhanced by marriage. Her mother was the daughter of the 17th Earl of Derby, the greatest owner-breeder during the first half of the twentieth century; she married the 2nd Earl of Halifax (whose father, the 1st Earl, had been foreign secretary). Together, Charles Halifax and their son Peter, the present earl and owner of Garrowby Stud in Yorkshire, bred the 1978 Derby winner, Shirley Heights.

Harry Rosebery had two Derby winners of his own with Blue Peter, the last winner at Epsom before the outbreak of war in 1939, and his son, Ocean Swell. The latter, who traced back six generations to Paraffin, won a substitute race at Newmarket in 1944. As president of the Thoroughbred Breeders' Association and one of the most high-profile owners in the country, Rosebery was in a strong position to advocate that racing should be allowed to continue for the duration of the war to ensure the essential continuity of bloodstock breeding and his strong lobbying undoubtedly influenced the top brass to maintain a degree of competition, albeit on a strictly regional basis.

Blue Peter, a most attractive chesnut standing just over sixteen hands, was out of Fancy Free, a mare purchased from Lord Wimborne when he decided to give up racing. A promising two-year-old, the Fairway colt looked to have classic potential and so it proved with convincing victories in both the Two Thousand Guineas and the Derby, followed by the Eclipse Stakes. It was a thousand pities that he was denied his chance in the St Leger, where he was due to meet the French invader Pharis II. However, war was declared on 3 September and the Doncaster St Leger Meeting was cancelled.

Most observers were convinced that Blue Peter would have landed the elusive Triple Crown despite the presence of Pharis. His proud owner-breeder was in no doubt. Remembering his old favourite some twenty years later, he said: 'He was just like a human being although a placid animal. Blue Peter was particular about what he ate. Give him something he didn't like and Blue Peter would take one look at it and turn away. He was the best horse I ever had and was the best I had ever seen and he only had half a career as a racehorse.'

Harry Rosebery had already won the St Leger with Sandwich in 1931. A yearling purchase, he had finished third in the Derby to Cameronian, owned by the Scottish whisky magnate, Arthur Dewar. When the land at The Durdans, where Rosebery's young stock had been reared, was sold after the Second World War, he bought another stud at Newmarket and named it Sandwich – this is where his two Derby winners Blue Peter and his son, Ocean Swell, went to be reared as weaned foals.

Latterly, with a steady complement of thirty or so mares at stud at any one time, Harry Rosebery had no need to buy yearlings, but Sandwich was by no means his only venture into the market place. Another inspired purchase was Miracle, who was a year junior to Sandwich. He cost a bargain 170 guineas from his owner-breeder, Lord

Beaverbrook, who became one of Harry Rosebery's closest friends. This colt won the Eclipse Stakes after finishing third in the Derby, but broke down prior to the St Leger. Both Sandwich and Miracle failed as stallions.

In the long term, Blue Peter's influence as a sire was through his daughters (he was champion broodmare sire of 1954), but his initial crop of foals did include Harry Rosebery's second Derby hero, Ocean Swell. Successful in a substitute running at Newmarket in 1944, he proceeded to win the following year's Gold Cup at Ascot before joining his own sire at Mentmore. Ocean Swell's major contribution at stud was to sire Fastnet Rock and this grey in turn became the maternal grandsire of Harry Rosebery's one and only Oaks winner, Sleeping Partner.

If ever there was a sentimental winner it was this grey in the 1969 Oaks. Prior to Sleeping Partner, her owner-breeder had had four runners-up in the fillies' premier classic as well as two thirds. Although Sleeping Partner had proved nothing exceptional as a juvenile, Jack Jarvis, shortly before he died, told her owner-breeder during their last telephone conversation that the grey could well win the Oaks. So it was a very moving moment for her eighty-seven-year-old owner when he and his homebred filly stood in the winner's enclosure at Epsom the following June.

Sleeping Partner was trained by Doug Smith, who took over the Rosebery horses at Park Lodge as well as continuing as a public trainer at Loder Stables. It was not a very practical arrangement and it was short lived. Not long afterwards Harry Rosebery decided to transfer the majority of his string to another Newmarket trainer. 'I want you to take them over by the weekend,' he instructed Bruce Hobbs, who somehow managed to accommodate an extra thirty-five horses at three days' notice!

During the brief period that Bruce Hobbs handled the Rosebery horses, he became the first trainer in the country to have over 100 horses in his care. One who presented a particular challenge was Tom Cribb. A good-staying handicapper and winner of the Northumberland Plate, he was a very tricky customer. When not equipped with a muzzle he would attempt to savage any rival who got in his way! Although Tom Cribb continued racing as a five-year-old, he somehow managed to remain an entire when exported to Italy.

Of course, Jack Jarvis was a hard act to follow as he and his principal patron had enjoyed a special rapport. The Mentmore horses were bred to be tough and sound and they had to be to survive the demanding training schedule that Jack Jarvis favoured. They invariably looked like the proverbial hat-rack, but they enjoyed an enviable record for winning races. Back home on the stud, the youngsters were never mollycoddled as two post-war managers would have verified – Clarence Hailey, a local bloodstock agent with an international clientele, and Clive Haselden, one of the best known equine veterinary practitioners in the Vale of Aylesbury. Clive Haselden acted as Rosebery's estate and stud manager for over three decades.

For many years the Rosebery horses dominated what was known as the Scottish fortnight in September. This coincides with the Ayr Western Meeting, which stages the Listed Harry Rosebery Stakes (formerly the Ladykirk Stakes). Over the years Jack Jarvis saddled over 100 winners for him at the Western Meeting. He always loved having runners in his native Scotland and, but for his patronage, his local course of Musselburgh (then a Flat-only course) would have long since ceased to exist.

One of his runners during the Scottish fortnight thoroughly disgraced herself. At the Hamilton Park Autumn Meeting in 1934 his two-year-old, Indiscretion, appeared on successive days, only to whip round at the start on both occasions. Having only once got off on equal terms in five juvenile starts, she was promptly covered by Sandwich and sold for 600 guineas at the following year's Tattersalls' December Sales. In 1947 her daughter, Imprudence, came from France to plunder the One Thousand Guineas and the Oaks. As a foal at foot, Imprudence had been in the front line of the fighting that took place in and around Nonant-le-Pin during the German invasion of Normandy in 1944.

It was not only in the hunting field that Harry Rosebery proved himself a heavyweight. As president of the Thoroughbred Breeders' Association from 1932 to 1955, he was so autocratic that few dared to question him, far less contradict him. Opinionated he most certainly was, but he proved a very able administrator on racing matters and, as a senior steward of the Jockey Club from 1932 to 1948, campaigned successfully for a number of reforms. Long term, he was instrumental in introducing the photo-finish camera; he advocated legislation on betting and the licensing of bookmakers; and he encouraged the advancement of the Tote.

Of course he liked a bet himself. Between the wars it would have been deemed out of order for a steward or member of the Jockey Club, far less a member of the aristocracy, to be seen placing a bet in Tattersalls' Ring. Like other serious backers in his position, he employed a commission agent to place any wagers on his behalf and it was a Scotsman, Johnny Marr, to whom he entrusted his instructions. 'Scotch' Marr was the son of a former Lord Mayor of Glasgow, an astute judge of the Form Book and all the different aspects of backing horses; he died a very wealthy man.

Lord Rosebery had not long been appointed senior steward when he was embroiled in a cause célèbre. In the event of any runner found to have been doped, the Jockey Club automatically warned off the trainer concerned. After scoring at Kempton Park on 13 August 1930, Don Pat stood in the winner's enclosure dripping with saliva. When a dope test proved positive, his trainer, Charles Chapman from Lavant in Sussex, had his licence withdrawn.

Charles Chapman then sued the Jockey Club for libel and the case was heard in the High Court in November of the following year. It produced a high-profile legal confrontation between Norman Birkett representing the Jockey Club (with Rosebery as its principal witness), and Patrick Hastings acting on behalf of Chapman. The jury returned a verdict in favour of the plaintiff and he was awarded substantial damages. However, in February 1932 the decision was reversed at the Appeal Court on a technicality regarding the relevant wording in the Jockey Club Rules.

Over the ensuing years, Charles Chapman made endless applications for the renewal of his training licence. It was all to no avail, despite the support of local grandees, the Duke of Richmond, owner of Goodwood racecourse, and the Duke of Norfolk, who ran a private stable at Arundel Castle. For his part, Lord Rosebery seemed to adopt an unremitting vendetta against the man who had had the temerity to challenge the Jockey Club's authority. In the end Charles Chapman, who always maintained his innocence, became a market gardener.

In 1951 another doping scandal reared its ugly head, but this time it involved a two-year-old filly belonging to Rosebery and trained by Jarvis. At the Newmarket Houghton Meeting on 31 October, Snap proved an uneasy favourite before finishing unplaced – the last of her three starts that season. It transpired that she had been doped. Her owner-breeder promptly put all the facts in the public domain, offered a £1,000 reward for any information, and made a personal request to Sir Harold Scott, chief commissioner of Scotland Yard, to implement extensive inquiries. The perpetrators were never found, but racecourse security at Newmarket was tightened up.

The circumstances surrounding Don Pat and Snap were significantly different. The former had been doped to win and the latter had been doped to lose; furthermore the Don Pat investigation had been initiated by the Kempton stewards, whereas Rosebery himself ordered a private dope test on Snap. However, to many observers it all smacked of double standards – after all, the Jockey Club did not differentiate between the two types of offence when it came to the automatic disqualification for life of the trainer in question. Jack Jarvis could count himself a lucky man!

It was certainly inadvisable to cross Lord Rosebery if one could avoid it. Just after the Second World War, Old Etonian Tom Nickalls – who had been invalided out of the army as a Lt-Colonel in the 17/21st Lancers – took up the post of Warren Hill on the *Sporting Life*. At some point he criticised Harry Rosebery's colt Midas, who had divided Dante and Court Martial at the finish of the substitute Derby of 1945. Evidently that opinion cost Tom Nickalls a position with bloodstock auctioneers Tattersalls. Whoever said that Rosebery could be a good friend but an implacable foe had a point.

In the 1960s, two of the last good colts bred at Mentmore were Fighting Ship and General Gordon. Even at that late stage the emphasis was still on producing the classic middle-distance and staying type of horse; sprinters never came into the equation, at least not intentionally. Both chesnuts suffered extreme bad luck. In normal circumstances Fighting Ship would probably have started favourite for the Gold Cup as a four-year-old, but injury forced him into retirement prior to the Royal Meeting and then the Gold Cup was abandoned due to a water-logged course. The very highly regarded General Gordon was an effortless winner of the Chester Vase before breaking a fetlock in his winding-up gallop for the Derby.

It is often said that a good horse has a good name and this was something to which Harry Rosebery always paid particular attention. The names he chose were always appropriate in terms of the sire and dam – General Gordon (Never Say Die – Camp Fire) was named after the man who was sent out by the British government to rescue the Egyptian garrisons in the Sudan and was killed at Khartoum. Surprisingly, bearing in mind the strait-laced attitudes of the time, many of the names were of a risqué nature. There was, for example, Bra for a filly by Ocean Swell out of Model, and Jolly Roger for a colt by Blue Peter out of Sonsie Wench – and there were many more of comparable ingenuity.

A love of racing and breeding was one of few pursuits that the Roseberys, father and son, shared and even then their approaches could be entirely different. The 5th Earl offered the filly, Popinjay, to Waldorf Astor (later Lord Astor) for £1,000, and was so amused when one of the world's richest men said he could only afford £800, that he capitulated. Harry was a harder nut to crack. When racing journalist Clive Graham, also acting for an American, was unprepared to pay the asking price of £20,000 for Fair Edith, Harry stuck to his guns, retorting, 'Don't forget, I'm bred by a Scotsman out of a Jewess, so I am not in the habit of giving anything away.' Incidentally both fillies proved well worth their money – Popinjay became one of the great foundation mares of the Astors' Cliveden Stud, and Fair Edith became the dam of Aunt Edith, one of the top racemares of the mid-1960s.

The 6th Earl of Rosebery died at Mentmore in May 1974 aged ninety-two. The principal beneficiary was his heir, Neil Primrose, the present Lord Rosebery, who lives at Dalmeny (which has a unique collection of Napoleon Bonaparte memorabilia) and has no interest in the Turf. He was Harry Rosebery's son, born to his second wife and widow, Eva. She was also mother, by her previous marriage, of the late Lavinia, Duchess of Norfolk, another leading racing personality of her era and the power behind the throne for so long at Castle Stables, Arundel.

In 1978 the Mentmore estate was disposed of to meet inheritance tax, Mentmore Towers being sold originally to Maharishi Mahesh Yogi – former guru of the Beatles – to become the headquarters of the Natural Law Party. The inevitable consequence was that this once great Rothschild property has been decimated at the hands of developers. The plan was for Mentmore Towers, a Grade I listed building, which has provided the backdrop for some blockbuster films, to be converted into a luxury hotel.

However, there is still a Rothschild legacy in terms of Thoroughbred breeding in these parts, once known as Rothschildshire due to the vast tracts of land owned by the Jewish banking dynasty. The 4th Lord Rothschild has a stud at Waddesdon and Sir Evelyn de Rothschild is part-owner of Southcourt Stud, near Linslade. The former is run by Jacob Rothschild's wife, Serena, and the latter was managed by Evelyn's sister and stud partner, Renee Robeson, who died in 2015. Both establishments were in the news in 2006. Waddesdon acquired a broodmare for a world record price of 4.6m guineas; and the Southcourt-bred Notnowcato was winner of three Group 1 races in 2006–7: the Eclipse Stakes, International Stakes and Tattersalls' Gold Cup.

8

A 100–1 JACKPOT AT EPSOM AND AINTREE

Few people can claim direct involvement with a Derby winner and a Grand National winner (in this instance two National winners), but that was the singular experience of Thomas Kennedy Laidlaw in the first half of the twentieth century. At the time these two historic races were of unrivalled interest and prestige worldwide, the relatively new medium of wireless enabling the action to be broadcast to the four corners of the globe. And the fact that Aboyeur and Gregalach both started at odds of 100–1 makes the Scot's achievement all the more sensational.

One of the first horses bred by Tom Laidlaw, Aboyeur triumphed at Epsom in 1913 in one of the most sensational Derbys of all time. This was the occasion when Emily Davison threw herself in front of the king's colt. Further drama ensued. A head and a neck separated the three principals as they flashed past the winning post. Initially the judge decreed that Craganour had prevailed over Aboyeur, but after much delay and deliberation, the stewards reversed that decision on the grounds of interference. This highly controversial episode remains the solitary disqualification in the colourful history of the Blue Riband.

Aboyeur raced for Alan Cunliffe, a director of Sandown Park and founder of the notorious Druid's Lodge stable on Salisbury Plain. The patrons of this remote outpost became known as the Druid's Lodge confederacy and they brought off some infamous gambles. Aboyeur, who achieved his only other success at Salisbury as a two-year-old, was sold at the conclusion of his three-year-old career for £13,000 to the Imperial Racing Club in St Petersburg. His ultimate fate during the revolution is not known, but the unsubstantiated story is that he was harnessed to a cart with another Derby winner, Minoru, and disappeared to Serbia.

It is doubtful whether Aboyeur earned any roubles in Russia. However, Craganour, named after a grouse moor in Scotland, did not run again before being exported to Argentina where he became an extremely successful sire. An unlucky racehorse, his disqualification after finishing first in the Derby followed a head defeat by Louvois in the Two Thousand Guineas when everyone apart from the judge thought that he had won. The previous season (1912) Craganour had proved the top two-year-old, but that was small consolation to his owner, Charles Bower Ismay. The Ismay family controlled the White Star Line, whose flagship, *Titanic*, met her end in such tragic circumstances that year.

Just like Aboyeur, Craganour was trained in a Wiltshire stable renowned for carefully planned betting coups in major handicaps, in this instance Jack Robinson's yard at Foxhill. Charles Ismay also had jumpers in training with Tom Coulthwaite at Hednesford. Indeed, it was one of his horses which was responsible for the Staffordshire trainer, a native of Lancashire, being temporarily deprived of his licence. Whereas Aboyeur had been sold privately as a foal by his breeder, Gregalach was one of two young jumpers that Tom Laidlaw had put on the open market in the spring of 1927 – he had decided to accompany his wife on a trip abroad in the hope that it would prove beneficial for her failing health.

That year, the main attraction at Tattersalls' April sale in Park Paddocks, Newmarket, on the morning of the Two Thousand Guineas, was a large consignment of horses in training. They were offered by the executors of Sir Robert Jardine, a fellow Scot from Lockerbie, one-time managing director of the great Scottish trading company, Jardine Matheson, who had died in January. They were followed into the ring by Gregalach and Grakle, a couple of five-year-old geldings from Tom Coulthwaite's yard, two very promising young chasers who had been acquired by their trainer on behalf of Tom Laidlaw as unbroken three-year-olds.

Gregalach had recently won three chases, including the Stanley Chase over the big Aintree fences. Grakle had fallen in that season's

National when leading on the first circuit – he had started favourite on the strength of finishing runner-up in the Cheltenham Gold Cup, a magnificent effort for a five-year-old. Another of Tom Coulthwaite's patrons, Cecil Taylor, a Liverpool cotton broker, was anxious to buy one or other of the pair, and after bidding up to 4,500 guineas for Gregalach, the first through the ring, he managed to secure Grakle for 500 guineas less. For 5,000 guineas, Gregalach passed into the ownership of another Scot, Mrs Gemmell. She was a sister of Norman Donaldson, who was chairman of the family shipping line based on the Clyde, and owner of the 1949 One Thousand Guineas and Oaks heroine, Musidora.

Amazingly both Gregalach and Grakle went on to win the Grand National. Gregalach's new trainer, Tom Leader at Newmarket, fielded no fewer than five runners in the 1929 National when, as the rank outsider of the quintet at 100–1, Gregalach stormed home in a record field of sixty-six runners from the hot favourite, Easter Hero. His rider was Robert Everett, an Australian amateur turned professional, who had gained much of his riding experience in South Africa. A former officer in the Royal Navy, he served in the Fleet Air Arm during the Second World War and was awarded a posthumous DSO.

Just to embellish this amazing story, when Grakle was victorious in 1931, Gregalach was the gallant runner-up. Previously Tom Laidlaw's own colours had been placed twice in the National by Fly Mask, who finished second in 1924 and third the following year.

Gregalach, who struck up an unusual relationship with a rough-haired terrier which accompanied him everywhere, and Grakle were two of the best Aintree chasers of their era. The former competed in five Grand Nationals and following his great triumph was allocated top weight of 12st 7lb in the next three runnings. The latter ran in six Grand Nationals, and was Tom Coulthwaite's third winner of the great race. His name lives on through the Grakle noseband, a device consisting of two crossed straps strategically placed on the bridle, which help to stop a horse from pulling unduly.

The circumstances by which the Laidlaws came to reside in Ireland were unusual. The family originated in the Borders and as a branch of the Black Douglas clan were contemporaries of Sir Walter Scott, who lived at St Boswells. Following the Napoleonic Wars they established a thriving iron foundry in Glasgow at a time when gas was becoming the principal source of commercial and domestic lighting. Not only did their cast-iron gas pipes serve many Scottish towns, but they were also supplied to such far-flung outposts as St Petersburg, Berlin and Milan.

R. Laidlaw & Sons' iron works also diversified in other areas, being involved in the construction of many of the splendid seaside piers around the coast of Britain, including Blackpool and Brighton. In 1905 the Admiralty, urged on by Winston Churchill, decided that oil rather than coal would be the fuel to propel the Royal Navy's new battleships and it was Laidlaws which supplied the vast oil tanks required to serve these monster warships at the new base at Rosyth on the Firth of Forth. Another member of the Laidlaw clan made his own special contribution to the Second World War by inventing and designing the burners for Frank Whittle's jet engines.

Tom Laidlaw was a graduate of Glasgow University – as were two of his brothers, and his cousin, Dick Allen, whose family owned the Allen Line which traded between Scotland and Canada. As a young man, Tom Laidlaw used to make regular trips from Glasgow to hunt and race in Ireland and his Irish expeditions were to have marked repercussions in later life.

Just outside Glasgow is Paisley which was famous as the home of the cotton thread industry, dominated in Victorian times by Coats' mills at one end of town and Clarks' at the other end. While J. & P. Coats monopolised trade in Europe, their rivals did likewise in North America. About 1890 the two companies joined forces to become the biggest cotton thread producers in the world. In due course the Clark family emigrated to New Jersey and Tom Laidlaw married William Clark's only daughter, a noted beauty. As he did not wish to live in America and she was disinclined to live in Scotland, they decided to move to Ireland where he had a number of friends amongst the local landowning community. After an interim period based in Dublin, they bought Somerton at Castleknock, Co. Dublin, from Sir George Brooke, whose family came from Co. Fermanagh in Ulster. It was here that he started breeding bloodstock in a small way.

The foundation mare of what became known as Abbey Lodge Stud was Carrick Shore (Kirk-Alloway – Terre de Sienne), a name derived from the works of Robert Burns. Kirk-Alloway was a homebred black horse out of Cantrip, an own-sister to Aboyeur, and he carried his breeder's colours to victory in the 1920 Irish St Leger. Terre de Sienne, a half-sister to an influential sire in Bruleur, was a French-bred mare Tom Laidlaw had procured from Evremond de Saint-Alary in 1928. The introduction had been afforded by that great Irish breeder, Jim Maher, breeder of a Grand National winner, Covertcoat (trained by Robert Gore, a descendant of the Earls of Arran), and a Derby winner, Manna.

When Thomas Laidlaw died in 1943, the stud, which had previously operated as the Somerton Estates Company and which he had greatly reduced in latter years, was taken over by two of his children, Robert and Elizabeth, and Robert's son, Thomas. From that time onwards the select broodmare band remained the exclusive preserve of Carrick Shore's descendants. Her daughter Dunure (unbroken like her dam) proved the mainstay. Dunure was named after a seaside town on the Ayrshire coast.

The last good horse bred by Tom Laidlaw Snr was Skoiter, who emulated Kirk-Alloway in 1939 by winning the Irish St Leger for the flour miller, James V. Rank. Skoiter, who became a useful sire of jumpers, was trained by Bob Fetherstonhaugh on the Curragh. He continued to handle the Flat horses retained to carry the Laidlaws' well-known colours of black with gold spots until his death in 1950. His successor was John Oxx and the Currabeg trainer became closely involved with all aspects of the Laidlaws' bloodstock affairs, right up to the 1990s.

In 1950 Abbey Lodge Stud gained its most prestigious victory on home soil with Dark Warrior in the Irish Derby. A smart two-year-old when he won the Beresford Plate, he had finished third in the Irish Two Thousand Guineas prior to his success in Ireland's premier classic. Dark Warrior scored by half a length from the Aga Khan's Eclat and Marcel Boussac's Pardal. The latter started favourite to augment his owner's great English classic double with Galcador in the Derby and Asmena in the Oaks – which was duly augmented by Scratch II in the St Leger.

Dark Warrior had been sold as a yearling from Abbey Lodge at Ballsbridge for 775 guineas (the underbidder had been Stephen Hill Dillon on the lookout for a prospective jumper for the Queen Mother). He failed to enhance his reputation when switched from Paddy Prendergast on the Curragh to Harry Wragg at Newmarket for the ensuing season. He was then sent to Brazil as a potential stallion. The deal was handled by his owner, Frank More O'Ferrall of the Anglo-Irish Bloodstock Agency, whose brother, Roderic, owned the famous Kildangan Stud in Co. Kildare, now the Irish breeding headquarters of Sheikh Mohammed.

Sixty-eight years after Tom Laidlaw bred the 1913 Derby winner, Aboyeur, Elizabeth Laidlaw bred Blue Wind, who brought off the English and Irish Oaks double in 1981. This Lord Gayle filly was readily identifiable with Abbey Lodge. While Dark Warrior was a son of Dunure, Blue Wind was a great-granddaughter of Dunure. She was foaled when her dam, Azurine, who was placed third in the Irish One Thousand Guineas, was twenty-one years of age.

Blue Wind changed hands twice at public auction prior to her two classic victories. She was sold by Betty Laidlaw as a yearling at Goffs for 5,600 guineas to Dark Warrior's trainer, Paddy Prendergast. She then realised 180,000 guineas in the same ring in November of the following year. Her greatly enhanced value was due to an interim success in the Silken Glider Stakes at Leopardstown. The price represented a record for one of her age group in the British Isles and an outright record for a horse in training in Ireland. Her new owner, Diana Firestone, sent her to be trained by Dermot Weld and in due course the filly took up residence at her Catoctin Stud in Virginia.

The Group 3 Blue Wind Stakes at the Curragh commemorates this outstanding filly, who also had a distinguished own-brother in Callernish. A very successful Irish-based stallion, he sired many winners under National Hunt Rules, highlighted by the 1996 Cheltenham Gold Cup hero, Imperial Call, trained by an Irish-based Scot, Fergus Sutherland.

Latterly, Abbey Lodge Stud was owned by Tom Laidlaw's daughter, Betty, in partnership with his grandson, Thomas, and the latter's daughter, Caroline Corballis. The dwindling number of broodmares were boarded on John Oxx's farm. Following Betty Laidlaw's death in 1959, the other members of the family decided not to persevere with the stud. However, the bloodline that made it famous was back in the headlines in 2004 when English-trained Wilko, a direct descendant of Azurine, won the Breeders' Cup Juvenile at Lone Star Park in Texas.

It was in 1950 that Tom Laidlaw Jnr had inherited Somerton's 400 acres comprising the farm and the stud, upon the condition that he went to live there. As a young man he had followed his father into the Royal Scots Greys. Robert, who was invalided out of the army towards the end of the First World War, used to spend half the year at home in Glasgow and half at Somerton. Chairman of the Coats/Clarks textile business, he was also involved in banking and was chairman of the Clydesdale Bank when he died in 1964. Tom took part in the Normandy landings, finishing up in the Baltic.

Tom Laidlaw Jnr of Gernonstown House, Slane, Co. Meath followed his father and his grandfather as a member of the Turf Club, the body which regulates Irish racing. He was also the last chairman of the panel of stewards at Phoenix Park, before this popular racecourse on the outskirts of Dublin was sold for development.

The status quo has been maintained by Caroline Corballis, the eldest of his four daughters and the fourth generation of this enterprising family to be members of the Turf Club. It is a unique Scottish/Irish liaison.

9

TURF IMMORTALITY AND A
SHARED BIRTHDAY

Mr McGregor, the gardener who famously chased Peter Rabbit, was never going to be one of Beatrix Potter's most endearing characters. His namesake, though, proved a very popular figure in the annals of the Turf. Indeed, as the owner-breeder (or part owner-breeder to be more accurate) of the 1932 Derby winner, April The Fifth, his background reads just like a work of fiction. Foaled on Sydney McGregor's birthday (hence the name), April The Fifth was trained, somewhat incongruously, by a member of the acting profession.

Sydney McGregor, who died aged eighty in 1970, lived at Lillington Stud Farm, close to Leamington Spa, in Warwickshire. Just down the road is the site of the old figure-of-eight jumps course. Time was when Leamington Spa was a prestigious meeting, with the Leamington Steeplechase, first run in 1835, attracting many top horses. Amongst the early winners was Lottery in 1840, who had triumphed in the inaugural Grand National only the previous year. The curtain finally came down at Leamington in March 1911, with a card devoted to chases.

Warwickshire has had its share of trainers down the years. One who made a significant impact during the early 1960s was an Irish interloper, Paddy Sleator, from Co. Wicklow. A very astute trainer, he used to operate a satellite yard from Arthur Thomas's Guy's Cliffe stables, near Kenilworth, and he won a multitude of jump races in England – so many, in fact, that trainers here made representations to the powers that be and the practice was disallowed. So much for open competition! One of Sleator's stars was the prolific scorer Scottish Memories (Mackeson Gold Cup), owned by Gerald Sanderson from Dunning in Perthshire.

Another jumping enthusiast from Warwickshire was Lord Leigh of Stoneleigh Abbey, near Kenilworth. His son, Ben, partnered his own horse, Rueil, to win the 1965 Grand Military Gold Cup before becoming a trainer in Lambourn. From his family home at Shipston-on-Stour, Charles Vernon Miller dispatched Bighorn to win the 1971 Hennessy Gold Cup for his father, who was also the gelding's breeder; Charlie had been assistant to Harry Whiteman at Cree Lodge, Ayr.

There used to be a number of well-known studs in the area too, including Dunchurch Lodge, subsequently moved to Newmarket; Offchurch Bury, later transformed into a polo ground; and Chesterton, home to the leading amateur rider, John Thorne – he partnered Spartan Missile, a son of his own stallion, Spartan General, to finish runner-up in the 1981 Grand National. It was also in Warwickshire, at Moreton Paddox in Moreton Morrell, that Bob McCreery bred the Two Thousand Guineas winner and highly influential sire, High Top.

A well-known figure out with the Warwickshire hounds, Sydney McGregor was a sporting farmer with a penchant for racing and he pursued all aspects of the business from owning and training his own horses, to buying and selling. Outwardly casual and cheerful, his appearance camouflaged an astuteness particularly so far as breeding was concerned. Also expert at bringing on young horses of all descriptions, he was a firm advocate of owning horses in partnership or leasing them to help defray expenses. Consequently a number of people benefited from his undoubted skills in breeding and acquiring good horses for a minimal outlay.

His family involvement with horses went back a long way, both literally and metaphorically. Sydney and his father were both born in Leamington and Sydney's birth certificate gives Edward's occupation as 'horse dealer'. Of course, it was an era when horses played an indispensable role in everyday life. The probably apocryphal story is that Sydney's grandfather – who looked after the horses belonging to affluent Glasgow businessmen when they took their annual summer vacation in those large Victorian mansions overlooking Loch Lomond – had travelled south over the border riding one horse and leading another. On reaching Leamington he managed to sell the pair for a handsome profit, whereupon he decided to make this popular Midlands spa town his permanent home.

Nothing exemplifies Sydney McGregor's consummate skill more than the redoubtable April The Fifth, whose modest background has the sort of romance associated with a National winner rather than a Derby winner. Of no account on the racecourse, his dam Sold Again had a prophetic name. She was given as a present to her Newmarket trainer, Sam Pickering. He sold her as a three-year-old at Tattersalls' 1923 December Sales, where she was bought for twenty guineas by a Worcestershire horse dealer. Two years later she reappeared at Tattersalls' June sale in Knightsbridge, where Sydney McGregor procured her for 230 guineas.

McGregor bought Sold Again not as a prospective broodmare, but to race under NH Rules. He leased her to Graeme Whitelaw – known as 'Grimy' – a Scotsman who trained his own horses near Lambourn. An Old Harrovian who had served in the Seaforth Highlanders, Graeme Stewart Lockhart Whitelaw came from Knockando – a sporting estate in Morayshire now owned by owner-breeder, Dr Catherine Wills. He had been a trainer first at Letcombe Regis and then at Ashdown Park, and was also joint-master of the Old Berks.

When Sold Again broke down after a solitary run over hurdles, Sydney and Grimy decided to breed from her jointly and to share any of her offspring. It was to a mating with Craig an Eran that she produced April The Fifth as her second foal – volumes 26 and 27 of *The General Stud Book* actually give G.S.L. Whitelaw as the official breeder.

In his autobiography, the leading amateur rider Frank Atherton Brown, who trained in the Cotswolds, recalls going over to visit Sydney McGregor at Leamington to see if he had any nice store horses for sale. 'We were walking round his farm together laughing and talking of this and that when we came upon a lanky looking black yearling colt standing by himself under a big elm tree, looking rather forlorn, as it was a wet day. "How do you like him?" quizzed Sydney. "Not much and he's black, anyway. Let's look at some three-year-olds," came the reply.' This unprepossessing youngster was April The Fifth.

As a yearling, the son of Craig an Eran was consigned to the

Newmarket July Sales to dissolve the partnership. Sydney McGregor secured the other half-share with a bid of 200 guineas. Returned to Lillington, he was then turned out for six months until joining Tom Walls the following January, by which time he had grown a thick winter coat. Tom agreed to take a half-share in the youngster in lieu of training fees, with any prize money to be shared equally. The instructions were not to hurry the colt and to keep the Derby and the St Leger firmly in mind, which must have seemed extraordinarily optimistic at the time.

The choice of Tom Walls, who trained a small string at Epsom, was a curious one. After a brief spell as a police officer in the Metropolitan force, he had embarked upon a stage career, his very first appearance being in a pantomime in Glasgow. During the 1920s and 1930s he was associated with a series of successful farces staged at the Aldwych Theatre. It was after one of his productions that Tom Walls named a horse Tons of Money, who wound up in Benito Mussolini's ownership, finally ending his colourful career as a charger in the Italian army.

After three modest runs as a juvenile, it was surprising that April The Fifth still retained his classic engagements. However, he grew over the winter and, following a fourth in a handicap at Birmingham, he ran unplaced behind Orwell in the Two Thousand Guineas, prior to winning a mile maiden at Gatwick. But it was a two-length victory over Firdaussi in the inaugural Lingfield Derby Trial that ensured his presence in the Blue Riband. Starting at 100–6 with Orwell the short-priced favourite at 5–4, he stormed home in the final furlong to win by three parts of a length from Dastur who, like Firdaussi, was owned by the Aga Khan.

The last Derby winner to be trained at Epsom (and the first to be trained there since Amato prevailed back in 1838), April The Fifth was also a one and only classic winner for his jockey, Fred Lane. Little did the crowd that thronged Epsom Downs that afternoon realise just how near April The Fifth had come to being a non-runner. Tom Walls' stable was a mile distant from the course, but the horse-box transporting him there was delayed by the sheer volume of traffic, so he had to be unloaded and led for the second half of the journey. Tom's cousin, who had been delegated to declare the horse, only reached the weighing room in the nick of time.

For a change of scenery after Epsom, the colt was sent with others of Tom Walls's horses down to Alfred Day's place at Fontwell Park (the racecourse was constructed on his old gallops). Unfortunately the Derby hero knocked himself below the knee, not once, but twice. With regular dips in the sea at nearby Selsey he soon became sound again, but there was little stable confidence behind his participation in the St Leger where he finished unplaced to Firdaussi. He never ran again.

Initially April The Fifth retired to stand at Jim Joel's Childwick Bury Stud in Hertfordshire at a fee of 150 guineas, but after an interim period standing at Abbey Chase in Surrey, he returned home to Sydney McGregor in Warwickshire where he spent the remainder of his days. The best of his progeny on the racecourse proved to be Lord Stalbridge's magnificent chaser, Red April, the winner of twenty-three races, highlighted by the newly instituted Queen Elizabeth Chase at Hurst Park.

In November 1931, when April The Fifth was a two-year-old, Grimy Whitelaw had relinquished his interest in the dam, Sold Again, and she was dispatched from his Antwick Stud at Letcombe Regis, on the Wantage side of Lambourn, to Lillington. She was accompanied by her foal by Erizo, a French-bred import who had scored three times for Grimy as a six-year-old before retiring to take up stud duties at his Letcombe Regis home.

One of Grimy's most memorable achievements as an owner-trainer was to bring off a double at the 1929 National Hunt Meeting at Cheltenham, with Castlederg in the County Hurdle and Big Wonder in the National Hunt Chase. Subsequently he had horses in training in various public stables. His name was to be commemorated by the Whitelaw Challenge Cup, a chase at Fontwell Park.

Viewed retrospectively, April The Fifth, who died in 1954 aged twenty-five, was a stud failure in Flat-race terms, but it was inevitable with a homebred Derby winner on the premises that his breeder would make the best possible use of his services. One mare who was mated almost exclusively with April The Fifth was Bright Spot. She produced two successive foals by him in Bright Lady and Good Days.

The younger of the pair, Good Days played a pivotal role in the ascendancy of the great Irish trainer Vincent O'Brien. Sydney and Vincent had met by chance at Tattersalls' 1943 December Sales, when the aspiring Tipperary trainer procured Drybob as a resubmitted lot for 130 guineas. Not only was Sydney instrumental in finding an owner to take a half-share in Drybob, but he also decided to send him Good Days with explicit instructions to prepare him for the following year's Irish Cesarewitch.

It is part of Irish folklore how Vincent O'Brien engineered a truly remarkable gamble in 1944, his first year with a licence, by landing the Irish Autumn double, Drybob dead-heating for the Cambridge-shire and Good Days landing the Cesarewitch. With ante-post odds of 800–1 about the double, a minimal outlay sufficed to bolster O'Brien's precarious bank balance by a significant amount! It was certainly fortuitous that wartime restrictions which had precluded horses trained in the south of Ireland from competing at the Curragh had been revoked.

Just as Good Days had set Vincent O'Brien's career alight at the outset of his training career, so his year-senior own-sister, Bright Lady, made a huge contribution when Vincent switched emphasis from jumping to the Flat in the 1950s. Bright Lady had proved a top-class staying filly during the war years when trained by Vernell Hobbs for Thomas Venn, winning substitute races for the Cesarewitch and Park Hill Stakes (then regarded as the fillies' St Leger). She was also runner-up in the Gold Cup to Umiddad, beaten a head. However, she produced an even better daughter in the great Gladness.

In 1954 Sydney McGregor sent Gladness (bred in partnership with Tom Venn), as a yearling to Vincent O'Brien. Big and backward, this rather plain Sayajirao filly ran just once as a juvenile at the Curragh in November and once as a three-year-old at Manchester twelve months later. On the second occasion she landed a colossal gamble, being backed down to 11–8 on in McGregor's amber and black hoops. It was a well-orchestrated betting coup as ostensibly the filly was journeying to England en route to her owner's stud in Warwickshire.

Over the next three seasons, Gladness proved an exceptional staying mare racing in the colours of the American, John McShain, an émigré from Ireland. Head of the giant construction firm that built the Pentagon in Washington, McShain at that time owned another outstanding horse in her stable companion, Ballymoss. Their careers dovetailed rather conveniently. While Ballymoss had a preference for top of the ground, Gladness, with her rounded joints, ideally required soft underfoot conditions – her trainer would never have risked her on firm going.

A big, rangy individual, Gladness won eight races altogether, highlighted by the Irish Champion Stakes at four years and the Ascot Gold Cup, Goodwood Cup and Ebor Handicap at five years – the previous season she had missed the Gold Cup due to the prevailing firm ground. To underline the relationship that existed between her trainer and breeder, it is interesting to recall that immediately prior to her great Gold Cup victory the mare did a gallop at Bericote, a piece of land next door to Lillington which Sydney McGregor used for his young stock.

Some would argue that Gladness put up her best ever performance when winning the Ebor in a canter by six lengths carrying 9st 7lb, conceding the runner-up 29lb. She also concluded her career on a high note. On a return visit to Ascot as a six-year-old, she finished second to Alcide in the King George VI and Queen Elizabeth Stakes. To bring her back to one and a half miles was a masterstroke of training, the more so as by that stage the mare had more than a suspicion of tendon trouble.

It was inevitable that when the time came Ballymoss and Gladness would have an assignation in the covering yard. Their union produced a useful colt in Bally Joy, successful in the Royal Whip. Whereas Bally Joy's career was marred by a wind problem, his own-sister, Merry Mate, won the Irish Oaks. With hindsight, Vincent O'Brien regretted that Gladness was not mated with stallions exhibiting more quality than Ballymoss. Perhaps Milesian qualified on that score – to this speedy horse she bred Glad One, who was second in the Oaks and Irish One Thousand Guineas and third in the Irish Oaks.

Whereas April The Fifth and Gladness were Flat horses of the highest calibre, Sydney McGregor was really more involved over the years with jumpers and his runners were much more likely to be seen at some Midlands jumping course than at Ascot, Epsom, Goodwood, York or Newmarket.

Mares by April The Fifth bred a number of good jumpers and the Derby winner made a particular contribution to the 1967 Cheltenham Gold Cup, as the sire of Verdant, granddam of the winner Woodland Venture, and as the maternal grandsire of the runner-up Stalbridge Colonist, one of an elite few to defeat Arkle over fences. Both Woodlander, the dam of Woodland Venture, and Verdant were bred by Sydney McGregor, who was also responsible for Woodlander's half-brother, Green Drill (Emblem Chase, Manchester), who finished third in the 1958 Grand National to Mr What.

Continuity is one of the perennial fascinations of bloodstock breeding and the modest female family to which April The Fifth belonged has re-emerged during the twenty-first century with the Queen's chaser, Barbers Shop, whom she inherited from her mother. He is a direct descendant of April The Fifth's own-sister Sybil. Bred by Sydney McGregor, Sybil was Sold Again's only other successful offspring on the domestic front, winning the Atalanta Stakes at Sandown Park and finishing third in the Park Hill Stakes. Like so many retired racehorses nowadays, Barbers Shop embraced an alternative career and he was a dual winner for the Queen at the 2017 Royal Windsor Horse Show.

10

SCOTLAND'S MOST HISTORIC
RACING STABLE

Although it seemed to make very little impact in the racing press at a national level, it was a sad day for Scottish racing when Linda Perratt vacated Cree Lodge stables at the end of 2007. Ayr's longest surviving training yard, it had been in existence for 100 years (it was built in 1908, the year after the racecourse came into being). Although there was no mention of it at the time, it seemed likely that it would be sold by the local council for residential or commercial development.

At one time the seaside town of Ayr contained a number of racing stables. Before the Second World War there were seven or eight trainers operating in the town or thereabouts, but by the 1950s there would have been about half that number – twenty years further down the road, only Cree Lodge, right opposite Scotland's premier racecourse, remained in business.

Historically the most significant Ayr stable was Clyde House. Here Snowy Clarke trained the 1900 Scottish Grand National winner, Dorothy Vane, whom he also rode. It was also from this yard that Charles Elsey gained his first important success with Westmead in the 1924 Ayr Gold Cup for Glasgow bookmaker Tom Queen. Charles's son, Bill, who succeeded him at Highfield Stables, Malton, was actually born at Clyde House. A former pilot, Bill was destined to train the classic winners Pia (Oaks) and Peleid (St Leger).

Cree Lodge owes its origins to John McGuigan (1863–1952), who was born at Whithorn in Wigtownshire. As a boy he drove a three-horse stage-coach for his father from Ayr to Prestwick. He started training at Ayr in 1893, building Cree Lodge on a plot of land in Craigie Road. Over half a century, he trained a multitude of winners under both Rules

– one of the more notable jumpers was Creebrae, winner of the 1928 Molyneux Chase at Liverpool.

John was succeeded by his son, David, but he was never as successful a trainer. David was a contemporary of Gordon Richards, the future record-breaking champion jockey who became a knight of the realm. For a while both young riders were attached to Martin Hartigan's stable at Foxhill in Wiltshire and when Gordon came north to ride at Ayr during the 1920s he invariably stayed with the McGuigan family. Through their joint association with the Hartigan family, David McGuigan rode one of Noel Murless's very first winners, Second Pop, in a seller at Carlisle in 1937.

Training was only part of John McGuigan's involvement in racing as he was an established dealer. In his younger days he travelled around the world keeping in touch with a clientele which stretched from South Africa to India, from America to Australia. He bought and exported Night Raid to the Antipodes, where he sired the New Zealand-bred Phar Lap, whom many consider the greatest racehorse in the history of Australian racing.

One of McGuigan's principal contributions occurred rather closer to home at Stockton (later Teesside) after Lord Derby's filly, Scapa Flow, had finished runner-up in a seller. 'It was only through the kindness of that good sportsman, Johnny McGuigan, that I got a friendly claim put in for her and she returned to Newmarket,' recorded her trainer, George Lambton. As the dam of Pharos and Fairway, Scapa Flow became one of the mainstays of the Derby family's great Stanley House Stud.

The next incumbent at Cree Lodge was an Englishman rather than a Scotsman. A former officer in the Royal Navy, Gerry Laurence trained polo ponies before turning to racehorses. Initially based at Balsham, near Cambridge, he then had spells in Berkshire at Aston Tirrold and in Upper Lambourn, before moving to Ayr in November 1954. A change of location coincided with a decided upturn in his fortunes.

By now training exclusively on the Flat, he bought most of his animals as yearlings and he proved a highly proficient judge. His best ever season was 1959 when his string won twenty-eight races, highlighted by Whistling Victor in the Ayr Gold Cup at the Western Meeting, by then Scotland's most valuable prize.

The new master of Cree Lodge concentrated principally on sprinters and two-year-olds. His two star juveniles proved to be King of the Clyde and Gay Mairi, both winners of the Ladykirk Plate (now Harry Rosebery Stakes), always a significant two-year-old race, again staged at the Western Meeting. King of the Clyde and Gay Mairi scored ten juvenile victories between them. King of the Clyde was a half-brother to Falls of Cruachan, a good handicapper trained in Scotland by George Boyd, and both were bred by the Laidlaws of Abbey Lodge Stud, the Scottish family domiciled in Ireland (see Chapter 8).

As Gay Mairi was passing the winning post at Ayr in September 1961, Gerry Laurence suffered a fatal heart attack – there had been racecourse rumours that he was about to retire due to poor health. Fortunately he had already implemented plans to try and ensure the future of Cree Lodge as a training stable. On purchasing the property he had promptly sold it to the local council and they in turn leased it back to him. Later the Western Meeting Club became the lessor and this sub-lease arrangement still functioned with the last incumbent, Linda Perratt.

One of the best ever Flat horses trained in Scotland, Gay Mairi was to triumph in the following year's Nunthorpe Stakes, the all-aged sprint championship at York, for Gerry Laurence's successor, Harry Whiteman. Unsuccessful when trained in France the ensuing season, Gay Mairi became the dam of Montgomery, one of the leading French sprinters of the early 1970s.

Harry Whiteman had served in the Royal Flying Corps during the First World War, and then spent twenty years as a professional jockey – much of it on the Continent, where he was stable jockey to Count Orrsich. He had retired from the saddle in 1932 when taking out a licence to train. His progression north was gradual – he started off at Fairlawne in Kent, and after spells at Russley Park in Wiltshire and Upper Lambourn, moved on to Wintringham, near Malton, before finally taking over the reins at Cree Lodge.

Harry had an extensive CV as a trainer long before he crossed the border. Whilst at Fairlawne in the years preceding the Second World War he handled the luckless Davy Jones for the Mildmay family from Devon. Anthony Mildmay, later Lord Mildmay of Flete, became the country's leading amateur in the post-war period and the Mildmay Course at Liverpool is named after him. Having made all the running, Davy Jones looked assured of victory in the 1936 Grand National when, on landing clear of the field at the penultimate fence, the reins parted at the buckle. His rider was powerless to prevent his mount from running out at the last, thus enabling Reynoldstown, partnered by another amateur, Fulke Walwyn, to secure his second successive victory.

Standing 17.1 hands, Davy Jones was an entire horse but was not particularly sound of wind or limb – he had, in fact, been tubed to help his breathing. He was retired to stand at Fairlawne at a fee of just nine guineas (applications to Harry Whiteman). Soon he was transferred to Lingfield Park Stud in Surrey, but the outbreak of war severely curtailed his stud career.

During the war Harry Whiteman occupied the historic Russley Park stables, which has had so many incumbents over the years, before making the short journey across the Wiltshire/Berkshire border to Park Farm stables, Upper Lambourn. As if to advertise his credentials for taking over at Cree Lodge, it was from Lambourn that he dispatched Irish Dance, a six-year-old entire, to justify favouritism in the 1949 Ayr Gold Cup.

Another Ayr victory that gave Harry Whiteman particular satisfaction came when Rosie Wings won the 1962 Usher Brewery Gold Tankard in June. The five-year-old carried the colours of her breeder from the Borders, Betty Tweedie, for whom she would prove an exceptional broodmare (see Chapters 20 and 28).

In 1967, Harry Whiteman's penultimate season, he had two particularly talented two-year-old colts in Mount Athos, a son of Rosie Wings, and Doon. While the former subsequently excelled for John Dunlop's stable, finishing third in the Derby, the latter was sold out of Harry Whiteman's yard mid-way through his second season for export to the USA and the price would have been considerably more than the 1,000 guineas he had cost as a yearling. Runner-up to Vaguely Noble in the Observer Gold Cup (now Racing Post Trophy) as a juvenile, he never quite lived up to his early promise here – after all, Vaguely Noble went on to prove the champion of Europe when winning the Prix de l'Arc de Triomphe.

Truth to tell, Harry Whiteman's most noteworthy protégé was human rather than equine. A native of Ayrshire, Sandy Barclay was still an apprentice when leaving Cree Lodge to join Noel Murless, to whom he would shortly become first jockey at Warren Place, Newmarket. Harry Whiteman had no doubts about the young rider's ability. 'Barclay's an absolute genius,' he commented at the time. 'I have been in racing for sixty-five years as jockey and trainer and I have never seen anyone like him.'

It was always assumed that Harry Whiteman's pupil assistant, Charles Vernon Miller, would succeed him, but there was a change of plan. Instead Charlie decided to take out a licence to train at his family home in Warwickshire where he soon made his mark by saddling Bighorn to win the 1971 Hennessy Gold Cup. So the opportunity arose for another Old Etonian, Nigel Angus, to fill the breach. Furthermore he had been born and brought up in Ayrshire.

With farming experience in Kenya and a spell at the Royal Agricultural College, Cirencester, Nigel Angus took out the licence to train at Cree Lodge in 1969. He had family connections with racing through his mother, Lady Moore. Penelope Moore was a sister of Gay Sheppard, clerk of the course at various tracks in the Midlands, and Dan Sheppard, the handicapper. She had installed Paddy Chesmore to train at the family home at Monkton, near Ayr, and Nigel used to ride for the stable as an amateur. His sister is the artist Pru Angus, who specialised in painting flora and fauna on the South African veldt.

One of the stable's owners was Charles Carlow, whose colours had been carried to victory at Ayr by the likes of Field Master (Galloway Cup) and Flight Master (Royal Burgh of Ayr Handicap). It was at his instigation that Nigel Angus became the new assistant, with a view to taking over when Harry Whiteman retired – Charles Carlow was a brother of Noel Murless's wife, Gwen.

It seemed incumbent on trainers at Cree Lodge to win the Ayr Gold

Cup and Nigel Angus managed to emulate his predecessors Gerry Laurence and Harry Whiteman not once, but twice, first with his own Swinging Junior as a five-year-old in 1972 and then with Roman Warrior as a four-year-old in 1975. Nigel retired from training two years later to indulge his other great passion, golf – he was a scratch player. Sadly the former master of Cree Lodge, who used to divide his time between South Africa and his home in Ayrshire, died in 2006 aged sixty-two.

Swinging Junior and Roman Warrior were entire horses, the former retiring to stand at Fort Union Stud in Ireland, and the latter to Sturt Farm Stud, near Burford, in North Oxfordshire; both establishments are now defunct. Neither Swinging Junior nor Roman Warrior excelled as stallions, but no one would deny that the latter was a truly magnificent individual and an exceptionally talented one, described by *Timeform* as 'a colossus of a horse with a heart to match'. This enormous chestnut measured over seventeen hands.

Roman Warrior was homebred by Dublin-based John Brown, whose colours had been carried to victory by Right Tack, the first to complete the English and Irish Two Thousand Guineas double. A horse who obviously appreciated a stroll across the Craigie Road to his favourite course, Roman Warrior excelled over six furlongs, winning the 1975 Ayr Gold Cup by a short head with a record weight of 10st – overnight he had been a doubtful runner owing to the prevailing heavy ground. Another highlight was to win the Canada Dry Shield Handicap at the Ayr July fixture on three consecutive occasions. He also dead-heated with the filly Swingtime for the Diadem Stakes at Ascot.

Nigel Angus's successor was his former head lad, Charlie Williams – a Welshman, he was an enormously experienced stableman, having held the same position with Harry Whiteman. One of the fillies that Charlie inherited was the useful Doogali and she provided him with significant early successes in the City and Suburban at Epsom and Harry Peacock Challenge Cup at Newcastle. Bred by Lord Strathalmond, Doogali was by the Harry Whiteman-trained Doon, who had been repatriated from the USA to stand as a syndicated stallion at Kingwood Stud, Lambourn.

Charlie Williams did not have an easy time at Cree Lodge due to persistent flooding. The stables were actually below sea level and whenever there was a combination of a high tide and torrential rain serious flooding used to take place. It was surely no coincidence that the inmates were also plagued with an unidentified virus, but fortunately the local council found an effective way of combating the flooding and everything took a turn for the better.

Due to ill health, Charlie Williams was forced to retire at the close of the 1984 season and he in turn was replaced by John Stoddart Wilson, who had been combining training under permit with working in the car trade at the family home in Motherwell – he had learnt the rudiments of training from Harry Bell at Hawick. When Nigel Angus retired, Cree Lodge (Scotland Ltd), the company that owned the stables, went into liquidation and it was a new enterprise, Ayr Racing Stables Ltd, that employed John Wilson.

Aged twenty, John Wilson was the youngest permit holder in the country. He looked like the new broom that would brush Cree Lodge's misfortunes away, but after a very promising start progress soon faltered. Despite saddling Harry Hastings to win the 1985 Supreme Novices' Hurdle at the Cheltenham Festival and Young Driver to finish a gallant second to West Tip in the 1986 Grand National, his long-term luck was out – both his stable stars soon succumbed to injury and during the summer of 1991 he handed over to his assistant, Linda Perratt.

Although the number of horses at Cree Lodge dwindled in recent years, Linda Perratt proved she could certainly train winners given the right ammunition. Particularly adept with sprinters, she saddled Ho Leng to win the 1998 Bunbury Cup, always one of the most competitive events at the Newmarket July Meeting. Another smart handicapper was his exact contemporary, Friar Tuck, bred in Ayrshire by James Thom and Sons. However, she was soon to vacate Cree Lodge for good.

From January 2008 through to November, Linda Perratt took the reins at Belstane Racing Stables at Carluke in Lanarkshire from Ian Semple, who remained on hand as her assistant. During that period she saddled a very commendable thirty-two winners. Two horses she inherited from her predecessor did particularly well. Appalachian Trail enjoyed Listed success in the Spring Trophy at Haydock Park, and then Big Timer gained a memorable victory in the Wokingham Stakes at Royal Ascot.

Commenting on Big Timer's triumph, his trainer, who was on duty at Ayr, commented, 'I couldn't believe the price he was, which was probably because he was trained up in Scotland.' All of 389 miles away in fact. Ironically the gelding carried the orange and blue colours of Gordon McDowall, the owner of Belstane Racing Stables, so it came as a shock when Linda Perratt's contract was terminated by her employer before the year was out.

However, it had always been the long-term plan for Linda to train from the family's North Allerton Farm, which is situated at Jackton, near East Kilbride, just down the road from Hamilton Park. Within five months Linda had reapplied for her licence and the new establishment was up and running.

The loss of Scotland's two most historic racing stables, Westbarns on the east coast and Cree Lodge on the west coast, could well have heralded the terminal decline of the indigenous training fraternity, but racing north of the border has shown extraordinary resilience in recent times. Despite such major setbacks and the uncertainty that both Ayr and Musselburgh have faced, enthusiasm amongst the public has never been stronger with Keith Dalgleish (see Chapter 34) at Belstane Racing Stables spearheading an amazing revival in the training ranks.

11

AN ICONIC TRAINER OF JUMPERS

In the 1950s two Scotsmen in Scotland put their homeland firmly on
the map so far as the list of leading trainers in the United Kingdom
was concerned. When it came to the number of races won during a
season, John Stewart Wight headed the statistics for the 1954–5 jumps
season with fifty-nine victories, and an identical total placed George
Henderson Boyd in second place on the corresponding table for the
1957 Flat season. These are truly astonishing figures.

Although Stewart Wight was close to Kelso and George Boyd was
no distance from Edinburgh (Musselburgh), all other race meetings in
the north involved travelling comparatively long distances on roads
that were far slower than those of today. Because of this both trainers
shared a common link – they were customers of Bobby Young from
the village of Yetholm, near Kelso. The firm maintained two very special
Foden horse-boxes, one for the exclusive use of Stewart Wight and one
for George Boyd. Since 1975 this flourishing livestock transport business has been known as Eric Gillie Limited, Eric having previously
been Bobby's right-hand man.

Back in the late 1950s and 1960s *The Berwickshire News*, which
covers local events north of the border (as opposed to its sister paper,
the *Berwick Advertiser*, which reports affairs on the English side) must
have devoted many column inches on its sporting pages to the enormous success enjoyed by Stewart Wight. Despite the proximity of the
A1 and the London (King's Cross) to Edinburgh (Waverley) railway
line, Grantshouse is a remote location. The winter backdrop is one of
the snow-capped Lammermuir Hills, as bleak and as beautiful a Low-
land landscape as one can imagine.

From Greenwood, his stables at Grantshouse, Stewart Wight trained the winners of over 1,000 races over a period of four decades, spanning the Second World War. By modern standards such a total seems insignificant, but it should be emphasised that seldom, if ever, did he have more than thirty horses in his charge, and more usually about twenty plus, at any one time; and, of course, there was far less racing in those days. Entirely self-taught in the art of training, his stable became one of the most powerful in the land and the most consistently successful in the north.

Like so many people involved with racing in Scotland, Stewart Wight came from a farming background. Indeed, he combined his training operation with running a mixed farm which provided home-grown hay, oats and straw for his string. Just as soon as the jump season ended (in those days there was a distinct demarcation period between the seasons), he concentrated on his farming activities and was much more likely to be seen in Edinburgh's Gorgie Market appraising the demand for pigs than attending a Flat meeting. Racing on the level was anathema to him while racing over hurdles was only a means to an end – part of a future chaser's early education.

The majority of his horses were bred in Ireland and that is where he procured them and in this respect Ken Oliver followed very much in his footsteps. Always a traditionalist, he favoured the old-fashioned stamp of chaser that took time to come to hand – but then patience was one of his hallmarks. Fortunately the great majority of his owners were country-loving people, with a background of horses and hunting, who were prepared to give their animals the necessary time to develop and pay the bills along the way without worrying about if and when they were going to get any return on their outlay.

Born in 1897, the son of a sporting farmer, Stewart Wight was hunting and riding in point-to-points from an early age and soon showed a remarkable aptitude in the saddle. However, it was not until after the First World War, in which he served with the Lothian and Border Horse, a yeomanry regiment, that he became professionally involved. By the time he took out a licence to train at Grantshouse in 1924 he had already made his name as an amateur jockey and for a brief period combined the two roles, albeit through force of circumstances rather than by choice – he would have much preferred to concentrate on one or the other.

A couple of Stewart Wight's first supporters were landowners from neighbouring East Lothian. The 12th Earl of Haddington's involvement ceased when he gave up race riding – he won the 1931 National Hunt Chase at Cheltenham on his own horse, Merriment IV, who also won the Valentine Chase at Liverpool. A much longer association developed with Robert Tweedie of Phantassie, East Linton, between Haddington and Dunbar, and his son, Reginald. Both stalwarts of National Hunt racing in Scotland, they became two of Stewart Wight's closest friends and patrons.

From 1919 to 1926 Stewart Wight rode as an amateur. However, in February 1927, the National Hunt Committee, which monitored jump racing at that time, mindful that he was at least earning a proportion of his living from training, refused to renew his amateur permit. Anxious to partner Robert Tweedie's Mr Jolly (on whom he had scored one of his earliest successes under Rules in the United Border Hunt Steeplechase at Kelso), in the forthcoming Grand National, he had no alternative but to turn professional.

Prior to Liverpool, homebred Mr Jolly provided one half of a winning double at Manchester for his Scottish trainer-rider in the Tweedie colours, along with the smart Ruddyman, his first two rides as a professional. Three weeks later he had his last ride as a professional when partnering Mr Jolly in the Grand National – well in contention on the first circuit, the gelding fell later on. Although Stewart never rode in public again, he did continue to ride schooling for many years to come.

Robert Tweedie's very first horse, Mr Jolly, won no fewer than seventeen chases and he had another prolific winner in Ballybrack; he raced until he was twelve, winning eighteen times over fences. Invariably ridden by Reg Tweedie, Ballybrack won the Liverpool Foxhunters' in 1932 and the Cheltenham Foxhunters' in 1934 – that season he won eight of his nine starts, seven of them consecutively; he was unbeaten in hunter chases.

Another good chaser to carry the Tweedie colours was Killadoon, successful in Manchester's prestigious Victory Chase. Reg also finished an unlucky fifth on the stable's Venturesome Knight in the 1940 Grand National behind Bogskar when his mount broke a blood vessel – runner-up for a second successive time was the all-Scottish MacMoffat (see Chapter 21).

It was not by chance that Stewart Wight's charges had the reputation as good jumpers, for he was meticulous in all aspects of the job. At Grantshouse the schooling fences resembled a miniature racecourse and it was not only the horses that were well taught. Over a period of time, Grantshouse became a schooling ground for many famous north country jump jockeys, both professional and amateur. Heading the former category were the stable jockeys, Dick Curran and Mick Batchelor, while amongst a coterie of leading amateurs were Reg Tweedie, Ken Oliver, Ewen Cameron, Adam Calder and Danny Moralee.

Dick Curran was retained as first jockey from 1945 to 1957 – during the 1952–3 season he partnered seventy-two winners when runner-up to champion Fred Winter. Dick Curran was a native of Yorkshire. That was where his contemporary, Jimmy Power, made his name as stable jockey to Bobby Renton, for whom he rode the great Aintree specialist, Freebooter, winner of the 1950 Grand National. Jimmy Power was also attached to the Grantshouse stable for an interim two years between leaving his native Ireland and joining Bobby Renton outside Ripon.

Two leading English amateurs also benefited from the Stewart Wight school of horsemanship. During the 1932–3 season both Frank Furlong, whose father owned and trained the great Reynoldstown, and Fulke Walwyn were serving army officers stationed at Redford Barracks outside Edinburgh. Regular visitors to ride work at Grantshouse, they were both destined to win the Grand National on Reynoldstown, the former in 1935 and the latter in 1936.

In 1938, the year after the stable won the Grand Sefton over the forbidding Aintree fences with Inversible, the master of Greenwood married Margaret Dodds. She was always known as Madge – her husband was invariably called 'Bossy', although it was not meant in any derogatory sense, but rather as 'the Boss'. Dark times were ahead and the Grantshouse stable was closed until the end of the war when jump racing was revived and the stable was quickly back on track.

The golden years for the Stewart Wight runners were from 1950, when Sanvina was a surprise winner of the Scottish Grand National ridden by her owner, Ken Oliver. There was a repeat victory in Scotland's premier steeplechase at Bogside in 1960, with Maude Milne Green's Fincham ridden by Mick Batchelor. Not many of Stewart Wight's charges had gone through the ring as yearlings, but this son of Devonian had realised 1,500 guineas at Goffs in Ireland in 1951.

The same owner-trainer combination was also responsible for Gigolo who finished fourth in the 1955 Grand National to Quare Times, Vincent O'Brien's third successive National winner following Early Mist and Royal Tan. An admirable stayer, Gigolo was successful in seven of his first nine starts including the Eider Chase, Newcastle, and Fred Withington Chase, Cheltenham, both severe tests of stamina and recognised National trials.

Considering how comparatively few horses she had in training at Grantshouse, Maude Milne Green had a surprising number of multiple-scorers. One of the most prolific in her 'royal blue, white sash and hooped sleeves, red cap', was Dove Cote, a black gelding whose twenty victories included the Cathcart Challenge Cup at what was then called the National Hunt Meeting. When Stewart Wight retired, the Edinburgh resident had her horses fairly close to home, with either Wilfrid Crawford at Haddington in East Lothian, or Bobby Fairbairn at Selkirk.

Two of the best hunter-chasers in the country were stable companions at Grantshouse and both advertised their prowess initially by winning the always competitive Heart of All England event at Hexham. Happymint, officially a Half-Bred (ineligible for *The General Stud Book* but registered in *The Half-Bred Stud Book*), was ridden by his owner, Danny Moralee, to win the Cheltenham Foxhunters' in 1954 and the Liverpool Foxhunters' in 1955. During that decade Danny Moralee was four times champion amateur, sharing the honours with Bob McCreery on the last occasion.

The other celebrated hunter was The Callant. Homebred by Charlie Scott, a farmer from Jedburgh and invariably ridden by Jimmy

Scott-Aiton of Legerwood, near Lauder, this grey had won a string of point-to-points before joining Stewart Wight for whom he justified favouritism in the Cheltenham Foxhunters' in both 1956 and 1957. The following season The Callant defeated Much Obliged at Hexham, Kerstin at Ayr and Wyndburgh at Haydock Park, but although he won sixteen races over fences (excluding point-to-points), he was never quite as good in open competition.

All too often there is little to differentiate between those living on opposite sides of the Tweed and just as Danny Moralee came from Northumberland (he belonged to an Alnwick farming family), so too did the 3rd Lord Joicey. Master of the North Northumberland Hounds on five occasions over a fourteen-year period, he lived at Etal Manor, near Ford, which has a Berwick-upon-Tweed address, but is actually much nearer to Coldstream across the border in Scotland.

Chairman of Albion Shipping and a member of the family whose vast coal-mining interests in Northumberland and Durham matched some of the largest in Europe, Hugh Joicey became one of Stewart Wight's principal patrons. Two outstanding chasers to carry his pink colours with olive green sleeves were Belhector (twenty-one chases) and Gold Bond (twenty-three chases), but the best of them was undoubtedly the gallant Bramble Tudor, an Irish-bred mare by that great sire of jumpers, King Hal.

Game and consistent, Bramble Tudor won nineteen races spread over six seasons and she was one of the market leaders for the 1955 Cheltenham Gold Cup, but ran below expectations – her preparation had been interrupted by a bout of coughing. Two years previously she had won the Cotswold Chase (now Arkle Chase) at Cheltenham. In 1954 and 1956 she won the Wetherby Chase and in between she gained another major success in the Great Yorkshire Chase at Doncaster. The second of those two victories at Wetherby over an extended three miles was arguably the best performance of her career as she defeated another outstanding mare in Kerstin, who was in receipt of 13lb. Kerstin, who proceeded to win the 1958 Cheltenham Gold Cup, was trained by Verly Bewicke, then based not so far from Grantshouse at Glanton in Northumberland.

Bramble Tudor produced six living foals and two of them, Tudor Deal and Tudor Fort, the winners of fifteen races between them, both scored at Hexham only a few weeks before Hugh Joicey died in October 1966. That pair were trained by Neville Crump at Middleham. He shared the Joicey horses with Stewart Wight when the latter was forced to relinquish his training licence during the 1960–1 season due to ill health – he temporarily took out a permit. At that time Neville Crump trained Hugh Joicey's Hennessy Gold Cup hero, Springbok.

That Newbury success came in November 1962 and the following January Stewart Wight died at home at Grantshouse, just three days before his sixty-seventh birthday. Someone who set the highest standards and expected them to be adhered to both in and out of the stable, he was also one of the most popular and respected figures on the racecourse, attired in his customary tweed suit and bowler hat.

A trainer of the old school, Stewart Wight is commemorated at Kelso, his local course, by the Stewart Wight Memorial Chase. Hard-working and conscientious, no one dispatched runners to the races looking in better fettle. With a flair for placing them to the best possible advantage, this Scotsman was the proverbial master of his craft and justifiably proud of his MBE, an honour accorded to comparatively few racehorse trainers of that vintage.

12

A COOL CUSTOMER WITH A ROYAL TAG

Every name tells a story and that is certainly true of the interrelated Stirling-Crawfurd and Stirling-Stuart families of Castlemilk, just south of Glasgow. William (Stuart) Stirling-Crawfurd (1819–83) was one of the leading figures of the Turf in the Victorian era and one of few people to own the winners of all five English classics, while his great-nephew, Douglas Stirling-Stuart, always known as Cuddy, owned Cool Customer, one of the most spectacular chasers immediately after the Second World War.

An extremely rich man, William Stirling-Crawfurd was able to indulge his passion for the Turf. He was only twenty-five when his representative, The Returned, finished second in the 1844 Grand National, only the sixth running of this great steeplechase. The following year his colours were actually carried to victory at Aintree by Cure-All, but this was a chance occurrence. As his intended runner had to be withdrawn at a late stage, it was agreed that his nomination could be transferred to William Loft's Cure-All, who was ridden by his owner, a Lincolnshire farmer. The following year Stirling-Crawfurd was out of luck again when Veluti, the favourite, broke down when leading at the second-last fence.

Thereafter Stirling-Crawfurd turned his attention increasingly to the Flat, gaining a first classic success with Mayonaise in the 1859 One Thousand Guineas. He was to gain seven further classic victories with horses trained by Alec Taylor Snr, who was based first at Fyfield in Hampshire and then at Manton in Wiltshire – Moslem and Gang Forward (Two Thousand Guineas), Thebais and St Marguerite (One Thousand Guineas), Sefton (Derby), Thebais (Oaks), and Craig Millar (St

Leger). Gang Forward started favourite for the 1873 Derby, dead-heating for second place behind Doncaster, owned by the Scottish ironmaster, James Merry.

Thebais and St Marguerite were homebred chesnut own-sisters. The latter became the granddam of Triple Crown hero, Rock Sand, who was homebred by another Scotsman, Sir James Miller. Stirling-Crawfurd was associated with two other Triple Crown winners. Having bought Isonomy for 9,000 guineas after he had completed a couple of seasons at stud, this dual Ascot Gold Cup winner proceeded to sire Common and Isinglass; he also sired Gallinule, the sire of that greatest of mares, Pretty Polly.

While in his late fifties, between the classic victories of Gang Forward (1873) and Sefton (1878), Stirling-Crawfurd married Caroline, widow of the 4th Duke of Montrose. A firebrand, she was commonly known as Carrie Red after the hue of her toupée (which must have clashed somewhat with her new husband's all-scarlet colours) and she owned a useful stayer in Corrie Roy. This inspired the popular verse: 'Corrie Roy and Carrie Red, one for the stable, t'other for bed, Carrie Red and Corrie Roy, isn't Craw a lucky boy?' Parodied in the musical comedy *The Sporting Duchess*, she is commemorated every year by the Carrie Red Fillies' Nursery run at the Doncaster St Leger Meeting.

Later Caroline, the leading lady owner of the late-Victorian period, with her own ideas about racing and breeding, raced under the *nom de course* of Mr Manton albeit her identity was common knowledge. Only seventeen on marrying the duke, she was in her mid-sixties at the time of her wedding to Stirling-Crawfurd; she married her third husband, Henry Milner, when she was seventy and he was twenty-four! But her true amour seems to have been Fred Archer. It is almost certainly apocryphal, but the great jockey was alleged to have enquired, 'Would he become a duke should he marry the duchess?'

Cuddy Stirling-Stuart's father, William Crawfurd-Stirling-Stuart had assumed the additional name of Crawfurd before reaching his majority. He was also a keen follower of racing, but any aspirations he may have entertained as a rider had been cut short by a serious fall when his mount rolled over on top of him and he broke both legs.

However, he is fondly remembered as an eccentric in both manner and appearance. Some of his many idiosyncrasies have been recorded for posterity.

With a penchant for outrageous tweed checks, he was invariably referred to as The Hatter on account of his unusual taste in hats which he wore either perched over his nose or on the back of his head. Invariably he had an oversize red silk handkerchief in his breast pocket and, as a direct descendant of the Royal House of Stuart, he frequently carried a Stuart tartan umbrella.

'Old Billy' was certainly a colourful character and at home he adhered to a strict routine. Every morning he emerged from the front door of the castle and stood momentarily sniffing the air. He would then proceed to relieve himself on the gravel forecourt. For more protracted operations he utilised his own lavatory at the back of the house where he would sit with the door wide open as he surveyed the loch and the glen. Any staff or guests who had the misfortune to witness these activities might have been embarrassed, but the laird most certainly was not!

A member of the Royal Company of Archers, the Queen's Bodyguard for Scotland, Cuddy Stirling-Stuart was not only proud of his royal connections, but also of his family ties with the Turf – one of his favourite possessions was a painting of Gang Forward by C. Lutyens, father of the famous architect. He and his elder brother, James, had grown up immersed in sport and racing. Both were educated at Eton and Oxford, Cuddy proving a highly competent all-rounder at games. It was at school that he acquired the nickname Cuddy.

On coming down from Oxford the two brothers joined the army. James went into the Scots Guards (he was killed early in the First World War), while Cuddy joined the Royal Scots Greys in which he served in both World Wars, being injured in the First. He had proved his aptitude for riding early on, winning the University College Grind three times (1912–14) on horses hired from an Oxford dealer. Racing took precedence over boxing; on the eve of the first of those three victories, he was knocked down in the ring, but allowed himself to be counted out. There were bigger fish to fry on the racecourse the following day!

Between the wars Cuddy lived the life of a country squire first in Gloucestershire, where his father-in-law, Herbert Lord, was Master of the Cotswold, and then at Bedale in the North Riding of Yorkshire, both good hunting counties. It was from his father-in-law that he acquired an unbroken homebred five-year-old in 1920 whom he named Extravagance, because he thought he had paid too much for him. Quite apart from being a wonderful hunter he was an excellent point-to-pointer – the combination scored thirteen times between the flags, including five open races in one season.

One of Cuddy's major contributions to the Bedale Hunt was to perform in the annual pantomime as a comedian to help raise funds, but buying horses was an altogether more serious affair. Certainly £2,500 was a great deal of money to spend for a novice hurdler early in 1945. The horse that attracted Cuddy's attention was Cool Customer, whom he had heard about through Dorothy Paget's advisor, Charlie Rogers. With the obvious stamp of a chaser, Cool Customer had won two bumpers (National Hunt Flat races) the previous year – as a neutral country, Ireland had continued to stage racing for the duration of the war.

Initially his new owner kept Cool Customer in Ireland, where he was ridden regularly by Aubrey Brabazon. Upon his recommendation the horse was placed with an up-and-coming young trainer in A.W. Riddell Martin. In the autumn of 1945 Cool Customer won three hurdle races off-the-reel, whereupon it was decided to turn his attention to fences. After the New Year, when he turned seven, he proceeded to win four consecutive chases including the important Leopardstown Chase.

Fortunately for Jack Fawcus, who suffered terribly in the war and had actually been repatriated as a prisoner of war due to his declining health, Cuddy Stirling-Stuart was anxious to have his horse trained closer to home. So Cool Customer joined Jack Fawcus's small string at Ashgill, outside Middleham, and he was to prove the best he ever trained. Belonging to a sporting Northumbrian family, this former

116

champion amateur rider who turned professional had partnered Southern Hero to win three Scottish Grand Nationals during the 1930s. His son, Charles, is a former *Sporting Chronicle* and *Daily Mirror* racing correspondent.

It was decided to give Cool Customer his first two outings from his Yorkshire base across the border in Scotland and he duly won at Bogside and Kelso. On the second occasion he made all the running but jumped indifferently, much to the consternation of his owner, who had the biggest bet of his life, laying the odds of £900–£400 twice with Scottish bookmaker Jimmy McLean. Runner-up at Kelso was Bruno II, owned and trained by Bill Anstruther-Gray (later Lord Kilmany) to whom he was conceding over a stone. Bruno proceeded to win the National Hunt Chase at Cheltenham.

Altogether Cool Customer scored nineteen victories, including the inaugural Great Yorkshire Chase in 1948, two runnings of another Doncaster feature, the Princess Margaret Chase, and the Victory Chase at Manchester, all prestigious events in those bygone days. Another outstanding performance was to win the Ewell Chase at Sandown Park in record time, carrying 12st 12lb, giving 16lb to a very fast horse in Rondo II. His owner was always present and no one could have got more enjoyment from the involvement.

In 1949 Cool Customer finished a gallant runner-up to Cottage Rake in the second of the latter's three Gold Cup victories (all with Aubrey Brabazon in the saddle). He had led Cottage Rake over the last fence, only to be outstayed in the final hundred yards of that uphill slog to the post. The previous year 'Coolie' had been favourite for the Gold Cup, but approached the first fence with his head in the air and paid the penalty – the one and only time he fell in thirty-four outings. Disaster has the unhappy knack of striking on the big occasion!

Notwithstanding this reversal, it was in the winner's enclosure at Cheltenham that Cuddy presented Aubrey with a pair of gold cufflinks to commemorate Cool Customer's Irish victories – in England Coolie was invariably ridden by Aubrey's compatriot, Joe Murphy. Ironically Cuddy had come very close to buying Cottage Rake. Had the Irish vet not spun the horse for his suspect wind, a deal would have been done at £3,000 – Cuddy always thought the circumstances were decidedly suspicious, 'a bit of a fiddle' as he put it.

In later life Cuddy Stirling-Stuart went to live near Malmesbury in Wiltshire, acting as a steward at a number of different courses in the south including Sandown Park. However, he did not sever all his connections with Yorkshire as his eldest daughter, Jean Burdon, was living at Jervaulx Abbey, near Ripon. This had been home to Hector Christie, trainer of the 1947 Gold Cup winner, Fortina, who started off in Fife.

The Burdons are related by marriage to the Joiceys – Lord Joicey owned that fine Scottish trained mare, Bramble Tudor. A strong racing connection persists down to the present day as two prominent jump trainers, Charlie Mann in Upper Lambourn and Henry Daly of Downton Hall, near Ludlow, in Shropshire, share a common family link with Cuddy Stirling-Stuart through their respective mothers. So does David Batten of bloodstock auctioneers Tattersalls.

13

THIS CLASSIC WINNER HAD TO WAIT FOR THE TIDE TO TURN

With racing back on an even keel after the severe disruptions of the Second World War, the domestic Flat racing scene in Scotland during the 1950s and 1960s was dominated to a very large extent by two stables. George Boyd's Tilton House was at Westbarns on the outskirts of Dunbar on the east coast, and Cree Lodge was at Ayr on the west coast, presided over by Gerry Laurence and then Harry Whiteman. The rivalry between the two camps was intense, but on balance George Boyd proved strongest of the three protagonists.

Beside the A1, the main arterial link along the east side of England into Scotland, Dunbar is in a strategic position where the Firth of Forth coastline merges with the North Sea. During the late nineteenth century and for two thirds of the twentieth century, Tilton House was a flourishing racing stable and its most successful incumbent within living memory was George Henderson Boyd. A small, dapper figure, like the majority of trainers of that era he always wore a trilby hat for racing and a tweed cap at home.

Dunbar was also the location of one of Scotland's historic racecourses. In 1871 the East Lothian and Scottish Yeomanry staged a Flat race meeting at Belhaven, which adjoins Dunbar and is the home of a preparatory school of that name. Racing under National Hunt Rules was inaugurated there in 1898. One of the principals behind these meetings was a Mr St Clair Cunningham, who lived locally at Hedderwick Hall, but following his death in 1906 the racecourse closed.

Cunningham had horses trained at Tilton House with John McCall, who presided over the establishment from around 1880 until his death in 1931. Born and brought up in Kelso, John McCall had been a professional runner and as a young man had won the prestigious Powderhall Sprint in Edinburgh and he graduated to training horses via greyhounds. His move to Dunbar from Edinburgh was precipitated by public concern for the danger caused by exercising his horses in the park.

One of his winners with a particular significance to *The Scots & the Turf* was Howcleuch, who won the Buccleuch Cup at Kelso in April 1899 for Andrew Oliver, uncle of Ken Oliver (see Chapter 19). John's sons, George and John Jnr, both served their apprenticeship at Westbarns before becoming successful jockeys in their own right – George rode Cherry Lass to win the 1905 One Thousand Guineas. In October 1901 he had gone through the card at Beverley, one of his winners running a dead-heat.

When John McCall died, John Boyd took over the reins at Tilton House, which was named after one of McCall's best horses. Bought out of a seller for thirty-eight guineas, Tilton was one of his trainer's three winners of the Ayrshire Handicap, then the most important race in Scotland. John Boyd's early experience of racing revolved around flapping – racing outside the jurisdiction of the Jockey Club and/or the former National Hunt Committee.

He and his family arrived at Dunbar from Cardrona Mains, their home beside the Tweed in Peeblesshire between picturesque Peebles, famous for its hydro and the Tweedale Museum, and the old mill town of Innerleithen. Cardrona Mains has since metamorphosed into a golf course. Next door is The Glen, a 5,000-acre estate which has long been in the Glenconner/Tennant family. Lady Tennant of Britwell Priors, near Andover, has enjoyed considerable success as an owner in recent times with the useful High Accolade trained by Marcus Tregoning.

Both the Boyd brothers were jockeys, Alec as a professional and George as an amateur. In due course Alec took over the training licence after his father's death in 1936, but with no racing in Scotland for most of the war he moved his string south to Middleham. One of his most notable victories came with the outsider, Backbite, in the 1944 Lincolnshire, a substitute affair run at Pontefract – the only other course operating in the northern zone at the time was Stockton. It was following service in the RAF that George eventually took control of Tilton House and a new era of prosperity dawned.

In April 1947 George Boyd saddled his very first winner, Backbite scoring in a seller at Bogside. Owned by his brother, this eight-year-old entire scored in three more sellers that season, at Hamilton, Lincoln and Doncaster, before being sold to South Africa. Three days after that initial success at Bogside, he had a double at his local meeting, Edinburgh (as it was called in those days). The die was cast. By the close of the season no fewer than twenty-nine winners had been accorded to G.H. Boyd, Dunbar.

In both 1947 and 1948, Pappatea, another full horse, won the Edinburgh Spring Handicap and over the next two decades George Boyd was to enjoy unprecedented success on his local course. Pappatea also provided him with his first major victory in England, winning the 1948 Northumberland Plate at Newcastle in June. Known as the Pitman's Derby, it was then regarded as the most prestigious race in the north-east and used to attract unprecedented crowds to the delights of Gosforth Park.

The following August, disaster struck at Tilton House when a freak storm hit the south-east of Scotland, causing the worst floods in living memory. Thirty-six hours of incessant rain, coinciding with exceptionally high tides, decimated the surrounding countryside, causing excessive damage to property, roads and the countryside generally with rivers and streams bursting their banks. The railway line proved particularly vulnerable – five bridges on the main east-coast line from London (King's Cross) to Edinburgh (Waverley) were swept away.

It was only through the sterling efforts of all the staff that none of the inmates of Tilton House stables lost their lives. Water levels were so high that there was imminent danger of the horses literally drowning in their boxes and with the water rising at an alarming rate they were let loose to take their chance. They dispersed in panic. Two of them actually went missing only to be found in a bedraggled state after plunging into the sea. Miraculously there were no serious casualties to man or beast, albeit the horses did seem to lose their form in the aftermath.

Pappatea retired to stud in England when seven years of age, standing briefly in Gloucestershire and Buckinghamshire before finding a permanent home outside Melton Mowbray in Leicestershire, blue-chip hunting country. Not a stallion of any great consequence in racing terms, he died in September 1971 at the advanced age of twenty-eight. As one of the very first horses that his trainer inherited, it is remarkable that Pappatea's lifespan exceeded George Boyd's innings as a trainer, but then George was forty years of age when he first took over the licence.

Adjacent to the old A1 and the GNER railway line, with Biel Water meandering its way in between, the Tilton House string had use of very limited grass gallops on a restricted piece of ground that had formed part of the former racecourse. Indeed, when George Boyd commenced training there the old starting gate and sections of the railings were still in evidence. However, the horses worked primarily on the seashore. Although somewhat ruled by the vagaries of the North Sea tide, there was a stretch beyond the sand-dunes which was described as 'level as a billiard table with perfect going'.

Early in his career, George Boyd handled a top-class colt in Barnes Park, who was probably the first to promote his name to racegoers in the south. Third to Nimbus in the 1949 Two Thousand Guineas, fifth behind the same horse in the Derby, and unplaced in Ridge Wood's St Leger, Barnes Park lost his form as a four-year-old whereupon he was transferred from his Australian trainer, R. Colven at Middleham, to Tilton House.

It had not been the intention to run Barnes Park in the 1951 Lincolnshire, but when he was allotted just 8st, which was much less weight than connections had anticipated, there was a fortunate change of plan – and in scoring by a half-length at 33–1 in a field of thirty-five runners on the Carholme at Lincoln, he emulated White Bud, who had been dispatched from Tilton House by John McCall to win the 1923 Lincolnshire. Later that year the latter's owner, George Dingley, a Glasgow bookmaker, was warned off over White Bud's running when a beaten favourite at Haydock Park.

Barnes Park was owned by Harry Lane, a building and engineering contractor from Stockton-on-Tees, and named after a housing development with which he had been involved prior to the war. One day at Kelso races, Harry Lane asked George Boyd to find him a chaser and for £2,000 or £3,000 (recorded figures differ) he procured nine-year-old Teal, a smart pointer and winner of the United Border Hunt Hunters' Chase. It was an inspired purchase as the following year the Yorkshire-trained Teal triumphed in the Grand National, the second leg of the Spring Double, to land his 22st owner a six-figure gamble.

The Lincolnshire hero, Barnes Park, set the standard for all the other major handicap winners saddled by George Boyd during the 1950s and 1960s. In those days, before the introduction of the Pattern system, such races were far more prestigious than they are nowadays. One has only to consider such historic events as Epsom's Great Metropolitan and City and Suburban Handicaps or the Rosebery and Great Jubilee Handicaps, now run on the all-weather at Kempton Park, to appreciate their sad decline. Continued success in these highly competitive handicaps reflected a trainer's ability to place his horses far better than the proliferation of weight-for-age and condition races nowadays.

Amongst George Boyd's big handicap winners during the 1950s were Chaseaway (Cumberland Plate, Carlisle), Dignitary (Salford Borough Handicap, Manchester), Blue Spot (Ayrshire Handicap, Ayr), Persepolis (Rufford Abbey Handicap, Doncaster, twice), Sunrise (Zetland Gold Cup, Redcar), Devonport (Rufford Abbey Handicap, Doncaster), Belleisle (Perkins Memorial Handicap, Newcastle), No Comment (Ayrshire Handicap, Ayr, Lanark Silver Bell), Staghound (Edinburgh Gold Cup) and Rexequus (Cambridgeshire) – the Lanark Silver Bell and the Cumberland Plate are two of the oldest established events in the racing calendar.

The grey Staghound was a particular favourite in the stable. He was owned by Charlie Tosh, who had been director of textiles for the Indian government during the Second World War and owned a jute business in Dundee. When George Boyd decided to concentrate on Flat horses only, his owner sent the grey son of Devonian as a prospective jumper to Ryan Price at Findon, for whom he won the well-endowed Henry VIII Chase at Hurst Park.

In 1952 Glasgow credit bookmakers, George and James McLean, masterminded a gamble on their two horses, Flush Royal and Cap of Gold, for the Autumn double. A month before the Cesarewitch, Flush Royal's trainer, Jack Fawcus, was seriously injured in a car accident at Pathhead, so the horse joined Cap of Gold at Westbarns. The arrangement was that Flush Royal would return to Jack Fawcus at Middleham should he come out of hospital in Edinburgh before the Cesarewitch, which he did. Three days later the horse landed the first half of this extraordinary gamble. Cap of Gold failed to oblige, saving the bookmakers liabilities estimated at £1 million.

The George Boyd bonanza in northern handicaps continued during the next decade with New Brig (Northumberland Plate, Newcastle), Falls of Cruachan (Manchester Cup; Lanark Silver Bell), Cagirama (Northumberland Plate, Newcastle; Tennent Trophy, Ayr), Rapanni (Old Newton Cup, Haydock Park), Milesius (Ayr Gold Cup) and Bestofive (Royal Burgh of Ayr Handicap).

Numerically speaking George Boyd's most successful season was 1957, when he saddled twenty-two winners of fifty-nine races. In November his owners all clubbed together to give their trainer a celebratory dinner at the Marine Hotel, North Berwick. It was an amazing achievement as only Charles Elsey won more races in Great Britain that season and the Malton trainer had more than twice the number of horses.

The victory of Rexequus two years later in the Cambridgeshire (like many of his stable companions he sported a sheepskin noseband) was a major landmark, not only for his trainer, but also for Scotland. The son of King of the Tudors, owned by Glasgow businessman Jack Adam, became the first horse trained north of the border to land the second leg of the Autumn double. Apart from Sayani (rated by his famous Australian jockey, Rae Johnstone, as one of the best he ever rode), Rexequus was then the solitary three-year-old to win the Cambridgeshire with as much as 8st 7lb during the twentieth century.

In 1961 the same trainer-jockey combination of George Boyd and Norman Stirk brought off an even more sensational triumph on the Rowley Course at Newmarket when Rockavon triumphed in the Two

Thousand Guineas at 66–1, with the Tote dividend representing odds of over 100–1. The generous starting price was understandable as in eight juvenile starts the colt had only managed to score at Hamilton, twice, and Stockton (Teesside Park), and failed to earn a rating in the Free Handicap – and prior to the Guineas, he had finished just fourth in the Northern Free Handicap at Newcastle.

Ironically, George Boyd was not at Newmarket to witness this great classic victory as he had postponed flying down until the morning of the race, but because of low cloud the flight up from London could not land at Edinburgh and was diverted to Glasgow; Norman Stirk had travelled down by train. In his trainer's enforced absence the colt was saddled by his friend, 'Boggy' Whelan, the Epsom trainer with whom he frequently stayed on his forays south – for Newmarket meetings he always stayed at the Rising Sun. It was a sensational race in more ways than one as the warm favourite, Pinturischio, was found to have been doped, while Rockavon was the longest priced winner in Two Thousand Guineas' history.

A 420 guineas foal, who was procured by George Boyd's patron, Thomas Yuill, a dairy farmer and small breeder from Strathaven in Lanarkshire, for 2,300 guineas as a yearling, Rockavon subsequently won a match at Newcastle in June. On his three remaining starts he was third of four in the King George VI and Queen Elizabeth Stakes behind Right Royal V and St Paddy, and fourth in the Doonside Cup at the Ayr Western Meeting and unplaced in the Champion Stakes. Syndicated to stand at Theakston Stud in Yorkshire in 1962, he was soon dispatched to France but made little impact as a sire.

One of George Boyd's owners, John Kennedy from Ayrshire, purchased a couple of yearling colts from Frank Tuthill's famous Owenstown Stud in Ireland. New Brig was an exact contemporary of Rexequus and Ayrshire Bard was an exact contemporary of Rockavon. New Brig was thought good enough to take his chance in the Derby and that had been Ayrshire Bard's objective too. Indeed, on the strength of Rockavon's Two Thousand Guineas victory that season, Ayrshire Bard was at one time ante-post favourite for the Derby, but after he was beaten decisively when favourite for the Dante

Stakes, he never ran at Epsom and was exported to New Zealand the following year.

The majority of George Boyd's horses were ridden by one or other of his two stable jockeys, Norman Stirk from Yorkshire, who had been apprenticed to his brother, and lightweight Norman McIntosh. Norman Stirk's very first winner was Las Vegas, trained by Alec Boyd, in an apprentice handicap at Newmarket in August 1946. The former plater concluded that season by winning the Manchester November Handicap.

Norman McIntosh, the son of a Banffshire farm worker, gained his first success at Hamilton in September 1949 on Highland Clan, trained by George Boyd, with whom he was then serving his apprenticeship. While Rockavon and Rexequus were the two top horses that Norman Stirk ever rode, Norman McIntosh rated Cagirama and Staghound as the best he partnered over a distance of ground, with Dignitary and Milesius the pick of the sprinters. A prolific winner, Dignitary was placed in the Ayr Gold Cup, and Milesius set the record straight when winning Scotland's premier sprint in 1966. At the time his handler described the short head victory as 'the biggest thrill of my racing career'.

The first Scottish-trained winner of the Ayr Gold Cup since Gerry Laurence's Whistling Victor in 1959, Milesius was owned by George Boyd in partnership with Archie Mowat, a bookmaker from North Shields. The colt had been procured through Epsom-based George Forbes, this bloodstock agent of Scottish descent having bought him out of Cecil Boyd-Rochfort's powerful Newmarket stable at the conclusion of a disappointing three-year-old career.

George Boyd did well with cast-offs from fashionable Newmarket stables, and two to excel during the 1950s were Chaseaway and Antagonist. A couple of homebreds belonging to the great Yorkshire breeder, Lionel Holliday, both were acquired as two-year-olds from his annual draft of horses in training at the Newmarket December Sales. One day at Hamilton Park, Antagonist, ridden by Norman McIntosh, started at 10–1 on, only to be beaten by his solitary opponent, ridden by Norman Stirk. Although few of them can have backed Antagonist at such prohibitive odds, some of the local Glaswegians were obviously none too happy with the outcome!

Local owner J.E. Fisher, from North Berwick, raced Dignitary and decided to start a public stud specifically to stand this smart sprinter. The chosen location was close at hand on the Duke of Hamilton's Archerfield estate at Dirleton, next door to Muirfield golf course. The Forth Stud opened for business in 1961 with Albert Ford from Burton Agnes in Yorkshire as stud groom. Local landowner and turkey producer Rupert Chalmers Watson, together with trainers George Boyd and Sam Hall, were also involved in an advisory capacity.

The following summer the Forth Stud acquired Dignitary's erstwhile stable companion, New Brig, who had embarked upon his stud career as a syndicated stallion at Midshiels Farm, Denholm. His credentials were altogether different. The Scottish Lowlands have a strong tradition of breeding jumpers and with two-mile victories to his credit in both the Northumberland Plate and Haydock Stakes, this son of Solar Slipper was bought with National Hunt breeders in mind. New Brig duly proved his worth, becoming an exceptionally successful sire of jumpers. Dignitary, by comparison, made little contribution at stud.

As a syndicated stallion under the management of Doncaster Bloodstock Sales, New Brig was the posthumous winner of the Thoroughbred Breeders' Association's Horse & Hound Cup for the British-based sire with the most steeplechase winners for the 1986–7 season. The stallion had died aged twenty-seven in 1983, by which time he was owned outright by former syndicate member, Bob McDonald of Kelloe Mains, Duns.

Every racehorse trainer is heavily dependent upon the veterinary profession and George Boyd employed a skilled practitioner in Alec Tully from Kelso. For a number of years Alec held a licence himself, training a small string at his home, Springhall. Invariably driven by his sister in his little green van, he was a regular visitor to Tilton House – as indeed he was to most of the horse fraternity living in the Borders, where his undoubted talents were recognised by all and sundry.

Here was a vet who knew his job and had a flair for prescribing the right treatment. Gossip being what it is, the suggestion was sometimes made that perhaps he had some special concoction to help a few of them run just that little bit faster! It is amazing the sort of rumours that can circulate without any foundation – at the time there was even the suggestion that Rockavon was a four-year-old when he won the Two Thousand Guineas! All sheer nonsense, of course.

George Boyd's stable also assisted the veterinary profession in an altogether different way. Barry Park, MRCVS – who was responsible for the creation of Lambourn's Valley Equine Hospital, a state-of-the-art establishment which became the nerve centre of Lambourn's now solitary veterinary practice – recalls that horses from Westbarns regularly put in an appearance at the famous Dick Vet College in Edinburgh (where he qualified) as live specimens participating in the practical part of the students' final examinations.

Looking back over George Boyd's illustrious career, which must have had the leading Scottish bookmakers in Glasgow and Edinburgh running for cover on so many occasions, it seems remarkable how few fillies he trained. Indeed, of all his major winners, only Blue Spot was a member of the fair sex. One totally lacking in distinction was False Evidence, who was destined to breed the champion two-year-old filly, Cry of Truth.

With 700 winners to his credit, George Boyd retired at the close of the 1969 season. He handed over to his nephew, Tommy Craig, his former head lad and assistant. It was just like old times when he saddled Goldhill's Pride to defeat some of the top sprinters in the country when landing the Portland Handicap at Doncaster in 1978. That provided Tommy Craig with the most high-profile success of his career which embraced both Flat and jumping; he retired at the end of 1992.

Tommy remembers his uncle as a hard taskmaster, but someone who was devoted to the job in hand. 'He was never ill or missed a day and everything was kept to a strict routine. Originally he had a dual licence, but he stopped training jumpers to concentrate on the Flat. He never married and he lived with his mother who died aged ninety-two.'

Tommy Craig continued to live at Tilton House, but the land where the stables were has been developed for commercial use. George Boyd died on 1 September 1990 – he was eighty-three.

Nowadays many horses are trained exclusively on a so-called all-weather surface, but this was not the case in George Boyd's era, when a gallop on some stretch of beach only ever occurred when prevailing snow and ice deemed it expedient. Indeed, many people considered that working horses on the seashore blunted their speed. Somehow George Boyd's unlikely achievement in training an English classic winner on the sands at Dunbar never seemed to have received the credit it deserved.

While wading in sea water has long been regarded as efficacious in terms of keeping horses sound it was not really until the advent of Red Rum that people began to realise that it was perfectly possible to get a horse racing fit exercising exclusively on the beach. At Stockport, Red Rum's handler, Ginger McCain, had no real alternative without resorting to the use of a horsebox.

Racehorses never received a mention as the popular BBC documentary programme *Coast* progressed up the east coast of Scotland past Dunbar. There were eulogies about St Abbs as a marine reserve and the history of the Bass Rock, the largest single-rock colony of gannets in the world. But how about the Two Thousand Guineas winner, Rockavon, or Bass Rock for that matter? Lord Rosebery's Bass Rock won the Victoria Cup when that major handicap was run at Hurst Park!

14

ALL THOSE SOLDIER RIDERS OWED HIM A
DEBT OF GRATITUDE

With one of the biggest and most successful Flat strings in the country, Richard Hannon Jnr has two yards on opposite sides of Collingbourne Ducis. The first is at East Everleigh on the edge of Salisbury Plain, close to the army ranges at Tidworth. The other is Herridge, high on the Wiltshire Downs, south of Marlborough. Here one can easily land and take off in a private aeroplane, the preferred means of transport to distant meetings for this busy trainer and his retinue during the summer months. The Shears Inn has been a very well patronised watering hole in between!

Richard Jnr took over from his father of the same name to whom he had been a long standing assistant for the 2014 season and astonishingly he managed to replicate his father's achievement of being champion trainer the preceding year. Richard Hannon Snr had also been top trainer in 2010 and 2011 as well as in 1992. Those more recent years were all the more commendable as they were achieved without Arab assistance – the stable has since attracted the patronage of these mega rich benefactors.

Richard Jnr's grandfather, Harry Hannon, used to train at East Everleigh, albeit he had an altogether smaller operation. The most prestigious winner he ever trained was the very smart sprinting mare, Ampney Princess. Successful in the Diadem Stakes at Ascot, she raced for Joane Wood, owner of Ampney Stud, near Cirencester, which she duly sold to the great Scottish jockey, Willie Carson (see Chapter 18), who renamed it Minster Stud.

Richard Hannon Jnr trains only on the Flat, but Herridge used to be exclusive to jumpers. In fact he bought the premises in 1990 from Alec Kilpatrick's two sons, Sandy and Jim. For a number of years they ran the place as a public (stallion) stud. The brothers had taken Herridge over when their father retired from training at the close of the 1972–3 season. His retirement was a short one as he died in 1976.

An international high-jumper in his day, Sandy has long been the best-known figure in the world of stallion advertising and he is responsible for the twin annual publications, the *Thoroughbred Stallion Guide* and the *Thoroughbred Business Guide*, as well as *European Bloodstock News*. Jim was assistant to their father from the time when Alec returned home from war-time service in the Argyll and Sutherland Highlanders.

Jim and Sandy used to break-in upwards of eighty yearlings per season for Richard Hannon Snr, amongst them the Guineas heroes, Don't Forget Me and Tirol. It was a far cry from their father's day, when he would never have had more than thirty horses in training there at any one time. But the old-fashioned stable block, with its indoor passageways and marvellous old wooden doors and partitions dating back to 1906, is still in use. But not much else has survived from those bygone days – even one of two enormous monkey-puzzle trees has disappeared, the victim of a lightning strike.

By no means the only old boy of George Watson's in Edinburgh to feature in *The Scots & the Turf*, Alec Kilpatrick will always be remembered for Galloway Braes, the fastest three-mile chaser of his generation, but he had another unique claim to fame. Being a Scotsman he was not one to miss an opportunity and, with its proximity to Tidworth, Herridge was the most convenient training establishment for all those young army officers who fancied themselves as jockeys. By no means all trainers are prepared to take time and trouble with aspiring amateurs, but in Alec Kilpatrick's case, it proved of mutual advantage.

Like so many jump trainers, Alec had a background of farming, hunting and point-to-points, but he had another equine connection. His father, James Kilpatrick, was a renowned Clydesdale breeder at his famous Craigie Mains Stud, at Kilmarnock in Ayrshire, which he founded in 1875. He exported horses to America, Canada, South Africa, Australia and New Zealand and bred a string of champions. In 1911, at Ayr Mart, in front of a crowd of over 4,000, he sold Baron of Buchlyvie for £9,500, a world record price for a draught horse. The stallion's skeleton can still be seen in Glasgow's Kelvingrove Museum.

In due course his elder son, also James, founded his own Clydesdale stud at Hawkrigg in Cumberland. Meanwhile his younger son, Alec, crossed the border in 1928 to farm at Stretton Manor, near Oadby, in Leicestershire, an ideal location for hunting with the Quorn and the Fernie.

There, Alec met Harry Beeby (his grandson of the same name is chairman of Goffs UK), who ran one of the biggest livery stables in the Shires. It was not long before Alec was riding some of Harry's horses out in the hunting field, where he showed them off to great advantage. A good judge of a horse, he was also competing in point-to-points and as an amateur under Rules, but his enthusiasm wavered somewhat after he wasted down to 9st 10lb to ride on a thoroughly miserable winter's day at Manchester!

With his aspirations turning more and more towards training, he laid down a tan gallop on the farm and was granted a licence to train for the 1932–3 season. His initial success came with Daniel, ridden by the season's champion jockey, Gerry Wilson, in a three-year-old hurdle race at Derby. He was then successful with a couple of homebreds over hurdles. Happy Home won four races in quick succession and a year later Ponessan won five races within a month and he went on winning over the ensuing years, invariably ridden by his lad, Jimmy Allen.

Disenchanted with farming, which was going through hard times, Alec was determined to make training his full-time occupation and he decided to rent a yard off Sonny Hall at Russley Park on the Wiltshire/ Berkshire border, close to the training centre of Lambourn. Installed at Russley for the 1938–9 season, he had brought with him from Leicestershire a colt named Jim Newcombe, whose owner, Tom Spiers, a precision engineer, had acquired him as part of a job lot. He showed no ability at two and three years on the Flat, so John McGuigan, who also came from the west of Scotland, was approached to buy him for £150, but with £100 the best offer, the deal fell through.

All of which was fortuitous for his original connections as Jim Newcombe soon found his true metier. A winning odds-on favourite in a three-year-old hurdle at Newton Abbot, he scored seven times over hurdles, and with stable jockey Ben Lay aboard, six times over fences. To give some indication of the value of races in those days the thirteen victories were worth a grand total of £980 – the stable did not manage to win a three-figure prize until his last victory, a chase at Taunton, worth £122 to the winner.

Very highly regarded by his trainer, Jim Newcombe was an entire and he became quite a successful jumping stallion. Initially he stood at Herridge at a fee of ten pounds and ten shillings, but by the time he was put down in 1953 aged nineteen he was located in Sussex. His best progeny was the Whitbread Gold Cup hero, Plummers Plain.

Jim Newcombe was amongst those making the move from Russley Park to Herridge Farm, but within a few months the war intervened and jump racing was put on hold until the advent of the 1945–6 season. Although Alec had been concentrating on farming, he did have a number of young horses about the place and soon jockeys like Bob Turnell and Glen Kelly came over to school them.

There was also a gunnery officer, Walter Skrine, who was madly keen to have a ride in the Grand National. So began the trainer's long involvement with soldier riders. Walter had a brother, Godfrey, who worked in a solicitor's office in Leicester and used to ride out for Alec at Oadby, and a sister, the novelist Molly Keane. The Collingbourne Ducis trainer must have had marked reservations about this budding amateur, as on his first appearance at Herridge in January 1945, he arrived on crutches, which hardly inspired much confidence.

Although he had ridden with considerable success in India, Walter Skrine had been badly wounded in the commando landings in Sicily. As the result of a serious operation, one of his legs ended up two inches shorter than the other. As this would have greatly inhibited his agility in the saddle, he promptly volunteered to have a second operation to literally redress the balance – in other words to have the other leg shortened by two inches!

To get Walter started, Alec had bought a schoolmaster called Post Horn from Ben Lay's wife. It was really a case of who would break down first, horse or rider, but in the cause of fitness the intrepid owner-rider completed a 600-mile tour of Ireland, walking and riding. Frequently Walter could be seen walking the fifteen-plus miles from Larkhill to Herridge. The demanding regime had the desired effect as at Fontwell Park the combination provided the stable with its first winner of the 1946–7 season. The pair were just beaten in the Kim Muir Challenge Cup at Cheltenham, but alas the old horse broke down on the eve of the Grand National.

Not long afterwards, a six-year-old replacement, Martin M, was bought at the sales in Dublin for 410 guineas. He served his purpose admirably as he won a totally chaotic Valentine Chase in November 1946 (Sandy Kilpatrick recalls that Walter Skrine went out to the paddock in a mac to cover up his walking stick). At their next attempt over the formidable Aintree obstacles, the pair of them completed the course in the following year's Grand National, won by 100–1 chance Caughoo. Job accomplished.

A heart condition enforced Walter Skrine's retirement, but he was succeeded by a whole platoon of competent soldier riders, notably Cecil 'Monkey' Blacker (father of world famous equine sculptor, Philip Blacker), Sir Nicholas Nuttall, and Sir Piers Bengough, who was to become Her Majesty's representative at Ascot. Between them they achieved a remarkable string of seven successes in the Grand Military Gold Cup at Sandown Park. Blacker won in 1954 on Pointsman; Nuttall won on Stalbridge Park in 1958 and 1961; and Bengough won on Joan's Rival in 1960, before completing a hat-trick on Charles Dickens in 1970, 1971 and 1972. During that period Alec hardly ever failed to have a runner and on one occasion he fielded six!

Another soldier who knocked on Alec Kilpatrick's door was Roscoe Harvey. After a very distinguished career in the Second World War, he had ended up as the army's senior Armoured Brigade commander. A competent amateur, he became the Jockey Club's senior stewards' secretary. That job precluded him from riding his own horses under Rules, but not in point-to-points. From 1946 to 1951 Aquilo, whom Alec Kilpatrick had bought as a two-year-old for just twenty-four guineas, and his owner scored twelve times between the flags. Tragically Roscoe Harvey's son had a fatal road accident after experiencing a fall on Aquilo on his first ever ride in a point-to-point.

Soldiers or no soldiers, the two outstanding horses trained by Alec Kilpatrick were for two titled ladies, Lady Orde, from Wherwell in Hampshire, with Galloway Braes, and Lady Sherborne, from Aldsworth in Gloucestershire, with Sidbury Hill.

Alec bought Galloway Braes as a four-year-old in Ireland in 1949 from Lord Rathdonnell. A half-share was then sold to Andrew McClure from Galloway, for whom he won a couple of races, before the Scottish draper decided to quit racing. Eileen Orde then bought him privately for £1,200. The Ordes had raced successfully in India where her husband was inspector general of police in the Punjab – one of his forebears, William Orde of Nunnykirk in Northumberland, owned the great nineteenth-century mare, Beeswing. Coincidentally both Walter Skrine and royal jockey, Harry Carr, had ridden winners in India for the Ordes. Only a few days after Galloway Braes changed hands, the six-year-old won the Royal Porcelain Chase at Worcester and Mrs McClure was immediately on the telephone claiming (unsuccessfully) the fine set of bone china that was part of the prize!

Galloway Braes and his old rival, Halloween, were the best staying chasers over park courses during the 1950s, although neither managed to win the Gold Cup. A raking, big dark-brown Irish-bred gelding, the son of Norwest was a confirmed front-runner with a tendency to make at least one serious jumping error. He twice won the newly instituted Queen Elizabeth Chase at now defunct Hurst Park, as well as the King George VI Chase in record time, a race in which he was second twice. He also won two Holman Cups at Cheltenham, where he finished third in two Gold Cups, in 1952 to Mont Tremblant and the following year behind Knock Hard.

Tragically, Galloway Braes fell and broke a shoulder at the last open ditch in the 1956 King George VI Chase on Boxing Day. His tally stood at nineteen victories and seventeen places from sixty-two starts. He had established new course records for three miles at Hurst Park, Birmingham, Kempton Park and Worcester. Great credit for Galloway Braes must go to stable jockey and regular partner, Bert Morrow, who scored on him sixteen times. After retiring from the saddle, this fearless rider went to work at Whitsbury Manor Stud, near Fordingbridge, in Hampshire.

By that time Percy and Eileen Orde had purchased Monkey Black-er's Grand Military Gold Cup hero, Pointsman, whom Alec had originally procured for £800 in Ireland from Willy Ashe in Co. Kildare. After his Sandown victory, Blacker felt he had to take a profit and the Ordes bought him for £2,500. Pointsman carried Percy's colours and, on his final start, he only just failed to emulate Galloway Braes when beaten a head by the great Mandarin in the 1959 King George VI Chase.

Sod's Law decrees that fatal accidents only happen to the very best horses and Sidbury Hill, a half-brother to Charles Dickens, provided another case in point. Bought privately from Charles Radclyffe, a well-known purveyor of potential jumpers from Lew, near Witney, in Oxfordshire, and named after a hill that is clearly visible from Herridge on a clear day, Sidbury Hill's career was short and sharp, but it was sufficiently long for his trainer to rank him amongst the very best he had handled.

Successful in three runs over hurdles when establishing course records at Cheltenham and Sandown, Sidbury Hill was put to chasing in handicaps as it was deemed unnecessary to risk him against other novices with the inherent danger of being brought down. As a six-year-old, he won first time out over fences at Birmingham and then twice at Newbury, although those victories were interspersed with two falls. However, he was allowed to take his chance in the 1961 Gold Cup. Ridden by stable jockey Tim Brookshaw, he was up with the leaders at the water second time round when he fell heavily and had to be put down. The Sherbornes lost four horses that year and the trauma put Lady Sherborne off ownership for good.

The Grand National proved a bogey race for Alec Kilpatrick. Time and again he had a fancied runner, only to be disappointed. His first attempt came with Newark Hill. Carrying the Jim Newcombe colours, he was brought down by two loose horses at Becher's second time round when going well. Two fine staying chasers, Whispering Steel, winner of the Mildmay Memorial Chase carrying the colours of Alec's wife, Mary, and Bassnet, winner of the Haydock Park National Trial, made three failed attempts each. In 1956 Must, winner of the Fred

Withington Chase, started favourite only to fall at the first and Bassnet met with the same cruel fate when second favourite in 1967 – yet both were experienced jumpers.

It is remarkable to reflect that Galloway Braes and Whispering Steel, together with Workboy, were exact contemporaries. Between them, this Irish-bred trio won a staggering thirty-nine races. Monkey Blacker, Pointsman's original owner, later bought Workboy, a fine two-mile chaser, and transformed him into an international showjumper, in which sphere his erstwhile stable companion, Prince Hal, excelled for leading lady showjumper Pat Smythe.

Alec Kilpatrick did train a Gold Cup winner in Four Ten, but his moment of glory had come in 1954 before arriving from John Roberts's yard at Prestbury. For his new stable, Four Ten won the Walter Hyde Chase at Kempton Park and the Golden Miller Chase at Cheltenham. Another to prove himself round Cheltenham's undulations was National Hunt Handicap Chase hero, Isle of Skye. He was owned in partnership by Sir Tommy Pilkington (later senior steward of the Jockey Club and brother to Sonia Rogers of Airlie Stud in Ireland) and Scots-born Ian Cameron, father-to-be of future prime minister, David.

At Ascot in the autumn of 1970, Charles Dickens became Alec Kilpatrick's 500th winner, but he was by no means the only multiple scorer at Herridge at that late stage. Three of them to do well were procured out of other stables. Fishers Lodge, who always had to work alone as he was such a tearaway, won nine races; Rosador, purchased in France from Hugh Leggat of Pirnie House Stud in Roxburghshire, proceeded to win half a dozen races, although originally the wrong horse actually arrived at the yard; and the highly strung little Stickler won eleven chases at Fontwell Park, having established a great rapport with stable jockey, Steve Jobar.

General Sir Cecil Blacker, who knew Alec Kilpatrick throughout his training career, described him in these succinct words: 'Alec is one of those rare people who are prepared to put up with the eccentricities and shortcomings of soldier-riders. He is tall, Scottish, impassive, and quite capable of speaking his mind; his kindness and generosity are more evident from his deeds than his words, of which he is in any case sparing.'

What he would have thought of all the hype that pervades racing nowadays does not bear thinking about. He was certainly lucky to be involved when he was!

15

A JAPANESE PRISONER OF WAR WHO
NEVER LOOKED BACK

During the 1950s, Galloway Braes and Halloween were arch rivals during a vintage era for staying chasers. Few people who saw them being saddled up prior to yet another fascinating confrontation would have appreciated that their respective trainers, Alec Kilpatrick and Bill Wightman, although training in the south of England, were both 'Scotsmen', one born and bred north of the border, the other by virtue of his lineage.

As described in the previous chapter, Alec Kilpatrick came from Kilmarnock in Ayrshire, whereas Bill Wightman, who was educated at an English public school, Dulwich, was born in England, but had strong Scottish parentage. His father came from Edinburgh, where the family owned a sheet-music business, while his mother, a talented artist and an exhibitor at the Royal Academy and the Hermitage, had strong connections with the Shetland Islands. She too had been at school and university in Edinburgh and her grandfather was the minister at Unst, the northernmost island of the British Isles, and Yell.

Even to those who knew him well, Bill always appeared the quintessential Englishman, yet he always regarded himself as a Scot who just happened to have been born in England. Taken at face value, he was an unlikely candidate to make a racehorse trainer. Born and brought up in Streatham in south-west London, he may have had a suburban background, but he was always a countryman by inclination. For some inexplicable reason, he exhibited a remarkable rapport with horses and dogs from the moment he became involved with them. He loved shooting and his hobby used to be training gun dogs, the first of them being acquired from the Waugh family.

At school he had excelled at games, particularly cricket. He was wicket-keeper of the celebrated Dulwich XI of 1932 that included S.C. (Billy) Griffith, who was to play for Sussex and the MCC. Leaving school without any academic qualifications, Bill became an office junior, working for the Wheat Commission in Westminster. Having always enjoyed the OTC (Officers' Training Corps) at Dulwich, he also joined the Yeomanry, the mounted section of the Territorials who had a riding school just off Sloane Square.

Bored with such a sedentary job, he enjoyed riding the army chargers and attending the occasional race meeting, whereupon he began to consider some sort of career in racing. But realistically, with neither the necessary funds nor any family connections, it all seemed a bit of a pipe dream. However, an unexpected invitation from an old school friend to play in a week of country-house cricket whilst on holiday in Sussex turned the dream into a reality. It was all thanks to two Old Etonians, Geoffrey Gilbey, a racing journalist and member of the gin family, and Evelyn Baring, a prominent member of the banking dynasty.

It was upon Geoffrey Gilbey's suggestion that Bill joined his trainer, Laing Ward, at Headbourne Worthy, near Winchester, in which part of Hampshire he would remain for the rest of his life. Having learnt the rudiments of training and shown a remarkable flair for the business in hand, Bill, who was still a teenager, was then presented with an unexpected proposition. Would he take over Geoffrey Gilbey's private string of racing ponies?

From Cloudbank, a yard at South Wonston, close to Headbourne Worthy, Bill Wightman saddled a bevy of pony winners, mostly at the well-appointed Northholt Park on the outskirts of London. In his first season he saddled no fewer than twenty-two winners under Pony Turf Club Rules, many of them well-bred individuals who were deemed too small to make their mark in racing proper. He even used to send them over on the Sandbanks ferry to work on the beach at Studland Bay for a change of scenery. However, before long he had bravely branched out as a public trainer of horses rather than ponies.

In May 1937 he saddled his very first winner under National Hunt Rules, when Sunny Peace scored over fences at Buckfastleigh, ridden by Bruce Hobbs. (The following year, aged seventeen, Hobbs became the youngest rider ever to win a Grand National when scoring on Battleship). Then, in September, Autumn was successful at Warwick to become Bill's first ever winner under Jockey Club Rules. Sunny Peace and Autumn had been acquired for fifty guineas and twenty-five pounds respectively. That was little money even for those far-off days!

At about this time Evelyn Baring bought Dean Farm, Bishop's Waltham, between Winchester and Southampton, as he was convinced that war was imminent and it would be advantageous to own a farm. The land was part of Sir Harry Warden Chilcott's estate, centred on the neighbouring village of Upham. Nowadays Dean Farm has a high profile in the bloodstock world as the Weinfelds' famous Meon Valley Stud. Another of the four original farms was Ower Farm, which duly became Bill Wightman's home and stables.

Bill had no sooner switched allegiance from South Wonston to Dean Farm than war broke out. Three days later, he signed up (in Newmarket of all places), but his wartime recollections as a young gunnery officer are chilling in the extreme. He spent three and a half years as a prisoner of war of the Japanese. This included a brief period in the notorious Changi Prison, with the final three years incarcerated at Kuching Camp at Sarawak in Borneo. Suffice to say that when this six-footer eventually returned home, he weighed just 7st 12lb. It says much for his outlook on life that many years later this former prisoner of war of the Japanese would be happily driving round in a Subaru car.

Thanks to Evelyn Baring and a remarkably quick recovery to full health, there was still a job awaiting him back home. By then the horses were stabled on top of the downs at Ower Farm rather than down in the valley at Dean Farm, on the other side of the Stephen's Castle Down gallops. During the war the horses had been entrusted to Harry Lowe, who had been Warden Chilcott's private trainer. Amongst them was the useful chaser, Southborough, and he duly provided Bill with his first winner on his resumption, when scoring at Wincanton in November 1946.

That victory was significant in a number of ways – not least because Southborough was owned by the Contessa di Sant Elia, who became the stable's most important patron, and was partnered by Desmond Dartnall, an indispensable cog in the wheel at Ower Farm as the stable's retained jump jockey. When it came to the Flat, Bill invariably employed the best that was available although he had a very able standby in Bill Anderson, who had considerable experience riding in France. Both Bill Anderson and head lad, Bill Nash, worked together for nearly fifty years.

A friend of the Warden Chilcotts, the Contessa di Sant Elia actually lived in the house at Ower Farm, which became Bill's home, as during his bachelor years he remained down at Dean Farm. The name may sound exotic, but Rosamund retained her down-to-earth Lancashire persona, rather than aspiring to the exalted-sounding status conferred upon her by marriage to an Italian aristocrat! She also became the owner of the best horse Bill ever trained and the one with whom he will always be associated.

In keeping with a number of top steeplechasers of that era, Halloween came into racing via the hunting field. Purchased from a local dealer by Dick Smalley, a captain in the Royal Marines, the combination had won a couple of point-to-points before Halloween joined Bill. By the close this bonny individual had scored seventeen victories under Rules and proved the best horse of his generation over three miles on a park course. Admirers of Galloway Braes might just dispute this, as their rivalry was legendary.

Initially Halloween was unbeaten in five hunter chases ridden by his owner, culminating with a rescheduled Cheltenham Foxhunters'. When the Smalleys sold him for £8,000 (equivalent to a substantial six-figure sum in today's money) to Rosamund di Sant Elia, it was with the proviso that he must remain with his trainer. The bay gelding was small of stature, but with the heart of a lion and sound as a bell. He and Fred Winter became one of the most celebrated partnerships in the annals of National Hunt racing. They achieved their greatest victories in the King George VI Steeplechase in 1952 and 1954.

A son of Court Nez, an HIS (Hunter Improvement Society) stallion, Halloween had proved he stayed well, but due to his lack of inches he was never risked over the big Aintree fences. He must also go down in the record books as one of the best three-mile chasers never to win the Gold Cup, in which he was placed on four consecutive occasions, twice finishing runner-up. Perhaps the undulations of Cheltenham did not suit him ideally, as he was always running on at the finish, having just been tapped for speed when they quickened up down the final hill. He was also a horse who liked to be left to his own devices – as several professional jockeys found to their cost!

Curiously the best Flat horse that Bill Wightman ever trained also came early in his training career – indeed Kingsfold was a contemporary of Halloween. Their trainer rarely had the luxury of being provided with smart homebred yearlings, so when Kingsfold's owner-breeder, Mrs L.W. (Lawrence Winsland) Smith from Coolham in West Sussex sent him this unfashionable bred colt by Kingsway, it must have seemed just par for the course.

Bill liked Kingsfold from the outset, although aware that he was never going to be a precocious two-year-old and that in the long term staying would probably prove his forte. The colt improved by leaps and bounds, scoring three times in his second season when finishing runner-up in the St Leger to the Aga Khan's Tulyar – the closest Bill ever came to saddling a classic winner. How unfortunate to be foaled in the same year as such a record-breaking champion! He was also underbidder at the yearling sales for the Two Thousand Guineas winner, Nearula.

Kingsfold's objective as a four-year-old was the Ascot Gold Cup, which had considerably more prestige to the breeding fraternity in those days than it does now. Following two preparatory victories at Newmarket, Kingsfold was installed ante-post favourite for the centrepiece to Royal Ascot, but tragically broke a leg doing a routine canter only a few days before. There was no alternative but to have him put down. Ironically the Gold Cup was duly won by Souepi, to whom Kingsfold had proved significantly superior on previous encounters.

Over the years Bill Wightman earned the reputation as one of the shrewdest of trainers. He knew the time of day and laid his horses out with commendable skill to get the better of the handicapper. True, he liked a bet and would advise his owners accordingly, and his record in the top handicaps was second to none, as the leading bookmakers found to their cost. However, he was the first to admit that this was a reflection on the class of horse he handled. He would never have jeopardised any horse's long-term prospects for the sake of a quick financial dividend.

Bill Wightman trained for two prominent lady owner-breeders. One was Florence Prior from Romsey in Hampshire. She was the compiler of *The Half-Bred Stud Book* and her trainer also became a sort of unofficial chauffeur! Flo Prior's outstanding horse was the smart grey sprinter, Runnymede (Palace House Stakes), who was ridden to all his victories by the Scottish jockey, Duncan Keith. Born and bred at Benham Stud, near Newbury – where his breeder kept her nucleus of mares including his dam, Dutch Clover, her foundation mare – Runnymede returned there to spend the duration of his stallion career. Another of Flo Prior's fillies was Greensward, who became the dam of the great Exbury. Greensward was so handy with her hind legs that she was never shod behind.

In similar fashion, Helen Fleetwood-Hesketh (later Helen Kennard) has enjoyed prodigious success with her foundation mare, L'Anguissola. The mare produced three fillies, all of whom did well at Ower Farm. Walk By became one of Bill's two winners of the Portland Handicap at Doncaster, while both Solar and Smarten Up were placed in the Cheveley Park Stakes, the traditional end-of-season championship for juvenile fillies. The latter proceeded to dead-heat for the Temple Stakes and finish runner-up in the Nunthorpe Stakes.

Subsequently, Smarten Up became the dam of that excellent sire, Cadeaux Genereux, and another filly to make her mark on the racecourse before doing likewise at stud was the Cambridgeshire heroine, Flying Nelly. She carried the colours of Simon Wingfield Digby, which are now utilised by his daughter, Venetia (Lady Hardy), of Sandley Stud in Dorset, later known as Scarvagh House Stud. Flying Nelly became the dam of his magnificent stayer, Further Flight, another grey.

Flat or jumping, sprinters, middle-distance performers or stayers, colts, fillies or geldings, Bill Wightman seemed to have the happy knack of doing well with all of them, a skill afforded to few trainers.

Additional big handicap winners included Air Trooper (Magnet Cup), Charlotte's Choice (Chester Cup), Import (Stewards' Cup, Wokingham Stakes), King's Ride (Lincoln), Privateer (Portland Handicap), Roxburgh (Rosebery Memorial), and Somersway (Ayr Gold Cup) – and that is by no means a comprehensive list.

One of his trainer's great favourites was Pneumatic, who is buried at Ower Farm. Purchased as a yearling for just sixty-five guineas, he was gelded shortly afterwards and proceeded to win seventeen of his seventy-eight starts and was ridden to victory on twelve occasions by Doug Smith. Owned by Bill's wife, Antoinette, at the beginning and the end of his racing career, he was a Newbury specialist, winning the Round Oak Handicap there on four occasions. He won at Newbury as a two-year-old in June 1953 and as a ten-year-old in August 1961.

Other Bill Wightman celebrities over jumps included Oscar Wilde (Welsh National), the front-running Badbury Rings, the ill-fated Fire Prince, and the staying hurdlers, Anthony Wayne and Hilarion. On the Flat, Fraxinus, Javata and Cathy Jane all won good races. Successful in the Brown Jack Stakes at Ascot, Cathy Jane was the first racehorse owned by Mick Channon, and the West Ilsley trainer is the first to admit that he owes a great deal to Bill's tutelage. Bill returned the compliment by sending him that durable handicapper, Digital, and he was still winning on the Flat in 2008 as an eleven-year-old.

Digital was homebred at Ower Farm and so too was the last of his more than 700 winners, Googly, who scored at Newbury in October 1993. Bill Wightman was then seventy-nine years of age and not only the last trainer in Great Britain to have started training pre-war, but also the senior member of that fraternity (in terms of years holding a licence), under both Rules, which is probably a record.

As the master of Ower Farm, Upham, said at the time, 'I've put my guns away, I've had the best shooting.' However, it was a measure of the man that despite advancing years he could not resist fielding the occasional point-to-point runner to win in his pale blue and white colours. The retired Hampshire trainer lived at his lovely home overlooking the picturesque brick and flint stable yard until he died on St Andrew's Day (30 November) in 2009, aged ninety-five.

There were many glowing tributes paid at Bill Wightman's funeral service at Upham church and in the press. Prior to his demise, a very succinct appraisal came from senior racing and breeding journalist, Peter Willett. In a private letter, he wrote: 'Bill is an extraordinary man because he is the only person I have met who spent a long time as a prisoner of war and appeared to be mentally completely unscarred by the experience. It certainly speaks volumes for his strength of character.'

16

THE FAIRY GODMOTHER OF
NATIONAL HUNT RACING

It is an extraordinary scenario for someone who became the personification of National Hunt racing. Never particularly keen on riding, either as a child or as an adult, the late Queen Elizabeth the Queen Mother did more to promote the cause of jump racing in Great Britain than anyone, yet she did not become involved in any meaningful way until she had reached her half-century. Many regarded her as the fairy godmother of the 'winter game', an image much enhanced by her liking for floaty chiffon dresses, hats adorned with a trademark veil, and not always the most practical of shoes.

When she was Duchess of York, racing would have been little more than a social diversion revolving around Flat racing in general and Royal Ascot in particular, but it was different once her husband had succeeded his elder brother as King George VI. It must have been incumbent on the sovereign to take an interest in the Royal Studs at Sandringham and Hampton Court. During the Second World War, when racing was severely restricted, the royal colours were carried to victory by Big Game and Sun Chariot (both leased from the National Stud), in four of the five English classics of 1942, all held on the July Course at Newmarket – the Rowley Course had been requisitioned by the RAF as an airfield. Four years later King George VI won the One Thousand Guineas with homebred Hypericum.

The ninth of Claude and Cecilia Bowes Lyons' ten children, Elizabeth was born on 4 August 1900, and she was just four years old when her father became the 14th Earl of Strathmore and Kinghorne on the death of his father. The family home was Glamis Castle in Angus, reputed to be one of the most haunted houses in the British Isles;

according to Shakespeare, this was where Macbeth, Thane of Glamis, murdered Duncan I, his predecessor as King of Scotland. Glamis is just north of Dundee, the only city in Scotland that faces south. On the other side of the border, the Strathmores owned two more homes, The Bury, a picturesque William and Mary house at St Paul's Walden Bury in Hertfordshire, and a London address at 20 St James's Square in Mayfair.

Elizabeth was brought up partly in England, where she was born, and partly in Scotland. Always an animal lover, she did have a favourite Shetland pony, Bobs, who followed her everywhere at Glamis, even into the house and up the stairs. During the First World War the castle was requisitioned as a hospital for injured soldiers and the young teenager witnessed the appalling suffering that war can inflict. There was also personal tragedy. Four of her brothers joined Scottish regiments and Fergus, one of two to serve in the Black Watch, was killed at Loos. Many years later their sister would become honorary Colonel-in-Chief of the Black Watch based in Perth.

The Earl and Countess of Strathmore maintained the status quo albeit they were not well off by the standards of the aristocracy and they could have ill afforded to indulge in racing had they felt so inclined. The Earl's uncle had been an enthusiastic amateur rider, who had competed in the 1847 and 1848 Grand Nationals. The 10th Earl of Strathmore owned and bred the 1803 St Leger winner, Remembrancer. However, Cecilia Strathmore (née Cavendish-Bentinck) had a more significant connection with the Turf. Her father, a clergyman, was a cousin of the 6th Duke of Portland. One of the great racing personalities of the Victorian era, the Duke owned the winners of eleven classic races in addition to St Simon, arguably the greatest racehorse of all time.

The Duke of Portland and the Earl of Strathmore were both popular figures who exhibited due concern for the welfare of their tenants, but their outlook differed. In view of Elizabeth Bowes Lyon's future role as the King's consort, it is amusing to reflect that whereas the Duke became Master of the Horse to the Royal Household at the time of the Jubilee and Diamond Jubilee celebrations, her own father had never been enamoured either with the ways of the court or with its courtiers. He was, in fact, an eccentric and retiring character, never happier than when out shooting a rabbit for supper or pottering about the garden – if Claude Strathmore could be described as a grandee he was a reclusive one.

It was during Ascot week in June 1949 – when the King's homebred filly, Avila, won the Coronation Stakes – that his wife's interest in jump racing, then very much the poor relation of the Flat, was first kindled. Amongst the guests at Windsor Castle for the Royal Meeting was Lord Mildmay of Flete. The leading amateur rider of his day, Anthony Mildmay suggested to Queen Elizabeth that she might like to have some amusement of her own with a jumper. His horses were trained by his old friend, Peter Cazalet, a contemporary at Eton and a brother officer in the Welsh Guards during the war.

Tall and frail in appearance, with a rather gaunt countenance, the 2nd Lord Mildmay overcame his obvious physical disadvantages to become the leading amateur rider in the period spanning the Second World War, when the racecourse echoed to the cries of 'Come on, m'lord'. On two occasions he had come agonisingly close to riding the winner of the Grand National. In 1936 on the tubed entire, Davy Jones, the reins parted at the buckle and the 100–1 outsider ran out at the last fence when holding every chance. Then in 1948, paralysed by cramp in his neck, he still managed to finish an honourable third on Cromwell. Both horses were trained at Fairlawne in Kent.

Anthony Mildmay was delegated to find a suitable horse for Queen Elizabeth and it was upon the recommendation of Tony Grantham, then Peter Cazalet's stable jockey, that they procured Monaveen for £1,000. This seven-year-old, who had once pulled a milk float in Navan, had given Grantham an extremely good ride in the Grand National of 1949 before falling at the nineteenth fence. Once sold out of training for thirty-five pounds, he was transformed by the application of a hood to aid his concentration.

Monaveen duly went into training at Fairlawne. As Peter's sister, Thelma, and Elizabeth were life-long friends, the new owner was already familiar with the lovely parkland setting of Fairlawne at

Shipbourne, near Tonbridge, in Kent, and the round of weekend house parties that took place there.

Comprising 1,500 acres, Fairlawne was certainly a grand establishment, the property boasting the country's only private Real Tennis court. Guests certainly knew what it was to be cosseted. The cook was none other than Albert Roux, who went on to preside over one of London's most famous restaurants, Le Gavroche, and as one of the last households in the country to maintain the munificence of the Edwardian era, standards of hospitality were unequalled. Within the portals of this rambling eighteenth-century house, one did not even have to place one's toothpaste on one's toothbrush!

Monaveen, whom Queen Elizabeth raced in partnership with her elder daughter, Princess Elizabeth, was unfortunate to have been a contemporary of the great Aintree specialist Freebooter, to whom he finished runner-up in the Grand Sefton Chase and fifth in the Grand National. In the interim the Royal runner had defeated Freebooter when landing the inaugural Queen Elizabeth Chase at Hurst Park, but tragically in the following year's renewal he fell at the water jump, breaking a leg. The horse was buried near the racecourse stables. When most of Hurst Park was given over to housing, a road, formerly part of the old car park, was named Monaveen Gardens. Somewhat ironically the construction firm involved in developing Hurst Park was Wates, a family closely involved in racing – Andrew Wates' Rough Quest won the 1996 Grand National.

It is fortunate indeed that such an introduction to ownership, a dream that quickly turned into a nightmare, did not deter Queen Elizabeth the Queen Mother from racing altogether. Fortunately for all concerned it seemed to have quite the reverse effect, otherwise she might well have concentrated her efforts on building up and expanding her prize-winning Aberdeen Angus cows on her farm adjoining the Castle of Mey in Caithness – the most northerly based herd of pedigree cattle and the most northerly castle situated on mainland Britain.

Following the death of King George VI in 1952, the Queen Mother's own racing colours, 'blue, buff stripes, blue sleeves, black cap, with gold tassel' (actually the Strathmore family's old colours) became an integral part of National Hunt racing and during the second half of the twentieth century she was to replace the redoubtable Dorothy Paget, who died in 1960, as jump racing's greatest single long-term patron. She may not have had the financial clout of the indomitable Miss Paget, but what she lacked in funds she more than compensated for with enthusiasm.

Peter Cazalet presided over a very grand racing stable at Fairlawne where he had an indispensable head lad in Jim Fairgrieve, a Scotsman (see Appendix). The Cazalets were Huguenots from the Basque region of France and came to England in the 1870s, when Peter's grandfather, Edward, built the stables at Fairlawne. Peter's father, William, had horses in training at Manton. Peter, an exceptionally talented all-round sportsman, both at school and up at Oxford, was a man of independent means and he decided to start a training establishment at Fairlawne in the 1930s for himself and like-minded friends.

In 1950 the racing world was stunned when Anthony Mildmay was drowned whilst taking his customary early-morning swim off Mothecombe, his family home on the south Devon coast near Ivybridge. Lord Abergavenny succeeded him as Queen Elizabeth's racing manager. As John Nevill, who lived at Eridge Park, close to Fairlawne, he was one of the stables' pre-war amateurs, who became a leading figure on the administrative side of racing (he was appointed Her Majesty's Representative at Ascot). He was also a director of Massey Ferguson, world-famous manufacturers of farm machinery. An Eton contemporary was Sir Martin Gilliat – he became the Queen Mother's private secretary and a permanent member of her racing entourage.

Anthony Mildmay bequeathed all his horses to Peter Cazalet, who duly passed Manicou on to Queen Elizabeth. Manicou was one of a number of successful French-bred horses associated with Fairlawne and acquired through the Maisons-Laffitte trainer, Wladyslaw Bobinski. His brother, Kazimierz, also a former Polish cavalry officer, was a world authority on Thoroughbred pedigrees through his magnum opus, *The Family Tables of Racehorses*, and he was the popular and much respected head of the British Bloodstock Agency's pedigree department.

A handsome entire, Manicou became the Queen Mother's initial winner in her own colours when scoring at Kempton Park in November 1950. The following month he returned to the Sunbury course to gain a major triumph in the King George VI Chase on Boxing Day. It was very disappointing that his subsequent career was marred by unsoundness. Never recapturing his early brilliance, he was retired to stand at C.W. Godden's Gables Stud Farm at Rotherfield in Sussex, where he sired a number of smart chasers.

In the spring of 1953 another French-bred was acquired and, like Monaveen and Manicou, his name began with the letter M; and like Manicou he was a Bobinski graduate. Seven-year-old M'As-Tu-Vu proved another useful staying chaser, but he fell on his only two attempts at the Grand National, in 1955 and 1956. On the latter occasion he capitulated at the nineteenth fence when still in contention, but it was his better fancied stable companion who was destined to cause one of the most sensational episodes in Grand National history – and remarkably they were two of only three horses that their owner had in training at that time.

There is no more iconic photograph in the annals of National Hunt racing than the Queen Mother's Devon Loch spreadeagled within fifty yards of the winning post – only seconds earlier he was being cheered home as the certain winner of the Grand National. Almost instantly, both horse and jockey were on their feet, apparently none the worse for their ordeal. Just why Devon Loch collapsed has remained a mystery ever since. Jockey Dick Francis's own explanation was that his mount was frightened by the noise from the cheering of an ecstatic crowd anticipating a royal victory. As a world-famous author of racing thrillers, it is certain that he would never have used such an implausible storyline in any of his best-selling novels.

Purchased in Ireland from Stephen Hill-Dillon, who specialised in young store horses, Devon Loch proved his worth round the park courses, scoring three times at Sandown. The horse suffered no long-term effects from his Aintree experience and was subsequently runner-up in the King George VI Chase. But like Manicou he later developed leg problems and was fired. In retirement he became a hack (albeit not a particularly reliable one!) for Sir Noel Murless, who trained the Queen's horses leased from the National Stud.

One of the Queen Mother's most durable stars was suitably named Double Star. Having won a bumper in his native Ireland, Double Star was acquired as a replacement for M'As-Tu-Vu – fortunately an initial scare that he might have defective vision proved unjustified. Although he was a hard puller, this Irish-bred won seventeen times for the Queen Mother, the last of three victories in the Ashdown Chase at Lingfield Park's December fixture contributing to a memorable royal chase treble in 1961 completed by The Rip and Laffy. Double Star had the enviable record of having never fallen in fifty outings.

Laffy, once the victim of a doping conspiracy, and The Rip were both good chasers, who attempted unavailingly to overcome the jinx that seemed to beset the Fairlawne Grand National runners – the former fell in 1964 and the latter finished seventh the following year. However, Laffy's twelve victories did include one 'National', the Northern Irish version at Downpatrick.

As a son of Manicou, The Rip was one of his owner's favourites. Bred by Jack Irwin – a hunting enthusiast whose family owned The Red Cat, a hostelry at North Wootton, near Sandringham – this confirmed front-runner excelled round the metropolitan tracks, scoring thirteen times altogether. The Rip was considered of sufficient class to run in the 1962 Cheltenham Gold Cup and he started second favourite on his only attempt at the Grand National in 1965. The Queen Mother had procured The Rip as a yearling for 400 guineas, having admired him greatly as a foal.

By the one-time HIS (Hunter Improvement Society) stallion, Game Rights, Game Spirit became Queen Elizabeth's property after winning at the local Alton show in Hampshire, where the three-year-old was judged to be the champion young hunter.

Game Spirit proved to be his owner's all-time favourite and most prolific winner, scoring twenty-one times. He also finished second in the 1976 Champion Chase and third in the 1974 Cheltenham Gold Cup. Unfortunately he fell between two stools as his ideal distance was two and a half miles and there was no Ryanair Chase in those days!

Sadly Game Spirit collapsed and died from a lung haemorrhage competing at Newbury, where he was regarded as something of a course specialist having scored there six times over fences. A charming individual, he had had a predetermined retirement as a hack for the Queen. This grand horse is commemorated by the Game Spirit Chase, invariably an important Cheltenham Festival pointer staged at Newbury's February fixture.

With the passing of the years, the Queen Mother became increasingly involved in breeding her own runners and she maintained a handful of broodmares at Sandringham and Wolferton, under the watchful eye of her daughter's long-time stud manager, Sir Michael Oswald (who can also claim Scottish ancestry). Much the most successful of her broodmares was Queen of The Isle, three of whose sons, Colonius, Inch Arran and Isle of Man, won no fewer than forty-two races between them – or fourteen races apiece to be more precise.

Colonius and Inch Arran were by Sir Winston Churchill's grand campaigner, Colonist II, while Isle of Man was by Manicou. A grey like his sire, who stood for an interim period at Sandringham, the Topham Trophy winner, Inch Arran, had the unusual distinction of establishing record times over both the National and the Mildmay fences at Aintree, as well as at Newbury. Rather appropriately, both Inch Arran and Isle of Man won the Dunkirk Chase at Ascot, named after Peter Cazalet's star two-mile chaser.

On 29 May 1973, Peter Cazalet succumbed to cancer at the age of sixty-six. Fairlawne was closed down as a training establishment (it was later sold to Prince Khalid Abdullah of Saudi Arabia, one of the country's top Flat breeders, as Juddmonte Farms), and the Queen Mother's horses were transferred to Fulke Walwyn at Saxon House, Upper Lambourn. A Welshman, Fulke Walwyn had been leading amateur rider three times, winning the 1936 Grand National on Reynoldstown, and was recognised as the country's top trainer of chasers. Like Peter Cazalet, he had trained three mega chasing stars whose names began with M – Mont Tremblant, Mandarin and Mill House.

During the 1960s the Queen Mother would have had as many as

twenty horses in training at any one time, with additional young horses waiting in the wings. However, over the following decade the numbers were gradually reduced by more than half and inevitably her annual tally of winners was correspondingly fewer for Fulke Walwyn than had been the case with Peter Cazalet. Doubtless the ever-increasing costs of keeping a horse in training had not escaped the notice of the royal bankers, Coutts!

Never particularly lucky at either Cheltenham (where her name has long been associated with the two-mile Champion Chase) or Aintree, Queen Elizabeth enjoyed contrasting fortune on the park courses around London which, of course, were much more accessible to her from Clarence House or Royal Lodge in Windsor Great Park. Her favourite racecourse was Sandown Park, where her horses won no fewer than seventy-nine races. A great supporter of the Grand Military and Royal Artillery Meetings, she always gave enormous encouragement to all the participants, presiding over the annual Grand Military cocktail party at Royal Lodge.

It was at Sandown, formerly home to the prestigious Anthony Mildmay/Peter Cazalet Memorial Chase, that her colours achieved one of their most memorable victories. Many seasoned racegoers could not recall a more exciting finish than the 1984 Whitbread Gold Cup (now Bet365 Gold Cup) when Special Cargo triumphed by two short heads after jumping the last fence in fourth place. Credit too to Fulke Walwyn, who had purchased Special Cargo as a five-year-old at Doncaster Sales for 13,200 guineas after he won a bumper in Ireland.

For Special Cargo to achieve his greatest victory at the age of eleven was astonishing enough, but to do so after breaking down, not once but twice, was a tribute to all concerned, not least Eldred Wilson, a tenant farmer on the Sandringham Estate, who had helped to get the old gelding sound again. Another local to play her part in the royal success story was Sylvia Palmer at Raynham Hall, who cared for the homebred young stock until they went to be broken by Charles Radclyffe.

Both Special Cargo and his owner are assured of posterity at Sandown as their respective statues preside over the area around the paddock – she also opened the new stand there. On 8 March 1986, Special Cargo gained one of his three victories in the Grand Military Gold Cup and this proved the second of a memorable Royal hat-trick that afternoon, topped and tailed by Insular in the Imperial Cup and The Argonaut in the Dick McCreery Cup.

The last time that Her Majesty attended the Grand Military Meeting (she won the Gold Cup there a record five times) was in March 2001 when her homebred mare, Bella Macrae, won the Barclays Handicap Hurdle. Named after the heroine of a bawdy Scots ballad, Bella Macrae is related to Barbers Shop, whom the Queen inherited upon the death of her mother and who was considered of sufficient merit to run in the 2009 Cheltenham Gold Cup.

Although the Queen Mother was primarily interested in steeple-chasers, a number of other smart hurdlers carried her colours. Antiar, winner of the Spa (now World) Hurdle was her only Cheltenham Festival winner, and three of her runners finished third in the Champion Hurdle – Worcran, Makaldar and Escalus. Makaldar, who won fifteen races altogether, was promoted to second. Chaou gained seventeen victories, including the Lancashire Hurdle. Tammuz (Schweppes Gold Trophy), Sunyboy (Fernbank Hurdle) and Insular (Imperial Cup) had all raced for the Queen on the Flat.

The most successful jockeys to wear Her Majesty's distinctive colours can be identified with the horses with whom their names are synonymous – although they were not necessarily exclusive partnerships: Tony Grantham (Monaveen), Bryan Marshall (Manicou), Dick Francis (Devon Loch), Arthur Freeman (Double Star), Bill Rees (The Rip), Richard Dennard (Inch Arran), Bill Smith (Game Spirit), David Mould (Makaldar), Kevin Mooney (Special Cargo) and Ally Branford (Colonius).

When Fulke Walwyn died in 1991, the Queen Mother continued to have a handful of horses in training at Saxon House with his widow, Cath. Mrs Walwyn retired a couple of seasons later, whereupon the horses were shared primarily between two other Lambourn trainers, Nicky Henderson and Tim Thomson Jones. By then the majority of her runners were homebreds.

On the very day that she celebrated her centenary in 2000, the Goodwood executive staged The Queen Elizabeth the Queen Mother's 100th Birthday Molecomb Stakes. As the runners went to post, the piper, Charles MacClean, played 'Scotland the Brave' and afterwards her chef at Clarence House, Michael Sealey, presented the winning trophy. How times changed during her lifetime. Back in the early days at Fairlawne, Peter Cazalet would never have gone racing without a bowler hat and any professional jockey would have enjoyed breakfast in the servants' hall!

Altogether the Queen Mother had ninety-eight individual winners of 461 races worldwide, including seven on the Flat. Monaveen, owned in partnership with the Queen, had opened the batting at Fontwell Park in October 1949, and homebred First Love, who scored at Sandown on 8 March 2002, was the last under NH Rules. The very last winner to carry her colours was actually in a point-to-point when Braes of Mar scored later that month at the Vale of the White Horse fixture at Siddington.

First Love was duly inherited by the Queen. When he scored at Folkestone in February 2003, he became the first chase winner in the royal colours since Ambush II (owned by her great-grandfather, the then Prince of Wales, later King Edward VII) won the 1900 Grand National. Meanwhile Monaveen's winning appearance at Fontwell in 1949 had even greater historical significance. He was the first runner for a Queen of Great Britain since Star won for Queen Anne in 1714!

There were plenty of other notable landmarks for the Queen Mother. Jack O'Donoghue saddled her 100th winner, Gay Record, at Folkestone in October 1964; Peter Cazalet was responsible for her 200th winner, Master Daniel, at Worcester in December 1969; her 300th winner, Sunyboy, at Ascot in 1976, was trained by Fulke Walwyn; and the honours for her 400th winner, Nearco Bay at Uttoxeter in 1994, belonged to Nicky Henderson. Her 450th winner was Fireball. Trained by François Doumen in France, he won at Le Pin au Haras in Normandy after which the band played 'God Save The Queen' on those extraordinary French hunting horns.

Queen Elizabeth the Queen Mother died aged 101 on 30 March 2002.

Always as magnanimous in defeat as in victory, she was charm personified and few could resist that engaging smile. She was loved by the racing public at large, not only as someone who adored her horses and whose primary concern was for their welfare, but also for her appreciation of all the jockeys who rode them and the dedication of all the staff looking after them. She was patron of the IJF (Injured Jockeys' Fund) and of the National Hunt Jockeys' cricket team, and it is a reflection of the genuine affection in which she was held that they chose her blue and buff colours to adorn their sweaters and caps. These colours also featured on her 'golf buggy', which she utilised for getting about a racecourse in her latter years.

Her Majesty's racing and stud manager, Michael Oswald, has always said that the Queen Mother chose National Hunt racing rather than the Flat because it was more fun and attracted such a diversity of characters. What was fun and what was funny mattered greatly to her. One of the more memorable remarks attributed to her concerned the use of a helicopter to get to the Cheltenham Festival. 'The chopper,' she said, 'has changed my life as conclusively as that of Anne Boleyn!'

17

THE MOST CHARISMATIC BOOKMAKER OF THEM ALL

Bookmaking underwent a radical change with the introduction of betting shops in the 1960s. Men in grey suits replaced the bright checks of the traditional bookmaker as 'Honest Joe' made way for the large multiples led by William Hill – who headed his own organisation, modestly described as 'the biggest bookmaker in the world' – and his arch rival, Cyril Stein of Ladbrokes. Then the dawn of a new century heralded an entirely new concept, with the advent of internet betting whereby one could equally well lay a horse to lose as back one to win, an open invitation to skulduggery if ever there was one.

On the rails, the days of Old Etonian Archie Scott and the popular Dickie Gaskell, the most courteous of men, who would invariably accommodate a valued customer at a shade over the prevailing odds, and the equally obliging Michael Simmonds and Jack Hawkins of Heathorns – layers who had an instinctive flair for the betting ring – were drowned on the incoming tide of corporate accountants for whom the bottom line was all that mattered. It seemed that the very heart of the business had been ripped apart; certainly for many much of the enjoyment of a tilt at the ring had disappeared.

But that was before the advent of John Banks. From Anderston, a not particularly salubrious district of Glasgow, this flamboyant character single-handedly brought back colour and panache into the on-course betting market. One of those larger-than-life characters with charisma to match, he was always prepared to back his own judgement – and to large sums. On the one hand he would lay a horse fearlessly, irrespective of whether his book balanced or not, and on the other he

159

was equally prepared to back his own fancy, particularly when taking up ownership himself.

At a time when many traditional bookmakers were forsaking their independence to gain employment as betting-shop managers, John Banks used his own initiative to prosper, both on course and in the high street. He had been brought up in a hard school. He was aged only eleven when his father dispatched him to the local street-corner bookie to place a bet of three pounds and ten shillings. As an inducement to return the following Saturday, the canny bookie gave the young schoolboy a commission of half a crown – a transaction that he never forgot.

On leaving Woodside Senior Secondary School in his native Glasgow, John Banks started working in a credit betting shop and by the age of twenty he had been promoted to manager. In no time at all he had a pitch in the Silver Ring at Ayr, operating under his own name. This larger-than-life character with his gravelly Scottish accent loved the cut and thrust of the racecourse, where his personality brought such a welcome breath of fresh air. Despite initial setbacks, business expanded rapidly and by the end of the 1960s he was established as the biggest and best-known independent rails bookmaker in Scotland, with over thirty betting shops in Glasgow, a business he duly sold for £1 million.

The next step up the ladder was to obtain a foothold in England, where he purchased twenty pitches at leading racecourses up and down the country. Almost immediately the Scottish bookmaker crossed swords with Cyril Stein who was in the process of transforming Ladbrokes from a relatively select credit betting organisation into a major commercial conglomerate, with a string of hotels and leisure facilities worldwide. Inevitably there was a clash of personalities between Cyril Stein and John Banks and a long-standing feud ensued. Never at a loss for words, the Scotsman famously quipped, 'While Cyril worries, John banks.'

Ladbrokes' modus operandi soon became apparent to the young Scots interloper. When a horse had been well backed with Ladbrokes, the firm would return a sufficient proportion of the money to the ring, thus shortening the starting price and reducing the firm's commitments in its betting shops nationwide. While Banks was invariably turned down when he approached Ladbrokes to lay off a bet, he nearly always accommodated them. In the long term, the ploy was successful and the Banks bank balance just went on multiplying.

Described by Channel 4 betting guru John McCririck (better known as an Old Harrovian and Newcastle supporter than for his Scottish ancestry) as 'brash, domineering, flamboyant, big-headed, tough and shrewd', Banks was a great self-publicist, handing yellow badges to his clients stating, 'John Banks is my bookie'. Inevitably he also acquired some of the more obvious trappings of success – the yellow Rolls Royce and the twin-engined Piper Aztec aeroplane – and it was a natural progression that he would own a few racehorses as well.

To many observers it seems an anomaly that jockeys are barred from owning racehorses and betting on them (in Victorian times they did both with abandon), whereas there is no such censure for members of the bookmaking fraternity, which in the dark old days had a background of intimidation and protection rackets. However, the canny Scot was not lured into purchasing an expensive yearling at the fashionable Newmarket sales. Instead he bought two horses in training in 1968. Both were acquired in rather different circumstances.

In August the two-year-old Cabouche won a three-horse seller at now defunct Teesside Park (Stockton) at 7–1 on and at the subsequent auction the Scottish bookmaker secured him for 950 guineas. Sent to be trained by Frank Carr at Malton, the colt proved no worldbeater, but his trainer knew the time of day. Over the next three seasons Cabouche won a seller every year with consummate ease and the starting price was never better than even money – mission accomplished.

Two months after procuring Cabouche, John Banks and Frank Carr went to the Doncaster sales, where they purchased Kamundu, a sixyear-old gelding who had won the Ayr Gold Cup three years earlier, for 5,000 guineas. He had lost his form at that stage, but the outlay was soon recouped with interest when the former top sprinter won a twomile hurdle race at Sedgefield at the rewarding odds of 10–1. One can rest assured that a considerable amount of guile and subterfuge was necessary to ensure such a rewarding starting price.

The following season, Kamundu took on a new lease of life as a miler. Third in both the Lincoln and the Cambridgeshire, he had his greatest moment of glory for John Banks in the Royal Hunt Cup. The strength of the market at the royal meeting afforded his owner an ideal opportunity to have a real old-fashioned plunge, but it was only on the morning of the race that he decided to back his horse thanks to the incessant rain that kept falling – Kamundu relished soft ground.

After much deliberation and the necessary financial inducement, Lester Piggott had agreed to ride Kamundu instead of Lorenzaccio owned by his great friend, Charles St George. These two protagonists finished first and second in a field of twenty-four, Kamundu with-holding Lorenzaccio's persistent late challenge by half a length. Banks had backed his horse from 14–1 down to 10–1 to win £50,000 (worth nearer a million pounds today), which ensured that the gelding went off as the 7–1 second favourite.

Sadly Kamundu died not long after he had won at Newmarket, carrying 10st on the final day of the season, but as far as John Banks was concerned his previous outing when third to Prince de Galles in the Cambridgeshire was to have serious repercussions. The following spring Prince de Galles was installed favourite for the Lincoln, but Banks, convinced that he was too high in the handicap, decided to oppose him.

In the event, New Chapter – ridden by the young Scot, Sandy Barclay, who had partnered Lorenzaccio at Royal Ascot – prevailed by half a length over Prince de Galles, who in this instance was ridden by Kamundu's Royal Ascot partner, Lester Piggott. No sooner had they passed the post than a stewards' enquiry was called with regard to possible interference between the two principals. The placings remained unaltered – otherwise, as John Banks was to admit later, he would literally have had to sell his house, such were his liabilities. As was the case with Kamundu, his winnings equated to about £1m nowadays.

His home was Whinshill House in fashionable Sunningdale, where he lived with his wife, Anne-Marie, a far cry from his Glasgow roots.

In his own inimitable way he used to describe betting shops as 'money factories'. Instead of having any adverse effect on business – as was the case when Gerald Ratner famously denigrated the merchandise in his own high-street jewellery shops – his operation continued to go from strength to strength.

Of course there are two sides of the coin. Always willing to offer better odds and lay greater amounts than his colleagues, Banks's innovative style made him vulnerable and his readiness to back his own judgement rather than balance his book was always liable to get him in trouble. It is reputed that he lost £80,000 in one hand when Persian War gained the third of his Champion Hurdle victories in 1970, but that did not deter him from sending a bottle of champagne that evening to owner Henry Alper.

In 1967, the year before acquiring Cabouche and Kamandu, John Banks paid a record 12,700 guineas at Doncaster in October for Hill House, who also joined Frank Carr at Malton. That season the seven-year-old had won the Schweppes Gold Trophy at Newbury (now the Tote Gold Trophy) in the most controversial circumstances for Findon trainer, Ryan Price. Dope-tested afterwards, he was found to have high levels of cortisone in his bloodstream, but further investigation by the Equine Research Station at Newmarket indicated that this, for him, was a natural phenomenon. His new owner probably got his money's worth in terms of publicity, but the horse never won again. He spent his retirement with Ryan Price, having failed to show any inclination as a showjumper for Harvey Smith, and died in 1980 aged twenty.

As was the case with Hill House, John Banks could not resist acquiring Gay Future. He had gained even greater notoriety in 1974 for Ayrshire permit holder Tony Collins (see Chapter 26) when the subject of a big betting coup at lowly Cartmel. For a reputed £9,000, Gay Future then joined the Epsom trainer, John Sutcliffe Snr, only to end up with Frank Carr – but just like Hill House, he died without winning again. On 20 January 1976, Gay Future took a heavy fall over hurdles at Wetherby – according to ground staff at the flight in question, it looked as though he had suffered a fatal heart attack in mid-air.

Never without an opinion – usually a valid one expressed in a no-nonsense manner – John Banks, who became chairman of the Rails Bookmakers Association, was adamant that it was in everyone's interest that all bookmakers (including those on the rails) should display prices on boards. Of course in his day tic-tacs still relayed prices in the ring and the occasional cloth-capped bookie did a runner when the cash ran out. It was all par for the course, an entirely different ball game from the sanitised world of internet betting that is the norm today.

But pride comes before a fall and in May 1978 John Banks was warned off for three years by the Jockey Club for consorting with champion National Hunt jockey, John Francome. Following the defeat in the Imperial Cup at Sandown Park of the favourite Stopped (the name defies belief!), trained by Fred Winter and ridden by his stable jockey, the bookmaker was found guilty of 'conduct likely to cause serious damage to the interests of horse racing'.

The High Court upheld the summary justice that had been administered in the confines of Portman Square, just to emphasise that when it came to affairs of the Turf, the Jockey Club wielded the rule of law. Banks was fined £2,500 and Francome £750. While the Glasgow bookmaker returned to the rails in 1981 adopting a somewhat lower profile, the multiple champion jockey was destined to earn even more plaudits as a Channel 4 television commentator and author of racing novels in the Dick Francis genre.

The man who replaced John Banks as the most fearless layer on the rails was another Glasgow bookmaker, Freddie Williams. Plagued by poor health for much of his life, 'Fearless Freddie' died at his Ayrshire home in June 2008, aged sixty-five. A workaholic, he suffered a fatal heart attack after returning from one of his old haunts, Glasgow's Shawfield greyhound stadium – earlier in the day he had been standing on the rails at Ayr.

It was John Banks who had introduced Freddie Williams to John P. McManus, the last of the big on-course gamblers, at Cheltenham in the late 1990s. At the time Williams' reputation as the most courageous man on the rails had snowballed after he accepted a £40,000 bet, handed over in cash in a Tesco carrier bag at Shawfield. The wager was a 10–1 double on Juventus to win the European Cup and Brazil to win the World Cup.

In sharp contrast to John Banks, Freddie Williams was a quiet, unassuming man, but a very popular and much-respected figure with bookmakers and backers alike. But just like John Banks, Freddie made his own prices and stuck to them – and when he laid another six-figure wager at the Cheltenham Festival from pitch number two on the rails, it would send John McCririck into a veritable frenzy of excitement. It is an extraordinary reflection on life that it is the Freddie Williamses of this world and not the John McCriricks who are prepared to put their money where their mouth is.

A stalwart character, always attired during the winter months in his familiar long black coat, Freddie was a miner's son and his mother was the daughter of a miner. He too would have gone down the pit but for failing the medical. A diseased pelvic bone caused him to miss much of his schooling, and in later life he had to overcome a number of serious operations including a quadruple heart bypass – but fortitude always seemed to pull him through.

A true leviathan of the betting ring, he was certainly a remarkable survivor. Over a thirty-five year period he graduated from sweeping the factory floor to manager of Currie's lemonade factory in his native Cumnock, where he started his own bottling plant, Caledonian Bottles, opened by Denis Law, a childhood friend. At the height of the alcopop boom he was employing a staff of eighty with sales of ten million cases annually.

At one time Fearless Freddie owned seven bookmakers' shops, but this was reduced to three in the Cumnock area. Besides the Scottish courses, he also had pitches at Cheltenham, York and Newbury, and he had horses in training with Jonjo O'Neill, Nicky Richards and Emma Lavelle. He also bought an upmarket restaurant in Glasgow for his daughter, Julie. But at the end of the day he and Julie were in their true element on the racecourse, rising to the constant challenge of the betting ring.

In 2006 Freddie Williams was the victim of a cowardly attack during the Cheltenham Festival which left him physically uninjured but severely shocked. As he drove back to his hotel in Bibury, his car was hijacked by a hooded gang armed with crowbars, who proceeded to steal a substantial amount of cash. Earlier in the afternoon he had laid J.P. McManus £600,000 to £100,000 about one of his runners, the grey Reveillez, who duly obliged. Win or lose, that's what John Banks would call a bet! The following year Freddie and Julie took the precaution of flying to and from the racecourse by helicopter.

For the first time since her father's death the previous June, Julie Williams was back in business at the 2009 Cheltenham Festival. It was a poignant occasion as this coincided with the inaugural running of the Freddie Williams Festival Plate, a chase over an extended two and a half miles, which with £90,000 in prize money was the most valuable handicap of the entire meeting.

Coincidentally John and Anne-Marie Banks, together with their daughter Joanna, were also the victims of an armed attack. In 1998 they returned home to Sunningdale after dining out in Knightsbridge, unaware that they had been followed from London by an armed assailant. A twenty-one-year-old drug addict wielding a gun, he relieved Mrs Banks of all the diamond jewellery she was wearing as well as a Rolex watch. Thanks to the wonders of DNA forensics, the culprit was eventually identified from a baseball cap left at the scene of the crime and in 2009 he was convicted at Southwark Crown Court and jailed for fifteen years.

Severely traumatised by the experience, John Banks died from cancer aged sixty-eight in August 2003, by which time both the Banks's credit bookmaking business and the racecourse pitches were controlled by his son, Geoffrey. He continues to be active on the rails at the bigger meetings in the south, but could never hope to emulate his father – the Betfair phenomenon has changed betting on the horses forever. Nowadays the really big punters at Royal Ascot and Cheltenham don't even bother to put in an appearance.

18

A 'STIRLING' CHARACTER IN AND OUT OF THE SADDLE

It was at the Battle of Stirling Bridge on the banks of the River Forth below the ancient castle that Sir William Wallace defeated the superior forces of King Edward I on 11 September 1297. Later captured through an act of treachery and executed in London, he became a national hero and to this day the Wallace Monument bears witness to one of Scotland's greatest patriots. Mary Queen of Scots was just nine months old when she was crowned at Stirling Castle in September 1543 – how incongruous that nowadays the backdrop to these historic battlements is the newfangled Braes O'Doune wind farm.

Born on 16 November 1942, in the county town of Stirling, north-east of Glasgow, William Fisher Hunter Carson, OBE, has enjoyed contrasting good fortune since travelling south over the border. A former racing commentator on the Flat for BBC television alongside Clare Balding, he brought a wealth of first-hand experience to the task. Yet many seasoned racegoers fail to appreciate just how brilliant the riding record of this one-time team captain of the BBC's *A Question of Sport* really was.

Willie Carson is not only the first Scotsman to be acclaimed champion jockey in the United Kingdom, but he also remains the only one to achieve that honour. Just for good measure, he was champion on five occasions from 1972 to 1983, a golden era dominated by two outstanding champions in Lester Piggott and Pat Eddery. What makes the Scot's achievement even more commendable is that while Piggott and Eddery have a background steeped in the Turf, Willie Carson had absolutely no family connections with racing and has achieved his exalted status through sheer application and determination.

During his riding days the five English classic races represented as good a yardstick of merit as any, and this intrepid Scot partnered seventeen winners at this exalted level. They comprise the Derby four times (Troy, Henbit, Nashwan and Erhaab), the Oaks four times (Dunfermline, Bireme, Sun Princess and Salsabil), the St Leger three times (Dunfermline, Sun Princess and Minster Son), the Two Thousand Guineas four times (High Top, Known Fact, Don't Forget Me and Nashwan), and the One Thousand Guineas twice (Salsabil and Sha-dayid). He also partnered the winners of eleven Irish classics.

Ascot proved a particularly happy hunting ground, with four winners of the King George VI and Queen Elizabeth Stakes, the most important all-aged race in the British Isles, a tally surpassed by an amazing eight victories in the Queen Elizabeth II Stakes, including dual scorer, Rose Bowl, and three winners of the Ascot Gold Cup. There have also been four winners of the Irish Oaks, three winners of both the Eclipse Stakes and Benson & Hedges Gold Cup (now Juddmonte International), two winners of the Irish Derby and one winner of the French Derby.

That is a formidable tally by anyone's standards, but two particular victories are etched in Willie's memory – on Erhaab in a rough race for the 1994 Derby (the last time the Blue Riband was run on the traditional first Wednesday in June), and on Bahri in the 1995 Queen Elizabeth II Stakes. On this occasion Willie demonstrated remarkable initiative. Following significant rain, the back straight on the round course at Ascot under the trees used to provide appreciably faster ground, and by adopting this circuitous route, Bahri enjoyed a crucial advantage.

Their partner can recall the precise moment when he decided to become a jockey. One evening back in 1954, as an impressionable schoolboy aged eleven, he went to see the racing film *Rainbow Jacket* at his local cinema in Stirling. The story of a young jockey's rise to the top of the tree, despite all the many vicissitudes along the way, so fired his imagination that he determined that this was the career for him. He never deviated from his resolve to become a jockey despite the many obstacles and early disappointments that ensued.

What young Billy (it is the racing fraternity who have always referred to him as Willie) would not have realised at the time was that a number of the stars in *Rainbow Jacket* were themselves racing fans in real life. Both Robert Morley and Wilfred Hyde White were enthusiastic if not particularly successful owners (subsequently Willie rode for both of them), while Teddy Underdown, a popular matinee idol of the time, was a proficient amateur on the Flat.

Back home he told his father, Tommy, a warehouse foreman for Fyffes Bananas in Stirling, and his mother, May, about his ambitions. His parents were surprised. As he was good with his hands they had often thought he might become a joiner; but he did have one obvious advantage – he was small. The trouble was that the only experience their son had of riding was on a bicycle. Every morning for two years this diminutive figure did a paper round which entailed cycling for the best part of three miles, most of them laden down with a heavy bag of newspapers. It seemed incredible that so small a figure could cope with such an awesome burden.

The routine involved leaving home on the Cornton Estate at about 7am, picking up the papers at Jim Hogg's newsagent's shop in Cowane Street, crossing the old Customs Bridge which spans the River Forth at the eastern end of Stirling Castle and delivering the papers in the sprawling suburb of Causeway Head. Most of Jim Hogg's paper boys only lasted a few weeks, but Willie proved determined and reliable, two qualities that were to stand him in good stead as a jockey.

If Willie was really keen to become a jockey, there was no alternative but to have riding lessons. May Carson worked at the Fourways restaurant at Dunblane, seven miles from Stirling. Upon the recommendation of the manageress, she contacted one of the regular customers, Thea McFarlane, who ran a local riding school. Mrs McFarlane explained that the prospects of ever becoming a jockey were remote in the extreme, but the Carsons would not be dissuaded. So Willie embarked upon a series of riding lessons at ten shillings and sixpence an hour compared to the twelve shillings and sixpence a week that he earned for the paper round. Doubtless all that cycling helped strengthen his legs, a good preparation for the future.

His early education in the saddle owed much to Jilly, a chestnut pony standing all of eleven hands high. As a complete novice on horseback, Willie had the inevitable falls, but he remained completely undaunted. Thea McFarlane's lasting impression of her young protégé was his innate determination and fearlessness. He also earned brownie points for being neat and tidy (he used to change in and out of his jodhpurs at the Fourways restaurant to avoid bullying by other boys), as well as being quiet and reserved – rather a different persona from the ebullient personality that emerged later!

When Willie left Riverside School in Stirling, it was upon Thea McFarlane's recommendation that his parents wrote off to three trainers in the hope that one of them might take on their fifteen-year-old son as an apprentice. Gerald Armstrong from Middleham in North Yorkshire answered in the affirmative by return of post and Willie duly arrived at his stables, Thorngill, on a bleak winter's day in 1957.

By the time that Gerald Armstrong retired at the end of the 1962 season, Willie had just a solitary winner to his credit. On 19 July that year, Pinker's Pond (named after a local landmark), equipped with blinkers for the first time, made all the running at Catterick to score by six lengths for his retained stable in a seven-furlong apprentice handicap. The race became the Willie Carson–Pinker's Pond Apprentice Handicap.

Just 5ft tall and able to go to scale at 7st 6lb, Willie then had his indentures transferred to Gerald's younger brother, Sam Armstrong, at Newmarket. At the time he and his wife Carole (the mother of his three sons) lived in a caravan next to the trainer's St Gatien stables – now occupied by Peter Chapple-Hyam. Sam Armstrong was prepared to give his apprentices the necessary opportunities to ride in public and Willie was soon established as one of the top young riders in the country. By the time he finished his apprenticeship in 1965 he had over 100 winners to his credit and the guv'nor had such a high opinion of him that he immediately signed him up as the stable's lightweight jockey.

This proved a watershed in his career. His reputation had escalated and so too had his finances – he was now living in Churchill Avenue. During the course of the 1966 season Sam Armstrong relayed a startling proposition to his young jockey from fellow Newmarket trainer Bernard van Cutsem. Would he consider the position as Lord Derby's retained jockey upon the pending retirement of Doug Smith? It was one of the most prestigious jobs in the business, and Willie Carson immediately accepted.

The plan was for Willie to join van Cutsem for the 1967 season to learn the ropes, in preparation for taking over from Doug Smith at the start of the following season. However, in the interim, Willie had bought a new Jaguar. Driving up the A1 to Durham on a foggy autumn day to see his wife's parents, they collided with a lorry. The car was a complete write-off and all the occupants, including his pregnant wife, Carole, and their two sons, Antony and Neil, sustained injuries. Willie, who had absolutely no recollection of the accident, broke a femur, his jaw, an ankle and a finger, and he spent a long period in the intensive care unit of Leeds Infirmary.

It is a great tribute to Willie's resilience that he was out of hospital within four months despite being unable to walk without the aid of callipers. Unbelievably, he was back riding in public only five weeks later. In fact he only missed the first three weeks of the new season and concluded his first year as Lord Derby's number one jockey with sixty-one winners. Six months after the accident Carole gave birth to their third son, Ross, and everything was back on track.

This time an unexpected stroke of good fortune was just around the corner. As the proprietor of the West Ilsley training establishment on the Berkshire Downs north of Newbury (now owned by Mick Channon), Lord Weinstock decided to replace the long-standing stable jockey, Joe Mercer, with 'someone younger' – much against the wishes of the resident trainer, Dick Hern. Willie Carson was chosen as his successor (fellow Scot Sandy Barclay had been second choice). By that stage he had already ridden one classic winner, High Top, in the 1972 Two Thousand Guineas for Bernard van Cutsem. This new appointment was to elevate him to the very top rungs of the ladder for the remainder of his career.

The new partnership got off to a fairytale start when the Queen's Dunfermline won the Oaks and St Leger in 1977, her jubilee year. This double was to be repeated six years later by Sun Princess, owned by Lord Weinstock's father-in-law, Sir Michael Sobell. In between, Willie had also partnered Troy, the first of his four Derby winners, for the Sobell/Weinstock interests. Significantly these classic winners were all homebred, Dunfermline by the Royal Studs at Sandringham, and Troy, hero of the 200th Derby, and Sun Princess at the Ballymacoll Stud Farm in Ireland.

Subsequently, Willie was to be associated with two other dual English classic winners in Nashwan and Salsabil, who were trained by Dick Hern and John Dunlop respectively. Both Nashwan, the only winner of the Two Thousand Guineas, Derby, Eclipse Stakes and King George VI and Queen Elizabeth Stakes in the same season, and Salsabil, winner of the One Thousand Guineas and Oaks, were owned by Sheikh Hamdan Al Maktoum. One of the brothers from Dubai, who have made a billion-dollar investment in bloodstock around the world, he owns the vast Shadwell Stud complex outside Thetford in Norfolk.

Sadly the three trainers with whom Willie Carson was most closely associated all experienced personal tragedy in their lives. A chain-smoker but always with a cigarette-holder, Bernard van Cutsem died prematurely from cancer; Dick Hern was confined to a wheelchair after being paralysed in a hunting accident which precipitated his death; and John Dunlop's eldest son, Tim, was killed in a motoring accident in France.

As so many patrons of West Ilsley and Arundel for whom he rode were owner-breeders, Willie Carson became increasingly interested in the breeding side of racing. It was Bernard van Cutsem, owner or joint owner of Northmore Stud Farm and Side Hill Stud in Newmarket, who first suggested that he should get involved. His very first mare was Hay-Hay. By then he had moved from Churchill Avenue to Falmouth Cottage (a house which went with Lord Derby's retainer) and for a while Hay-Hay lived in a shed at the bottom of the garden before finding more suitable quarters at Red House Stud at Exning, where she produced a number of small winners.

In the autumn of 1980 the champion jockey bought his present home at Barnsley, near Cirencester, in Gloucestershire, from Joane Wood.

Previously known as Ampney Stud, which had been home to a handful of modest stallions, the property had fallen into disrepair and the new owner promptly set about transforming it into a private stud with all modern amenities. Based on idyllic limestone land with its own water supply from a borehole, it now extends to more than twice the original sixty acres. He also gave it a new identity as Minster Stud – it had previously been a church property known as Glebe Farm.

One of the first mares to take up residence at Minster Stud was the minor juvenile winner, Honey Bridge, who had been procured for 10,000 guineas as a filly out of training. In 1988 her colt, Minster Son (named after the stud), triumphed in the St Leger. This was an historic occasion as Willie Carson became the only jockey to win an English classic on a horse he had bred himself – and, of course, the St Leger is the oldest of the five classic races. What a feeling of satisfaction Willie must have experienced as he drove his mount to such a glorious victory.

At Doncaster, Minster Son defeated the English and Irish Oaks winner, Diminuendo – and there was no fluke about it. Lady Beaverbrook's colt had earlier won Goodwood's Predominate Stakes and Gordon Stakes to add to his success in the Newmarket Stakes, all recognised classic trials.

Willie Carson values insider knowledge when it comes to bloodstock breeding, particularly with regard to temperament. He certainly knew more than most about Minster Son whom he sold as a yearling for 36,000 guineas. He had ridden his sire, Niniski, to win the French and Irish St Legers for the Dick Hern–Lady Beaverbrook combination. Furthermore the stallion stood at Kirsten Rausing's Lanwades Stud at Newmarket, and it was Willie Carson who rode Niniski's son Petoski, bred by Kirsten Rausing, owned by Marcia Beaverbrook and trained by Dick Hern, to win the 1985 King George VI and Queen Elizabeth Stakes.

When Willie Carson won the Derby on Nashwan, the runner-up at a monumental 500–1 was Marcia Beaverbrook's grey Terimon, who became a useful sire of jumpers. Mated with the Niniski mare, Misowni, Terimon sired a useful chaser for Minster Stud in Scots Grey. He gave his breeder enormous pleasure when winning the 2007 Aintree Fox

Hunters', as did his half-brother, Scots Dragoon, also a grey, in winning the 2010 Grand Military Gold Cup.

Another Minster Stud mare to keep the bandwagon rolling is Bathilde. She is the dam of the dual Group winner, Tungsten Strike (Henry II Stakes, Sagaro Stakes), who was actually foaled in America, and Al Shemali. The latter hit the jackpot when winning the Group 1 Dubai Duty Free at the inaugural Dubai World Cup Meeting at Meydan in March 2010.

The only untoward aspect concerning Minster Son was that he was trained not by Dick Hern, but by his assistant, Neil Graham. He had taken charge temporarily following his employer's serious hunting accident in Leicestershire and subsequent heart problems. These were dark days for all concerned at West Ilsley and there was great public consternation when Dick Hern was forced to vacate West Ilsley (then owned by the Queen) and move to Kingwood Stables overlooking Lambourn – a new purpose-built yard belonging to Hamdan Al Maktoum – for the 1991 season.

Nowadays a St Leger winner does not have sufficient cachet to stand in Newmarket and Minster Son was soon winging his way north from Longholes Stud to Acrum Lodge Stud, Co. Durham. By the time he died there in 2006, aged twenty-one and suffering from equine asthma, he was gradually gaining momentum as a sire of staying chasers.

An exact contemporary of Minster Son, Unfuwain was one of the first good horses that Willie Carson rode for Sheikh Hamdan. Both colts made their two-year-old debut in the same race at Newbury and there was a remarkable result. In a field of twenty-seven runners, Willie finished runner-up on the favourite, Unfuwain, to his unconsidered stable companion.

A half-brother to Nashwan, Unfuwain was an obvious choice for his rider to use as a stallion and in partnership with Dick Hern, Willie Carson bred a very smart filly by him in Shadow Dancing. A real handful in training, she proved quite a feather in the cap of Dick Hern's young successor at Kingwood, Marcus Tregoning, finishing third in the 2002 Oaks.

Owning and breeding racehorses is certainly unpredictable. Chriselliam, whom Willie owned in partnership, had to be put down in February 2014 when an infection in her off-hind foot failed to respond to treatment and spread to the pedal bone. Rated the best two-year-old filly of her year after winning the Group 1 Fillies' Mile at Newmarket, she greatly enhanced her reputation by also winning the Grade 1 Breeders' Cup Juvenile Fillies Turf at Santa Anita.

Chriselliam's victory in California came at the beginning of November. Only the previous month Willie Carson had sold a yearling by Halling at Tattersalls' October Yearling Sale (Book 2) for 60,000 guineas and Jack Hobbs as he was named developed into a racehorse of the highest class with a comparable rating as a three-year-old to Minster Son.

Later sold on to Godolphin, Jack Hobbs won the Irish Derby after finishing runner-up in the Blue Riband to his stable companion Golden Horn. But, just like Chriselliam, Jack Hobbs met with a serious setback. On his four-year-old debut he suffered a pelvic injury; on his only other appearance that season he finished third for a second time in the Champion Stakes.

Jack Hobbs brought his earnings to over £4m by winning the Group 1 Dubai Sheema Classic at Meydan in Dubai on his 2017 debut. Meanwhile his dam Swain's Gold produced a Sepoy half-sister to Jack Hobbs who sold for 200,0000 guineas as a yearling in 2016. Next time she had a filly foal by Dubawi, prior to being mated with Jack Hobbs's Epsom conqueror, Golden Horn. To compensate for Jack Hobbs's disappointing run at Royal Ascot in 2017, Minster Stud-bred Snoano scored on the final day.

Willie Carson continued under contract to ride for Sheikh Hamdan for whom he won the One Thousand Guineas, Oaks and Irish Derby with Salsabil, the One Thousand Guineas with Shadayid, and the Derby with Erhaab, all trained by John Dunlop in the beautiful park at Arundel. Not that he ever rode work there. That is something that this most urbane of trainers never encouraged – in his view jockeys belong on the racecourse!

It was John Dunlop who trained the filly Habibti, one of two exceptional sprinters ridden by Willie Carson, the other being the colt

Dayjur, trained by Dick Hern. As three-year-olds, both won the Prix de l'Abbaye de Longchamp, Haydock Sprint Cup and Nunthorpe Stakes. *Timeform* rated Habibti 'Horse of the Year' and 'Best Sprinter' in 1983, giving the same two accolades to Dayjur in 1990. But for jumping a shadow within yards of the winning post, Dayjur would have won that season's Breeders' Cup Sprint at Belmont Park; instead he was beaten a neck.

One of few omissions from Willie's impressive CV is victory in the Prix de l'Arc de Triomphe. He was placed on four occasions, finishing second on Sun Princess, third on Troy and Ela-Mana-Mou (all for the Sobell/Weinstock family) – Troy started an odds-on favourite, but the prevailing soft ground was against him. He also finished third on Awaasif.

Two of his most memorable rides in Epsom classics also ended in defeat. In 1974 he was desperately unlucky not to win the Oaks on Dibidale – two furlongs from home, her saddle slipped, dislodging the weight cloth and yet Willie still managed to ride her bareback into third place, followed by the inevitable disqualification. Three years later, he was just denied victory on Hot Grove in the Derby when, sandwiched against the rails, Lester Piggott did him no favours on The Minstrel.

Both Bernard van Cutsem and Dick Hern encouraged their stable jockey to take up hunting as a relaxation and it was the latter who introduced Willie to the Quorn. He took to riding across country like a duck to water. His very first hunter, Sollys Clump, was a five-year-old loaned by Mimi van Cutsem. A colossus of a horse standing 17 hands, he was once ante-post favourite for the Grand National. There was nothing that Willie and his second wife, Elaine, enjoyed more than to spend a good part of the winter out with the Cheshire hounds – her father, John Williams, farmed near Tarporley. This was one of their favourite haunts and at one time they had a couple of terriers called Chester and Roodeye.

Willie Carson continued to race ride until he was fifty-three, but the decision to retire was not of his own making. At Newbury on 20 September 1996, he was just about to mount Meshhed, one of Hamdan Al Maktoum's homebred two-year-olds fillies, when she kicked him in the stomach, hurling him under the paddock rail. Rushed to Basingstoke Hospital, he was in intensive care for eight days. He had hoped to return to the saddle the following spring, but the injuries sustained in that freak accident terminated his riding career – very probably the body-protector he had been wearing saved his life. Back in August 1981, he could thank his crash helmet for salvation when he sustained a fractured skull in a horrific fall from Silken Knot in the Yorkshire Oaks, the filly breaking both her forelegs.

W.F.H. Carson had the deserved reputation of not making many mistakes when the chips were down. A brilliant judge of pace, who was as effective as any of his contemporaries when push came to shove, he had an inimitable style, goading his mount on with hands and heels. At times he could do a convincing impression of a whirling dervish as he got one home in the dying strides, but horses ran well for him and importantly they tended to recover quickly from their exertions. He was also an incisive rider, always prepared to take a calculated risk where there was an advantage to be gained.

During a long and distinguished career from 1962 to 1996, Willie Carson rode 3,828 winners in Great Britain to occupy fourth place on the all-time honours list – behind Sir Gordon Richards, whose total stands at 4,870 winners, Pat Eddery (4,632), and Lester Piggott (4,493). The only other rider to breach the 3,000 tally was Doug Smith (3,111). Like Doug Smith, on whom he modelled his style to some extent, he benefited considerably from being a natural lightweight, which not only avoided the debilitating practice of wasting, but also ensured a steady supply of rides in handicaps from outside stables, which helped greatly to augment his tally of winners.

His best seasonal total was 187 as late as 1990 – on 30 June that year he rode six winners at Newcastle, including the Northumberland Plate, for five different trainers. Those six winners formed part of a truly remarkable sequence when he notched up twelve victories from four-teen mounts. He also rode four winners one day at the 1986 Ayr Western Meeting. Like many of his colleagues he used to ride in India during the winter and on another memorable occasion in Madras he partnered eight winners on the nine-race card.

Somewhat incongruously, Willie Carson became chairman of

Swindon Town Football Club from 2001 until 2007. But another more likely appointment in retirement was as UK representative to the Thoroughbred Corporation. Amongst the outstanding horses in Europe to represent this American-based organisation owned by Prince Ahmed Salman of Saudi Arabia were the 1999 Derby winner, Oath, and the previous year's St James's Palace Stakes hero, Dr Fong.

Willie Carson would almost certainly have been known as Jock Carson, had it not been for a contemporary of that name when he first went to Newmarket. For a while he had the soubriquet 'Never Say Die' Carson – which was an extremely accurate description of his style as he never gave up in a race – but in the end his own name came to personify his own special brand of skill and perseverance in the saddle. It was a worthy tribute to the most successful professional Flat jockey that Scotland has ever produced.

Willie's eldest son Antony trains a small string in Newmarket and he lives in the same house in Churchill Avenue as did his father ('the first house I ever bought,' he says). It is very much a family affair as Willie is one of his owners and Tony's son William is the stable jockey. A proficient lightweight with forty-six winners for the calendar year 2016, he gained the first important success of his career in Scotland when winning the 2008 Ayr Gold Cup on Regal Parade for a group of enthusiastic colleagues working in the fishing industry in Aberdeen. Ironically this valuable sprint handicap was one of the few top events to elude his grandfather.

FOUR SCOTTISH STALWARTS OF THE TURF

Willie Carson

Alan King

Mark Johnston

The Queen Mother

Mat Dawson The greatest trainer of the Victorian era with the winners of twenty-eight classics to his credit.

The Beckhampton triumvirate *Left to right:* Reginald Macdonald-Buchanan, Fred Darling, Arthur Dewar.

Waugh family c. 1898 *Back row:* Alec, Charlie, Richard, Isabel, Willie, Hugo. *Front row:* Tom, Janet, James, Grace, Dawson.

Left: **Hurry On** (Joe Childs) 'The best I have ever trained, the best I am ever likely to train' – high praise indeed from Fred Darling.

Below: **The 6th Earl of Rosebery** He and his father owned five winners of the Derby, all homebred.

Lord Woolavington Founder of Lavington Stud in Sussex to which his daughter, Catherine Macdonald-Buchanan, added two Newmarket studs.

Tom Laidlaw An Irish domiciled Scot who bred a 100–1 Derby winner and sold a 100–1 Grand National winner.

Sir Malcolm McAlpine Provided the McAlpine clan with a first high profile winner, Shaun Spadah, in the 1921 Grand National.

Stewart Wight
A legend amongst
National Hunt trainers.

© ROUCH WILMOT

April The Fifth (Fred Lane) The 1932 Derby winner
whose romantic background was more in keeping with
a Grand National hero.

Rockavon (Norman Stirk) The surprise 1961 Two Thousand Guineas winner
trained on the sands at Dunbar.

George Boyd
The trainer with
the three-year-
olds Rockavon
(N McIntosh, left)
and Ayrshire
Bard (N Stirk).

Left: **Bill Wightman**
A master trainer on
the Flat and over
jumps.

Right: **Alec Kilpatrick**
The leading jumps'
trainer who showed
enormous patience
with soldier riders.

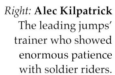

Devon Loch (Dick Francis)
A rare portrait: most
photographs depict the
luckless pair prostrate on the
run-in after looking assured
of victory in the 1956 Grand
National.

Minster Son
(Willie Carson) A unique combination – the only winner of an English classic to be ridden by his breeder.

Ken Oliver 'Uncle Ken' to some, 'The Benign Bishop' to others.

Sandy Struthers Owner of the top-class colts Mount Athos, Scottish Rifle and Pitcairn.

Merryman II
(Derek Ancil) How many racing enthusiasts realise that the 1960 Grand National winner was bred within sight of the mighty Forth Bridge?

Wyndburgh
(Tim Brookshaw) But for a broken stirrup iron, this gallant combination would surely have won the 1959 Grand National.

Rubstic (Maurice Barnes) The first of only two Grand National winners to be trained in Scotland.

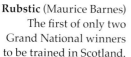

Attraction The Duke of Roxburghe, left, greets his homebred winner of the 2004 One Thousand Guineas.

Susan Crawford The celebrated equine artist in front of her Joshua Reynolds' easel.

Brigadier Gerard (Joe Mercer) The greatest British racehorse of the 20th century?

Lucy Alexander The first girl to become champion conditional jockey in the UK over jumps.

Lucinda Russell Edinburgh-born and only the fourth lady to train a winner of the Grand National.
One for Arthur The Scottish-trained and owned winner of the 2017 Grand National.

Keith Dalgleish has very quickly become a record-breaking Scottish-based trainer.

19

UNCLE KEN – THE BENIGN BISHOP

There are successful businessmen and there are successful racehorse trainers. The two seldom go together, but the late James Kenneth Murray Oliver, OBE, of Hassendean Bank, Minto, near Hawick in Roxburghshire, was both. Furthermore, in his youth he was a top-flight amateur rider as well as a competent all-round sportsman, which again is a rare combination. 'Win or lose – have some booze,' was his favourite catchphrase and he never needed an excuse to have a party or open a bottle. For his energetic lifestyle twenty-four hours in the day were totally insufficient.

Someone once said, 'Ken has two speeds – full ahead or fast asleep,' and there was nothing in between. Considering that he only had a limited amount of time to devote to racing, his contribution was enormous. Once he had given up race riding as one of the top amateurs in the north, he achieved two unimaginable goals – to become one of a handful of leading National Hunt trainers in the British Isles and to restart sales of bloodstock at Doncaster. Today the new Doncaster/Goffs consortium (Goffs UK) provides real competition to Tattersalls, the very company that renounced Doncaster in the first place.

At Merchiston Castle School in Edinburgh, his sporting prowess was more in evidence than any academic achievement. On leaving, young Ken joined the family firm of livestock auctioneers, Andrew Oliver & Son in Hawick, founded by his great-grandfather in 1817. For over 150 years this was one of the biggest auction markets in the north, and it continued in business until the 1980s. (The site is now a supermarket.) It owed its prosperity to sheep – over three days in August

1907 over 60,000 sheep went through the ring. At the centenary sale of rams at Hawick in September 1945, over 1,000 head were offered.

As a child, Ken's riding experience had been confined to a Shetland pony, but as so many of his clients were sporting farmers and followers of the Buccleuch Hunt it seemed a good opportunity to combine business with pleasure. Inevitably hunting led to point-to-pointing. Successful on his first ever ride, on a one-eyed horse called Delman at the Lauderdale meeting at Blainslie, he was immediately smitten and henceforth he pursued his hobby with characteristic fervour.

As was the case for every able-bodied person, the war disrupted life to a degree that no one could possibly have envisaged. He joined up along with his old school friend, Alan Innes, whose sister, Joan, was to become his first wife and the mother of his two children, Stuart and Susan. The Innes family farmed at Windywalls, near Kelso, after whom they named a homebred mare, the future dam of a spectacular grey hunter-chaser, The Callant. Ken was commissioned in the Yorkshire Hussars and his wartime excursions embraced North Africa for the desert campaign; then Sicily and the successful landings in the south of Italy, where he was wounded.

On returning home to Denholm House, just across the River Teviot from Hassendean Bank, Ken assumed added responsibilities in the family firm which was then expanding rapidly. However, he was determined to start race riding again. In 1948 he was having no luck in point-to-points on his eight-year-old mare, Sanvina, so he sent her to Stewart Wight in Berwickshire with a view to disposing of her in a selling chase. In the absence of her owner who had to attend to business, Sanvina duly won at Perth in September, only to be bought in for 160 guineas. Not long before, the trainer had telephoned prophetically to say that she should be retained whatever the outcome.

By the end of her career Sanvina, who had originally cost £350, had won twelve chases, providing her amateur jockey with a memorable victory in the 1950 Scottish Grand National, run in those days at Bogside, near Irvine. Sanvina scored by six lengths at Tote odds of over 60–1 carrying 12st 2lb, the highest weight to be carried to victory since the war. The same owner-rider-trainer combination completed a memorable double in the last race on the card when Johnnie Walker III won the hunter chase. A few bottles of Johnnie Walker were downed afterwards!

Johnnie Walker's objective was the following season's Foxhunters' at both Cheltenham and Aintree. Unfortunately on the last day of the hunting season the gelding injured a knee jumping a stone wall out with the Buccleuch and had to be boxed home. Bobby Fairbairn, who at the time ran a livery yard at St Boswells, helped to get him sound again, whereupon he joined Stewart Wight. Despite everything, horse and rider did extremely well to finish runner-up at Cheltenham and third at Aintree after being remounted. Sadly Johnnie Walker broke his back when falling at the water jump at Manchester.

On taking out at permit to train, Ken Oliver saddled and rode his first winner, Stockwhip, scoring over hurdles at now defunct Rothbury Park in 1953. But the real catalyst for his training career proper, which numbered around 1,000 winners, was his marriage in May 1958 to Rhona Wilkinson, who brought that great National campaigner, Wyndburgh, with her to Denholm. His story is told in Chapter 21. Without the publicity that Wyndburgh generated – not to mention the huge hands-on contribution that his second wife brought to the training regime at Hassendean Bank – her husband would never have become one of the country's top trainers. He simply would not have had the time.

Training is always a team effort and there were two essential cogs in the wheel. The first was his old friend, Padge Berry, from Co. Wexford in Ireland, from whom he bought so many young horses over the years, following the success he had enjoyed with Johnnie Walker. The other was head lad George Hogg – he worked at one time as a shepherd for Stewart Wight, for whom he also rode as an amateur. The golden years for Hassendean Bank were the 1960s and 1970s, when there were invariably fifty horses in the yard and inevitably all the leading jockeys were queuing up for rides.

Ken and Rhona always concentrated on chasers rather than hurdlers and they were for the most part staying chasers. This is indicated by no fewer than five winners of the Scottish Grand National, Scotland's premier steeplechase. In only his second full season with a licence, Ken won with Pappageno's Cottage at Bogside in 1963 ridden by Tim Brookshaw. This was followed by the Ayr victories of The Spaniard (Barry Brogan) in 1970, Young Ash Leaf (Peter Ennis) in 1971, Fighting Fit (Chris Hawkins) in 1979, and Cockle Strand (David Dutton) in 1982 – the latter beat his stable-companion, Three To One, by half a length.

Pappageno's Cottage had changed hands for 500 guineas after John Sheridan, the first outside owner for whom Ken trained a winner, sold him privately when the gelding failed to find a buyer at the Kelso horse sales. Invariably equipped with blinkers, 'Old Pappa' also won the four-mile Fred Withington Chase at Cheltenham twice. Prior to becoming a chaser, The Spaniard won nine consecutive times over timber, including the George Duller Hurdle at the Cheltenham Festival.

A courageous little mare, Young Ash Leaf recorded a record time in winning the Scottish Grand National. She also won the Greenall Whitley Chase, Haydock Park, was second and third in the Whit-bread and runner-up in a Hennessy; in addition she competed in the Colonial Cup at Camden in South Carolina. Fighting Fit, the next Scottish National winner, also triumphed in the Hennessy Cognac Gold Cup.

Arguably the most talented horse ever trained at Hassendean Bank was Arctic Sunset, whose owner, Jimmy McNair, farmed near Mus-selburgh. A brilliant novice, he won the Cotswold Chase (now Arkle Chase) at the Cheltenham Festival, where he was third in the following year's National Hunt Two-Mile Chase (now Queen Mother Champion Chase). Normally ridden out by his trainer at home, he tragically broke a fetlock at Sandown Park and had to be put down.

By contrast Even Keel enjoyed a happy retirement, hunting with Edmund Vestey, MFH, in Essex. A real tearaway in training, who refused to start on occasions, he recorded the most important of his twenty-three victories in the Benson & Hedges Gold Cup, Sandown Park, and Kirk & Kirk Chase, Ascot.

On the same day that Ken procured Even Keel from Padge Berry, he also bought the enormously talented Drumikill. He too became a proficient chaser, but first he made a great name for himself over timber, winning the Liverpool Hurdle at the Grand National Meeting and finishing runner-up to Persian War in the second of the latter's three Champion Hurdle victories.

Another very smart hurdler was Billy Bow, despite being hobdayed (a wind operation). Sadly he collapsed and died after winning the Ladbroke Hurdle at Newcastle, where a race was named after him. It is only when reviewing the careers of such a bunch of talented jumpers that one realises just how many fall by the wayside through mis-adventures of some description – accident, injury or just plain stress certainly take their toll.

Other outstanding performers include Fort Rouge (Grand Annual Chase, Cheltenham), a close relative of Arctic Sunset; Happy Arthur (George Duller Hurdle, Cheltenham), runner-up in the Scottish Grand National; High Edge Grey (Charlie Hall Memorial Pattern Chase, Wetherby); Meridian II (Fred Withington Chase, Cheltenham); Grand National runner-up, Moidore's Token; Prize Crew, winner of eight chases at Wetherby; Roaring Twenties (County Hurdle, Cheltenham); Tom Morgan (Mildmay Chase, Liverpool; Grand Annual Chase, Cheltenham); and Tregarron (Greenall Whitley Chase, Haydock Park).

A grey as the name implies, High Edge Grey was special as he provided Ken's granddaughter, Sandy Forster, a very proficient point-to-point rider, with a first ever winner under Rules. Nowadays Sandy holds a full training licence at Yetholm, near Kelso, where her partner, Clive Storey, is her assistant as well as being a successful trainer of point-to-pointers.

Few days brought more pleasure to the Olivers than 11 November 1968. It is a long journey from Hawick to Wolverhampton and back so when it was decided to run Drumikill at Dunstall Park, Rhona entered four other horses to help defray the travelling expenses, much against the better judgement of her husband, it has to be said. He had mixed feelings about the Midlands course, having once finished second there in his riding days, only to be called before the stewards for not trying!

All five horses, including Drumikill and Even Keel, made it to Wolverhampton and by the close of the afternoon all five had won, ridden by stable jockey, Barry Brogan – a flawed genius in the saddle, in the same mould as that great footballer, George Best. One of the benefactors of this 'famous five' was Simon Fraser, a patron of the stable who had backed the quintet in an accumulator to win £7,000, worth at least ten times that amount in present-day values. It was a nice touch when Simon sent the Olivers a horse he named Wolverhampton. Subsequently Wolverhampton joined Ginger McCain's stable. On the eve of the 1975 Grand National in which he and the great Red Rum were due to run (Red Rum finished second), they were working together on the Southport sands when Wolverhampton dropped down dead.

Simon Fraser was the son and heir of the Second World War hero, the 17th Lord Lovat, chief of Clan Fraser. By the time of Simon's premature death he had sold Beauly Castle in Inverness-shire, which had been in the family for 500 years, to Ann Gloag of the Perth-based bus company, Stagecoach. At one time Simon was a leading owner with Vincent O'Brien; he also bought a nucleus of mares from the Canadian, Max Bell, with the intention of establishing a stud at Beauly, but this rather enterprising plan never came to fruition.

The Benign Bishop was special for two reasons. First he was named after his trainer, who acquired the lasting soubriquet from a magazine article, and second he was homebred, being a grandson of his faithful old partner, Salvina. Retired due to a suspicion of leg trouble, she became the cornerstone of Ken's breeding operation. Sent to Ken Oliver's great Irish benefactor, Padge Berry, her only offspring were three filly foals produced in successive years. Two of them, Honeytown and Melgund Glen, once scored over hurdles on the same afternoon at Kelso.

By the Cheltenham Gold Cup hero, Fortina, Honeytown started off in point-to-points. Rhona was all set to win on the mare's first race between the flags at the demanding Friars Haugh course in the shadow of Floors Castle, when they collided with the rails after jumping the last fence. Some years later, misfortune also befell Honeytown in the Scottish Grand National at Bogside. Going ominously well, she was brought down at the third-last fence.

Honeytown was only a pony in stature, never measuring more than

15 hands, but she proved an exceptional broodmare although she was anything but a regular breeder. Three of her five winners were by another great Irish-based jumping sire, Arctic Slave, including Bally-owen and The Benign Bishop. Ballyowen won five consecutive races in Ireland, trained by Padge Berry. The Benign Bishop won sixteen races – a brilliant novice, he won the champion novice chases at both Ayr and Chepstow. He was given by Ken to his son Stuart, who also won on him. Another of Honeytown's prolific winners was Chandigar. He raced for Ken's daughter Susan, winning twenty-one races, all bar one of them over fences.

A winner seven times under NH Rules, Bannow Bay, an own-sister to Ballyowen and The Benign Bishop, produced a real star in Deep Sensation. This son of Deep Run was offered for sale as a yearling from Hassendean Bank at Doncaster in November 1986 when procured by Irish agent, Jack White, for 23,000 guineas, a European record for a store yearling. Resubmitted in the same ring two years later, he failed to find a buyer, but Ken Oliver was instrumental in him being sold privately to Findon trainer, Josh Gifford.

In the spring of 1993, Deep Sensation brought off the big double of the Queen Mother Champion Chase at the Cheltenham Festival, followed by the Melling Chase over the Mildmay Course at the Liverpool Grand National Meeting. Previously he had won the Tote Gold Trophy at Newbury. Altogether Deep Sensation earned over £360,000. It was a tremendously proud moment for Ken Oliver when the home secretary, Michael Howard, presented him with the Queen Mother's Silver Cup as the leading British-based National Hunt breeder at the annual awards luncheon of the Thoroughbred Breeders' Association in London in January 1994. Towards the end of his career he trained for the Queen Mother.

Ken Oliver was hardly looking for any fresh challenges when his friend and colleague, Willie Stephenson, suggested that they should join forces and start a rival sales company to Tattersalls, operating from Tattersalls's old hunting ground at Doncaster. Willie, who trained at Royston in Hertfordshire, was one of an elite band to have saddled both a Derby winner (Arctic Prince), and a Grand National winner

(Oxo) – indeed it was Wyndburgh who had finished an unlucky runner-up to Oxo at Aintree in 1959.

So against the advice of almost everyone, Doncaster Bloodstock Sales Limited came into existence in 1962 with Ken and Willie each contributing a capital sum of just £500, a figure that seems inconceivable nowadays to launch a serious new business venture. All along, the plan was for the administrative offices to be in Hawick with the sales conducted at Doncaster. Apart from Botterills, based in York, with monthly sales conducted at Ascot, Tattersalls, whose offices were still in Knightsbridge in central London, then had a virtual monopoly of all bloodstock offered at public auction in the UK.

From the outset Ken Oliver realised that for DBS to succeed it would need support from across the Irish Sea (a precursor of the Doncaster/Goffs merger that was to take place more than four decades later). It was certainly ironic that one of the first Irish breeders to sign up for the inaugural St Leger sale in 1963 was Peg Watt. A cousin of Tattersalls' partners, Ken and Michael Watt, the Limerick breeder was an enormous help in getting this particular sale established and in the first six years from 1963 to 1968 she was the top vendor.

However, the founders' most significant long-term decision was the recruitment of the present chairman, Harry Beeby, whose son, Henry, was to succeed him as managing director; between them they have made the enterprise the enormous success that it is today. Harry's father, George, the son of a horse-dealer in the shires, trained at Compton in Berkshire where he enjoyed great success under both Rules. Always associated with Lord Bicester's magnificent chasers, he also trained the wayward Grey Sovereign who proved a surprisingly influential sire.

The new Doncaster St Leger Yearling Sales, which always used to coincide with the oldest classic on Town Moor, quickly established a reputation as the sale for precocious two-year-olds. It really came of age in 2006, when the three principal juvenile events at Royal Ascot – the Coventry Stakes, Norfolk Stakes and Queen Mary Stakes – were all won by St Leger graduates. But these yearling sales had long before become serious competition to the erstwhile monopoly enjoyed by Tattersalls.

Nonetheless the bread and butter of DBS has always been National Hunt horses and the Spring Sales in May have long offered the best possible selection of stores available anywhere and again there is always a strong Irish element. Over the years it has created records for jumpers in every department. The highest individual price of 530,000 guineas was paid for Garde Champetre in May 2004, a new world auction record for a jumper in any category, proven or unproven.

An occasion which gave Ken Oliver particular satisfaction in his latter years was the dispersal in May 1993 of 127 horses, following the death the previous year of leading National Hunt trainer, Arthur Stephenson, Willie's cousin, conducted at his Crawleas stables at Bishop Auckland in Co. Durham. Amongst them was One Man and this grey proceeded to win the King George VI Chase twice, the Queen Mother Champion Chase and Hennessy Cognac Gold Cup, to qualify as one of the best jumpers ever sold by the firm.

DBS passed two important milestones in 2008. January saw the opening of a new £6m sales complex, a far cry from the inaugural year of 1962 when business was conducted from a draughty marquee! Then in the summer the firm merged with Irish rivals Goffs, albeit they retained separate identities. It was not until April 2016 that the company changed its name, selling for the first time as Goffs UK at that year's Grand National meeting. Henry Beeby is a strong advocate of these boutique sales. Since 2014 another has been held annually on the eve of Royal Ascot at The Orangery at Kensington Palace – ironically this is just down the road from Hyde Park Corner, historically the site of Tattersalls' regular Thoroughbred auctions.

Uncle Ken to some and The Benign Bishop to others, Kenneth Oliver died aged eighty-five in 1999, when he ranked as the oldest licence-holder in the country. A man of many parts, he was involved with virtually everything that happened to the Borders farming community. Certainly no one had more zest for life or put more into it and for him racing was primarily fun. Until the end of 2006, his widow trained in her own name from Hassendean Bank, albeit on a much reduced scale, but she continued to breed a few stores for sale, thus maintaining the family association with DBS. She died in 2003.

20

BONNIE AND CLYDE

There was a decidedly Scottish flavour so far as the result of the 1979 Oaks on Epsom Downs was concerned. The winner was James Morrison's Scintillate and the runner-up was Sandy Struthers's Bonnie Isle. It was a pretty remarkable outcome all round, as both were homebred fillies produced by their respective owners from just a handful of inexpensive broodmares – resident in England rather than Scotland, it has to be said.

Jim Morrison, later the 2nd Lord Margadale, was a Scot by inclination if not by birth (the name Margadale is taken from the family's spiritual home, the Isle of Islay, the location of some world-famous whisky distilleries), and this picturesque island off the west coast of Scotland is just across the water from the mainland. To the north of Glasgow, from where the Morrison clan migrated to England, is Craigmaddie at Milngavie, Sandy Struthers's home of long standing.

All his working life Sandy Struthers has been involved with the family shipping line, J. & A. Gardner, based on the Clyde. Founded by his great-grandfather in 1860 to transfer stone from their quarry at Ballachulish, the business expanded to as many as fifteen ships carrying cargo around British coastal waters. Modern times, however, have not favoured independent operators and the business dwindled to just two vessels both based in the Falkland Islands, one operating on behalf of the Falkland Islands' government and the other under contract to the British army, with all repairs and maintenance being carried out in Chile.

Sandy's in depth knowledge of shipping resulted in his appointment in 1989 as chairman of Caledonian MacBrayne, whose Glasgow based fleet of ships and ferries provide an essential lifeline to all the Western Isles. The organisation is heavily subsidised by the government and any chairman of Cal-Mac is answerable to the Secretary of State for Scotland.

His organisational skills were also recognised by racing's hierarchy. He was deputy senior steward of the Jockey Club at the time that Lord Hartington (now the Duke of Devonshire) was negotiating the transfer of power to the British Horseracing Board (now the British Horseracing Authority). First recruited to serve as a racecourse steward at Hamilton Park, he earned promotion to Newmarket and has served as both a member and a steward of the Jockey Club.

Many a love affair with racing has been kindled through Cambridge University's proximity to Newmarket, but by the time Sandy Struthers went to Trinity College, he had already acquired a fascination with racehorse pedigrees as a schoolboy at Stowe. As an undergraduate he was to gain a hands-on experience with Thoroughbreds when leading up some of the yearlings which had gone into training with George Colling, whose Stanley House string at that time included the likes of Mossborough, Saturn and Wilwyn.

His first venture into ownership came in 1959 with a leased filly, Bon Star, who scored twice in the colours of John Henderson, a fellow Glasgow businessman. The first to score in Struthers's own colours – grey, pink sleeves, check cap – was Ratcatcher. Also trained by Gerry Laurence at Cree Lodge, Ayr, this grey colt scored four times as a juvenile in 1961.

In the long term two people were largely responsible for keeping the Struthers's ship on course in the world of racing and breeding – Arundel trainer John Dunlop and Christopher Philipson, one-time chairman and managing director of the British Bloodstock Agency. The three of them were close friends as well as business colleagues when it came to racehorses and that may well have been a major contributory factor in their shared involvement, with no vast expenditure incurred along the way.

From 1966 to 1970 Sandy enjoyed an amazing run with the progeny of one broodmare. When Betty Tweedie's Rosie Wings, one of the most popular performers of her generation in the north, retired to stud (see Chapter 28), she was sent over from Berwickshire to Ireland as a temporary boarder at Jim McVey's Woodpark Stud, Co. Meath (now one of the Maktoum family's studs) where in her first two seasons she was covered in turn by the resident stallions, Tamerlane and Sunny Way.

The first mating resulted in a colt, Scottish Sinbad, who was procured on Sandy Struthers's behalf as a yearling at Newmarket in a draft from Woodpark Stud for 3,400 guineas by Harry Whiteman, Gerry Laurence's successor at Cree Lodge. The following season Scottish Sinbad was joined there by his year junior half-brother, Mount Athos (by Sunny Way), whom Sandy Struthers bought privately after he failed to make his reserve as a yearling.

Mount Athos was an exact contemporary of a smart colt at Cree Lodge called Doon. The pair were due to meet in the Knockjarder Plate at Ayr's Glasgow Fair Meeting in July, when Mount Athos, who had won his only two starts, was set to concede 13lb to the once-raced Doon. Despite his owner's protestations, Mount Athos ran at Ayr, finishing runner-up to his stable companion. As a direct consequence of this altercation, Sandy Struthers transferred both Scottish Sinbad and Mount Athos to John Dunlop at Arundel at the end of the season.

That was certainly a retrograde step from the point of view of Scottish racing, but had Scottish Sinbad not changed stables it seems singularly unlikely that he would have been sent down on the long journey south to compete at Goodwood. It was here on the Sussex Downs, just down the road from Castle Stables, Arundel, that Scottish Sinbad won the Chesterfield Cup, the most important of his seven victories, before being exported to Singapore.

Meanwhile, Mount Athos proved a very good three-year-old in 1968, far better than anyone could possibly have envisaged. Following success in handicaps at Nottingham and Newcastle, he finished third at 45–1 in the Derby to Sir Ivor and Connaught. In midsummer he proved that was no flash in the pan by winning the Princess of Wales's Stakes and Gordon Stakes. At Goodwood, he completed a memorable double initiated by his half-brother in the Chesterfield Cup. Tailed off last in the St Leger behind Ribero, his enthusiasm was once more called into question the following season when he tried to run out and virtually pulled himself up in the Ascot Gold Cup. Previously he had divided Park Top and Connaught when second in the Coronation Cup.

Only hours after Mount Athos's disappointing run in the St Leger, his owner walked from the racecourse to the sales across the road, purchasing his Sing Sing half-brother, John Splendid, for 8,300 guineas. A sprinter like his sire (bred by fellow Scot, Bill Stirling), John Splendid achieved a memorable victory as a three-year-old in the 1970 Ayr Gold Cup, a race that all Scottish owners are always bent on winning. Only a neck and a short head deprived him of a second Ayr Gold Cup victory the ensuing season, in a field of twenty-eight.

Both Mount Athos and John Splendid became stallions a long way from home – the former in Argentina and the latter in Australia. However, for an interim period John Splendid did a stint covering at Neville Dent's Hart Hill Stud, near Shaftesbury in Dorset. Coincidentally, John Dunlop had learned the rudiments of training with Neville Dent when the latter handled a small string of jumpers at Brockenhurst in the New Forest. It was Dent who was instrumental in the introduction of the 5lb sex allowance for mares and fillies over jumps.

Sentiment was undoubtedly a factor regarding the purchase of John Splendid and so it was with Scottish Rifle. Named by Sandy Struthers after his old regiment, the Cameronians (Lanark used to stage an annual Cameronian Meeting with the Cameronian Cup as the feature event), Scottish Rifle was by Mount Athos's sire, Sunny Way, and was also bred by Woodpark Stud. Acquired for 3,600 guineas at the Newmarket October Yearling Sales, he was to prove an even better performer than Mount Athos.

One of the top middle-distance horses amongst the older division, Scottish Rifle scored three times at Goodwood in his second season, including the Gordon Stakes, and was runner-up in the Irish Sweeps Derby. On the Curragh the surprise winner, Steel Pulse, turned the tables comprehensively on Roberto, who started a hot favourite to confirm the superiority he had demonstrated in winning the Derby at Epsom.

Scottish Rifle really excelled the following season, bringing his tally of Group victories to six. They were headed by the Eclipse Stakes, which was staged that year at Kempton due to rebuilding work at Sandown. He was also placed second in the Prince of Wales's Stakes and Benson & Hedges Gold Cup (now Juddmonte International), and third to that great mare, Dahlia, in the Washington DC International. All these are Group or Grade 1 races nowadays.

John Dunlop has particularly fond memories of Scottish Rifle as he had two commendable traits. He was blessed with the kindest of dispositions and he was never sick or sorry during three busy seasons at Arundel – and the fact that he incurred no vets' bills was doubtless appreciated by his owner! Originally retired to stand at Sussex Stud, near Horsham (formerly an annexe to the National Stud), Scottish Rifle was then transferred to Lavington Stud nearby, only to be exported to Czechoslovakia.

Good horses that Mount Athos and Scottish Rifle undoubtedly were, their owner's favourite was Pitcairn, whose dam, Border Bounty, was a popular racemare owned and raced by Betty Tweedie's elder sister, Lorna Fraser of Ladyrig, near Kelso. Irish-bred Pitcairn cost 3,500 guineas as a yearling, an almost identical sum to Scottish Rifle. It was at Sandy's request that Christo Philipson went over to the Dublin September Sales to inspect the colt. At the time the youngster had an unattractive skin condition and that probably explains his relatively modest price.

Successful twice as a juvenile, Pitcairn was placed in three of the season's top events, finishing runner-up in the Dewhurst Stakes and Middle Park Stakes and third in the Champagne Stakes. The ensuing season he proved a top miler, winning the Blue Riband Trial Stakes by a staggering eight lengths, Hungerford Stakes and Goodwood Mile, and was second in the Irish Two Thousand Guineas and third in the Champion Stakes.

Pitcairn was retired to stand in his native Ireland at Greenmount Stud, Co. Limerick. At first no one seemed interested in standing the horse. Lord Harrington of Greenmount only agreed to have him on the understanding that payment for a three-quarter-share was delayed until his fourth covering season. Pitcairn was represented by only his first crop of runners when he was exported to Japan in 1978. That year he was the leading first season sire thanks to Ela-Mana-Mou, but he did have fertility problems.

Due to the exploits of Ela-Mana-Mou and Cairn Rouge, Pitcairn succeeded his own sire, Petingo, as the champion sire (Great Britain and Ireland) in 1980. Petingo stood under the auspices of Tim Rogers's Airlie Stud, the breeder of Pitcairn, and Sandy still keeps in touch with Tim's widow, Sonia. It was at the old BBA offices in Charing Cross Road that Sonia Pilkington, as she then was, studied Thoroughbred pedigrees under Bobby Bobinski – that is when she was not lunching with Tim at the Mirabelle! Although Sonia has long since handed over the reins at Airlie to their son, Anthony, she is still a leading figure in Irish bloodstock circles and is a director of auctioneers, Goffs UK.

Meanwhile, Sandy Struthers had been establishing a small band of boarding mares at Christo Philipson's Lofts Hall Stud, near Saffron Walden in Essex. One of them was Ruddy Duck, whom Christo had acquired as an in-foal mare at the 1972 Newmarket December Sales for just 4,000 guineas. Her bargain price might just have had something to do with the fact that the eight-year-old was the very first lot through the ring on the Saturday morning, not the most propitious place in the catalogue.

In due course Ruddy Duck produced winners to John Splendid, Scottish Rifle and Pitcairn. Matings with Pitcairn proved an inspiration, producing two ultra distinguished own-sisters in Flighting (Princess Royal Stakes), and the Oaks runner-up, Bonnie Isle. Initially the latter looked the superior of the pair, but by the end of Flighting's career when placed in numerous prestige events, their trainer, John Dunlop, would have been hard pressed to separate them in terms of ability. Both Flighting and Bonnie Isle were sold privately to the USA and that would certainly have helped to balance the books.

The connection with the Philipsons' Lofts Hall Stud is interesting as Mary Philipson, Christo's widow, is a daughter of Sir Reginald Macdonald-Buchanan (see Chapter 6). Lofts Hall has another Scottish link as Stuart Thom, who is stud groom at Lofts Hall, is a son of Gordon Thom from Pettochside, near Ayr. The latter is one of the sons of James Thom and Sons of New Hall Stud, breeders of the 2005 Cheveley Park Stakes heroine, Donna Blini.

21

A GRAND NATIONAL VICTORY AT LAST

To the cognoscenti of the Turf who value tradition, the Derby remains the greatest race in the world. There is no need for the qualification Epsom Derby, just as the word racing need never be extended to horse-racing. To the jumping enthusiast the equivalent Blue Riband of steeplechasing is the Cheltenham Gold Cup run at level weights with an allowance for members of the fairer sex. For the general public, however, nothing rivals the Grand National, one of the greatest sporting spectacles on Earth, with a worldwide television audience estimated at hundreds of millions.

It is amazing that the very first Grand National at Liverpool in 1839 was won by a horse called Lottery, for this is exactly what the race has proved to be over the years. This is not surprising for a handicap run over four and a half miles and sixteen of the most formidable fences to be found on any racecourse anywhere – all of which are jumped twice, with the exception of The Chair and the water jump. In the interests of safety, both horse and rider now have to qualify to compete, but in the old days there were no such restrictions, a situation that undoubtedly contributed to the romance of this legendary sporting event.

Until 1960 the unique spruce and gorse fences at Aintree (as Liverpool is equally well known) were even more formidable than they are today. They were absolutely upright, without the apron in front which encourages a horse to stand off, but – notwithstanding these and other alterations in an endeavour to obviate quite so many falls – the race remains the ultimate racecourse test for horse and rider. Do the obstacles anywhere else have such emotive names as Becher's, The

Chair, Valentine's and the Canal Turn? The very mention of them sets the adrenalin flowing.

For generations Scotland's racing enthusiasts have had a love affair with the Grand National, but for 140 years it was a story of unrequited love. That is, if one adheres to the popular notion that the nationality of a horse depends entirely on where he or she is trained. For some inexplicable reason, the fact that the winner was bred in Scotland, is Scottish-owned or indeed was ridden by a Scot (or has identical connections with any other country for that matter) is irrelevant.

This aspect is well illustrated by the 1896 Grand National winner The Soarer, who was owned by William Hall Walker (later Lord Wavertree) and ridden by an army subaltern David Campbell (later General Sir David Campbell). Campbell became the first serving cavalry officer to win the National, his father having been a major in the Cameron Highlanders. Despite his own Scottish ancestry, William Hall Walker took his title from a district of Liverpool, to which he was a great benefactor, most notably with the Walker Art Gallery.

Hall Walker financed his considerable involvement in racing through the family brewing business Peter Walker & Sons. An eccentric, he became the leading breeder of his day. Despite his dependency on horoscopes when formulating his broodmare matings, he defied the critics by breeding the winners of all five English Classics. In the end he gave away his stud at Tully in Kildare which duly became the Irish National Stud, while most of the stock was donated to the British government to become the foundation of the National Stud in England.

One of the most memorable renewals occurred in 1911 when the great race was won by the one-eyed Glenside, who was also reputed to have a wind problem. The only runner not to capitulate in the atrocious conditions, he was bred by William Kincaid Lennox of Campsie Glen in Stirlingshire. Instead of Lennox, *The General Stud Book* gives the surname Peareth, but later the breeder made the change of name to comply with the conditions of an inheritance. Glenside was trained by Robert Collis at Kinlet in Worcestershire.

In 1921 there was an action replay of Glenside's year when the winner, Shaun Spadah, was the only one of a then record thirty-five runners to complete the course without coming to grief. Once again, the handful of placed runners were remounted. Shaun Spadah carried the tartan colours of Malcolm McAlpine, a member of the eponymous Scottish construction firm. The horse, who had had three previous owners, was trained a long way from Scotland by George Poole at Lewes in Sussex on the south coast.

One of the most exciting finishes ever came in 1930, when Shaun Goilin defeated Melleray's Belle by a neck. That season the gallant runner-up had won the Cheltenham Foxhunters', ridden by George Owen (who was destined to train the 1949 Grand National winner, Russian Hero). Owned by William Wilson of Castlehill, Ayr, and trained in Yorkshire, Melleray's Belle, who had finished fourth in the 1929 National at 200–1, was a popular mare, who had a race named after her at Ayr.

The irony is that when a Scottish-trained horse did eventually prevail at Aintree after so many years of endeavour and near misses, the winner was trained by an Englishman from the West Midlands! Rubstic, who scored in 1979, was dispatched from Bedrule – in the Borders, between Hawick and Jedburgh – by John Leadbetter, but the trainer was actually born in Staffordshire. Furthermore, Rubstic's training quarters had alternated between England and Scotland, but this time Scotland enjoyed the rub of the green.

When discussing Scotland's long list of disappointments, people invariably recall MacMoffat, who finished second to Workman in 1939 and to Bogskar in 1940, ridden on both occasions by Ian Alder from Hawick who served in the Gordon Highlanders during the war. MacMoffat, like so many jumpers before and after, was bred in the Borders, by Major Moffat Thomson, and owned and trained by his neighbour, Captain L. Scott Briggs – in those bygone days it was *de rigueur* to let it be known that one belonged to the officer class, just in case, heaven forbid, anyone should think otherwise!

With an excess of young horses running on his farm, MacMoffat's breeder asked Scott Briggs if he would care to buy any of them. Not greatly taken by the numerous horses he was shown grazing out in the field, he changed his mind when MacMoffat broke into a canter. He promptly bought him for sixty guineas.

Not the only Scottish horse to have hunted with the North Northumberland and to have won the Heart of All England Hunt Cup at Hexham, MacMoffat was unlucky to be born when he was. He was only a seven-year-old when competing in the first of those two Nationals and there were no further opportunities from 1941 to 1945 as the great race was cancelled. He did return to the fray aged fourteen along with Bogskar, but both were fallers.

Luck was not on the side of Wyndburgh, who, from a Scottish viewpoint, was the most iconic performer so far as the Grand National was concerned. He shared much in common with MacMoffat – he was bred in the Borders and enjoyed an education in the hunting field; he also had a suitably Scottish-sounding name, in this instance taken from a hill in the Cheviots near his original home on the Wilkinson family's farm, Whitehaugh, on the Carlisle side of Hawick.

It was in 1943 at Hawick auction market that 'Wilkie' Wilkinson paid just twenty-two guineas to buy the unbroken six-year-old mare, Swinnie, from a neighbour, Marjorie Robson-Scott. Subsequently the major gave Swinnie to his younger daughter, Rhona, to help her with shepherding their flock of North Country Cheviots. Then, just before leaving home to study for a farming diploma at Moulton Agricultural College in Northamptonshire, Rhona had her mare covered by Maquis, who stood just down the road with the Bell family at Midshiels.

The result of this twenty-five-pound mating was Wyndburgh. Destined to become part of Aintree folklore, he competed in six consecutive Grand Nationals, finishing runner-up three times. One would never have singled him out as a typical Aintree horse as he was close-coupled and barely measured sixteen hands. Indeed, that very fine judge, Stewart Wight, thought his future would be as 'a good hill hunter', an assessment that he soon had to rectify!

Having been partnered by Rhona to finish second in two point-to-points, Wyndburgh was trained officially under permit by her father, but she really held the reins and rode him in all his work. Saddled by her father, Wyndburgh showed a marked preference for some cut in the ground. He was to finish second in the 1957 Grand National ridden by Mick Batchelor behind Sundew, having gained his first victory under Rules in a chase at Cartmel over Whitsun.

On the strength of winning the Grand Sefton over the big Aintree fences, Wyndburgh started 6–1 favourite for the 1958 National, finishing fourth to Mr What. That May, Rhona Wilkinson married Ken Oliver, whereupon her pride and joy left Whitehaugh to join the newly married couple at Denholm House, situated a few miles out of Hawick towards Kelso, before they moved to Hassendean Bank.

Two more Grand National seconds for Wyndburgh came in 1959 behind Oxo, ridden by Tim Brookshaw, and on his final appearance as a twelve-year-old in 1962 to Kilmore, partnered by Tommy Barnes. To complete the record the horse unseated Michael Scudamore (father of Peter and grandfather of Tom) behind Merryman II in 1960; and was sixth to the grey Nicolaus Silver in 1961. Wyndburgh has the unfortunate distinction of being the only horse to be runner-up three times without actually winning.

An unforgettable incident in 1959 almost certainly deprived Wyndburgh of Aintree glory. At Becher's Brook on the second circuit, a stirrup iron broke and Tim Brookshaw rode virtually bareback for the remainder of the race, only to be beaten one and a half lengths. But for this misfortune Ken Oliver would have become the first permit-holder to saddle a Grand National winner. Next to Aintree, Wyndburgh seemed most effective at Newcastle and he was successful twice in the four-mile Eider Chase, then known as the Tote Investors' Handicap Chase. Wyndburgh is buried at Hassendean Bank where he died at the advanced age of thirty-one.

In 1960, Merryman II was the last winner of the Grand National over the old-style upright fences which were so uncompromising and put such a premium on jumping ability. It was also the first National to be televised live by the BBC. More importantly, he could so well have been Scotland's first Grand National winner, but fate decreed otherwise. Early on in the gelding's career Neville Crump from Middleham witnessed Merryman winning the Buccleuch Hunter Chase at Kelso by a distance and was so impressed that he approached his owner, Winifred Wallace, with an offer to train him. The die was cast and it was Yorkshire rather than Scotland that received all the plaudits!

In 1959 Merryman demonstrated both his aptitude for jumping the big fences and his staying ability by winning the Liverpool Foxhunters', partnered by Borders farmer Charlie Scott, and the Scottish Grand National at Bogside, ridden by Neville Crump's stable jockey, Gerry Scott (no relation). It was the latter who rode the handsome bay with a distinctive white blaze when he won the Grand National, justifying favouritism by fifteen lengths. The previous December he had been diagnosed by the Royal (Dick) Veterinary College with a bone inflammation in one of his front hooves, but fortunately this healed just in time.

The following year Merryman was runner-up to Nicolaus Silver despite the absence through injury of his regular partner (he was ridden instead by the popular Oxfordshire trainer-rider, Derek Ancil, an outstanding horseman) and receiving a nasty kick on his stifle down at the start. The third of Neville Crump's three Grand National winners (following Sheila's Cottage and Teal), Merryman died in retirement at the age of fifteen on a day out with the North Northumberland hounds.

Winnie Wallace's involvement with Merryman mirrored that of Rhona Wilkinson with Wyndburgh, as she hunted him and rode him in point-to-points. She did not breed him, however. That role was performed by the Marquess of Linlithgow of Hopetoun at South Queensferry, on the outskirts of Edinburgh. It seems the former viceroy of India, then in his eighties, announced at breakfast one morning, quite out of the blue, that as he could not afford to try and breed a Derby winner, he would quite like to breed a Grand National winner instead!

At about that time the family was given a mare, Maid Marion, whom Lord Linlithgow's daughter, Lady Joan Hope, hunted with her local pack, the Linlithgow and Stirlingshire. She later put her in foal to Carnival Boy, then standing as a Hunter Improvement Society stallion at Alnwick Castle, owned by the Duke of Northumberland. The result was Merryman.

Carnival Boy had the comparatively rare distinction of winning on the Flat, over hurdles and over fences – in fact he won the Gloucestershire Hurdle at Cheltenham (now Supreme Novices' Hurdle) and was runner-up in the Champion Hurdle. However, at the time of his great

Aintree victory, Merryman could not even claim to be a Half-Bred, the official terminology for horses entered in Miss Prior's *The Half-Bred Stud Book*, far less *The General Stud Book* itself – the breeding of his dam only came to light afterwards.

Merryman, who was foaled in 1951, was bred officially by Lord Linlithgow, but he died the following year. Meanwhile his daughter (by then Lady Joan Gore Langton) had joined her soldier husband on an overseas posting. After spending four years at Hopetoun, the Carnival Boy gelding joined George Beveridge, a well-known nagsman and landlord of the Plough Hotel at Yetholm in the Borders. When he failed to find a buyer for the youngster, he was sold to Winifred Wallace, a friend and neighbour of the Linlithgows, for £470.

No sooner had the great Wyndburgh departed the scene than Scotland had another formidable standard-bearer in Freddie. Like Merryman he had a distinctive white blaze and received his early education in the hunting field, in this instance out with the Buccleuch. Unlike Merryman he was Irish-bred, but was never trained in a professional stable, his entire racing career being spent with Reg Tweedie of Middlethird, Gordon, in Berwickshire.

Robert Reginald Tweedie, whose brother, Lex, farmed at Eweford, just above George Boyd's stables at Dunbar, personified all that is best about the farming and racing fraternity in the Borders and the country thereabouts. Reg followed in the footsteps of their father, Robert Waugh Tweedie. Both were stalwarts of National Hunt racing in every aspect of the sport, from owning and training to breeding and stewarding, as well as hunting and farming the family's 1,000 acres.

Living in close proximity to Stewart Wight at Grantshouse, father and son had a close association with Scotland's premier trainer of jumpers. It was through their old friend that Reg originally acquired Freddie as a young horse for £350. Unfortunately the Grantshouse trainer did not live to witness Freddie's two seconds in the Grand National, as he died in 1963 – only the previous year Freddie made his first appearance in public at his local point-to-point.

Successful in seven consecutive hunter chases spread over two seasons, Freddie won the 1964 Cheltenham Foxhunters' in commanding fashion as a seven-year-old at 3–1 on. This provided amateur Alan Mactaggart, from West Nisbet, near Jedburgh in Roxburghshire, with the most important success of his riding career. Immediately afterwards this star hunter was put in at the deep end. Installed favourite for the Scottish Grand National despite top-weight, it was only by half a length that he failed to concede 22lb to the smart Popham Down.

Freddie and his regular professional partner, Pat McCarron (Irish not Scots), won two Sandown Park feature races – the Mildmay Memorial Chase and Gallagher Gold Cup – and the Great Yorkshire Chase at Doncaster, to prove one of the top staying chasers in the country. He was also runner-up to Arkle in the Hennessy Gold Cup. However, he is best remembered for a titanic struggle in the 1965 Grand National when, as 7–2 favourite, he was beaten three-parts of a length by the American interloper, Jay Trump. On that occasion he was conceding the winner 5lb, while the following year, when the testing going was against him, he occupied the same berth albeit twenty lengths behind Anglo, who was in receipt of 21lb.

Freddie's career ended due to a heart murmur, but he enjoyed a long and happy retirement at home on the farm, part of it shared with Betty Tweedie's wonderful broodmare, Rosie Wings. He died in 1985 aged twenty-eight – strange how so many of these grand old Aintree warriors survived to such a ripe old age!

The Tweedies will always be associated with their local course of Kelso. Reg, a former chairman, who has a stand there named after him, died in 1999 and Betty, a patron of this popular Borders course, died in 2009 at the grand old age of ninety-six.

For a fourth time during the 1960s a Scottish-trained horse was to finish second in the Grand National. It was Moidore's Token, trained by Ken Oliver. A former showjumper, he was owned by Pat Harrower from Heriot in Midlothian and she used to take him hunting when, much to the trainer's consternation, the pair of them would jump everything in sight. A giant of a horse, he went into the 1968 Grand National undefeated in three seasonal starts. At the advanced age of eleven he ran the race of his life with stable jockey Barry Brogan, to finish runner-up to Red Alligator, beaten twenty lengths, despite making serious errors at the last two fences.

The result of the 1978 Grand National had a particular significance for anyone waving a blue flag with a white saltire, as the Scottish-owned Lucius defeated the Scottish-trained Sebastian V. If not a vintage renewal, it was certainly one of the most exciting finishes ever witnessed at Liverpool, with just three lengths separating the first five home. Lucius's owner, Fiona Whitaker, bought him as an unbroken three-year-old at the Doncaster Sales for 1,800 guineas through her trainer, Gordon W. Richards, from Penrith in Cumbria.

At that time Fiona and her husband, David, lived at Aberdour in Fife, overlooking the Firth of Forth, which was convenient for her husband David's work as a chartered accountant in Edinburgh. With the building of the liquefied gas terminal at Braefoot Bay right next door to their home, the Whitakers later moved to Glenfarg, no distance from Perth racecourse, where her father was chairman and where Fiona used to be a steward. Lucius ended his days hunting in Fife; he died peacefully in his sleep aged twenty-seven.

More recently Fiona Whitaker's homebred Macgregor The Third won the popular cross-country Sporting Index Chase at Cheltenham three times. He was the last of nine winners of over sixty races that his owner has bred from her original foundation mare, Arctic Dawn, who gained her solitary success at Perth. Arctic Dawn also won her owner the TBA's annual National Hunt Broodmare of the Year award for the 1985–6 season.

Fiona Whitaker originally had horses with Fred Winter at Lambourn, as did her mother, Irene Dewhurst, a member of the Dewar whisky family (see Chapter 6). It was upon Fred Winter's recommendation that Mrs Whitaker transferred her horses to Gordon Richards, when she and her husband moved back to Scotland. Nowadays she has horses with her daughter, Lucy Normile, at home at Duncrievie – she has a public licence, having previously trained point-to-pointers. One of her staff, Stephen Freeman, became the first representative for Scotland on the National Association of Stable Staff, the former Stable Lads' Association.

Sebastian V, the runner-up to Lucius, is one of those characters whose place of abode alternated between England and Scotland. He was owned by Richard Jeffreys, a farmer from West Lilburn, near Alnwick, and at one time he had horses in training with Andy Scott just down the road at Wooperton. However, Sebastian was trained by Harry Bell at Midshiels, near Hawick, so qualifies for the Scottish tag. Previously Sebastian had won the 1977 Scottish Grand National, and the same colours were carried to victory in the 1962 Scottish Grand National by Sham Fight, ridden by his trainer, Tommy Robson, Gordon Richards' predecessor at Greystoke.

It had proved a long haul but finally in 1979 Rubstic became the first ever Grand National winner to have been trained in Scotland. But further investigation reveals that this was a very tenuous state of affairs, as the horse was originally trained in England, and after an interme-diate spell with Sebastian's handler, Harry Bell, he recrossed the border to join Lucius's trainer, Gordon Richards, before finally retracing his steps to Roxburghshire. This time his destination was Bedrule on the opposite side of the River Teviot to Hassendean Bank.

Much of the credit for Rubstic (named after the Swedish equivalent of a Brillo Pad) must go to Harry Bell. He originally bought the colt as an unraced three-year-old for 1,050 guineas at Newmarket in July 1972 – the vendor, Peter Calver, had bought him as a yearling for 500 guineas. Not long after, John Douglas saw him out in a field at Midshiels and bought him privately for 1,300 guineas.

In due course, Harry Bell saddled Rubstic to finish second in the 1975 Scottish Grand National, in which event he was runner-up for a second time in 1978. An Edinburgh businessman, John Douglas was familiar with Hawick as a former Scottish rugby international, who had played for the British Lions. Meanwhile in retirement, Rubstic put in a personal appearance at Hampden Park for a Scottish Cup Final; he also graced the official opening of a new telephone exchange in Edinburgh.

Not many people have two future Grand National winners through their hands, but Rubstic's previous owner, the Scottish veterinary surgeon, Peter Calver, owned and rode Highland Wedding to win a handful of point-to-points. Despite a tendency to break blood vessels, Highland Wedding proceeded to win the 1969 National as a twelve-year-old for Toby Balding. What is more, he was bred in Scotland by John Caldwell, a farmer from Prestwick in Ayrshire, by the local premium stallion, Question, out of a Half-Bred mare.

One of Highland Wedding's intermediate owners was Jim Love, a vet from Paisley, who had acquired him through Tom Foster, a Glasgow horse-dealer, for fifty pounds. Jim Love subsequently sold him to Peter Calver for £185. One of Highland Wedding's joint owners when he triumphed at Aintree was a Canadian, Charles Burns, and it was in Canada that the horse spent his retirement.

The racing world is a close-knit community so it is not surprising that so many of these Scottish horses have links. For example, Rubstic was ridden by Maurice Barnes whose father, Tommy, had finished runner-up on Wyndburgh. Freddie was partnered by Pat McCarron, and he had served his apprenticeship with Harry Blackshaw, as did Rubstic's handler, John Leadbetter. In his time John also worked for Neville Crump, trainer of Merryman, as well as Ken Oliver, trainer of Wyndburgh and Moidore's Token – it is all very much a case of wheels within wheels.

There is little glory in finishing second in the Grand National, though it is an heroic effort nonetheless. Two further Scottish-trained runners-up are the 66–1 outsider, Young Driver, in 1986 – a first runner for John Wilson of Cree Lodge, Ayr – and Blue Charm in 1999, trained by Susan Bradburne, near Cupar, in Fife. Blue Charm, who was 16lb out of the handicap, was named after a salmon fly commonly used by anglers on the Tay. The 1989 Grand National hero Little Polveir took his name from a Scottish salmon-pool.

So for a very long time Rubstic remained the solitary Grand National winner trained in Scotland. But thirty-eight years later that achievement was to be trumped by a second hero, and this time the winner was trained by a Scot rather than an Englishman (see Chapter 32).

22

WHAT NEWMARKET OWES TO AN INDIAN CAVALRY OFFICER

The most prestigious of the Thoroughbred Breeders' Association's much-coveted annual awards is the Andrew Devonshire Bronze – known in his lifetime as the Duke of Devonshire Bronze. The trophy, which depicts the 11th Duke's outstanding racemare, Park Top, is presented to someone felt by members of the TBA council to have made a major contribution to the British racing and breeding industry. Needless to say the roll of honour features many distinguished names from home and abroad.

The Devonshire award for 1993 went to Douglas Gray, former director of the National Stud, but he was not the only Scotsman to be honoured that day. Another recipient was Hawick trainer, Ken Oliver, winner of the Queen Mother's Silver Salver as the National Hunt Breeder of the Year. Furthermore, the owners responsible for the winners of the two broodmare awards also bore the Scottish stamp – the H.J. Joel Silver Salver for the Flat went to the late Sir Robin McAlpine, and Walter Aitken from Langton Mill in Berwickshire took the Dudgeon Cup, the equivalent National Hunt prize.

Not everyone would have realised that Charles Robert Douglas Gray was a Scot, for his background was a cosmopolitan one. Since first going to live in Newmarket, he had always been known as Douglas Gray, to differentiate him from another Colonel Gray – a former chief of police in Malaya, who was then agent to the Jockey Club. Although his parents came from Edinburgh, Dougie, as he was called by his friends, had been born in December 1909 in Peking, where his father, an army surgeon and a veteran of the Boxer Rebellion, was medical officer to the British Ambassador to China.

Destined to follow his father into the army, Dougie was an

accomplished athlete as a young man. He played rugby for Fettes (he was a Scottish schoolboy international at both rugby and hockey) and for the Royal Military College, Sandhurst; and while attending a crammer in Sussex he also played rugby for the county.

There had not been many opportunities for riding in Scotland, but at the RMC he became keen on hunting and competing in point-to-points. Then in 1930, when adding another string to his bow as a qualified pilot, he was commissioned into the army and posted to the Seaforth Highlanders in India. After a year he transferred to Skinner's Horse (1st Duke of York's Cavalry), also known as the 1st Bengal Lancers, which was the only Commonwealth regiment to wear a yellow tunic. Thus began a love affair with India in general and with horses in particular.

Pay in the Indian army was better than the British and the life of a young cavalry officer, even one of relatively modest means, offered wonderful opportunities. Astride a horse all day on parade, Dougie received every encouragement to indulge in mounted sports and he competed in the regimental polo team, rode in races (winning the prestigious Lucknow Chase on Curragh Rose), and engaged in pig-sticking, which was regarded in much the same light as fox-hunting. It was accepted as the most sporting way to dispatch such a formidable four-legged adversary.

In 1934 the twenty-four-year-old subaltern became the youngest rider ever to win the Kadir Cup – or rather his grey steed Granite did (traditionally the credit is given to the horse and not the rider). The Blue Riband of hog-hunting involved a series of heats consisting of four competitors apiece, leading to a final, the winner being the first to draw blood. It was inaugurated in 1869, but discontinued after 1939. The winner received a silver cup presented by the Royal Calcutta Turf Club – this found a permanent home at the Cavalry and Guards Club. From a record entry of 120, Douglas and Granite defeated Roscoe Harvey in the final.

Many years later Roscoe Harvey (10th Hussars) was to become a familiar figure on racecourses at home as the senior stipendiary steward. However, Roscoe and his old friend, 'Babe' Moseley (Royal Dragoons)

– who also took part in that particular Kadir Cup competition – gained rather more notoriety back on the home front many years later by endeavouring, unintentionally, to negotiate a motorway in the wrong direction. Miraculously there were no casualties!

Three years as ADC to the governor of Burma, Sir Archibald Cochrane, entitled Dougie to a period of leave back home, where he sought a suitable mount for the 1938 Grand National. He bought ten-year-old Emancipator, who had been ridden in three Nationals without much luck by Peter Cazalet, and sent him to be trained by Peter Thrale at West Horsley in Surrey. One day he finished third on Emancipator in an amateur riders' chase at Lingfield Park, prior to winning over hurdles on his stable companion, Bob Each Way. Unfortunately all his wasting to ride at Aintree was in vain as Emancipator was brought down at the fence before Becher's on the first circuit.

When war was declared, Skinner's Horse was quickly mechanised and dispatched to the Sudan to confront the Italians in Eritrea and Abyssinia, and this particular soldier was wounded at the Battle of Keren. Keen to be back with horses, he then transferred to the remount department. After serving in Burma and Siam, helping to organise thousands of captured Japanese horses and mules, he was appointed District Remount Officer in the Punjab (now Pakistan), which involved over seventy stallions and 3,500 mares spread over a vast area. He was still there in December 1947 after the partition of India and Pakistan and the end of British rule.

For the next three decades Dougie and his wife, Joan, integrated into life at Newmarket. It was through an introduction to Jack Jarvis – who with Lord Rosebery as his principal owner was one of the leading trainers in the country – that he met his young patron, David Wills. Like Jarvis, he duly received a knighthood. A member of the Bristol tobacco family, Wills bought Hadrian Stud, then in a very dilapidated state, and installed Douglas Gray as manager. It was the beginning of a long and happy association, although David Wills' subsequent decision to support a number of altruistic causes rather than spend the money on bloodstock had obvious repercussions.

Early on, David Wills, who had served in the Cameron Highlanders, owned three runners-up in Newmarket classics – Growing Confidence, Unknown Quantity and Subtle Difference – and then he hit the jackpot with Happy Laughter. A 3,500 guineas yearling, Happy Laughter was rated the leading member of her sex after winning the 1953 One Thousand Guineas. It was a remarkable achievement as she had not long undergone a major sinus operation. Happy Laughter looked to have all the credentials to make a worthy foundation mare, but it was not to be – in fact she was a complete failure at stud.

Situated on prime stud land between Duchess Drive and Woodditton Road, Hadrian Stud was transformed into one of the best appointed private studs in Newmarket (it is now part of Sheikh Mohammed's vast Dalham Hall complex). But in 1958 the owner decided to sell a large proportion of his bloodstock at the Newmarket December Sales when top price of 11,000 guineas was paid for Auld Alliance. At the time she had a two-year-old in the USA named Tomy Lee and he was destined to win the following year's Kentucky Derby, the first British-bred to win America's most prestigious race since Omar Khayyam in 1917.

Much of the emphasis at Hadrian Stud during the 1960s and 1970s revolved around boarders, many of them owned by foreign nationals. They yielded a real star in Noblesse, who was bred and reared on behalf of one of Hadrian's American clients, Mrs P. G. Margetts – the success of Tomy Lee had brought the Newmarket stud to the notice of many influential breeders in the USA. One of the easiest Oaks winners in living memory, Noblesse became the ancestress of three Khalid Abdullah celebrities in Rainbow Quest, Warning and Commander In Chief.

Just a couple of miles away from Hadrian, Dougie and Joan also ran Stetchworth Park Stud from 1960 to 1982 as an independent operation. At first they leased the property from Lord Ellesmere, heir to the Duke of Sutherland, a substantial landowner around Newmarket, whose Scottish home, Mertoun, is near St Boswells on the Borders. The Grays then bought the stud, which they ran as a commercial boarding establishment specialising in sales preparation, before selling the property to the present owner, Bill Gredley, owner-breeder of the 1992 Oaks and Irish Oaks winner, User Friendly, as well as Big Orange, the 2017 Ascot Gold Cup hero.

Douglas Gray was a perfectionist and he was very much hands-on when the occasion arose. Amongst his American clients was Danny van Clief who had horses with Geoffrey Brooke, amongst them Crocket, the unbeaten champion two-year-old of 1962. The following year one of van Clief's yearlings at Stetchworth proved so intractable that it was decided to have him cut and Dougie broke him in himself. Red God's progeny had the reputation of being difficult so it was a relief to everyone when Red Skipper joined his trainer without mishap. After winning three consecutive races as a juvenile, Red Skipper went berserk on the gallops one morning and had to be put down.

Dougie much enjoyed having students at Hadrian. Three of them were stud owner Peter Player, stud manager Michael Bramwell, and David Minton, who became a high-profile bloodstock agent, now operating as Highflyer Bloodstock. Peter Player, a member of the Nottingham tobacco family, took over as manager of Hadrian Stud when Dougie stepped down in January 1971. It is at Peter's Whatton Manor Stud in Nottinghamshire that art historian Dr Catherine Wills, David's daughter, maintains a nucleus of the family mares to this day. The Wills own Knockando, a sporting estate in Morayshire, and many of their horses have Scottish place names.

No sooner had Dougie handed over to Peter Player at Hadrian than he was approached by Lord Wigg, chairman of the Horserace Betting Levy Board, to succeed Peter Burrell (another Duke of Devonshire award-winner) as caretaker director of the National Stud. This short-term appointment had long-term benefits. It was through his American connections that he persuaded Paul Mellon to stand the great Mill Reef at the National Stud, heralding a new era of posterity there. And as his assistant, he chose Michael Bramwell who duly succeeded him as director.

The outstanding middle-distance horse of his generation was Mill Reef, whose victories included the Prix de l'Arc de Triomphe, King George VI and Queen Elizabeth Stakes, Eclipse Stakes and the Derby at three years. He broke a foreleg in training at Kingsclere the ensuing season, but miraculously was saved for stud. He spent the duration of his stallion career at the National Stud and was twice champion sire thanks to two homebred Derby winners, Shirley Heights (1978) and Reference Point (1987). The latter was a posthumous affair as Mill Reef died in 1986.

In his capacity as director of the National Stud, Douglas Gray's diplomacy was sorely tested. Not infrequently, he found himself 'piggy in the middle' between the Levy Board, who financed the operation, and various members of the Jockey Club, who regarded the environs of the stud as their personal property. It had been the practice to rear a few pheasants there. On one memorable occasion a pheasant got up, spooking Tudor Melody as he was being led in hand out at exercise. As a result of this incident, which could have had such serious repercussions for one of the stud's most prestigious stallions, Dougie had the unenviable task of trying to placate a very irate Lord Wigg!

Thirty-seven when he first arrived in Newmarket, Dougie soon resumed point-to-pointing; indeed, he continued to do so until breaking his neck at the Moulton fixture in 1963. In the interim he had made another valiant attempt at the National fences. In the summer of 1948, he acquired the winning hunter chaser, Adam's Caught, who had finished second in the Liverpool Foxhunters', then run over the full National course. Prepared for the following year's Foxhunters' by local trainer and former jump jockey George Archibald, the new partnership were twenty lengths clear of the field approaching the third last fence only to fall. So near and yet so far!

No one could doubt Dougie's sense of commitment and over the years he made a tremendous contribution to the Newmarket community as a whole. Nowadays members of the public have ready access to go round stables and studs, and the opportunity to look behind the scenes owes much to Douglas's pioneering endeavours. During his term as a council member of the Thoroughbred Breeders' Association he arranged and looked after the Newmarket end of tours by overseas visitors, then a totally novel concept.

During his long innings at Hadrian Stud, the former Indian cavalry officer had a staunch ally in secretary Eileen Riley, who subsequently occupied the same position at Sir Robin McAlpine's Wyck Hall Stud, managed by John Waugh. Later, Eileen married the former Newmarket trainer, Geoffrey Barling. When he died she went to live at Fortrose on the Black Isle overlooking the Moray Firth, a long way from her native Devon, but very convenient for a spot of fishing on the Wills' estate!

No one professionally involved in racing benefited more from Douglas Gray's willingness to help than Bruce Hobbs. When Bruce was unceremoniously sacked by Sir David Robinson – at that time the biggest owner in Newmarket, with three private trainers – Dougie coerced a handful of influential owner-breeders, including David Wills, Jim Philipps, Jocelyn Hambro and Tom Blackwell, to form a consortium and establish Bruce Hobbs in the historic Palace House Stables in the middle of town.

Outside racing, the colonel was involved in all sorts of good works, for which he received an OBE in 1998. He was president of the Newmarket British Legion for nearly thirty years; latterly he was also president for the whole of Suffolk and the most effective Poppy Appeal organiser ever. Upon leaving to live closer to his daughter at Greywell, near Basingstoke, he worked tirelessly as president of the Indian Cavalry Officers' Association, making regular trips to India. In 2001, four years after the death of his wife, Joan, he married Helene Wilson, the widow of a brother officer in Skinner's Horse.

Douglas Gray died aged ninety-four in October 2004. With the National Horseracing Museum, of which he was a prime instigator, and the statue of Mill Reef at the National Stud, he should not be forgotten in his adopted home. He had originally conceived the idea of this award-winning museum while visiting the American equivalent in Lexington, Kentucky.

Mill Reef is a direct male-line descendant of the great Eclipse. Douglas was instrumental in the skeleton of this celebrated Thoroughbred being transferred from the dusty vaults of the Natural History Museum in London to become an early exhibit at the new museum in Newmarket High Street. It was later transferred to its present home at the Royal Veterinary College, near Potters Bar in Hertfordshire. From about 1860 to the turn of the century, Eclipse's skeleton was actually owned by the newly established veterinary college in Edinburgh, where Douglas went to school.

23

THE FAMILY THAT CHANGED THE FACE OF BRITAIN

Everyone must have seen a hoarding advertising McAlpine, probably the most instantly recognisable name in the field of construction and civil engineering in Great Britain during the twentieth century. The patriarchal figure is Sir Robert McAlpine. Founder of the eponymous company, he was created a baronet in 1918. His forebears had been forced to migrate from the Highlands to the Lowlands in the mid-eighteenth century following Culloden, that darkest of chapters in Scottish history.

Born in 1847, the original 'Bob the Builder' was brought up at Newarthill, near Motherwell in Lanarkshire – close to Glasgow, the centre of Scotland's industrial heartland. He started work down the coalmines at the age of seven, earning one penny a week. Later he became a bricklayer, would rise at four in the morning and proceed to lay 2,000 bricks during the course of a single day. Robert's first wife was a strict Presbyterian like her husband (both taught at Sunday School). She was the daughter of a stonemason who was an elder of the local kirk.

By the age of twenty-two Robert was self-employed and within six years he owned two brickyards and employed 1,000 men. An intimidating figure as he patrolled his building sites in a dark suit, brandishing a rolled umbrella, he would castigate any workman whom he thought was slacking. Many were Irish labourers and the McAlpine maxim was, 'Keep Paddy on the mixer!' Progress was halted, however, when the collapse of a local bank rendered him bankrupt. Such an occurrence would have been the ruin of most businessmen in those days, but his fortune was fully restored by the time of his death in 1934.

In Scotland, one of the most iconic structures attributed to the McAlpine building expertise is the Glenfinnan viaduct, which carries the popular Fort William to Mallaig railway line, skirting some of the most picturesque countryside in the Highlands. Comprising twenty-one arches, the tallest of which is 100ft, the viaduct was constructed in 1901 and was one of the first structures to bring concrete to the fore as a revolutionary building material. Not for nothing was McAlpine called 'Concrete Bill'.

In 1931 the old firm completed the construction of the Dorchester Hotel. An innovative building, it was constructed of reinforced concrete instead of traditional Portland stone, and insulated with seaweed. Not only did the Dorchester become a favourite rendezvous for the social elite, but it also served as the best air-raid shelter in the metropolis for the duration of the Second World War. As 'new money' the McAlpines did not have a grand London house in the aristocratic tradition, but this hotel on Park Lane overlooking Hyde Park was to serve them well as a luxurious alternative.

As the McAlpine clan prospered down the years, so various family members, all of whom were to become decidedly Anglicized as is the fashion, took up not only racing but also Thoroughbred breeding, with varying degrees of involvement. The four principals have been Sir Robert's third son, Malcolm McAlpine, the latter's son, Robin McAlpine, a grandson, Edwin McAlpine, and a great-grandson, Bobby McAlpine. Extraordinarily Sir Robert and his heir (of the same name) died within a fortnight of one another; the latter owned Richmond II, who finished third in the 1929 Grand National.

Robert Jnr, Malcolm, Robin and Edwin were all directors of the original family firm which became known as Newarthill. They were collectively responsible for a few of London's most prominent edifices beside the Thames: the National Theatre and the Shell Centre on the South Bank, and Canary Wharf in Docklands, a joint venture with Canadian partners. Another famous building was the old Wembley Stadium with its iconic twin towers, which was demolished at the beginning of the twenty-first century. More recently, 'Team McAlpine' has been responsible for the Emirates Stadium built for Arsenal FC, and the circular Olympic Park stadium at Newham in East London, the colossal centrepiece for the 2012 Olympic Games.

Sir Robert Snr's fourth son, Alfred, branched out on his own with the creation of Sir Alfred McAlpine & Sons in 1935. This was to become another hugely successful organisation of which his grandson, Bobby McAlpine, was chairman and chief executive until his retirement in 1994. At one time the two family firms apportioned the country between them so as to avoid direct competition, but they have long since gone their separate ways. Sir Alfred McAlpine & Sons' lasting testimonial is the nationwide motorway network. It also diversified into property and housing with a particular involvement in the USA.

The McAlpine tartan first made its mark on the racecourse with the victory of Malcolm McAlpine's Shaun Spadah in the 1921 Grand National. It was a sensational renewal as Shaun Spadah, a long-backed bay with a Roman nose and a prominent white blaze, was the only one of the thirty-five runners to complete the course without mishap – the remaining three finishers were remounted. Owned by a Scotsman, Shaun Spadah was bred by an Irishman (Paddy McKenna), trained by an Englishman (George Poole) and ridden by a Welshman (Fred Rees). Trained at Lewes, he was buried up on the downs beside the old racecourse.

Proficient at tennis, golf and curling in his day, Malcolm was also a keen angler, either fishing the Usk in South Wales for salmon, or his stretch of the Test at Whitchurch in Hampshire for trout. But racing became his principal relaxation and it took on a new dimension when, before the Second World War, he started breeding bloodstock in Newmarket. Originally he kept his mares at Scaltback Stud and then he leased the adjacent Wyck Hall Stud and Cemetery Stud from the Jockey Club – incongruously for a builder, he never actually owned a stud of his own.

During the war, Malcolm's homebred Seneca gained a sensational victory in the 1941 Champion Hurdle – it was only a second ever appearance over timber for this four-year-old gelding, who was trained by Victor Smyth at Epsom and ridden by his nephew, Ron Smyth. After the war, Vic Smyth provided the McAlpine colours with their first classic success when Zabara won the 1952 One Thousand Guineas and was runner-up in the Oaks. Rated the leading two-year-old filly of her generation, Zabara had been acquired privately as a foal and she was to play a significant role for McAlpine breeding in future generations.

Two of the best homebred colts (both bred officially by McAlpine Farms Limited, representing Malcolm and his sons) were Ratification and Infatuation. There were marked similarities between the pair, quite apart from their names. Both were top two-year-olds trained by Vic Smyth; both won the Greenham Stakes, Newbury's Two Thousand Guineas trial, but were otherwise disappointing three-year-olds; and both stood at Hamilton Stud, Newmarket, before being exported to Japan. An unplaced favourite for the Two Thousand Guineas, Infatuation then injured himself irreparably prior to the Derby, for which he had been very well fancied.

Malcolm McAlpine played an essential role in the Derby being reinstated on Epsom Downs in 1946. The requisite building licence to repair the grandstand had been refused by the Ministry of Works as it was classified as 'non-essential work'. However, Sir Malcolm, representing the Jockey Club, engineered a rethink. Using his own labour, he returned the Derby to its traditional home for the first time since 1939, on schedule. In the long term, he wielded more influence as one of the joint founders with James V. Rank of the Racehorse Owners' Association. Malcolm had been under-bidder to the flour miller for the 1938 St Leger hero, Scottish Union, when that colt was sold as a yearling.

By an extraordinary coincidence Robin McAlpine's one and only classic winner, Circus Plume in the 1984 Oaks, was a granddaughter of his father's solitary classic winner, Zabara. However, Circus Plume was not homebred. Her dam, Golden Fez, was a yearling when Robin's father died in 1967. Successful as a three-year-old at Longchamp, she was culled at the 1977 Newmarket December Sales for 15,000 guineas – and the purchaser was Circus Plume's breeder, Camilla Drake of Somborne Stud in Hampshire.

In the circumstances it must have rankled her Scottish owner that he had to pay no less than 98,000 guineas to secure Circus Plume as a foal. But the expenditure was justified as, in addition to the Epsom classic, she won the Yorkshire Oaks and was runner-up in the Irish Oaks. As a weanling, Circus Plume was reared at Northmore Stud Farm at Exning on the outskirts of Newmarket. This once belonged to James Borland Walker of Johnnie Walker whisky, based in Kilmarnock, and he bred some useful horses there during the 1930s.

Another of Robin McAlpine's culls was Zabara's granddaughter, Amazer. The latter became the foundation mare of John Moore's Biddestone Stud in Wiltshire, breeding the outstanding middle-distance champion, Mtoto, who was trained by a Scotsman, Alec Stewart. Review was another significant broodmare to slip through the net. For Peter Fitzgerald's Mondellihy Stud in Ireland, she produced Pourparler and Fleet, both winners of the One Thousand Guineas in the 1960s, as well as Display, who was runner-up in the same Newmarket classic.

Even though the bloodlines he nurtured often seemed to provide more success for others, Robin McAlpine was a major player, both as an owner and a breeder. During the 1960s John Waugh (see Chapter 5) was his private trainer in Newmarket, and he subsequently took over the management of Wyck Hall Stud, which continued to be leased from the Jockey Club.

Over a period of time Robin became disenchanted with the overheads incurred at home, so that latterly both his racing and breeding stock were divided between Newmarket and France. His principal trainer in England became Geoff Wragg – John Dunlop had handled Circus Plume. At Chantilly his trainers were Alec Head and Edouard Bartholomew. The mares were boarded at the Head family's Haras du Quesnay, near Deauville, where the progeny benefited from the generous French breeders' premiums. Two of his best French-trained performers were the fillies First Waltz (Prix Morny) and Ranimer (Sun Chariot Stakes). At one time the McAlpine horses in France were managed by John Ciechanowski, who was still riding work in Lambourn in his eighties.

Robin McAlpine, on the other hand, never went racing in old age, albeit he kept close tabs on both his racing and breeding stock. He adhered strictly to a policy of retiring his mares aged sixteen, however successful they had proved. He divided his time between his London home in Bloomsbury and a house in Newmarket's Bury Road, next door to Geoff Wragg. Right up to the time of his death in February 1993, aged eighty-six, he continued to do the matings of his substantial broodmare band, a task which gave him enormous pleasure. He used to pore over his private stud book (bound in green leather with gold leaf), giving his secretary and the compiler apoplexy in the process. Whether his bark was worse than his bite is a matter of opinion!

Sir Robin died just a few months before one of his greatest achievements as an owner-breeder. At Royal Ascot two homebred half-brothers brought off a sensational double, Beneficial winning the King Edward VII Stakes and Jeune winning the Hardwicke Stakes. Their dam, Youthful, was awarded the 'Broodmare of the Year' award by the Thoroughbred Breeders' Association. Further accolades were in store as Jeune was then sold to Australia where he was voted 'Horse of the Year' for the 1994–5 season when he triumphed in Australia's most high-profile race, the Melbourne Cup.

This was not the first time that a McAlpine-bred horse had made an impact in the southern hemisphere, as Infatuation sired Showdown, a dual champion sire in Australia. Jeune too became a successful sire 'down under'. Meanwhile Beneficial has become a leading sire of jumpers in Ireland, based at Knockhouse Stud in Co. Kilkenny.

Surprisingly neither Beneficial (by Top Ville) – who had established a new course record when winning the Dee Stakes at Chester in May – nor Jeune (by Kalaglow) were entered for the Derby, but they typified the sort of classic horse that their owner was always striving to produce. As his manager John Waugh said at the time, 'You need to have middle-distance horses to keep improving the breed, don't you?'

Robin McAlpine bequeathed his substantial bloodstock holding equally between his stepdaughter, Rebecca Philipps, and his adoptive daughter, Carolyn Elwes. It comprised over 100 head of stock. Both enthusiasts have changed emphasis to breeding commercially, albeit on a greatly reduced scale. Rebecca operates as Highbury Stud, after the part of London where she lives and runs her publishing house,

Short Books. She is a granddaughter of Harold Nicolson of Sissinghurst in Sussex, the co-founder of publishers Weidenfeld & Nicolson.

Carolyn is married to Nigel Elwes, former chairman of the Thoroughbred Breeders' Association, and before moving to Dorset, they used to live at Sir Robin's former country home, Aylesfield, near Alton, in Hampshire. They trade as Aylesfield Farms Stud. Like Robin, both Rebecca and the Elwes board their mares at Newmarket, the former at John Troy's Willingham House Stud, and the latter at Lord Derby's Woodlands Stud. The best winner to have emerged from this inherited stock since Sir Robin's death is Indian Creek. Bred by Rebecca, he proceeded to emulate Jeune by winning the 2003 Hardwicke Stakes at Royal Ascot.

Lord Edwin McAlpine of Moffat headed the Newarthill branch of McAlpines and was closely involved with the design and construction of Britain's nuclear power stations. In comparison with his cousin Robin, he raced on an altogether smaller scale and a minimal investment. Consequently Edwin McAlpine enjoyed much less success despite having a stud of his own, Dobson's Stud, at his Fawley home, near Henley-on-Thames, in Oxfordshire, which was managed by one of his trainers, Michael Pope.

During his lifetime Sir Robert McAlpine had transferred his allegiance from the Liberals to the Conservatives (his daughter, Roberta, married the eldest son of the Liberal politician and coalition prime minister, David Lloyd George). In the latter part of the twentieth century, both Edwin McAlpine and his son, Alistair, became prominent figures in the Tory hierarchy. In fact they became the first father and son combination to be appointed to the House of Lords in their own right.

The outstanding racehorse to carry Edwin McAlpine's 'yellow, green sleeves, red cap' was Devon Ditty. She cost 7,800 guineas as a yearling and proved the joint champion two-year-old filly of 1978, winning the Cheveley Park Stakes, Flying Childers Stakes, Cherry Hinton Stakes, Lowther Stakes and Princess Margaret Stakes – a truly astonishing haul. Much coveted as a potential broodmare by some of the well-heeled members of the breeding fraternity, she then became the property of Robert Sangster's Swettenham Stud, before joining Khalid Abdullah's fledgling Juddmonte Farms at Wargrave-on-Thames just upstream from Henley-on-Thames.

A succession of second-division stallions stood at Dobson's Stud, amongst them the smart sprinters, Welsh Abbot – who was homebred by Sir Winston Churchill – and Daring March. Another was the popular grey, Birdbrook, trained by Michael Pope. Birdbrook sired a smart homebred filly for Edwin McAlpine in Star Bird (Challenge Stakes). Some useful handicappers carried his colours in the 1950s and 1960s, amongst them Luxury Hotel (Great Metropolitan Handicap), Golden Leg (Wokingham Stakes) and Royal Ridge (Queen's Prize), all prestigious races in those bygone days.

Two years before he died (there was a very grand memorial service at St Paul's Westminster in May 1990), Edwin McAlpine had decided to give up breeding and all his stock were dispersed at Doncaster's 'York Race' Sales in August 1988. Eleven of the mares had been covered by the resident Dobson's Stud stallion, Tremblant.

In their time, both Malcolm and Robin were president of the Racehorse Owners' Association. As one of the country's foremost employers, Robin was one of the first to recognise the essential role played by stable staff and the headquarters of Racing Welfare in Park Lane, Newmarket, is named Robin McAlpine House. Edwin for his part was chairman of the trustees of the British Racing School in Newmarket. Nigel Elwes was to become chairman of both Racing Welfare and the British Racing School, for which he received the CBE in 2008.

Edwin McAlpine's sporting aspirations were confined to an occasional round of golf (he is best remembered for his annual cocktail party in November, held not at the Dorchester but at the Hotel Intercontinental). By contrast, his relative Bobby McAlpine (a grandson of Sir Alfred McAlpine) was an accomplished all-round sportsman in his younger days. Unbelievably for a Scotsman, he played in a squash tournament in Edinburgh representing Wales, qualifying to do so as he was actually born there.

However, it was through playing cricket that he became involved in racing. One of his cricketing colleagues was Ian Lomax, who in the

1950s and 1960s held the licence for his wife, Rosemary, then training at Baydon above Lambourn. Prevailed upon in an unguarded moment to take a share in a jumper called Marnrack, Bobby unwittingly became a racehorse-owner overnight and despite the gelding's limited success his enthusiasm for racing never wavered.

Bobby hit the jackpot when he procured a grey colt at the Newmarket yearling sales for 2,800 guineas. He named him Precipice Wood after the best pheasant stand on his Llanarmon Estate in North Wales. A highly strung individual who required careful handling, Precipice Wood enabled Rosie Lomax to become the first lady to train a winner at Royal Ascot when scoring in the 1969 King George V Handicap. The following season he won the Gold Cup from the previous year's Derby winner Blakeney, the first winner of the Blue Riband to compete in this marathon for a quarter of a century.

Bobby was so enamoured with Precipice Wood that he then acquired his own-brother, another grey, whom he called Coed Cochion (Welsh for 'Precipice Wood') and he joined Jeremy Hindley at Newmarket. Although not as good a racehorse as Precipice Wood, Coed Cochion also gained a Royal Ascot victory, winning the 1976 Queen Alexandra Stakes, the longest Flat race still run in Great Britain. He might well have completed the Ascot Stakes and Queen Alexandra double that year had his jockey, Paul Cook, not listened to Lester Piggott, who observed that they were all going too fast, thus enabling Coed Cochion's pacemaker to score at 66–1!

As half-brothers to the leading National Hunt sire, Spartan General, both Precipice Wood and Coed Cochion stood for a time at Emral Stud, near Wrexham, scene of a historic mining disaster. In fact both stallions died prematurely, but Precipice Wood, who also had brief periods standing in England and Ireland, did well as a sire of jumpers. His outstanding progeny was Forgive'N Forget (1985 Cheltenham Gold Cup), whom Bobby sold in utero. He also featured as the maternal grandsire of Red Marauder (2001 Grand National). Another of his offspring was the top hunter-chaser, Compton Lad. The last National Hunt runner saddled by Michael Dickinson, this grey was bred by Bobby's aunt, Jackie Brutton, and duly inherited by him.

Emral Stud was managed for many years by Jean Broad, with Harry Beeby of Doncaster Bloodstock Sales handling the promotion of the stallions. Emral is situated just a mile into Wales, sandwiched between Cheshire and Shropshire, and this is very much Bobby McAlpine country as he has always lived thereabouts and has long been a familiar figure, stewarding at Bangor-on-Dee, Chester and Haydock Park. He has also played a major role in racecourse management. Chairman of both Bangor and Chester for many years, he was instrumental in both courses being united under the same umbrella.

In 1980 Bobby bought Swettenham Hall, near Congleton, from Robert Sangster. That was just as convenient for Sangster – then involved with the family's Vernons Pools based in Liverpool – as it was for McAlpine: the head office of Sir Alfred McAlpine and Sons was on the outskirts of the city at Hooton. Later Bobby moved back to Cheshire to his present home, Tilstone Lodge, near Tarporley. Nowadays his mares – trading as Tilstone Lodge Stud – are kept just down the road at Goldford Stud, near Malpas.

It has never been altogether clear whether Bobby is trying to breed Flat horses or jumpers. Witness the case of Quarry Wood, the dam of Cormorant Wood and River Ceiriog. Cormorant Wood triumphed in four races which nowadays have Group 1 status: the Champion Stakes, Benson & Hedges Gold Cup (now International Stakes), Lockinge Stakes (dead-heat) and Sun Chariot Stakes. River Ceiriog excelled over timber, winning the Supreme Novices' Hurdle and Scottish Champion Hurdle.

Just like Edwin McAlpine with Devon Ditty, Bobby decided Cormorant Wood was too valuable to keep, but he did retain her half-sister Cormorant Creek. In 2000, her yearling colt by In The Wings was sold for 130,000 guineas from Goldford Stud. As Inglis Drever, he became one of the best hurdlers in the country for Graham and Anthea Wylie, winning the World Hurdle at the Cheltenham Festival in 2005, 2007 and 2008. That is all the more remarkable as he missed the 2006 renewal due to a serious tendon injury. A champion staying hurdler, Inglis Drever was the inaugural winner of the National Hunt 'Order of Merit' award.

Cormorant Wood – who owed her name to an invasion of cormorants which decimated the fish population on the river at Swettenham – was leased to and then bought outright by the late Sheikh Maktoum Al Maktoum of Gainsborough Stud. In 1991 and 1992 her son, Rock Hopper, won the Hardwicke Stakes, the Royal Ascot feature also won by Jeune and Indian Creek.

There were four occasions per annum when Bobby McAlpine never allowed business to take precedence over pleasure – Royal Ascot and the Chester May Meeting, together with the Cheltenham and Liverpool Festivals. It was at Cheltenham that Bobby's sister, Valerie Shaw, twice won the Queen Mother Champion Chase with Pearlyman – and that particular Chester fixture is just as popular with Bobby's long-time friend and one time trainer, Barry Hills.

The McAlpines are by no means the only ones who have been attracted to racing as a family, but they are unusual in so far as they seem to have been keen on both Flat and jumping, and that is probably a fair indication of the real enthusiast. Not everyone enjoys the sport all year round, whatever the weather, but then the Scots are a hardy race. Traipsing round all those construction sites in the middle of winter is not everyone's cup of tea, but obviously it has its compensations!

24

THE MASTERMIND BEHIND A GREAT CHAMPION

Anyone compiling a short list of the greatest racehorses of the twentieth century would have to include Brigadier Gerard and a very high percentage of well-informed opinion would conclude that 'The Brigadier' was the greatest of them all.

In their informative book *A Century of Champions* to celebrate the millennium, joint authors John Randall and Tony Morris of the *Racing Post* listed the top 200 horses to have raced in Great Britain and Ireland during the 1900s. John and Jean Hislop's homebred colt was the chart-topper and fourth in the world rankings – some achievement for a stud which only ever had a handful of modest mares and never patronised the most high-ranking stallions.

Brigadier Gerard was named after the swashbuckling character in Sir Arthur Conan Doyle's historical novels, who served as a cavalry officer in Napoleon's army. Better known as the creator of Sherlock Holmes, the most famous fictional detective of all time, Conan Doyle had a degree in medicine from the University of Edinburgh and evidently the character of Dr Watson was autobiographical.

But that is by no means the only Scottish connection concerning Brigadier Gerard, as both of John Hislop's parents were Scots. His father came from Castlepark, Prestonpans, no distance from Musselburgh. Brought up in a strict Presbyterian household, he was educated locally at Edinburgh Academy, where he was captain of rugby. John's mother hailed from Aucheneck, Drymen, in Stirlingshire, not far from Glasgow with distant views of Loch Lomond.

John himself was born on 12 December 1911, at Quetta in Baluchistan, where his father was serving the British Empire in the 35th Scinde

Horse, having started out as a young officer in the Royal Scots. The original intention had been for John to attend the same school before following his father into the army. But circumstances changed and he went to Wellington College in Berkshire instead.

John was only seven years old when his father, who never enjoyed the best of health, died from pneumonia in March 1919, aged only forty-two. Mother and son returned from India, eventually acquiring a permanent home at Gerrards Cross in Buckinghamshire. As a schoolboy he lived a dual existence in the holidays, spent partly in suburbia, where a neighbour introduced him to the delights of racing at Sandown Park, and partly in Scotland with his mother's sister, Katie, and her husband, Charles Galbraith.

The Galbraiths lived in some style with a full complement of staff at The Barony, just off the road from Dumfries to Moffat. With encouragement from his aunt, a keen follower of the Dumfriesshire hounds, and her Scottish groom, John rode well enough to be a reasonably proficient horseman by the time he arrived at Sandhurst. However, the removal of a kidney (an operation performed in Edinburgh) put paid to his military career. Though his mother had more conventional alternatives in mind, her nineteen-year-old son was determined to pursue his aspiration to become a racehorse trainer.

John Hislop was always slight and dapper and rather effete in appearance. It was through his cousin, John Galbraith, that he became a pupil with Victor Gilpin, initially at Clarehaven Lodge, Newmarket, and then in West Sussex when Victor moved down to train at Michel Grove, part of the Duke of Norfolk's estate near Arundel. All the while he had been perfecting his riding technique by hunting and competing in point-to-points and under Rules, enjoying a modicum of success.

Thanks to Victor Gilpin, John met that accomplished nagsman, Tom Masson, who trained at Lewes in Sussex on the south coast, having been brought up in Perthshire where his father was a farmer. Victor and Tom proved his two great mentors, helping to promote John's aspirations as an amateur jockey, along with two more seasoned trainers, George Todd and Sam Armstrong.

Although he partnered a number of winners over jumps and finished third on Tom Masson's Kami in the 1947 Grand National, John really made his name riding as an amateur on the Flat. The ultimate exponent, he was champion for thirteen consecutive seasons. From 1946 until his retirement in 1956, he won on eighty-seven of his 177 mounts. Most of these winners were insignificant horses in the general scheme of things, but one, Domaha, later made a name for himself as a sire of jumpers.

During the war he served in the Sussex Yeomanry as a gunner, finally joining Phantom, the Special Air Services (SAS) unit responsible for transmitting information from the front line. He was awarded the MC. He returned to live at Lewes after the war when he took up race riding again, but instead of turning to training for a living, he embarked upon a new career writing about racing. It was probably a decision which had more to do with available funds than anything else, as a notepad and pen cost rather less than setting up a racing stable!

The author of a number of erudite books providing a unique perspective into the art of race riding, he was also recognised as an authority on bloodstock breeding, contributing to the *Sporting Chronicle* and the *Sporting Life*. But perhaps his biggest following came through his Sunday racing column in the *Observer* and then the *News of the World*. The latter seemed an unlikely medium for his talents, but doubtless he received an offer that was too good to refuse.

He also became general manager of the glossy periodical, *The British Racehorse* (later the *European Racehorse*) published by Turf Newspapers of which he was a director. Turf Newspapers, which had a shop in Curzon Street, Mayfair, were also responsible for publishing that indispensable work of reference, the *Register of Thoroughbred Stallions*. In association with the *Sporting Chronicle*, then an alternative daily racing paper to the *Sporting Life*, it also published *Raceform* and *Chaseform*.

As an accomplished rider and journalist, he also blazed the trail for two Old Etonians, John Lawrence (later Lord Oaksey) and Marcus Armytage. Both racing correspondents for the *Daily Telegraph*, they likewise excelled in the Grand National, the former finishing second on Carrickbeg in 1963 and the latter achieving the ultimate goal for any rider, professional or amateur, by scoring on Mr Frisk in 1990.

But for John Hislop, who died in 1994, his lasting testimonial will be as the breeder of Brigadier Gerard, although the prime ingredients in this particular story were unquestionably sentiment and luck. No one in their wildest dreams could have envisaged that such an outstanding champion would materialise from such a pedestrian mating.

When John was at his preparatory school in Hemel Hempstead, he took riding lessons and, sharing a fondness for racing, his lady instructor regaled him with the feats of that wonderful filly, Pretty Polly. It so happened that a number of Pretty Polly's descendants were in training at Clarehaven during the 1930s – the filly herself had been trained there by Victor Gilpin's father, Peter. So John resolved that if and when he ever started breeding bloodstock he would endeavour to buy one of her descendants.

The opportunity occurred at Tattersalls' Newmarket December Sales of 1945 when Pretty Polly's five-year-old great-granddaughter, Brazen Molly, who had never seen a racecourse, was acquired as a barren mare for 400 guineas. Brazen Molly, who became progressively blind, was owned in partnership with a friend to help defray expenses and the progeny were offered for sale. However, when John and his second wife, Jean, purchased a small stud of their own at East Woodhay, near Newbury, they decided to breed to race rather than to sell.

So they bought out Pat Dyke Dennis, their partner in Brazen Molly's last foal, a filly by Prince Chevalier. Two years' training bills from George Todd at Manton was just about all that the Hislops had to show for the racecourse exertions of La Paiva as she was called. Certainly there could have been no particular aspirations when La Paiva was mated with Queen's Hussar, who stood just down the road from East Woodhay at Lord Carnarvon's Highclere Stud. The result was Brigadier Gerard.

As Dick Hern had trained his year-senior half-brother, Town Major, to score on his two-year-old debut for Jean Hislop, it was decided to send Brigadier Gerard to join him in training at West Ilsley. His career was to be one of unbelievable brilliance. Ridden exclusively in public by stable jockey Joe Mercer, carrying Jean's violet and cerise colours, the son of Queen's Hussar was beaten only once in eighteen starts.

As a two-year-old, the Brigadier won his only four outings, culminating with victory in the Middle Park Stakes. That season he was rated third on the Two-Year-Old Free Handicap behind an unusually outstanding pair of juveniles in Mill Reef and My Swallow. They were expected to dominate the following season's Two Thousand Guineas, but in finishing second and third respectively at Newmarket they were comprehensively beaten by the Brigadier who was making his seasonal reappearance.

That classic victory did not come out of turn. During the war John Hislop had acquired his very first broodmare, Orama, privately for £370, together with a filly foal at foot. As Respite, the latter was destined to become the dam of the 1953 Two Thousand Guineas winner, Nearula. Two years earlier Brazen Molly's son, Stokes, had finished runner-up in the Newmarket classic – like Respite, he had been sold as a yearling. Rather foolishly John never retained any of Orama's female relatives.

Connections avoided the temptation of running the Brigadier in the Derby (he was not bred to stay the distance), leaving the way clear for Mill Reef to gain a memorable victory. Instead he went to Royal Ascot to win the St James's Palace Stakes and was unbeaten in his remaining starts that season, the Sussex Stakes, Goodwood Mile, Queen Elizabeth II Stakes and Champion Stakes. The only chink in his armour proved to be soft ground. Such were the prevailing conditions when he only just scraped home that season at Royal Ascot and Newmarket.

As a four-year-old he won the Lockinge Stakes, Westbury Stakes, Prince of Wales's Stakes, Eclipse Stakes, King George VI and Queen Elizabeth Stakes, Queen Elizabeth II Stakes and Champion Stakes, an unprecedented haul of Group trophies.

Midsummer provided two sensational performances – victory in the 'King George' where his sheer class enabled him to prevail over one and a half miles, and the Benson & Hedges Gold Cup (now International Stakes), where he was beaten by that year's Derby winner, Roberto, the solitary reversal of his entire innings. Both protagonists finished in record time so the superiority of the inconsistent Roberto that afternoon seemed totally inexplicable, but then again horses are not machines.

Not surprisingly the Brigadier established all sorts of precedents. He became the only English classic winner of the twentieth century to remain unbeaten in ten or more races at two and three years old, and the only classic winner in that period to win seven or more races at four years old. His record of consistency at the highest level was breathtaking and it is a great tribute to his soundness that he never seemed to have a day's illness all the time he was in training.

As small-scale owner-breeders, who had beaten the big battalions at their own game, the Hislops were widely applauded not only for the way in which they had campaigned their horse over three seasons, but also for fending off all offers for their champion when the time did come for him to go to stud. Having declined a substantial £250,000 for him at the conclusion of his two-year-old career and, in an age when American-breds like Mill Reef and Roberto dominated the racing scene, they could have literally named their price.

Brigadier Gerard was retired for the 1973 season to stand at Lady Macdonald-Buchanan's Egerton Stud, Newmarket, adjacent to the National Stud, where his great contemporary Mill Reef embarked upon his innings as a stallion. Ironically the former, who retired completely sound, totally failed to come up to expectations as a progenitor, whereas the latter, who was saved for stallion duties after pioneering surgery for a broken leg, proved a dual champion sire.

The Hislops were intent on controlling Brigadier Gerard as a stallion in the same way that they had mapped out his racing programme. They syndicated the horse amongst essentially English-based breeders, retaining sixteen of the customary forty shares, but their expectations that he would prove nothing less than the saviour of British bloodstock proved to be wishful thinking. Indeed, one of the only two Group 1 winners that he managed to sire, Light Cavalry (St Leger), was home-bred by Jim Joel – it was not just coincidence that John did all the matings for Joel's Childwick Bury Stud.

There had been some unfortunate repercussions following a falling-out with Dick Hern. The most public was the Hislops' refusal to subscribe to the European Breeders' Fund, by which the price of an annual stallion nomination helped contribute towards owners' costs as prize money, with corresponding prizes for breeders. So Brigadier Gerard became the only British-based stallion of note whose progeny became ineligible for the qualifying races. The Hislops saw the system as a restrictive practice and they were not prepared to be press-ganged into compliance.

It was also reputed that Brigadier Gerard had become difficult to handle as a stallion. Indeed, rumour had it that he had actually become savage. At one time there was a story doing the rounds that Jean Hislop, a formidable lady at the best of times, had marched into his box despite being forewarned of the stallion's increasingly dubious temperament and that he had soon deposited her on the ground. If true, it must have been a very frightening and rather humiliating experience.

In 1984 the Hislops sold the house and stud at East Woodhay to Juliet Reed, who renamed it Woodhaven Stud (four years later she won the Grand National with Rhyme 'N' Reason), moving to Regal Lodge, Exning, on the outskirts of Newmarket, previously home to the National Stud director, Michael Bramwell.

The Hislops brought with them their life-size bronze of Brigadier Gerard, sculptured by their good friend, John Skeaping. The imposing statue now stands proudly in the pre-parade ring on the Rowley Course, a lasting testimonial to one of the truly great horses to have graced the Turf in the twentieth century. Brigadier Gerard died in retirement in October 1989, aged twenty-one.

25

DIFFICULT STALLIONS WERE HIS BREAD AND BUTTER

If ever a man was hoist by his own petard it was Ian Muir, who operated for so long as the master of Fawley Stud, next door to Whatcombe, home to a succession of Thoroughbred stallions on the Oxfordshire/Berkshire border, above the Newbury to Wantage road.

On the other side of the valley are the famous Woolley Down gallops. Historic Whatcombe is where Dick Dawson (no relation to the Scottish Dawsons) trained two of his three Derby winners, Trigo and Blenheim, between the two World Wars; where Arthur Budgett trained two more in the half-brothers, Blakeney and Morston, in 1969 and 1973 respectively; and where Paul Cole maintained the tradition with Generous in 1991.

The numerous stallions to have stood at Fawley Stud never aspired to anything quite so prestigious as a Derby winner. Because Ian Muir could never resist a challenge, he earned a very deserved reputation for being able to handle difficult horses, be they savage or merely idiosyncratic, and so he was always in demand to take on some wayward individual whom no one else wanted. Consequently, Fawley, which operated as a family concern for so many years, became a sort of remand home for temperamental stallions and the high success rate that Ian Muir achieved bears testament to his unstinting dedication to their welfare.

Ian Muir was just six months old when his parents and sister moved to Fawley from the hamlet of Combe, just a mile distant, where he was born. He was actually christened David John, but has always been known by the Gaelic form of his second name. By a remarkable coincidence, the original Farnborough Downs Farm at Combe is owned by Jessica White, one of the late Lord Howard de Walden's daughters, and generations of the Muir family were tenants of the Howard de Waldens, near Kilmarnock, in Scotland.

Ian Muir's father was brought up on that farm in Ayrshire, his mother came from Galloway, and his wife, Agnes, also hails from Ayrshire. No one who knew Ian could fail to recognise all his admirable Scottish qualities – the hard work ethic, the preference for plain speaking and the flair for innovation; he also had a deep religious conviction. And like Alec Kilpatrick (see Chapter 14), that noted trainer of jumpers who came down from Ayrshire, Ian Muir had a background in which Clydesdales played a prominent role. His father was a well-known Clydesdale breeder, but the era of workhorses was coming to an end when he died.

Ian left school aged fourteen during the Second World War, as there was no one else to drive the new tractor and he soon exhibited his skills by winning the championship at the Lambourn ploughing match. A few years later a road accident was to change Ian's life forever – someone ran into the car he was driving, killing his father. Fortunately the Wroughtons, whose Woolley Estate owned the land at Fawley, agreed that the Muirs could continue with the tenancy of this farm of nearly 1,000 acres and gradually they built up the dairy herd to 125 cows to augment the arable and sheep side.

As local landowners, the Wroughton family of Woolley Park have played a 'behind the scenes' role in terms of racing locally. They made a major contribution as owners of the Woolley Down gallops, but their influence extends further as Philip Wroughton was one of the original patrons of Newbury racecourse when it opened for business on 26 September 1905. Indeed, the very first race on that memorable afternoon was the Whatcombe Handicap over five furlongs, worth a princely £160.

The Muirs always had a great love of horses and as children they all rode and hunted, but breeding Thoroughbreds really started as nothing more than a hobby. Back in the 1950s, Ian went to see the stallion, Coup de Myth, owned by Alec Pope, the father of Streatley/Blewbury trainer Michael Pope, with a view to buying him, but the horse failed the vet on account of his wind. A few days later Alec Pope telephoned to say that Ian could have the horse as a present provided he, Alec, could send five mares per season free of charge. The deal was done.

Although Coup de Myth was not fashionably bred, he had shown some ability as a racehorse. Successful on the Flat and over hurdles in England, he had also won a mile nursery at the Curragh where he was runner-up in the 1945 Two Thousand Guineas and Derby. Coup de Myth, who had been standing at Upper Basildon, near Pangbourne, at a fee of eleven guineas, was advertised initially at the same figure at North Farm Stud, Fawley, and this eventually rose to twenty-one pounds.

It was following a succession of matings with Coup de Myth that What A Din, an old mare that Ian Muir had procured for twenty-seven pounds and ten shillings to settle a bad debt, foaled What A Myth. As an unbroken three-year-old he was sold privately for £1,000 to the Findon trainer, Ryan Price. The chesnut gelding then raced for Sir Archibald James and Lady Weir from Kilwinning in Ayrshire. The partnership was dissolved when Ryan Price brought him back on Lucy Weir's behalf for 4,200 guineas at the Ascot Sales in November 1964. By the close of the 1967–8 season, he had won twenty-one races, including the Whitbread Gold Cup, Mildmay Memorial Chase, Rhymney Breweries' Chase and Mandarin Chase, to prove one of the best staying chasers around.

At that point What A Myth appeared to lose his form, but a spell of hunting in Leicestershire rekindled his enthusiasm to such good effect that he proceeded to win two hunter chases prior to a glorious victory in the 1969 Cheltenham Gold Cup, where he encountered the soft ground that he relished. That very year Ryan Price also trained Lord Weir's brilliant and unbeaten juvenile, Quarryknowe, who was by Quorum, sire of triple Grand National hero Red Rum.

Retired immediately after Cheltenham, twelve-year-old What A Myth has the distinction of being the oldest winner of the Gold Cup, along with Lord Bicester's great Silver Fame, who scored in 1951. The race was first run in 1924. Tied Cottage was also twelve years of age when he finished first in 1980, only to be disqualified.

The only other memorable winner sired by Coup de Myth, who died suddenly in 1966 aged twenty-four, was Baulking Green. Another chesnut and one of the most popular and prolific winning hunter-chasers of his generation, Baulking Green was bred in the village of that name in the Vale of the White Horse and raced for his breeder, Jim Reade, a hunting farmer in the Old Berks country. Baulking Green was the first good horse trained by Tim Forster, then based locally at Letcombe Bassett, and he saddled him to win the United Hunts' Cup at the Cheltenham Festival four times.

Over a period of time Ian Muir became great friends with Ryan Price, a fine all-round horseman, and it worked to their mutual advantage. Many of the Findon trainer's most famous horses would spend their summer holidays at Fawley and two of them – Nuage Dore and No Worry – became stallions there. Ryan Price never suffered fools gladly and he dispensed plenty of good advice. One view he strongly advocated was, 'Always fill your yard with other people's horses.' Whenever possible Ian Muir adhered to this dictum – to such good effect, in fact, that he was eventually able to buy his rented property outright.

Two other personalities who feature prominently in the development of Fawley Stud were Patrick and Doris Honner, who lived locally at Lovelocks, under the south side of the M4 at junction 14, the turning for Hungerford and Lambourn. Lovelocks is now home to one of Nicky Henderson's owners, Christopher Hanbury. An independent bloodstock agent, Pat Honner and his wife boarded a handful of broodmares at Fawley, trading as Shamrock Stud. Previously he had been more involved with breeding jumpers and in fact he was responsible for Fighting Line, winner in 1949 of the first Welsh National to be run at Chepstow.

Much of Shamrock Stud's success revolved around the mare, Codicil, who did well with Fawley stallions. To the grey Zeus Boy she bred Grandpa's Legacy, the dam of triple Group scorer Consol (Geoffrey Freer Stakes), and to Sahib she produced Mary Green. Mated with yet another Fawley resident, Lombard, Mary Green foaled Ian Muir's homebred Destroyer. Successful in the Henry II Stakes and third to two outstanding stayers in Gildoran and Longboat in the 1985 Ascot Gold Cup, Destroyer became a stallion in Ayrshire.

235

Grandpa's Legacy, Consol and Destroyer were all first foals. Much the best filly bred by Shamrock Stud was Himawari, whose sire, Derring-Do, had been trained next door at Whatcombe by Arthur Budgett. Sold for 17,000 guineas as a yearling, a very substantial sum in those days, Himawari won the Falmouth Stakes and was runner-up in the Coronation Stakes and Nassau Stakes, all Group 1 races nowadays.

Additional stallions resident at Fawley included Three Cheers, Tacitus, Silver Cloud, Crisp and Even, Track Spare, Andrea Mantegna, Supreme Sovereign, Buckskin, Tender King, Satin Wood, Northern State, Faustus, Reprimand, Northern Game and Averti. It would be fair to say that few of them qualified as premier-division stallions. Some were not well enough bred to make the grade, while others were not sufficiently good racehorses to attract the necessary support. One horse who had all the credentials to make a top-class stallion was Supreme Sovereign, but alas he had another shortcoming.

A grey, Supreme Sovereign was not the first or the last stallion to arrive at Fawley with the reputation for being a handful. Indeed, a huge notice outside his box proclaimed, 'Beware – this horse is dangerous. Only authorised persons to handle this horse.' In the old days savage stallions were not uncommon, which was probably more a reflection on the way they were kept in solitary confinement than anything else. Whatever the cause for Supreme Sovereign's behaviour, he had commenced his stallion career in Ireland where he had actually mauled someone, inflicting a broken arm and three broken ribs in the process.

Successful in the Lockinge Stakes, which is run at Newbury, the racecourse closest to Fawley, Supreme Sovereign put the fear of God into everyone. Silver, as he was known on the stud, would strike out, bare his teeth and roar like a lion. However, he was a hydrophobic and as long as one was equipped with a running hosepipe or carrying a bucket of water he would beat a retreat. For added protection, a semi-circular wire-mesh barrier was erected round his stable door with free access to a paddock behind and an ingenious chute to provide access for covering his mares. He refused to be shod by the farrier and in the end his hooves were kept trimmed with an electric grinder.

After four traumatic seasons at Fawley, this enigmatic grey was sold to Hungary, and against all the odds completed the long road journey to Budapest accompanied by two broodmares, without mishap. There was probably relief all round when 'Jaws', as he was called by some, died a couple of years later. His outstanding progeny was the 1975 One Thousand Guineas heroine, Nocturnal Spree, another grey.

Someone else who benefited considerably from Ian Muir's expertise was Roger Denton of now defunct Benham Stud, to the west of Newbury, no distance from Fawley. Initially Jellaby, also a grey, who had been bought out of Ryan Price's stable, refused to cover mares. Having acquired the horse from the insurance company, Roger then put him back in training and he gained a second victory in the Brigadier Gerard Stakes. Somehow an interim season at Fawley cured the horse's aversion to covering and in due course he was sold for an appreciable sum to Kuwait – mission accomplished.

During the 1980s Fawley Stud changed hands not once but twice. First Ian Muir sold it to Esal Commodities, which was primarily a bookmaking concern, and when that organisation went into liquidation the stud was bought by John Deer, managing director of precision engineers Renishaw. The first good horse he bred there was Averti and this sprinter, who was trained in Lambourn by Ian Muir's son, William, stood at Fawley, until his owner-breeder sold the stud, transferring the mares to his own Oakgrove Stud, next to Chepstow racecourse. Averti is the sire of Avonbridge, a half-brother to Patavellian, both of whom won John Deer the Prix de l'Abbaye de Longchamp, a race in which Averti finished second.

Ian and Agnes Muir had five children, fourteen grandchildren and numerous great-grandchildren, and at one time all were living within fifteen miles of Fawley. Indeed, this hamlet seemed to be inhabited exclusively by Muirs, with many of them working on the stud. For a number of years when Ian was manager, his two sons Iain and William shared responsibility as stud groom, the former looking after the breeding stock and the latter taking charge of the youngsters and horses out of training.

In 1990 Willie took out a licence to train in Lambourn at Stan Mellor's old base, Linkslade, next door to Barry Hills at the foot of the historic Faringdon Road gallops. Three Group winners trained by Willie are the top sprinter Averti (1997 King George Stakes), and the middle-distance performers Enforcer (2005 Darley Stakes), who was placed in a number of Group 1 events, and Enroller (2009 John Porter Stakes). Other stable stalwarts include Almaty, Material Witness, Texas Gold and Zargus.

Nowadays Willie (father-in-law of jockey Martin Dwyer) is also a director of Heatherwold Stud at Burghclere on the other side of Newbury, where Iain is stud groom. The stud is actually owned by Michael Caddy, a Hong Kong banker. It was at Heatherwold that the 1990 Prix de l'Arc de Triomphe winner, Saumarez, was bred – he features as the maternal grandsire of the 2007 Derby hero, Authorized. The late Ann Jenkins, for so long manager of Heatherwold Stud, subsequently bred an outstanding filly in Lush Lashes.

Meanwhile, Ian Muir remained at Fawley, having retained that part of the property known as North Farm Stud, which only came into being after protracted negotiations with the local planning authority. Extending to over 200 acres and nearly 100 boxes, this is managed by Ian's youngest daughter, Grace, but nowadays she has another increasingly time-consuming role. Ian died in 2014.

Grace is the founder and chief executive of HEROS (Homing Ex-Racehorses Organisation Scheme). This is one of four welfare centres funded by Retraining of Racehorses, the British Horseracing Authority's official charity for the welfare of horses who have retired from racing. Based at North Farm, this enterprise was granted charitable status in July 2006 and was officially launched at Newbury racecourse that September.

HEROS handles in the region of 100 ex-racehorses per year. Many go on to excel in a wide variety of disciplines, while others, who because of accident or injury are unsuitable for riding, find a permanent home at North Farm where they are cared for indefinitely. Fortunately the essential role that such centres now fulfil is well recognised by the racing public and HEROS has benefited enormously through charity race days sponsored locally at Newbury as well as other racecourses in the south.

26

NOT SUCH A GAY FUTURE

It is not particularly surprising that Old Harrovians have made, and continue to make, a marked contribution to Turf affairs. Heading the league table is Sir Winston Churchill, which is astonishing considering how late in life he became involved and how little time he had to devote to racing. Not only was he the owner of that popular grey, Colonist II, but he was also an owner-breeder of note. Amongst the horses he bred at his Newchapel Stud, near Lingfield, in Surrey (later Churchill Stud), were that top-class pair of chestnut contemporaries, High Hat and Vienna.

At present there is a clutch of old boys in the Newmarket training ranks – Sir Mark Prescott, Bart, William Haggas, Willie Jarvis and James Eustace. Meanwhile, the media can claim such familiar faces as the late Julian Wilson, John McCririck and Nick Luck. Far less well known, not being television 'personalities', are Peter Player of Whatton Manor Stud, where the sensational Hungarian-trained sprinter, Overdose, was bred, and Rhydian Morgan-Jones. Both have made their mark on the administrative side of affairs.

However, Antony Collins from Ayrshire is one Old Harrovian who will be remembered for a rather different reason – 'The Gay Future affair' as it became known. Just like his uncle, Ian Collins, a patron of Atty Corbett's stable, Tony had experience as an amateur rider and permit-holder – that is, he had a licence to train under Rules horses owned by himself or immediate members of his family. Along with fellow Scots John Hislop and the Stirling brothers, who also feature in this book, Ian served with distinction in the SAS (Special Air Services) during the war.

Ian Collins subsequently became vice chairman and managing

director of the eponymous publishing house, William Collins, but eschewing the opportunity to join the family business, Ian's nephew Tony, an inveterate bon vivant, decided upon a career as a stockbroker. For him the racecourse and the challenge of taking on the bookmakers has always had an irresistible appeal. Amusing and hospitable, he has always entertained guests at his home for the Ayr Western Meeting and down south at Royal Ascot, the July Meeting at Newmarket or the Cheltenham Festival.

Tony Collins enjoyed the hands-on experience as a permit-holder too, albeit he never had more than a handful of moderate horses at his yard, Torley at Southwood near Troon, home of the famous golf course. It was at the Newmarket July Meeting of 1974, as a guest of the Curragh Bloodstock Agency, that he mentioned to one of the directors, Johnny Harrington (whose widow Jessica has made such a name for herself as a trainer in Ireland), that he was contemplating buying a potential jumper to add to his modest string.

Johnny Harrington also trained a small string of jumpers in Ireland at that juncture. That January, he had bought a chesnut gelding by Bally Joy – who had just celebrated his fourth birthday – out of John Oxx's stable. The day after Harrington and Collins met at Newmarket in the summer, Irish trainer Edward O'Grady bought Gay Future – as the Bally Joy gelding was called – for £5,000, less a commission of five per cent. The purchase was made over the telephone on behalf of three owners from Cork, headed by builder Tony Murphy.

Unknown to one another at the time, Collins and Murphy were to become the principal conspirators in the Gay Future affair. The Cork confederacy decided to execute an audacious gamble and not long afterwards Edward O'Grady flew to Scotland to discuss plans for Gay Future. An inveterate gambler, Tony Collins agreed to join in the fun and games. Gay Future was sold to him for a nominal one pound and shortly afterwards a chesnut contemporary by Arctic Chevalier arrived at his Ayrshire stables, while the real Gay Future remained in Edward O'Grady's care.

The planned betting coup was an extremely ingenious one. Gay Future was one of three horses, all ostensibly trained by Tony Collins, to be entered to run on the August Bank Holiday Monday – Gay Future at Cartmel, Opera Cloak at Plumpton and Ankerwyke at Southwell. Gay Future would be backed in doubles and trebles with the other two, but Opera Cloak and Ankerwyke would then be withdrawn on the day, whereby all the multiple bets would automatically became single bets on Gay Future.

The whole success of the operation depended on three contingencies. Firstly getting sufficient money on Gay Future at a price that justified the execution of such a daring scheme; secondly ensuring that such a volume of money wagered off course did not get back to Cartmel to reduce the starting price (hence the choice of a minor meeting at one of the busiest times of the season); and last but not least, making sure that Gay Future actually won without suspicions being raised that anything untoward had taken place.

It was a tall order, but Gay Future himself was in good hands. Edward O'Grady was an experienced trainer, who knew exactly how to prepare a runner for a specific objective. The horse had already proved himself in bumpers (NH Flat races) when in five outings for Johnny Harrington he had never finished out of the first four, having scored at Thurles and finished runner-up at Limerick Junction. At that stage Gay Future had never left the ground in public, but he showed his handler that he was a natural when schooled over hurdles.

Here was a promising novice who was probably good enough to go to the National Hunt Meeting at Cheltenham, never mind a nondescript event, the Ulverston Novices' Hurdle, at lowly Cartmel. So the countdown began to Monday, 26 August. On the day, Gay Future himself came across on the ferry from his home outside Thurles in Co. Tipperary and the horse-box proceeded to the prearranged rendezvous, a telephone kiosk near the racecourse, where he changed places with the horse that had been masquerading as Gay Future at Tony Collins's stable.

So far so good. Meanwhile the members of the syndicate delegated to actually put the money on left their temporary headquarters at a hotel in central London, to place bets to the tune of £30,000 in betting shops within a ten-mile radius. So as not to draw undue attention to

241

their activities, these wagers included some single bets, but they were mostly doubles and trebles, with stakes of five pounds, ten pounds or twenty pounds only. As neither Opera Cloak nor Ankerwyke had any worthwhile form, the bets individually appeared harmless enough.

The tension at Cartmel must have been excruciating. Again no stone was left unturned and all sorts of red herrings were laid. In fact Gay Future went to post at Cartmel with Racionzer, a 'stable companion' who was backed sufficiently in the ring to suggest that he and not Gay Future was the stable fancy, a diversion that was enhanced by the fact that it was Gay Future's jockey and not the rider of Racionzer who wore the distinguishing cap.

Gay Future himself had been sweating profusely in the paddock (thanks to the careful application of some soap flakes), and his 'inexperienced' amateur jockey mounted with very long leathers – this was actually Ireland's champion amateur, Timmy Jones! Meanwhile Tony Collins had added to the subterfuge by travelling all the way south to Plumpton, which implied that Opera Cloak was fancied more than his two runners at Cartmel. It was all very cloak and dagger!

By the time the bookmakers realised something was amiss, the result was a *fait accompli* and Gay Future had romped home by fifteen lengths at the rewarding odds of 10–1. However, fate intervened. It just so happened that a journalist telephoned Collins's stables to enquire about the two non-runners, only to be told by an innocent party that both horses had never left the yard. Immediately alarm bells began to ring and consequently most of the off-course payment was withheld. What had appeared to be the perfect starting-price coup had come gloriously unstuck.

In fact many people sympathised with the perpetrators of this enterprising scam. The Director of Public Prosecutions took a long time to decide that a prosecution was justified and eighteen months elapsed before the case was heard at Preston Crown Court on 3 February 1976. Although there were as many as eight co-conspirators only Tony Murphy and Tony Collins stood in the dock, charged with conspiracy to cheat and defraud bookmakers – Edward O'Grady was deemed to have no case to answer. Meanwhile Tony Murphy expressed concern that the trial should take place so close to Birmingham, as totally unfounded rumours spread that the coup had been engineered so that the proceeds could help the cause of the IRA.

The English judicial system seemed rather more favourably disposed to the accused than the Jockey Club. In his summing up, the trial judge, Mr Justice Caulfield, pointed out that racing was a self-regulatory body and that doubtless it would administer its own summary justice. He also emphasised that the modus operandi of placing bets piecemeal on a horse running at a meeting where there was no 'blower system' in operation exhibited cunning and cunning was not illegal. In other words the onus was on the bookmakers to ensure that they had their own safeguards in place against any such eventuality. Notwithstanding the judge's comments, which seemed to direct the jury towards an acquittal, the two miscreants were found guilty by a majority of ten to two.

The culprits each received a fine of £1,000 and were ordered to pay £500, which represented a very small proportion towards the costs of the prosecution. Predictably the Jockey Club took a far more serious view of the whole affair. Both Collins and Murphy were warned off for ten years, which meant that they were banished from all British racecourses and from Newmarket Heath, albeit the ruling did not include Ireland. Within six years Tony Murphy was dead. Meanwhile Tony Collins must have rued the day that he got involved as he found the sentence a long and painful one.

Not long afterwards Gay Future was acquired by the flamboyant Scottish bookmaker, John Banks (see Chapter 17), but not before he had scored by fifteen lengths at Hexham, ridden by Jonjo O'Neill. The gelding started even-money favourite, with Tony Collins wagering £4,000 at 11–10. Detective Chief Superintendent Terence O'Connell of Scotland Yard, who was still investigating the case, had quizzed Tony Collins as to whether Timmy Jones would be coming over from Ireland to ride Gay Future. His owner therefore thought it prudent to substitute Gordon W. Richards' stable jockey, thus forging a long-lasting friendship which has survived down to the present time.

Another leading racing personality who stood by Tony Collins during all these trials and tribulations was his good friend, Robert Sangster. They had known one another during National Service when both failed to get a commission. Many years later, Sangster invited his old friend to take a stake in some of his horses, and this Tony did, so frequently in fact that he was dubbed 'Mr Ten Percent'. His most rewarding involvement came during the 1990s thanks to one of Sangster's Swettenham Stud mares, Kanmary.

A grey, Kanmary had three smart sons, Colonel Collins, Captain Collins and Commander Collins, all named by Sangster in honour of his old army chum (he always referred to him as 'The Colonel'). All were trained by Peter Chapple-Hyam at Manton. Two of them were top-class: Colonel Collins finished third in the Two Thousand Guineas, the Derby and the Irish Derby, and Commander Collins won the Racing Post Trophy. Kanmary had her last foal, City Leader, at the advanced age of twenty-two, and he won the 2007 Royal Lodge Stakes in the Sangster colours.

The Sangster connection also provided Tony Collins with a memorable day on Sunday, 25 May 1997, when Single Empire, carrying his own colours of green, white sleeves, red cap with white hoop, won the Italian Derby by a nose. However, that afternoon Tony Collins chose to be at the Curragh, where Romanov, in whom he had an interest, carried the Sangster colours into third place in the Irish Two Thousand Guineas. So it was Tony's daughter, Gay, who led Single Empire into the winner's enclosure at Rome's Capannelle racecourse.

Despite all those high days and holidays shared with Robert Sangster, it is that August Bank Holiday Monday in 1975 for which Tony Collins will always be remembered. In 1995, twenty years to the day after that never-to-be-forgotten occasion, the former permit-holder from Troon was back at Cartmel for rather a different reason – as sponsor of the Gay Future Hurdle. Obviously 'all was forgiven' so far as the Cartmel executive was concerned.

Tony Collins says, 'It was all a long time ago, but whether justice was done is open to question. Whatever the rights and wrongs of the verdict, ten years' suspension was a savage sentence compared to the modern tariff for misdemeanours.'

they had four children, Susan and her three brothers, George, William and Charles. Their mother's maiden name was McCosh – she came from a family of prominent steel manufacturers from Glasgow.

Over the years Wilf Crawford trained mainly for family and friends, but as far as he and his wife were concerned, virtually all the success they enjoyed stemmed from the purchase of one individual. In August 1954 he bought an unraced three-year-old filly by Etoile de Lyons out of Singing Sword at the bloodstock sales of Messrs T., S. and L. Petch in Stockton for 150 guineas. In due course Singing Sword would feature as the granddam of the 1964 Welsh National winner, Rainbow Battle.

Duly named Lothian Princess, the Etoile de Lyons filly developed into quite a stable star, scoring eight times – twice over hurdles and six times over fences. She also became responsible for a veritable dynasty of homebred winners with the first name Lothian – a means of identification frequently associated with breeds of livestock rather than bloodstock. Her first two offspring were the smart geldings, Lothian Prince and Lothian Brig, the winners of eighteen chases between them.

Lothian Princess's remaining produce were all fillies, three of them including Lothian Lady being own-sisters to Lothian Brig, who was by Scotland's leading National Hunt sire, New Brig. Not only had New Brig been trained by George Boyd at Dunbar just down the A1 (in adverse weather conditions the Crawford horses would work on the sands at Westbarns), he was also standing at that time at the Forth Stud at Dirleton, which is even closer to Haddington. So here was a Scottish-trained horse earning renown as a stallion in Scotland, quite an unusual occurrence.

Although Lothian Lady never managed to win, she proved a prolific broodmare before she died in May 1989 aged twenty-two. She had no fewer than ten 'Lothian' offspring, while ensuing generations produced a multitude of additional ones. The best of her sons were Spartan Prince and the unfortunate Lothian Captain, who broke his back when still comparatively young. The former was by Spartan General and the latter by Roscoe Blake. They stood at John Thorne's Chesterton Stud in Warwickshire and with Jean Broad at Emral Stud in North Wales respectively, two public studs that Wilf Crawford patronised on a regular basis. Subsequently the family sprang back to prominence with the talented chaser, Lothian Falcon.

Few of Wilf Crawford's patrons were in the major league as owners, but that is not to say some had not enjoyed success at the top level. One such owner was Richard Stevenson from Perth. A former RAF Wing Commander who had been awarded an Air Force Cross, and an enthusiastic golfer, he had owned a top performer in Wise Child, trained by Verly Bewicke. The best chaser he had with Wilf Crawford was Final Approach. Another of his owners, Maude Milne Green from Edinburgh, had enjoyed conspicuous success with Stewart Wight.

Looking back over his career, Wilf Crawford nominated Final Approach as one of his stable stars along with such stalwarts as Hamilcar, Mirval, Dunrobin, Off The Cuff, Kildrummy and Wayward Lad. True they were campaigned mostly in the north, but nothing gave their handler greater pleasure than to score at Kelso or Perth, two of his favourite courses. It is at Kelso that he and his wife are commemorated by the Wilfrid and Patricia Crawford Memorial, the trophy for which is an imposing Philip Blacker bronze.

One of Wilf Crawford's least distinguished inmates was a filly named False Evidence. Placed twice on the Flat for George Boyd, she was saddled by the Haddington trainer to run four times unplaced over hurdles. Scheduled for the Kelso horse sales, False Evidence was sold privately beforehand to the Bedfordshire owner-breeder, Pearl Lawson Johnston, for whom she bred the grey, Cry of Truth, the champion two-year-old filly of 1974!

Someone who knew all these Crawford horses as well as anyone was Roy Barrett. Head lad at Haddington for twenty-five years, he was to win the inaugural Stable Employee of the Year award at the annual Stable Staff Awards in 2005. By that time he had joined Scotland's leading jump trainer, Len Lungo, who has since retired. Roy moved just across the border to assist Rose Dobbin at Chatton, near Alnwick.

Of the jockeys whom Wilf Crawford employed, the most celebrated was the brilliant Irishman, Ron Barry, who commenced his British riding career at Haddington. Subsequently stable jockey to Fulke Walwyn, Ron Barry was twice champion prior to becoming an inspector of courses. Neil Doughty was another leading jump jockey to be retained, while others associated with the stable included Colin Hawkins, Ridley Lamb, Steve Taylor, Dennis Atkins and Steve Charlton. Two Scots to ride for the stable were Geordie Dun and Swannie Haldane. It was at Perth on a Crawford runner that Jonjo O'Neill rode his 150th winner.

Long before Wilfrid Crawford died in 1992 (latterly he had forfeited his full trainer's licence for a permit), his daughter was recognised as one of the world's great equestrian artists, a reputation earned almost exclusively by her classic oil portraits of famous racehorses. By then she was living in the Wiltshire village of Tisbury, the capital of the Nadder Valley west of Salisbury. It overlooks the River Font, which gives its name to Fonthill Stud, owned by the Morrisons, another racing family which has close ties with Scotland.

However, in the autumn of 2010 she returned to her native Scotland to Bonchester Bridge, just south of Hawick. A few years ago, she and her husband bought a dilapidated shepherd's bothy and converted it into a house with a purpose-built studio. The Crawfords' new home is also much more convenient for presenting the trophy that commemorates her parents at Kelso!

Susan Crawford has been busier than ever since moving back north of the border. Just about the first commission was the 2009 Oaks heroine Sariska for owner-breeder Lady Bamford. Her biggest patron though has been Prince Khalid Abdullah of Juddmonte Farms. His two eminent stallions Dansili and Oasis Dream were followed by various depictions of Frankel himself, as well as one of his dam Kind. There is also a painting of the champion with his owner-breeder which hangs in the Jockey Club Rooms in Newmarket and a portrait of the horse's trainer Sir Henry Cecil. The most recent stallion portrait is of another Banstead Manor Stud resident, Kingman.

While her exceptional talent is obviously a God-given gift, the fact that Susan Crawford always wanted to paint horses is not that surprising. She grew up at Haddington surrounded by racehorses, ponies and hunters, and there was already evidence of artistic talent in the family. Her grandfather taught drawing at the Royal Military College, Woolwich, and illustrated books of poetry with his own watercolours, while her mother had an uncle who was recognised as a highly competent amateur artist.

On leaving Prior's Field School at Godalming in Surrey, the aspiring young artist rented a small flat in Edinburgh from 1959 to 1963 and embarked upon her career. To start with, she concentrated on murals, three of her first commissions being for a ship, a milk bar and the Forth Bridge motel. She then completed a couple in London – one for Selfridges in Oxford Street, and another for The Saddle-Room, a fashionable West End night club.

All the while she was conscious of the fact that to make the grade as a professional painter, she would have to improve her technique. During eighteen months in Florence she had a celebrated tutor in an ageing Signorina Simi. The mornings were spent sketching nudes and the afternoons were devoted to drawing portraits – and whenever possible she took the opportunity to visit art galleries to study the works of the Old Masters, but remarkably she never had any formal painting lessons per se.

By the time Susan left Italy in the late summer of 1965 she realised that her ultimate ambition was to concentrate on equestrian art, mesmerised as she was by the works of George Stubbs and Sir Alfred Munnings. Her preference for painting horses rather than people perplexed the Italian portrait painter Pietro Annigoni, famous for his 1956 portrait of Her Majesty The Queen. Obviously he did not share the experience of the famous eighteenth-century horse painter, Ben Marshall. He had discovered that whereas a patron would pay ten sovereigns for a portrait of his wife, he was quite willing to part with fifty guineas for a painting of his favourite steed!

One of Susan Crawford's first paintings on her return home was of the previous year's Derby and Irish Derby winner, Santa Claus, who was standing at Tim Rogers's Airlie Stud outside Dublin. Tim bought the picture, the first of twenty-three Derby winners that Susan Crawford has painted. The most recent is Golden Horn. Initially she went to Ireland for two weeks and stayed for two years. 'That is where my horse painting really started,' she recalls, 'and where I learnt to drink whiskey!'

Back in England, Susan utilised Julian Barrow's studio in Tite Street, Chelsea, before buying her own studio south of the Thames, near Albert Bridge. It was while living there that she married Jeremy Phipps of the Queen's Own Hussars (subsequently the Jockey Club's head of security) and a new nomadic lifestyle ensued. Before taking up residence in Tisbury, she reckoned that they had moved homes seventeen times in twenty-five years! It all proved too much for the *Dictionary of Scottish Arts and Artists* which listed her as 'having died tragically at the height of her career in 1986' – whereas in fact she was busier than ever.

Commissions to paint famous racehorses have taken Susan Crawford on numerous visits to North America. Two of her most celebrated subjects have been Ribot, then standing in Kentucky, and Northern Dancer, who was twenty-eight when she visited him at home in Maryland. They were two of the greatest racehorses during the second half of the twentieth century and just for good measure she has also painted Northern Dancer's two outstanding sons, Nijinsky and Sadler's Wells.

Of course she has also painted many celebrated jumpers. Just about her very first commission was to paint Freddie, one of the most popular horses ever trained in Scotland, for the Tweedies. Perhaps her best-known painting in the public domain depicted the heads of Arkle, Red Rum and Desert Orchid, probably the three most iconic steeplechasers of the post-war period. Commissioned by the Injured Jockeys Fund for its annual Christmas card, 'We Three Kings' broke all records as a best-selling print.

Susan says she owes a considerable debt to the Tryon Gallery in London's Dover Street where she has exhibited consistently over the last four or five decades, first under the auspices of Aylmer Tryon and then with fellow director, Claude Berry. Amazing as it may seem, Claude and his then wife, Caroline, used to breed Thoroughbreds themselves up in the Borders (see Chapter 28), no distance from the Crawfords' new base at Bonchester Bridge.

No one who is *au fait* with Susan Crawford's work would be surprised to find one of her paintings hanging in the National Portrait Gallery, such is her ranking in the eyes of the establishment. In her time she has completed portraits of the Queen, together with her mother, her sister, and her two eldest children. The Queen and Prince Charles are two of her greatest admirers and patrons and the Queen Mother owned a striking triptych of Prince Charles painted in the manner of Van Dyck's famous masterpiece of King Charles I.

One of Susan's royal portraits that gives her particular satisfaction is of the Queen Mother, commissioned by the Black Watch, a regiment of which she was honorary Colonel-in-Chief. More recently she has painted the Queen riding her grey Highland pony, Jingle, with Balmoral in the background. More controversial perhaps is a portrait of the Duchess of Cornwall. Susan's cousin, James Duncan Millar, served as a regular in the Black Watch when he was one of the Queen Mother's equerries. He now runs the family estate, Remony, near Aberfeldy in Perthshire, at the bottom end of Loch Tay.

If and when the time eventually comes for Susan Crawford to put down her brushes and stow away her easel (once owned by Sir Joshua Reynolds no less!) for good, she will have the immense satisfaction of knowing that not only will her works live on to give pleasure to future generations, but also that her creative talents have been inherited by both of her children. Jemma is an established portrait painter in her own right and Jake is a furniture designer. As they say, it must all be in the genes.

28

THEY BREED GOOD FLAT HORSES
NORTH OF THE BORDER TOO

Quite often individual jumpers, invariably chasers, become great favourites with the racing public. One of the reasons, of course, is because they happen to be around so much longer than their average Flat counterparts. Only occasionally does a Flat performer catch the public's imagination. In recent years this occurred with three distinguished stayers: Further Flight, Persian Punch and Sergeant Cecil. All three were geldings and all of them enjoyed extended careers much more in keeping with a jumper.

In 2007, a four-year-old filly, Turbo Linn, achieved considerable popularity when remaining undefeated in eight consecutive starts. These ranged from the Grade 1 bumper (NH Flat race) at the Aintree Grand National Meeting to the Group 2 Lancashire Oaks, transferred from a waterlogged Haydock Park to the Newmarket July Meeting. Ten days later, the filly with the oversized ears completed a magnificent course and distance double in the Aphrodite Stakes (Listed) carrying a penalty.

Admirable as those achievements were, they would not normally be sufficient to win the hearts and minds of hardened racegoers. But Turbo Linn was homebred on the proverbial shoestring by James Nelson, a Dumfriesshire farmer from Lockerbie. One of the most endearing qualities of the British psyche is empathy for anyone who is perceived as the underdog. It was certainly a disarming experience to see James Nelson standing proudly in the winners' enclosure at Newmarket in high summer, clad in a tweed coat and cap.

In terms of breeding, Turbo Linn certainly set the cat among the pigeons, but as far as her owner-breeder is concerned she is no flash in the pan. By an obscure sire out of a bumper winner, the filly goes back three generations to an unraced mare who was bred by James Nelson's uncle of the same name. He had acquired the fourth dam, Negara, who was also unraced, some forty years before and from her he bred a very smart jumper in Bishops Pawn, who scored fourteen times over jumps.

Historically no one would claim that Scotland has made a major impact in producing high-class Flat horses. Animals like Turbo Linn are few and far between. Realistically, breeding for the Flat requires a substantial financial outlay, so it probably makes little appeal to the Scottish psyche – better to leave such a speculative undertaking to the Sassenachs! However, between the present Duke of Roxburghe at one end of the scale (see Chapter 29) and the Nelsons at the other, there are many who have made a significant contribution.

As the winner of the English and Irish One Thousand Guineas, Guy Roxburghe's Attraction takes top billing, but over the last fifty years horses bred in Scotland have also been placed in the Derby, Oaks and St Leger. There have also been a champion race mare; two winners of the Italian Derby within the space of three years; a winner of the International Stakes, who was an ante-post favourite for the Derby; winners of the Dewhurst Stakes, Cheveley Park Stakes and Phoenix Stakes; and the dam of a champion sire. All these races are now rated Group 1. Nearly all these winners were bred in the Borders and all came from a comparatively small mare base.

Two to perform with credit in English classics were Bounteous (Dewhurst Stakes) and Queen Anne's Lace, who were placed in the St Leger and Oaks respectively. They were bred by Hugh Leggat or his wife at their Pirnie House Stud outside Kelso. In the 1950s and 1960s this was the biggest fully fledged private stud breeding exclusively for the Flat in Scotland – in 1966 the private Pirnie House stud book listed seventeen mares, probably the stud's optimum ever complement.

Frances Innes, one of Hugh Leggat's daughters, who still lives in the Borders and used to work part time for the Duke of Roxburghe, estimates that her father bred some 360 winners of over 770 races. Her own daughter, Melissa, is also a racing fan. Brought up near Jedburgh, she worked for Doncaster Bloodstock Sales, for trainers Nicky Henderson and Roger Charlton, and as secretary to Prince Khalid Abdullah's racing manager, Teddy Grimthorpe.

Essentially an owner-breeder operation, Pirnie House Stud was started with the unraced mare Spyado, dam of Spy Legend, winner of the 1949 Free Handicap. However, in the long term the three foundation mares proved to be Marie Elizabeth (dam of Bounteous), purchased as a foal in 1948, and the two half-sisters, Mary Tavy and Fairnington, daughters of the noted foundation mare, Henriette Maria. Mary Tavy resurfaced as the third dam of Florida Son, sire of the top Irish chaser, Florida Pearl.

As a juvenile, Bounteous defeated the future Derby winner, Psidium, for the Dewhurst Stakes and was then runner-up to Aurelius in the St Leger. Sent to be trained in France by Mick Bartholomew as a four-year-old, he won two major events at Deauville: the Grand Prix and the Prix Kergorlay. Another smart homebred performer for Hugh Leggat in France was Montevideo II, successful in the prestigious Prix du Rond-Point at the Prix de l'Arc de Triomphe meeting. He appears in the distaff pedigree of the 2008 French Derby hero, Vision d'Etat.

A son of Rockefella, also sire of the Scottish-trained Two Thousand Guineas winner, Rockavon, Bounteous was repatriated to stand at the Princess Royal's Stables Houses Stud at Harewood, near Leeds. He then moved to Ticklerton Stud in Shropshire, en route to Japan in 1969. His stud innings here was notable for the champion filly sprinter, Abergwaun, a strange anomaly considering that her sire stayed so well.

Any Ascot victory is always much coveted and Hugh Leggat's royal blue and scarlet colours excelled there. Amongst his homebred winners was Current Coin (Cork and Orrery Stakes, now Golden Jubilee Stakes) – also successful in the Phoenix Stakes and Larkspur Stakes in Ireland, where he was trained by John Oxx and retired to stud. Others include Baron's Folly (Queen Anne Stakes in record time for the straight mile); Vhairi (Princess Royal Stakes, run that year at Newbury); Pirnie (Wyndham Stakes, Golden Gates Nursery); Jock's Lodge (Red Deer Stakes); Marie Therese (Fern Hill Stakes); and Rose Petal (Golden Gates Nursery).

At the Newmarket December Sales of 1967, Hugh Leggat sold a young in-foal mare, Byblis, for 5,700 guineas to the Freedman family and she was to have an extended influence at their Cliveden Stud beside the Thames. She was to become the third dam of their 1987 Derby winner, Reference Point, and the sixth dam of the 2008 Eclipse Stakes winner, Mount Nelson, by which time Cliveden Stud itself had been sold.

Lorna Fraser of Ladyrig, near Kelso, a near neighbour of Hugh Leggat's, sent her broodmare B Flat to be covered by Bounteous to produce Border Bounty. Placed in the Yorkshire Oaks, Border Bounty became the dam of top-class miler Pitcairn, who was bred by Tim Rogers of Airlie Stud and raced for Scottish-based Sandy Struthers (see Chapter 20).

In due course Pitcairn and his sire, Petingo, became champion sires, Petingo in 1979 thanks to Troy and Pitcairn in 1980 courtesy of Ela-Ma-na-Mou. Pitcairn and Ela-Mana-Mou both started off as stallions under Tim Rogers's management. He was really the first person to put Ireland on the stallion map and the Scottish-bred Border Bounty certainly made her own contribution.

That was by no means the end of the story however. In 1981 Border Bounty's Artaius foal became the first filly of her age to realise a six-figure sum at public auction. Nearly three decades on, the mare is still involved with record breakers. Her granddaughter, Rafha, winner of the French Oaks, bred Invincible Spirit (Haydock Park Sprint Cup), a record-breaking sire for the Irish National Stud in 2006 and now one of the most sought-after stallions in Europe, as is his half-brother, Kodiac.

Hugh Leggat's younger brother, Alex, known as Tanny, who rode in point-to-points and was a former permit-holder, also bred Thoroughbreds at his home, Lindsaylands, near Biggar, in Lanarkshire. A brick manufacturer, he was a director of Lanark racecourse for twenty-five years and chairman when it closed in 1977. Although he was never involved in breeding to the same extent as his brother, Tanny, who died in 1991, did particularly well in the north. Two homebred half-brothers to score in his red and grey colours at the Ayr Western Meeting were Hundalee (Bogside Cup) and Frascadale, twice winner of the Ayrshire Handicap.

Royal Ascot in 1978 was a particularly memorable occasion for Tanny and his wife, Belle, when their homebred Mountain Cross won the Ascot Stakes and Queen Alexandra Stakes. The marathon double (the Queen Alexandra Stakes over two miles, five and a half furlongs is Britain's longest Flat race) had not been completed since the legendary Trelawny in 1963, and would not be repeated again until Baddam in 2006. The latter had three full days to recover from his initial exertions, whereas Trelawny and Mountain Cross had a day less.

The Leggats' daughter, Jane, married the Malton trainer, Jimmy Fitzgerald, who rode Brasher to win the last Scottish Grand National held at Bogside. In fact the first good horse owned by the Leggats was a jumper, Cruachan, trained by Bobby Renton in Yorkshire, finishing third to Clair Soleil in the 1955 Champion Hurdle and fourth to Limber Hill in the 1956 Cheltenham Gold Cup.

It was purely by chance that the Tweedies, whose name is indelibly linked with that great chaser, Freddie (see Chapter 21), became involved with breeding for the Flat. As chairman of the Buccleuch Hunter Breeding Society, Reg was on the lookout for a potential stallion to produce hunters and point-to-pointers in this part of Scotland. For 500 guineas he bought seven-year-old Telegram II at Botterills' May Sale in 1954 from a consignment of horses offered by the redoubtable Dorothy Paget.

At the previous year's Newmarket July Sales he had paid 160 guineas for the six-year-old winning mare, Wynway. In 1956 she foaled a colt by Telegram, who broke his pelvis and never ran, but the following year she produced an own-sister whom Reg gave to his wife as a foal for a birthday present.

Named Rosie Wings, she went into training with Harry Whiteman at Malton and then moved with him to Cree Lodge, Ayr. She proved extremely versatile, winning seven times at distances from one mile to one mile seven furlongs. She was at her best as a five-year-old, landing the Usher Brewery Gold Tankard (then Scotland's richest Flat race) on her local course in commanding fashion despite carrying a penalty. But it was as a broodmare that she really made her mark.

Rosie Wings' first three offspring were the colts Scottish Sinbad (by

Tamerlane), Mount Athos (by Sunny Way), and John Splendid (by Sing Sing). Between them they won eighteen races in the colours of Glasgow ship-owner, Sandy Struthers (see Chapter 20). Mount Athos and John Splendid were a particularly talented duo, the former finishing third in the Derby and the latter winning the Ayr Gold Cup.

The decision to send Rosie Wings to Ireland for her first three coverings nearly ended in disaster as she proved a very bad traveller. Betty Tweedie, who once broke her neck in a point-to-point, had the greatest difficulty in restraining her on the outward bound ferry crossing to Dublin. The return journey proved even more hair-raising. On the flight from Dublin to Cambridge, accompanied by a batch of yearlings scheduled for the Newmarket sales, she panicked at some point over the Irish Sea and it was touch and go whether her handlers would have to resort to a lethal injection.

In later years Rosie Wings proved a poor breeder. She was leased to Guy Reed of Nidd Hall Stud in Yorkshire and mated exclusively with his homebred grey stallion, Warpath. She was twenty-six years of age when retired from the paddocks in 1983. This coincided with the last of her nine individual winners, No More Rosies – she in turn became a useful broodmare, particularly with her jumpers. In retirement Rosie Wings used to share a paddock at Middlethird with Freddie himself.

It is extraordinary that two winners of the Italian Derby should have been bred within a few miles of one another in Roxburghshire. The first of them was Old Country in 1982, whose breeder, Claude de Pomeroy Berry, owned the Firth Stud at Lillieslief, near Melrose. Old Country was trained at Newmarket by Luca Cumani. At the time Claude and his wife Caroline bred both Flat horses and jumpers; she also bred Shetland ponies. (Their son is the Newmarket trainer, John Berry.) As a director of the Tryon Gallery, Claude Berry was a prominent figure in the world of sporting art.

A former amateur rider, Claude Berry had started breeding bloodstock at Lillieslief when he relinquished his permit to train in the early 1970s. Between them Claude and Caroline bred some very successful jumpers, but with the passing of the years he became more involved in producing Flat horses for the commercial market. Old Country (by Quiet Fling) was consigned as a foal to Tattersalls' 1979 December Sales where he realised 13,500 guineas. It was at the same sale in 1974 that his dam, Little Miss, had been procured for 2,000 guineas.

Old Country also did his bit to promote the family fortunes, both at home and abroad. Following his Italian Derby victory, he remained in training for an additional three seasons, winning the Prix Royal Oak (French St Leger) at four years, the Jockey Club Cup at five years, and the Premio Roma at six years. Not surprisingly, he was eventually sent on a one-way ticket from Newmarket to Italy as a prospective stallion.

Catherine Napier of Kippilaw, near St Boswells, who was brought up at Melrose and died in 2008, was another successful small-scale breeder. An owner with James Bethell and Ernie Weymes, she did well with the progeny of her unraced broodmare, Toccata, who was bred by the greatest of Yorkshire breeders, Lionel Holliday. Two to excel in her 'cerise, black and white striped sleeves' were Abercata, winner of the Zetland Gold Cup, Redcar, and Tockala, successful in the Weir Memorial Trophy at the Ayr Western Meeting.

Just down the road from Kippilaw is Mertoun, where the late Duke of Sutherland used to maintain a handful of mares operating as Dryburgh Stud; following his death it was continued on modest lines by his widow, Evelyn. Not the luckiest of owners, he won the 1969 Dante Stakes with Activator, but this homebred colt died before the year was out. Two more useful colts to race for Lord Ellesmere (as he then was) were Whitehall and North Cone. The former was bred at Mertoun and the latter was a yearling purchase.

The Sutherlands are large landowners around Newmarket, and on the Stetchworth side of town land leased from their estates has played a prominent role on the veterinary front. This trend began with Mertoun Paddocks, home to the Equine Fertility Unit which folded in 2007 due to lack of funding. It was resumed with the Newmarket Equine Hospital, which opened its doors in 2008. In charge of the EFU was a New Zealander, Professor Twink Allen of Cambridge University, whose daughter Catherine married Frankie Dettori.

Over the last few decades the marked decline in farming and agriculture generally has encouraged farmers to diversify, indeed many of them were forced to do so out of sheer necessity. Gordon Thom used to milk 300 cows on as many acres in a renowned dairy farming area no distance from Ayr, but in 2000 he decided on a whole new strategy. He retained seventy acres of his grassland and turned them into New Hall Stud. Trading as James Thom and Sons, this enterprise specialises in boarders of all descriptions. Clients past and present have included trainers Ian Semple, Jim Goldie and Linda Perratt. The Thom family also runs a nucleus of its own mares, selling the offspring as yearlings. Amongst them is Donna Blini (20,000 guineas), winner of the Cheveley Park Stakes and Cherry Hinton Stakes in 2005.

Although Simon Fraser (later Lord Lovat) made an unavailing attempt to start a fully fledged stud at Beauly, near Inverness, Flat breeding in Scotland has almost always revolved around the Lowlands. However, a notable exception is provided by Robert Gibbons, owner of the Lawers Estate at Comrie (home of the Scottish Tartan Museum), between Loch Earn and Crieff in Perthshire.

The former chairman of Highland Spring raced that admirable mare, Hunters of Brora (named after the retailers of fine Scottish tweed). She won the 1998 Lincoln as an eight-year-old, due compensation for no fewer than three placings in the Cambridgeshire. The first two offspring of Hunters of Brora, Scotland The Brave and Little Bob, also trained by James Bethell, completed a double for Gibbons' red, white and blue colours, when scoring at Ayr in October 2005.

One of the soundest philosophies when it comes to breeding blood-stock is the oft-quoted maxim of long-term National Stud director, Peter Burrell: 'Mate the best with the best and hope for the best.' Of course, that involves serious capital expenditure, but diversification from farming could make Flat breeding in Scotland an attractive alternative to the more traditional pursuit of producing jumpers. Good Flat horses have been bred north of the border and there is absolutely no reason why the trend should not continue, given the necessary investment.

29

THIS STATELY HOME HAS A UNIQUE ATTRACTION

In 2007 the Royal Mint issued a limited edition of collectors' coins to commemorate notable landmarks in British history, including the 100th anniversary of the Scout Movement, the 200th anniversary of the abolition of the slave-trade, and the 300th anniversary of the Act of Union between the old adversaries, Scotland and England.

A racing connection exists with all three. The 2nd Lord Rowallan, the Chief Scout, was the father of Atty Corbett, the man who trained Queen's Hussar, the sire of Brigadier Gerard. Bristol, the headquarters for Wills' tobacco imported from Virginia, was one of Britain's key 'slave' ports. The late Sir David Wills and his daughter, Catherine (who breeds under the title St Clare Hall Stud), besides owning the Knockando Estate in Morayshire, have named many of their horses after locations in the Western Isles and the Highlands. And it was the 1st Duke of Roxburghe, the owner of Floors, who signed the Act of Union three centuries ago.

That momentous step coincided with the creation of the dukedom upon a man who was described as 'the best accomplished young man of quality in Europe'. Then secretary of state for Scotland, he commissioned another Scotsman, William Adam – father of that most celebrated of all British architects, Robert Adam – to build beautiful Floors Castle in the 1720s, with subsequent embellishments by the Edinburgh architect, William Henry Playfair. It was spelt 'Fleurs' until the middle of the nineteenth century, and the French pronunciation remains *de rigueur*.

The largest inhabited castle in Scotland, with 200 rooms, Floors is a magnificent Georgian edifice accommodating a particularly fine collection of Belgian tapestries, many of them bought by Mary Goelet, the American heiress wife of the 8th Duke. Situated just outside the old market town of Kelso, the house was described by Sir Walter Scott as, 'the most romantic, if not the most beautiful place in Scotland'. It has an idyllic setting by the banks of the River Tweed. The imposing, often snow-capped, Cheviot Hills rise in the distance. In the 1990s Floors was also the scene of a daring and much publicised burglary.

The estate of 50,000 acres comprises a large swathe of prime agricultural land divided between an extensive arable and hill farming enterprise and forty-five tenanted farms. Over 2,000 acres are devoted to woodlands and forestry. Grouse moors and two beats on the Tweed stretching three miles upstream from Kelso provide prime shooting and fishing. The Junction Pool, where the rivers Tweed and Teviot converge, is regarded as the Holy Grail for salmon-fishing. There is also Kelso racecourse, which enjoys tremendous local support, one of Scotland's finest country house hotels and a championship golf course.

The sale of valuable fishing rights helped Guy Roxburghe, the 10th Duke, to meet the substantial death duties that accrued following his father's demise in September 1974 – he died while out grouse-shooting. At the time Guy Innes-Ker was a nineteen-year-old subaltern in the Blues and Royals, the Household Cavalry. A keen cricketer, he had been in the XI at Eton and had won the Sword of Honour at Sandhurst. Having completed a short-service commission in the army, he proceeded to Magdalene College, Cambridge, where he obtained a degree in land economy.

On leaving university, he immediately took over responsibility for the Roxburghe Estates. Apart from opening the castle to the public, he has initiated a number of flourishing business ventures – The Roxburghe Hotel, with its own golf course, a garden centre in the castle grounds, and the building of a number of executive homes. A very keen golfer himself, he also follows the professional game with great enthusiasm. Another innovation is producing bloodstock for the commercial yearling market, which comes under the classification, Floors Farming.

Guy's father was always known as Bobo Roxburghe and likewise inherited the title at a young age. He had bred Thoroughbreds at Floors since the mid-1950s, but the one-time senior steward of the Jockey Club was a traditional owner-breeder whose two principal trainers were Matthew Peacock and his son Dick, at Middleham. The latter trained two of his best homebreds in Erudite, winner of the Free Handicap, and Sweet Story, winner of the Yorkshire Cup and the Northumberland Plate.

Sweet Story actually stood as a stallion at Floors, where he replaced another good stayer in Guide, both of them proving popular with the local hunting and point-to-point fraternity. Guide, twice winner of the Royal Caledonian Hunt Cup at the Ayr Western Meeting, was twenty-one when he died at Floors from heart failure in 1970. He had been a yearling purchase and Guy Roxburghe recalls that his father had been underbidder at the sales for his much more distinguished half-brother, Ballymoss, one of the outstanding horses of his generation.

As an owner-breeder, Bobo Roxburghe had no regard for fashion. His sole objective was to win races in his silver and green colours, and a victory in the north gave him just as much, if not more, pleasure than one down south. After his death, Guy was advised by his new step-father, Jocelyn Hambro (whose mother drowned in Loch Ness) that the only viable course, should he want to continue with the stud, was to operate on a commercial basis. So the existing stock was sold and the new enterprise started with a clean sheet.

Jocelyn Hambro, a member of the banking dynasty, had many years' experience of breeding bloodstock himself. Owner of Waverton Stud in Gloucestershire (previously William Hill's Sezincote Stud), he had moved there from Redenham Park Stud in Hampshire, where Bridget Swire later boarded her mares. Latterly Waverton was run in conjunction with Cotswold Stud by Jocelyn Hambro's daughter-in-law, Mary Hambro – at one time she was the largest yearling consignor to Tattersalls' sales. In conjunction with Alan Lillingston of Mount Coote Stud in Ireland, Jocelyn Hambro bred the 1979 One Thousand Guineas winner, One in A Million, and her relative, Deep Run, a multiple champion sire of jumpers.

It was not only Guy's late stepfather who had an interest in Thoroughbred studs. His first wife, the former Lady Jane Grosvenor, is also involved – via her brother, the late 6th Duke of Westminster. The 1st Duke started the now defunct Eaton Stud in Cheshire and owned four Derby winners in the 1880s and 1890s, Bend Or, Shotover, Ormonde and Flying Fox. He also bred the outstanding racemare, Sceptre. More recently, Anne, Duchess of Westminster, the fourth wife of the 2nd Duke, owned Arkle, the greatest steeplechaser of all time.

As an undergraduate, Guy Roxburghe raced the colt, False Witness, who was foaled the year after his father's death and had been retained at that year's Newmarket December Sales for 5,200 guineas. A relative of Sweet Story, he was trained by Bruce Hobbs at Newmarket and became his owner's very first winner when landing the odds as a two-year-old at the Newmarket July Meeting. That whetted his owner's appetite for racing and breeding and gradually he built up a nucleus of broodmares at Floors with a view to selling their offspring as yearlings.

Guy Roxburghe quickly made his mark as a serious commercial breeder thanks to the purchase of a mare, Norfolk Light, for 12,000 guineas at the 1977 December Sales. Prior to selling her for 23,000 guineas five years later (in the interim her half-sister, Yanuka, had finished third in the One Thousand Guineas), he sold her 1982 yearling colt by Welsh Pageant at Newmarket for 25,000 guineas. Named Welnor, he excelled in Italy as a three-year-old, winning the Derby, Gran Premio d'Italia and Premio Emanuele Filiberto. Remarkably, that was a second winner of the Derby Italiano to be bred in Roxburghshire within the space of three years, following Old Country in 1982.

All top studs keep culling and restocking to maintain forward momentum – it is said that a stud is either in the ascendant or on the decline, it is never static. One acquisition that certainly helped Floors to keep in the front line was Vaguely. Purchased for 28,000 guineas back in 1980, she was consigned by her breeder, Sir John Astor. The mare was out of a half-sister to his St Leger winner, Provoke, from the immediate family of that great stayer, Trelawny, a line developed by the Astor family at their famous Cliveden Stud in Buckinghamshire.

Vaguely is entitled to be regarded as one of the foundation mares of the present Floors Stud as she attained the dual objectives of all commercial breeders – she delivered the goods both in the sales ring and on the racecourse. The catalyst for this success was her Shirley Heights colt, Shady Heights, sold at the 1985 Highflyer Sales for 110,000 guineas to join the Newmarket stable of Robert Armstrong. His wife Mary was a cousin of Guy Roxburghe – tragically she died a few years later.

Shady Heights was a highly promising two-year-old when runner-up in the Dewhurst Stakes. He became ante-post favourite for the Derby, but encountered all sorts of problems as a three-year-old. However, in the ensuing season he proved ultra consistent, finishing in the frame in eight Group races, winning the Tattersalls' Rogers Gold Cup at the Curragh, and being awarded the International Stakes at York upon the disqualification of Persian Heights. 'Shady' was exported for stallion duties in Japan.

In strictly monetary terms, Vaguely proved a tremendous benefactor to Floors. Basking in the reflected glory of Shady Heights, three of her yearling colts were sold for an aggregate of 735,000 guineas, amongst them Rahif, an own-brother to Shady Heights, who realised 380,000 guineas. In addition, Jdaayel, an Ajdal filly, was sold privately to Sheikh Hamdan Al Maktoum of Shadwell Stud. This would have brought the total revenue to something in the region of £1m.

The 1990s proved a quiet decade for the stud, but its re-emergence from the doldrums came from a most unexpected quarter. Back at the 1983 Newmarket December Sales, the non-winning Eastern Shore had been bought for a substantial 155,000 guineas, carrying her first foal. The mare was consigned by David McCall (one-time racing manager to the American Charles Engelhard), part-owner of her covering sire, Ile de Bourbon.

Towards the end of her otherwise uneventful stud career, Eastern Shore produced a filly called Flirtation. The duke grades his mares A, B and C in terms of quality and because Flirtation failed to win and belonged to a family that had not done well for him, she was classified in the lowest category – cheap and cheerful. However, to a mating with Efisio in 2001 she produced Attraction. Rejected by Doncaster Bloodstock Sales on account of her dubious forelegs, she was dispatched to

John Hills in Lambourn with a view to leasing her. When that option came to nothing, she joined Mark Johnston at Middleham.

Against all the odds, Attraction proved the sort of individual that any breeder can only ever dream about. Unbeaten in five juvenile outings, she gained commanding victories in the Queen Mary Stakes and Cherry Hinton Stakes. On the very afternoon that she scored at Royal Ascot, her owner was officiating as a steward at Ascot for the very first time, and his wife, Virginia, received the trophy at the Newmarket July Meeting as her husband was away fishing in Norway.

It was at this stage that the wheels nearly came off altogether, which was always a possibility with those fragile-looking forelegs. As it turned out, her juvenile career came to a grinding halt in mid-season. Having already won a Group 2 and a Group 3, her owner was keen to tackle a Group 1 in France, but she then suffered an overreach while swimming and precautionary X-rays revealed bone chips in her knees. Finally plans to compete for the Cheveley Park Stakes were abandoned when she cracked a pedal bone a week before the race. Despite these setbacks, the daughter of Efisio was rated the champion two-year-old domestically and the champion two-year-old of her sex in Europe.

On her first two starts the ensuing season, Attraction brought off a sensational double, winning the One Thousand Guineas and the Irish One Thousand Guineas, to become the first ever winner of these two classics. Up till then, Attraction had only ever raced over a straight course and some experts considered that, with such suspect-looking forelegs, it would be inadvisable to subject her to the added strain of running round a bend. But nothing ventured, nothing gained, and on a return visit to Royal Ascot she won the Coronation Stakes over the round mile; she concluded the season with victory in the Sun Chariot Stakes.

It was a very sporting gesture to keep Attraction in training as a four-year-old, when her target revolved around the million-dollar bonus for the new Asian Mile Challenge. This comprised the Champions Mile in Hong Kong and the Yasuda Kinen in Japan, which would be run to suit her front-running style. However, she was never in contention at Sha Tin. Subsequent lameness followed by a bruised foot caused her to miss Royal Ascot and York, but she bowed out with a sensational victory in September, beating the winners of that season's One Thousand Guineas and Irish One Thousand Guineas in the Matron Stakes in Ireland. That proved her finale due to recurring lameness, the precise cause of which remained a mystery.

The Leopardstown race was her fifth individual Group 1 victory in a career which earned just under £900,000. The proverbial model of consistency, she won ten times and was placed three times from a total of fifteen starts. Never raced beyond a mile, she was also rated the champion three-year-old filly of her generation in Ireland, and the champion older mare in Ireland from seven to nine furlongs at four years.

Floors Stud has sold many six-figure yearlings, but the seven-figure barrier was breached in 2016 when a Frankel colt out of Attraction realised an astonishing 1.6 million guineas. Both his parents had won a Guineas over the Rowley Mile. The unbeaten champion was then represented by only his second crop of yearlings and this was a record price for one of his progeny at public auction. The purchaser was Sheikh Hamdan Al Maktoum of Shadwell Stud who named the youngster Elarqam and he duly followed in his mother's footprints by joining Mark Johnston.

At that stage Attraction was responsible for six winners from as many runners headed by Group 3 winner Fountain of Youth, a 420,000 guineas yearling who stands as a stallion in Shropshire, and the Grade 3 placed Cushion, now a Floors broodmare. While she is the only one of Attraction's daughters in the stud, three of Attraction's half-sisters have been retained. Since producing Elarqam, Attraction has foaled a 2016 colt by Dubawi, and a 2017 filly by Invincible Spirit – the latter has been named Motion and her dam was then tested in foal once more to Frankel.

In 2002, the year after Attraction was foaled, Floors Stud came up with another star in Comic Strip. Only a modest performer at home, this gelding became a veritable icon in Hong Kong. Renamed Viva Pataca he was twice voted champion older horse, his earnings equating to about £6 million. In 2013 his half-sister Laughing excelled in the USA, winning two Grade 1 events, the Flower Bowl Invitational Stakes,

Belmont Park, and the Diana Stakes, Saratoga. In 2016 their yearling half-brother by Dubawi realised 750,000 guineas.

Comic, the dam of Comic Strip/Viva Pataca and Laughing, was bred by and is owned jointly with Lord Hartington (now Duke of Devonshire), they having procured her dam Circus Act as a three-year-old in 1988 for 48,000 guineas. Guy Roxburghe is a great believer in shared ownership of broodmares and he bred the 2017 Royal Ascot winner Rare Rhythm (Duke of Edinburgh Stakes), in partnership with Highclere Stud on the Hampshire/Berkshire border, where the dam actually resides – to many Highclere Castle is synonymous with the fictional Downton Abbey.

Highclere, just south of Newbury, is the family home of the Earl and Countess of Carnarvon and the stud is managed by his sister, Lady Carolyn Warren – her bloodstock agent husband John, is the Queen's stud and racing manager (he succeeded his father-in-law) and their son Jake focuses on the resident stallions. Both husband and wife have had a long time involvement with the Roxburghe bloodstock. Indeed Highclere was the home of Attraction's sire Efisio and John acts as Guy Roxburghe's advisor.

The major contribution made by stud staff should never be underestimated and in this respect Floors Stud is no different from any other high-class private stud. The two linchpins of the establishment, both long serving employees, have been former stud grooms, Paddy Sullivan and his successor Barrie Hosie. The current man in charge is David Trouton, who arrived in 2012 and combines the duties of manager and stud groom. He previously worked at Robert Barnett's Fair Winter Farm in Buckinghamshire.

It remains relatively feudal up on the Borders, so what Bobo Roxburghe (memorably his private telephone number was Kelso 1) would have thought about his son and heir owning a hotel called The Roxburghe defies description. Here was someone who once declared that it was *infra dig* to eat in other people's houses, let alone restaurants. He would almost certainly have had apoplexy had he witnessed the present Duke fishing the Tweed alongside the celebrity chef, Ainsley Harriott! But times move on.

30

THE MAN WHO RESURRECTED MIDDLEHAM

Two trainers who have done as much as anyone to perfect their trade in the last quarter of a century are both non establishment figures and they had to fight their way to the top without any of the more obvious advantages. In the same way that Martin Pipe, the son of a West Country bookmaker, revolutionised the old fashioned ideas of training jumpers, so too has his counterpart on the Flat, Mark Johnston, although he did have the benefit of being a graduate of Glasgow Veterinary School.

Their technique was to get horses far fitter than was possible using traditional training methods. That degree of superior fitness was manifest on the racecourse by their being able to go out and make the running without capitulating when the ultimate pressure was applied towards the finish of a race. And there is no doubting their toughness – there is nothing unusual about the Mark Johnston runners having two bites of the cherry at festival meetings when exceptional well being, both physical and mental, must be the key.

There is a popular misconception that Mark Steven Johnston, BVMS, MRCVS, works his horses far harder than his colleagues, but he certainly feeds them more frequently – four times per day including a night-time feed. As anyone who has travelled behind one of his horseboxes will verify, the Mark Johnston maxim is 'Always Trying', and there is no denying their characteristic front running and free going way of performing. How often has it been said, 'It's so difficult to pass a Mark Johnston horse once they hit the front.'

Front running is the hallmark of the Johnston runners. It is also accepted that training racehorses is a numbers game and generally

268

speaking it is impossible to remain consistently at the top without the necessary horsepower in modern parlance – and one is talking here in terms of a hundred horses or even twice as many, unheard of numbers in the past. He also thinks it is preferable to run his horses frequently rather than expending that energy at home for no remuneration.

Competition is more acute now than it has ever been so how does someone without any connections with racing or significant financial resources manage to attain such a goal? The answer is with the greatest of difficulty, but as Mark Johnston would surely testify, it is not a course to be entertained by the faint-hearted. Nowadays the master of Kingsley House estimates that should his string plummet to below 150 he would be losing money.

Until Mark took up residence in 1989, Middleham in North Yorkshire was languishing as a training centre. The death of Dick Peacock only four years previously had marked the end of an era – three generations of his family had trained at Manor House over a period of one hundred years, and such a void was never going to be filled despite the arrival of younger trainers from the south like Patrick Haslam and James Bethell.

By that stage Middleham was better known for jumpers, a legacy from the time that Neville Crump was based opposite Kingsley House at Warwick House whence he dispatched three Grand National winners, including the Scottish owned and bred Merryman II.

Warwick House owes its name to Anne Neville, daughter of the Earl of Warwick, who married King Richard III and Middleham Castle was their favourite residence. Immortalised by Shakespeare in the soliloquy from Richard III 'A horse! A horse! My kingdom for a horse!' as he lay mortally wounded at the battle of Bosworth Field in August 1485, his death terminated the Plantagenet succession and the Wars of the Roses.

Patrick Haslam's son, Ben, now trains adjacent to the castle ruins. Close by is Manor House Stud, owned and managed by Lenore Peacock, the widow of Dick Peacock, where Dante (Derby), trained at Manor House by his father, Matthew Peacock, and Dante's own-brother, Sayajirao (St Leger), were bred and raised – in 1945 Dante became the last northern trained winner of the Derby, albeit a substitute affair at Newmarket. Also bred at Manor House Stud was Tirol, who brought off the Two Thousand and Irish Two Thousand Guineas double in 1990.

Middleham had been a training centre since the eighteenth century and regular race meetings were held on the High Moor from as early as 1739 until 1873 when disputes arose over grazing rights. The town's historic past resurfaced in a most unexpected way. It was on Lennie Peacock's land that an extremely rare fifteenth century gold and sapphire reliquary pendant was discovered. Known as the Middleham Jewel, it realised £1.2m at Sothebys in December 1986. Resold for £2.5m this diminutive medieval treasure was soon on display in the Yorkshire Museum in York.

Once the Deanery, Kingsley House derives its name from a former owner, Charles Kingsley, author of *The Water Babies*. In 1955 Avril Vasey moved there from the other side of town. Subsequent incumbents were Ken 'Window' Payne, Steve Nesbitt and George Moore. Mark Johnston's immediate predecessor, George Moore was private trainer to George Dawes, who had won the football pools, but was later declared bankrupt.

Kingsley House was in a dilapidated state when Mark Johnston took up residence. Here was an outsider from some remote corner of Lincolnshire, who seemed determined to revolutionise the way things had been done in Yorkshire for generations and to exacerbate the situation he was an outspoken Scotsman! At the time his principal patron was Hinari Consumer Electronics, owned by Mark's business partner, Brian Palmer. Rumour soon spread that the yard had been taken over by some consortium from the Far East which did not inspire too much confidence so far as the locals were concerned!

Up till then Mark's experience of training amounted to two seasons based at North Somercotes, near Louth, on the Lincolnshire coast, fifteen miles south of Grimsby. There were no gallops at Bank End Stables, so instead he utilised the beach just a mile distant – the young trainer was less fazed than he might have been as, when a veterinary student, he had ridden out on the sands at Dunbar for George Boyd's nephew, Tommy Craig. Still, care had to be taken as this part of Lincolnshire was a Ministry of Defence live bombing range!

The Johnstons recorded their very first winner when the two-year-old Hinari Video scored at Carlisle in July 1987. The following season the tally rose to five winners. Success for Brian Palmer's colours was imperative and without his financial backing the move to Middleham could never have been entertained.

Bank End was certainly an unorthodox launch pad to Mark's training career in which his wife Deirdre has been very much the second in command – nowadays they are assisted by their elder son Charlie. It is no coincidence that they both come from similar Scottish backgrounds and both father and son are graduates of Glasgow Veterinary School.

Mark was born and brought up in East Kilbride to the south of Glasgow. His parents were both Glaswegians and they had met when Mark's father was working as a steward for BOAC (British Overseas Airways Corporation) and his mother was an air hostess with BEA (British European Airways) – the forerunners to British Airways. Later, Ronald ran his own TV aerials' business in Glasgow. By then the family had moved to Gartmore Bridge, north of the city, where Ronald had an occasional horse in training with Paddy and Susan Chesmore at Drymen.

Deirdre Ferguson's parents lived near Aberfoyle, no distance from Gartmore Bridge. She and Mark had a shared interest in horses from an early age. He was determined to become a trainer encouraged by the success he had enjoyed racing whippets, and she had always adored horses and riding. They were married in 1985, just a year before buying their stables in Lincolnshire by which time her husband had three years' experience as a veterinary surgeon in general practice.

Since arriving at Middleham, Mark Johnston has established himself as one of the very top trainers in the country. To appreciate the extent of these achievements one has to remember that many leading trainers have the inestimable advantage of homebred horses as ammunition, but before the Maktoums became established patrons of the stable, Mark had to rely mostly on yearlings bought at public auction with strictly limited funds, virtually always selected by himself.

Mark Johnston recorded his first Group success with Marina Park in the Princess Margaret Stakes at Ascot in July 1992. That autumn one of his original owners, Paul Venner of Baileys Horse Feeds, retained a Robellino colt at the Newmarket October Yearling Sales for 10,500 guineas, 500 guineas more than he had paid for him as a foal. He named the colt Mister Baileys.

Mister Baileys won the 1994 Two Thousand Guineas by a short head from Grand Lodge to become the first English classic winner to be trained north of the River Trent since Mrs McArdy won the 1977 One Thousand Guineas. The colt looked a Derby prospect on the form book after winning the Royal Lodge Stakes as a juvenile. However, Epsom, where he finished fourth after being third in the Dante Stakes (behind Erhaab on both occasions), proved his nemesis.

Both Mister Baileys and Grand Lodge established a new course record for the Rowley Mile and with hindsight his trainer regretted running him at Epsom. In preparation for the Guineas it had only been possible to give Mister Baileys three serious pieces of work on grass (the all-weather facilities had been waterlogged), so the Newmarket classic was his seasonal reappearance. Prior to the Derby he had worked 'the wrong way round' on Middleham Moor, that is downhill left-handed to replicate the Epsom terrain.

Following a tendon injury, the intention was for Mister Baileys to take up stallion duties at the National Stud, but he contracted grass sickness, became the subject of an insurance claim, and went to stud in the USA. He was eventually repatriated to stand at Whitsbury Manor Stud in Hampshire, but only covered there for a brief period before proving infertile and being retired to his owner's home, Petches Farm Stud, near Braintree, in Essex. He died aged eighteen in 2009.

One of the most popular horses Mark has trained is Double Trigger and he had a magnificent understudy in his year junior own-brother, Double Eclipse. Both Ela-Mana-Mou colts were bought as yearlings at Goffs in Ireland, Trigger for IR7,200 guineas in 1992 and Eclipse for IR17,500 guineas in 1993; both were owned in partnership by Kent businessman Ron Huggins.

Between them Double Trigger and Double Eclipse won an

astonishing twenty-one races. Twelve of Trigger's fourteen victories came in Group events. The last of them was the Doncaster Cup as a seven-year-old when he became only the second horse in history to win the marathon more than twice. He also has the unique twentieth century distinction of winning three Goodwood Cups.

Such was Double Trigger's impact at Goodwood that the restaurant in the new paddock complex was named after him. There is also a Double Trigger Trophy at Redcar in September which corresponds to the very race that this great stayer won on his two-year-old debut. But perhaps the biggest compliment of all is to have a GNER railway engine named in his honour.

The first of Double Trigger's Goodwood Cup victories in 1995 was a truly memorable occasion as he prevailed by a neck over Double Eclipse in a pulsating finish. Had the positions been reversed that would have cost Trigger the stayers' Triple Crown as his Goodwood victory was sandwiched between wins in the Ascot Gold Cup and Doncaster Cup. For some inexplicable reason Trigger, who was always a poor worker at home, was not named as that season's 'Stayer of the Year'.

Royal Ascot, the Newmarket July Meeting and Glorious Goodwood are three midsummer festivals that Mark targets annually and at that time of year the ground is invariably on the firm side which the Middleham trainer thinks favours his horses' style of running. The stable has a particularly strong following during Goodwood week where he has an unrivalled record, having never failed to have a winner at the festival meeting from 2000 right through to 2017 when he was crowned leading trainer for the eleventh time. Altogether he has saddled seventy-three winners at Glorious Goodwood.

The Queen's Vase and Princess of Wales's Stakes have proved very popular Group targets and the stable has provided the winner of the Queen's Vase on no fewer than seven occasions with And Beyond, Shanty Star, Melrose Avenue, Soapy Danger, Holberg, Namibian and Hartnell. Namibian also won the Gordon Stakes at Goodwood and Hartnell became a celebrity in Australia. They typify the sort of staying three-year-olds with whom Mark Johnston excels.

Double Eclipse retired to stand at Emral Stud in North Wales in 1998, and Double Trigger took up residence at East Burrow Farm on the edge of Exmoor the following year. Briefly both stallions cohabited in Devon, but Eclipse subsequently moved to Northern Ireland before crossing the border to Co. Limerick. Double Eclipse became the first of the brothers to sire a Grade 1 winner when Go Native won the Supreme Novices' Hurdle at the 2009 Cheltenham Festival.

The next celebrity was Royal Rebel, who was by Mister Baileys' sire, Robellino, and he emulated Double Trigger in winning the Gold Cup, not once but twice. Purchased as a yearling from his breeder, the Duchess of Bedford, Royal Rebel cost Peter Savill, then chairman of the British Horseracing Board, a substantial 145,000 guineas.

An enigmatic individual, who was gelded as a backend three-year-old, Royal Rebel was inconsistent, but he proved an exceptional stayer on his day and his going days invariably occurred at Ascot. Frequently equipped with blinkers or a visor, he carried no such appendage when winning the Gold Cup in 2001 and 2002. He showed the utmost resolution in those two Gold Cups yet somehow he never received much credit for his endeavours.

Mark Johnston loves the Royal Meeting. In addition to three Gold Cups, he has gained two more Group 1 victories with Two Thousand Guineas third Bijou d'Inde (St James's Palace Stakes), and the brilliant One Thousand Guineas heroine, Attraction (Coronation Stakes). Homebred Attraction, who was frequently ridden at home by Deirdre Johnston, is discussed in detail in Chapter 29, but suffice to say that like Mister Baileys, she gained her classic victory at Newmarket on her seasonal reappearance.

Runner-up in the Eclipse Stakes, Bijou d'Inde was bought by Mark Johnston as a yearling for a bargain 20,000 guineas on behalf of Stuart Morrison, an advocate from Glasgow for whom he had won the Ebor Handicap with Quick Ransom. Bijou d'Inde defeated the winners of the English, Irish and French Two Thousand Guineas at Royal Ascot. Brought down in the Dubai World Cup spraining a tendon, he retired to Elsenham Stud in Hertfordshire (once owned by Dorothy Paget), before being exported to Turkey.

Two more durable middle distance performers Fruits of Love and Bandari excelled at Royal Ascot, the former winning the Hardwicke Stakes twice and the latter once. Both also won the Princess of Wales's Stakes. On his way home after winning the 1999 Dubai Turf Classic, Fruits of Love escaped virtually unscathed when jumping a partition in the horsebox and landing upside down alongside the driver – he had to be extricated in the most dramatic circumstances by the Hertfordshire fire brigade.

Both Fruits of Love and Bandari retired to stud in Ireland. The latter, who was frequently led round the paddock in a lip chain and taken to the start equipped with earplugs, kept his form remarkably well for a seven-year-old entire. Sadly he had little opportunity to make his mark as a stallion as he died after just two covering seasons.

Bandari raced for Sheikh Hamdan Al Maktoum and Kingsley House has enjoyed the patronage of the ruling family of Dubai since the beginning of the twenty-first century. This ensured a substantial annual influx of blue-blooded youngsters together with the financial benefits that that engenders, but the drawback was that any showing exceptional promise would be whisked away to pursue his or her career in the Godolphin colours.

The downside is well illustrated by Shamardal, who is the best horse Mark Johnston has trained. Unbeaten winner of the Dewhurst Stakes for Sheikh Maktoum Al Maktoum's Gainsborough Stud when rated the champion two-year-old of Europe in 2004, he left Middleham for Newmarket to win Godolphin the following season's French Two Thousand Guineas and Derby as well as the St James's Palace Stakes. Astonishingly, as a foal Shamardal had been diagnosed as a wobbler (the manifestation of the condition is a loss of balance and coordination).

Another classic winner to follow in Shamardal's footsteps was the 2009 St Leger hero, Mastery. Two more outstanding colts to switch allegiance to Godolphin were Fly to The Stars and Lend A Hand. In the case of Lend A Hand, Mark retained him long enough to saddle him to finish second in the 1998 Two Thousand Guineas.

In 2008 Kingsley House drew an uncharacteristic blank at Royal Ascot when former inmate, Campanologist, won the King Edward VII Stakes for Godolphin. However, there was the reverse side of the coin. On only her second start for Mark Johnston, the Maktoum-owned Nahoodh won the Group 1 Falmouth Stakes at the Newmarket July Meeting.

The following year Mark Johnston trained two individual Group 1 winners in the three-year-old Jukebox Jury (a grey like Nahoodh), who won the Preis von Europa, while Awzaan won the Middle Park Stakes. Jukebox Jury went on to dead-heat for the Irish St Leger as a five-year-old.

Mark is only too happy to travel abroad with his runners in pursuit of lucrative prize money. Both Quick Ransom and Double Trigger made unavailing attempts at Australia's greatest race, the Melbourne Cup, as did Yavana's Pace. A temperamental individual, Yavana's Pace amassed a fortune campaigning all over Europe. As a ten-year-old he scored in Cologne to become the oldest winner at Group 1 level, not bad for a gelding by the Irish jump stallion, Accordion!

Their trainer also has a soft spot for the remarkable sprinter, Branston Abby, who is buried at Kingsley House. A quirky individual, she was always exercised early in the morning before the rest of the string arrived on the gallops. Kept in training as a seven-year-old, she won a total of twenty-four races, a post-war record for a British-trained mare. Six of her eleven Listed victories came in Germany albeit she was disqualified from one. Sadly Branston Abby died from grass sickness before ever producing a foal.

Nowadays there are around 200 horses in training at Kingsley House in any one season. Since 2008 there has been a huge dependency on Sheikh Mohammed's son Sheikh Hamdan Bin Mohammed Al Maktoum. The significance of this new liaison was evident at Royal Ascot in 2010 when Monterosso won the Group 2 King Edward VII Stakes and Rainfall won the Group 3 Jersey Stakes.

Other patrons of Kingsley House are the top breeders, Kirsten Rausing of Lanwades Stud, Newmarket, and Renata Jacobs of Newsells Park Stud in Hertfordshire. In 2006 the latter's Soapy Danger won two of Mark Johnston's favourite races, the Queen's Vase and the Princess of Wales's Stakes. In 2010 Kirsten Rausing's homebred mare Lady Jane Digby won a Group 1 in Germany – her two-year-old Frankel filly Francophilia is one of Kingsley House's two-year-olds of 2017.

After a few seasons when Group winners were rather thin on the ground, Mark Johnston Racing produced two star juveniles in 2015, both Darley homebreds. Buratino won the Coventry Stakes at Royal Ascot, and the grey Lumiere, whose sire Shamardal was such a good two-year-old for Kingsley House, won the Cheveley Park Stakes.

When Lumiere was a foal, Mark Johnston procured her dam Screen Star from Darley at the 2013 Newmarket December Sales for 52,000 guineas. He then sold the resulting colt foal for 70,000 guineas only to buy him back as a yearling for 105,000 guineas. Doubtless he was attracted to Screen Star having trained a relative, Systematic, to win the Cumberland Lodge Stakes and Ormonde Stakes.

Lumiere's triumph at Newmarket was the stable's first Group 1 winner since Jukebox Jury dead-heated at the Curragh in 2011. She was also the first domestic Group 1 winner since Awzaan won the 2009 Middle Park Stakes. The stable then produced the 2016 Middle Park Stakes winner The Last Lion – that was his tenth juvenile outing, having made a winning debut at Doncaster on the opening day of the season. Unfortunately both proved disappointing three-year-olds.

By now there were two significant changes regarding the large complement of horses at Kingsley House owned by Sheikh Mohammed's son Sheikh Hamdan (whose uncle of the same name remains a patron of the stable). His colours of green and red have been replaced by all grey. The second change is that Mark Johnston is now regarded as one of Godolphin's own trainers, so he is able to keep training anything that shows exceptional promise.

Mark Johnston's resolve to win races with some of the less talented members of his team is exemplified by his record on the all-weather tracks, notably the winter season which runs from the end of October through to finals' day at Lingfield Park on Good Friday. One can only assume that the rewards justify the enormous amount of travelling involved, but one thing is certain – not many people would want to be confronted by the diesel bills involved!

There must be all sorts of logistical problems in training such a huge string of horses this far north, not least the financial implications and the availability of competent staff, as well as adverse weather conditions. However, modern facilities can make all the difference and even during the heavy snowfalls during the winters of 2008–9 and 2009–10, horses of all age groups were able to work either on the Park Farm Tapeta gallop or the all-weather strip on the Low Moor.

Investment at Kingsley House is always ongoing and Kingsley Park's new exercise centre housed in a purpose built barn was up and running for the start of the 2017 season. This new complex includes a swimming pool, water walker and treadmill, all facilities which can equally well be used as an adjunct to the routine training schedule or for horses with physical problems. They have been declared indispensable aids by the two in-house vets, Neil Mechie and John Martin.

Nowadays fewer trainers follow the old fashioned routine of evening stables when inspecting every horse in the yard accompanied by the head lad. For a start there is an insufficient number of hours in the day to make this feasible even if the trainer was permanently at home. But Mark has to attend race meetings all over the country on a daily basis, helped admittedly by piloting his own aeroplane.

The master of Kingsley House is full of surprises and one of his favourite pastimes is bicycling. Unfortunately for him high days and holidays provide scant opportunities for such leisure activities even when there is no racing – on Easter Monday, the rescheduled date for Middleham's annual open day now organised by Racing Welfare, he conducts a question-and-answer session from the back of one of his own horse-boxes.

Any Flat trainer's ammunition is largely dependent on what he or an agent select at the annual round of yearling sales. Needless to say Mark has his own ideas about what he looks for in a potential racehorse and his priorities when it comes to choosing yearlings are based on a combination of his own veterinary knowledge and first hand experience. He has never been constrained either by tradition or convention and buys many of his yearlings 'on spec'.

Surprisingly he places greater emphasis on pedigree than conformation. His preference is for the sire to be proven rather than fashionable and to be a Group 1 winner; he is also an advocate of stayers. On the distaff side he likes any of the dam's progeny to have earned a Timeform rating of over 80.

Another priority is the overall appearance of the individual and he favours an athlete and is not necessarily dissuaded by minor conformation defects. Back at the knee is one fault that most yearling buyers will not countenance, but Mark associates it with inherent speed. And he is not too concerned about OCD (bony enlargements commonly found in the limbs of young stock) considering it only an indication of excessive growth at an early stage of development rather than an inherent problem.

As the runners walk round the paddock, a commentator will frequently say 'and that is a typical Mark Johnston horse' meaning that he or she is a well made 'good-topped' individual, a horse with a certain size and substance (with its mane and tail invariably plaited). When it comes to yearlings, he always attaches importance to weight. He has never had a good filly under 400 kilos and he likes them to be 450 kilos. His motto is, 'the bigger they are the faster they go'.

A one-time regular guest columnist on the *Sporting Life* and the *Racing Post*, who produces his own monthly magazine, the *Kingsley Klairon*. Mark always has an opinion, invariably controversial, but always well reasoned, and he is not concerned should it contradict the accepted view of the majority. It was a disagreement over the perceived wrongs to stable staff that caused his fall out with the *Racing Post*.

Other controversial issues to which he is strongly opposed are the use of drugs in the training regime, the present declaration system and the indiscriminate watering of courses. Conversely he is a great supporter of staying races, narrow band handicaps and the overall diversity that racing in Britain affords. However, he thinks that the promotion of racing to the general public focuses far too much on the betting aspect rather than the horses themselves.

For whatever reason jockeys who ride regularly for Mark Johnston seem to engender less publicity than those employed in other top yards and he is a great believer that there are jockeys for courses in the same way that there are horses for courses. There was a time when he had first call on the services of Jason Weaver and Kevin Darley, respective riders of his two classic winners, Mister Baileys and Attraction.

During the summer of 2007 Kevin Darley, one of the senior members of the weighing room, decided to ride as a freelance and then retired. This left Joe Fanning top of the pecking order at Kingsley House, but subsequent injury enabled the stable's Greg Fairley, a Scot, to become the season's top apprentice. Greg started on the flapping circuit in which sphere his father, Andrew, was many times champion. Today the stable relies to a large extent on Joe Fanning, Franny Norton and P. J. McDonald.

Kingsley House is run on modern business lines with an administrative manager and individual yard managers, who supervise some thirty horses apiece. They convene every week to exchange views and targets – with so many horses, delegating responsibility has to be a key factor. All the staff wear uniform riding kit at home and matching tartan waistcoats on the racecourse, which helps to engender the ethos of team spirit. Every four months there is a special prize for the most deserving member of staff chosen by fellow employees.

Traditionally a racing stable is always identified by the trainer's name, but Mark Johnston would be equally happy to have the corporate title, Kingsley House, so that any future transfer to one of his two sons, for example, could be effected without incurring a change to the identity of the business. Furthermore this would enhance the value of the operation as there would be a certain good will attached, something that does not exist under the prevailing system.

Experience gleaned at Kingsley House has proved quite a stepping stone. Jason Weaver is now a racing pundit for ITV, while his former riding colleague, Keith Dalgleish, has done tremendously well as a trainer in Scotland. Also two former in-house vets have become successful trainers. James Given started off at Willoughton in Lincolnshire from a yard that used to be part of Limestone Stud, while James Tate is virtually a private trainer at Newmarket for associates of the Maktoum family.

Mark is proud of his own heritage and he has a great affinity with Glasgow. This is manifest by his support of the pioneering endoscopy project undertaken by his alma mater, the veterinary school at Glasgow University. Just for good measure the university's pipe band wears the distinctive Mark Johnston Racing logo. And he certainly could not resist the invitation to become a director of Hamilton Park, which is one of the most progressive racecourses in the country.

Since Mark Johnston embarked upon his training career, the goal posts have been moved to such an extent that it is almost impossible to chart his annual position on the leading trainers' list in Great Britain (prize money earned) year on year. In 2003 and 2006 he finished runner-up to Sir Michael Stoute (albeit £1m adrift both times) and he has featured in the top ten from 1994 to 2016 when he registered a record 23 consecutive centuries of domestic winners.

Prior to 2007 the official trainers' championship was determined by the duration of the Turf season only, but with the increasing importance of all-weather racing it now runs for the calendar year. In 2009 that enabled Mark to become the first trainer in Great Britain to break through the double century barrier with a grand total of 216 wins.

But what the master of Middleham values above all else are winners at Royal Ascot and after an abortive 2016 he was back on the score sheet in 2017. Dante Stakes hero Permian, who had run disappointingly in the Derby, gained due compensation in the King Edward VII Stakes (the Ascot equivalent) and that grand old stager Oriental Fox completed the double in the Queen Alexandra Stakes – he had won Britain's longest Flat race two years previously. This brought the stable's tally of Royal Ascot winners to a sensational forty-one, Double Trigger having opened the batting in the 1995 Gold Cup.

Memories of Mark Johnston's very first Group winner were revived when Nyaleti ran away with the 2017 Princess Margaret Stakes on 'King George' day at Ascot to emulate Marina Park, who prevailed in the same race a quarter of a century before. The filly Nyaleti looks a great prospect as indeed does another juvenile, this

31

A SCOTTISH KING PRESIDING OVER
AN ENGLISH CASTLE

Landlord and tenant do not always see eye to eye. So often when it comes to training, 'he who pays the piper calls the tune' and Wiltshire-based trainer Alan King has certainly had to be resilient. Having been ousted in double quick time from his original base in Gloucestershire, he was momentarily faced with an uncertain future yet again when his present quarters were sold in 2016. Fortunately for all concerned the new owner was only too happy for the status quo to be maintained.

Nowadays the trainers' championship has polarised to such an extent that just a handful of names dominate thanks to the patronage of a clutch of very rich owners. Despite this, Alan King can claim a record of consistency that few can match. In the last fourteen seasons (2003–4 to 2016–7) he has never been out of the top ten NH trainers in Great Britain in terms of earnings and has twice occupied third place. And in Yanworth he seems to have a horse with the potential to go right to the top.

Born in Lanarkshire, Alan King is the youngest of three brothers who were brought up on the family's South Netherburn Farm, which ran a dairy herd of Friesians, situated to the south-east of Glasgow between Larkhall and Stonehouse. Just occasionally there were racecourse visits to Hamilton and Ayr, as well as Lanark which then staged trotting races. The three boys were all members of the Pony Club through which, very fortuitously, Alan met trainer-to-be John Wilson.

Mad keen on racing from the age of seven or eight, the young Alan King would spend his Saturdays at home watching racing on television. Inevitably he had his boyhood heroes and they tended to be trainers rather than jockeys, headed by Henry Cecil on the Flat and Fred Winter over jumps. Prophetically, when it came to horses his favourites were mostly jumpers, like the Grand National stalwarts, Red Rum and Crisp, and Edward Courage's gallant Spanish Steps.

After a year milking cows at home, Alan joined John Wilson, who was then based up the road at Motherwell prior to taking over the famous Cree Lodge Stables at Ayr (see Chapter 10). At that stage Alan had aspirations as an amateur rider and it was John Wilson's suggestion that he should go to David Nicholson to receive some well needed tuition. 'I went down in August 1985 planning to return at Christmas, and stayed fifteen years,' he recalls, 'not that it did anything to improve my riding technique!'

The address of Alan King's training quarters, Barbury Castle Stables, Wroughton, Swindon, is somewhat misleading in a geographical sense. Wroughton, once the site of an RAF base and now a dismal collection of disused Ministry of Defence buildings, is an isolated spot on the North Wiltshire Downs some way removed from the urban sprawl of Swindon. Formerly the enormous workshop of the Great Western Railway, nowadays Swindon is the manufacturing base in the United Kingdom of the giant Japanese car corporation, Honda.

Barbury Castle, the site of an Iron Age hill fort, is situated to the south of the M4 which skirts Swindon, running up to the historic Ridgeway, north of the old coaching town of Marlborough. Just like the neighbouring Berkshire Downs, this is racehorse country, although there have been changes in occupancy over the last few years. Three erstwhile trainers in the vicinity to have retired are Jim Old, who shared a Wroughton address with Alan King, while across the valley at Broad Hinton, Jeff King (no relation) was succeeded briefly by Andy Turnell. Contemporaries, both were top ranking professional jump jockeys.

To the south of Wroughton is Ogbourne Maizey, where Andy Turnell's father, Bob, also used to train. The only surviving yard there now is Bonita Racing Stables which Peter Makin sold to Emma Lavelle in 2016. Across the Marlborough Downs from the famous

Ogbourne gallops once utilised by Sir Gordon Richards, are Manton and Beckhampton, two of the most historic training establishments in the country with a great classic tradition. Since the Manton Estate was sold by the Sangster family, it is now shared by Brian Meehan and George Baker, while Beckhampton has long been presided over by Roger Charlton.

Wroughton, by comparison, has always been associated with jumpers. Aubrey Hastings won the 1906 Grand National on Ascetic's Silver whom he also trained. He was to send out three more National winners from Wroughton with Ally Soper, Ballymacad and Master Robert. Subsequently he found and trained two 'Jacks' who became 'Aces', Brown Jack and Kellsboro' Jack. Winner of the 1928 Champion Hurdle, Brown Jack has a race named after him at Ascot to commemorate an unprecedented six consecutive victories in the Queen Alexandra Stakes. And members of the local Wroughton football team were called the Brown Jacks.

Aubrey Hastings' successor at Wroughton was his former assistant, Ivor Anthony. Amateur champion in 1904 and professional champion in 1912, Ivor inherited Kellsboro' Jack whom Aubrey Hastings considered the best exponent he had ever seen over the formidable Aintree fences, a view that was vindicated when the gelding won the 1933 Grand National. Ivor Anthony saddled a second National winner with Royal Mail in 1937. He was also successful with Morse Code in the Gold Cup and with Chenango in the Champion Hurdle.

With absolutely no family connections with racing, Alan King's career as a trainer owes everything to David Nicholson, another top professional rider who took up training just like his father before him. 'Frenchie' Nicholson, who was apprenticed at Chantilly and whose own father had been master of the Pau Foxhounds in the shadow of the Pyrenees (hence the nickname), gained his most important victory on Lord Sefton's Medoc II in the 1942 Gold Cup. During the time that he trained at Prestbury his stable star was the same owner's Irish Lizard.

However, Frenchie Nicholson had another string to his bow as a jockeys' tutor, champion Pat Eddery being his greatest protégé. Over jumps his pupils included his own apprentice son, David. One of the strongest jump jockeys of his generation and completely fearless, he had few superiors over fences. In 1968 David took out a licence to train at Cotswold House, Condicote, Stow-on-the-Wold. Initially he continued riding, only to give up the unequal struggle with his weight.

It was one of Frenchie Nicholson's lads who, when David was at school at Haileybury, referred to him as 'The Duke', as he was known ever after. The Duke was even more successful as a trainer than as a jockey – his proudest moment in the saddle had been to win the Whitbread Gold Cup on Mill House. However, nearly two decades elapsed before he saddled a winner on his local course at the National Hunt Festival. In fact he had two winners at the 1986 meeting, the second of them, Charter Party, going on to win the Gold Cup two years later, the individual highlight of his training career.

It was during his first two full seasons, 1993–4 and 1994–5, at Jackdaws Castle, Temple Guiting, which is nearer to Cheltenham, that David Nicholson became champion trainer, the only time in seventeen consecutive seasons that Martin Pipe was knocked off his perch. A purpose-built establishment, Jackdaws Castle belonged to Colin Smith, a construction magnate and part-owner of Charter Party. His racing enterprise was called Ford Farm Racing and his breeding involvement, which included some top jumping stallions, operated as Ford Farm Bloodstock.

Aged eighteen when he first worked for David Nicholson as a stable lad, Alan King stayed on as his assistant until David's retirement in 1999 following an acrimonious split with his landlord. At that juncture Alan took over the licence together with such celebrities as Relkeel, Anzum, Go Ballistic and Mulligan, but it was only a temporary arrangement. He was soon replaced by Richard Phillips, until Jackdaws Castle was sold to John P. McManus, who installed fellow Irishman, Jonjo O'Neill, as the resident trainer.

Until David Nicholson's untimely death in August 2006, he remained a tremendous supporter and advisor to Alan King. It must have been a nerve-racking time when, with the patronage of mostly inherited owners, Alan transferred his operation on 1 June 2000, from Jackdaws Castle to Barbury Castle. Owned by Konrad Goess-Saurau, an Austrian count, the yard had previously been occupied for brief spells by two aspiring trainers, Michael Heaton-Ellis and Clive Cox.

Alan King started out in Wiltshire with about thirty horses, but no sooner had he assembled a nucleus of staff and adequate tack to keep the wheels turning than everything came to a grinding halt – the foot and mouth epidemic ravished the countryside culminating with the cancellation of the Cheltenham Festival and much else besides. Then two years later his landlord decided to sell the 2,000 acre Barbury Castle Estate set in an idyllic amphitheatre of downland, farmland and woodland, retaining Temple Farm next door.

Fortuitously one of Alan King's owners, Nigel Bunter, who lived locally (they met originally over a drink at the Wheatsheaf Inn in Ogbourne St Andrew), had just sold his mobile telephone business, Cellular Operations, to Vodafone, and, looking for an alternative involvement, he jumped at the opportunity to purchase Barbury Castle. But as agriculture represents such a poor return on capital investment the new owner looked at alternate sources of income and arable farming and training racehorses became only part of the enterprise.

Unfazed by the fact that Goess-Saurau's attempt to introduce American-style timber racing never caught on at Barbury Castle, Nigel Bunter revitalised the old point-to-point course and started the Barbury Castle Horse Trials, soon an established fixture in the eventing calendar. The facilities also served as the quarantine quarters for the horses belonging to the American team competing at the 2008 Beijing Olympics.

Alan King's stable numbers eventually multiplied to nearly two hundred horses. Unlike David Nicholson, the Scot did not have to wait long for his first Cheltenham Festival winner, Fork Lightning scoring in the 2004 William Hill Handicap Chase, and in 2005 he won the Triumph Hurdle with Penzance. Then in 2006 Voy Por Ustedes won the Arkle Trophy and My Way De Solzen won the World Hurdle, a first Cheltenham stable double for stable jockey Robert 'Chocolate' Thornton.

The stable's early achievements at Prestbury Park in March soon had such leading owners as Trevor Hemmings, Sir Robert Ogden and John Hales beating a path to his door and J.P. McManus was not far behind. Of course not everything is sweetness and light. Some things in life seem to have no rational explanation and the stable's tremendous record at Cheltenham was matched over a prolonged period by an equally abysmal one at Sandown Park.

However, there was no stopping the Festival bonanza with trebles in each of the next two seasons, five of the six winners being partnered by Choc Thornton. In 2007 My Way De Solzen won the Arkle Trophy; Voy Por Ustedes won the Queen Mother Champion Chase; and Katchit won the Triumph Hurdle, all Grade 1 events. Victory for My Way De Solzen in the Arkle, in which he put up a better time than Voy Por Ustedes managed in the Champion, fully vindicated his trainer's controversial decision to bring the previous season's World Hurdle winner back from three miles to two miles.

Barbury Castle's winners in 2008 comprised Katchit (Champion Hurdle), Old Benny (National Hunt Chase), and Nenuphar Collonges (Spa Hurdle). That was a fifth victory from six starts at Cheltenham for the diminutive Katchit and in so doing he became the first to bring off the Triumph-Champion double in successive years since Persian War in 1968 – and seventy-three five-year-olds had been beaten in the Champion Hurdle since See You Then prevailed at that age in 1985.

Another stable star during the 2007–8 season was Blazing Bailey who was successful in the Liverpool Hurdle and the World Series Hurdle – his victory at the Punchestown Festival provided his trainer with a notable landmark, a first ever success in Ireland.

Conversely the 2009 Cheltenham Festival was the most frustrating that Alan King has ever experienced. On all four days he had saddled a runner to finish second in a Grade 1 contest, but that elusive first winner did not materialise until the very last race of the entire meeting, Oh Crick landing the Grand Annual Handicap Chase. This just happened to be Alan's 700th career win and the same horse had provided him with a 500th winner on New Year's Day 2008.

Two of those four Cheltenham runners-up were Voy Pur Ustedes and Walkon and they redeemed themselves at the Liverpool Grand National Meeting by winning the Melling Chase and the Anniversary Novices' Hurdle respectively, two more Grade 1 events – Voy Pur Ustedes was winning the Melling Chase for a second consecutive year having defeated Master Minded on the first occasion. Oh Crick, who had provided Alan King's second jockey, Wayne Hutchinson, with his first ever Cheltenham Festival winner also contributed to the Aintree bonanza by winning the Red Rum Handicap Chase.

In April 2014, Choc Thornton had a fall at Chepstow from Say When, a gelding owned by Alan King himself. The jockey (37), who had endured a series of recent injuries, suffered a broken vertebrae. This was to terminate a riding career embracing well over 1,000 winners. So his deputy, Wayne Hutchinson, who had been getting an increasing number of mounts, became the number one stable jockey. It was a watershed for Barbury Castle as Alan King and Darlington-born Choc Thornton had been colleagues with David Nicholson, Choc having been both champion amateur and champion conditional jockey.

The mid-way point of the National Hunt season, the Christmas period has also proved a rewarding time for Barbury Castle. In 2006 and 2007 Voy Por Ustedes won the first two runnings of the Desert Orchid Chase at Kempton Park while Halcon Genelardais was just denied a winning double in the Welsh National – at the second attempt he failed by a head carrying top-weight. Not surprisingly Alan King is a tremendous advocate of these French-breds and they account for a substantial proportion of his NH string.

In the old days the Duke enjoyed a very successful association with David Minton of the British Bloodstock Agency, when the market for jumpers revolved mostly around Irish-breds. David then set up his own independent agency, Highflyer Bloodstock, in partnership with his former BBA colleague, Anthony Bromley, who has exploited the availability of French-bred horses with quite spectacular success and Alan King has certainly been one of the principal beneficiaries.

Quite apart from the fact that French breds tend to be extremely athletic with an inherent ability to jump from an early age, they had, up till that time at least, represented very good value for money. For example, My Way De Solzen cost £32,000 and Halcon Genelardais £22,000, not big sums by present day standards. Voy Por Ustedes was originally trained by Alan King for the David Minton-managed Million In Mind Partnership, but returned to Barbury Castle after changing hands at the 2005 Doncaster Spring Sales for 106,000 guineas.

These French breds have continued to serve Alan King well. One of the stable's current stars is Uxizandre, winner of the 2015 Ryanair Chase at the Cheltenham Festival. He was sandwiched between two greys who seemed to be a permanent fixture there, Medermit and Smad Place – the latter was making his seventh consecutive appearance at the meeting in 2017 when lining up for a third time in the Gold Cup. Smad Place had his moment of glory when winning the 2016 Hennessy Gold Cup at Newbury. It was also at the Berkshire course that another French bred, Messire des Obeaux, was successful in the Grade 1 Challow Hurdle.

Alan King, whose stable is sponsored by Ultima Business Solutions, has trained the winners of 1,282 races under NH Rules to the close of 2016–17 season. These include thirty Grade 1 wins and fifteen wins at the Cheltenham Festival. Of course any Festival winner is a cause for celebration and the handicaps are no exception so it was a great feather in Alan's cap when Medinas and Meister Eckhart finished first and second in the always competitive Coral Cup.

For a top stable it is essential to have a flagship horse and the popular chaser Smad Place has been replaced at Barbury Castle by a star hurdler. Like Uxizandre, Yanworth is owned by John P. McManus and his trainer was aware from an early stage that he was something special. During the 2016–17 season Yanworth won the Grade 1 Christmas Hurdle, Kempton Park and Stayers' Liverpool Hurdle, as well as the Grade 2 Ascot Hurdle and Kingwell Hurdle, Wincanton.

On his only other seasonal appearance Yanworth was the unplaced favourite in the Champion Hurdle. There was a sting in the tail as a routine test revealed the presence of a drug which, while permitted for horses in training, is forbidden on the racecourse, an infringement of the rules that cost Alan King a £2,000 fine.

Although Flat horses do not play a major role at Barbury Castle in the general scheme of things, the stable has a good strike rate. It was quite a training feat to keep Nigel Bunter's five-year-old Shipmaster sound enough to win the 2008 Sagaro Stakes, a first Group winner for both owner and trainer – in 2015 came the 50–1 Cesarewitch winner Grumeti and the following year Primitivo won the King George V Handicap, a first Royal Ascot triumph.

Back at the ranch the horses are accommodated in two separate yards about a mile apart. Alan's house cum office is a state of the art development where the impressive facilities include three American-style barns together with an indoor school and a horsewalker. This is regarded as the main yard. The other complex, which comprises five barns converted from cattle sheds, is called Sharpridge – Nigel Bunter built himself a house there.

There is a comprehensive selection of gallops. The principal ones on grass are Sharpridge Five, a 5 furlong incline with a sweeping left-hand turn and the Barbury Mile where the terrain is much more undulating. On old downland turf they can be guaranteed to provide wonderful going in the driest of spells, but they would be compromised by sheer weight of numbers during a prolonged period of extreme weather conditions. This is when the two all-weather gallops come into their own. The most recent climbs 350 feet over a distance of nearly 5 furlongs. Nowadays the horses come up that hill towards the top of the Ridgeway six days a week.

There is nothing new about so-called interval training as the concept was first utilised by Paddy Prendergast, that master trainer of two-year-olds in Ireland, long before Martin Pipe applied it so successfully to the training of jumpers. However, it is all a far cry from those early days at Condicote. Alan King recalls that when he started out with the Duke, traditional roadwork was an integral part of the fitness programme and this was the strict schedule three times weekly. Now all that has changed irrevocably.

Additional facilities include a one and a half furlong sand circle, which is utilised for conditioning and stamina work, while a field is set aside specifically for schooling. The youngsters start off over a row of logs and then progress to a line of three hurdles before attempting a series of portable hurdles and fences on a grass strip. The necessity for thorough schooling was one of the Duke's priorities to which the Wiltshire-based trainer has always adhered.

All trainers seem to have their own methods and foibles and despite the considerable numbers involved, the Wroughton handler remains very much hands-on, making all the entries himself and compiling the work-lists on a daily basis. Unlike some of his major rivals, he has never had to rely on one or two principal owners and if he has a really fancied runner in a big race he is unlikely to watch the proceedings in their company – he prefers to keep his own council!

Although Alan King never did become proficient as a jockey (the best he could manage was third in a hunter chase at Kelso), his record as a trainer of jumpers is truly remarkable. Just like his kinsman, Mark Johnston, Alan King has solid family support behind him. Once again he is indebted to David Nicholson as he met his wife, Rachel, when she was employed by him. They have two children, Henry and Georgia. She was already a member of the Pony Club at the tender age of six, so who knows, one day there may well be a Queen of the Castle.

32

HE SHOULD HAVE BEEN NAMED
AFTER ARTHUR'S SEAT

Saturday 8 April 2017 was a glorious spring afternoon under a clear blue sky and it coincided with a momentous occasion at Liverpool as One For Arthur became only the second Grand National winner trained in Scotland. Thirty-eight years had elapsed since Rubstic prevailed back in 1979, but whereas he was trained by an Englishman, this latest Aintree hero was handled by Lucinda Russell, who was born and brought up in Edinburgh and trains on the opposite side of the Firth of Forth.

Lucinda Russell's partner and assistant is the eight times champion jump jockey and occasional *Daily Mail* racing correspondent Peter Scudamore, MBE. He is the son of Michael, who won the 1959 Grand National on Oxo (from his popular Scottish rival Wyndburgh), and father of Tom. Peter was stable jockey to Martin Pipe and in due course his own son Tom took over the same role for Martin's son David.

The 2017 result of the world's greatest steeplechase was dominated by women as One For Arthur is owned by 'Two Golf Widows', former school friends Deborah Thomson from Gullane and Belinda McClung, who lives near Jedburgh and acts as a racecourse steward. They became the owners of the gelding after he joined the Lucinda Russell team for £60,000 at the Cheltenham horses in training sale in December 2013. The four-year-old had previously been sold twice at public auction in his native Ireland: for €14,000 as a yearling and €34,000 as a three-year-old.

Arthur, as he is inevitably known at home, was partnered at Aintree by 24-year-old Derek Fox. He was having his first ride in the National having finished fifth on the horse over these unique fences in the

293

shorter Becher Chase in December. On that occasion the jockey was censured by the stewards for anticipating the start. This performance was sandwiched between victories for the partnership over extended distances at Kelso and Warwick, a fact that was reflected in his 14–1 starting price in the Grand National.

The modification of the Aintree fences means they are nothing like as formidable as once they were. Consequently there is more emphasis nowadays on being in a prominent position throughout the race rather than the old fashioned concept of hunting round towards the rear of the field for the first circuit. But despite their joint inexperience of the course, this is exactly the way that Derek Fox rode Arthur in a forty runner field, a vindication of the stable's confidence in his ability.

One additional factor must have tested the stable's loyalty towards its new stable jockey. On 9 March, just thirty-one days before the National, Derek broke his left wrist and right collarbone in a fall at Carlisle. That he was able to pass the doctor to ride at Aintree speaks volumes for his determination to get race fit again and to the dedication of all concerned at Jack Berry House, the jockeys' new rehabilitation centre in Malton.

Previously a conditional jockey to the stable, Derek Fox from Sligo took on the mantle of number one rider at Arlary House upon the retirement of long standing stable jockey Peter Buchanan at the close of the 2015–16 season. Despite his name, Peter hails from Northern Ireland, and according to Peter Scudamore he was the best schooling jockey in the business.

Early in her career Lucinda had a call on such top jockeys as Richard Johnson, Andrew Thornton and Tom Scudamore, but with an ever increasing string it became mandatory to have someone who was readily available at home and she always has a strong contingent of conditional riders. One of the stars was Campbell Gillies from Edinburgh who died tragically aged twenty-one in a swimming pool accident while on holiday in Corfu in 2012. A tree was planted at Arlary House in his memory.

Based at Arlary House, Milnathort, at Kinross on Tayside, whence she moved in 1979 and built the stables, Lucinda Russell's yard is sponsored by Ian Macleod & Co., a family business chaired by Lucinda's father Peter Russell and synonymous with Isle of Skye and Glengoyne whiskies.

'The business is very keen to promote this brand through racing and by sponsoring our yard,' explained Lucinda. Edinburgh Gin also comes under the same umbrella and on Derby Day 2017 the firm was responsible for a richly endowed card at Musselburgh highlighted by the £80,000 Edinburgh Cup. The business is also a generous sponsor at Perth, Lucinda's local course.

One might hazard a guess that One For Arthur was named after that spectacular Edinburgh landmark Arthur's Seat, but not so. In fact one needs to look to another capital city as the nomenclature is owed to Arthur Guinness, the founder of that ubiquitous Dublin brewery.

Lucinda Russell is only the fourth lady to train a National winner following Jenny Pitman with Corbiere in 1983 and Royal Athlete in 1995, Venetia Williams with Mon Mome in 2009 and Sue Smith with Auroras Encore in 2013. The latter was ridden by Ryan Mania. Born in Galashiels, he started out with Howard Johnson in County Durham, before joining Sue Smith's Yorkshire stable. Not long after his National triumph he retired from race riding aged twenty-five to become master and huntsman of the Berwickshire Hunt.

While Ryan Mania gained his first riding experience in point-to-points, Lucinda Russell came into racing after competing in three-day events. She first took out a licence to train in August 1995 and was quickly off the mark, her very first winner being her first ever runner, Fiveleigh Builds at Perth. When she started out at Arlary House, she had about a dozen horses, and it is indicative of her success (over 600 winners to date) that at one time their number exceeded three figures.

Lucinda Russell has always favoured staying chasers and in 2005 the stable had high Grand National expectations with Strong Resolve who started one of the favourites at Aintree. Had he prevailed he would have become only the third grey National winner. This popular front-runner, who was also owned by a group of old school friends (in this instance from Perth) was successful eight times and earned over

£100,000. Sadly Strong Resolve had to be put down in August 2008 following a freak accident at home.

The highlight of Strong Resolve's career came when he finished runner-up in the Welsh National at Chepstow, a feat repeated by another of the stable's greys in Silver By Nature in the 2009 renewal. Also strongly fancied for the Grand National, Silver By Nature gained his most important success in the Blue Square Gold Cup, Haydock Park – the Lancashire course is the furthest south that the stable runners can manage without an overnight stay. Silver By Nature was homebred by Geoff Brown of Kinfauns. Owner and chairman of local St Johnstone Football Club, he has a rising star in Silver By Nature's close relative Sammy B.

Despite the usual, rather inadequate, fortnightly interval between the two events, there is always the temptation for a National runner to take his chance in the Scottish equivalent at Ayr, but One For Arthur's owners were not to be seduced by that particular double – Lucinda had already saddled the runner-up in Scotland's premier chase with Kerry Lads.

The day after One For Arthur's historic Aintree victory his admirers came from far and wide to welcome him home. His exertions were far from over as in the ensuing weeks he was paraded at all four of Scotland's NH courses, Musselburgh, Ayr, Perth and Kelso, with the Grand National trophy itself making an appearance at Hamilton Park, all in the cause of promoting jump racing north of the border. Then it was off for his summer holidays to enjoy a well earned break.

Needless to say the result of the 2017 Grand National was not such good news for Scotbet, Scotland's largest independent bookmaker. The two hardest hit of its fifty shops were in Kinross, just three miles from Lucinda Russell's yard, and North Berwick, close to where One For Arthur's owners live. Ladbrokes too reported substantial payouts in its branches in Fife with Glenrothes, Cowdenbeath, Kelty and Perth particularly hard hit. Evidently Rubstic's success all those years ago was a rather less painful affair for the bookmakers!

It is a fact of life that racing, particularly jump racing, is a high risk business for the participants, both human and equine, but the racing fraternity is extremely generous in supporting charities which benefit injured jockeys and horses alike. So the number twenty-two saddlecloth which One For Arthur wore to victory at Aintree was auctioned on line in aid of the Great North Air Ambulance Service.

It is generally recognised that training racehorses is very much a numbers game. It is also a fickle business and Lucinda Russell's current string falls some way short numerically of her optimum. It is certainly a reflection on the ups and downs of the game that she had no runners at the 2017 Cheltenham Festival. Yet in 2012 she saddled a winner there in Brindisi Breeze only for that horse to be killed in an horrific road accident.

One For Arthur's historic victory at Aintree in colours incorporating the Scottish saltire, seems to exemplify all the positive qualities that the *Braveheart* concept conjures up and this was a much deserved shot in the arm for Scottish racing. Remarkably One For Arthur's owners are good friends of the Douglas family, and it was John Douglas who owned the only other 'trained in Scotland' Grand National hero Rubstic – in fact John's son Struan was one of the Russell/Scudamore party at Aintree.

Lucinda Russell has certainly experienced the ups and downs of racing over the last few years. Despite the fact that financial considerations dictate that training horses has to be a business rather than a sport these days, she is always as gracious in defeat as in victory. But when fortune smiles, she is always the first to emphasise that any credit should be attributed to her wonderful team at home.

33

BRING ON THE GIRLS

With so many top National Hunt jockeys speaking with that characteristic soft Irish brogue it is not surprising that Ireland should have produced such talented lady riders as Nina Carberry and Katie Walsh. After all they were born and bred to be jockeys and it would surely have been a travesty had the rules continued to exclude them from competition.

Female Flat jockeys have long been part and parcel of the scene on this side of the Irish Sea with Hayley Turner, now a regular TV racing presenter, achieving the highest profile so far. But it has been a different story when it comes to jumping. Such was the prejudice against jump jockeys of the fairer sex in the UK, that it is unlikely that the two leading protagonists, Lucy Alexander and Lizzie Kelly, could ever have made a name for themselves without family connections.

Geographically the two girls are poles apart as Lucy is stable jockey to her father Nicholas Alexander in Fife and Lizzie is attached to her step-father Nick Williams's Devon stable. Whereas Lizzie's success has been achieved largely through the stable star Tea For Two in whom her mother is joint owner, Lucy made history by becoming champion conditional jockey for the 2012–13 season with thirty-eight winners, an auspicious fast track rise to the top.

Lucy Alexander's career in the saddle is a mirror image of her father's involvement in training. He substituted his permit to train (the conditions restrict one to training for oneself and one's immediate family) dating from 2002 for a fully-fledged licence for the 2007–8 season. Lucy herself turned professional in 2011 having previously gained invaluable experience in point-to-points and as an amateur under National Hunt Rules.

The Alexanders have a corinthian tradition which spans about seventy years of hunting and point-to-pointing in Scotland, and Nick won the permit holder's national award for Best Horse in both 2003–4 and 2006–7. His initial coup de grace was to saddle Fearless Foursome to win four consecutive races within the space of twenty-four days in December 2006.

Representing the fourth generation of an equine distaff family that the Alexanders have developed, Fearless Foursome was named after Nick and his three brothers, who memorably competed against one another in the Fife members' race in 2002, all wearing distinguishing versions of the family's scarlet and royal blue colours. A journalist pointed out in his column that the 'fearless foursome' were beaten by the only other runner in the race!

It was Lucy's grandfather Cyril Alexander who bought Dysie Mary, the third dam of Fearless Foursome as an unraced four-year-old at Botterill's Ascot Sales in June 1973 for 1,350 guineas. Placed in a point-to-point, she broke down on her only other appearance between the flags before producing Fearless Fortune's grandam Lillies Brig. Hunted regularly by Nick, a former stockbroker and businessman, she won a hunter chase and a couple of point-to-points before producing Harrietsfield (named after a Perthshire village), the dam of Fearless Foursome.

Such female families provide a wonderful sense of continuity and during the 2016–17 season Fearless Foursome had four siblings amongst Kinneston's forty-strong team with the mare Little Glenshee, and the geldings Here's To Harry, Clan Chief and Clan Legend. The latter won the 2017 Cyril Alexander Memorial Chase at Kelso. After one of Fearless Foursome's victories the trophy was presented by Monica Dickinson whose son Michael rode numerous winners for Cyril Alexander back in the 1970s.

This family involvement is maintained down to the present day by Lucy's uncle Jamie and brother Kit. Both ride as amateurs for the stable and there is nothing unusual in seeing all three competing against one another at some meeting in the north. Kinneston itself is located in beautiful countryside at Leslie, near Glenrothes – Lucinda

Russell is based on the other side of the bird sanctuary of Loch Leven with its island castle in which Mary Queen of Scots was imprisoned in 1567.

By the end of the 2016–17 season Lucy had ridden 143 winners under Rules. About sixty of them have been for her father, including the very first, when as a nineteen-year-old amateur, she scored on Seeking Power over fences at Kelso in February 2010. Initially progress was slow and she only had one solitary winner the following season.

At about this time she enrolled at Edinburgh University to read biology, but her enthusiasm for lectures waned after about eight weeks. She then set about gaining some expert tuition in various top yards, spending six months with Aidan O'Brien in Ireland followed by short spells with Sir Michael Stoute in Newmarket and Kevin Ryan in Yorkshire.

Rose Alexander, Lucy's mother, is always concerned whenever her daughter is race riding which is understandable as she has experienced more than her fair share of injuries. But Mrs Alexander also knows just how focused and determined Lucy is with the job in hand. She recalls how she won the victor ludorum for athletics at school and on her point-to-point debut aged sixteen was tailed off for most of the contest only to get up for a dead-heat in the shadow of the post.

Lucy says that becoming champion conditional has been the most satisfying aspect of her career so far. 'It shows you have been riding winners consistently all season, not just on one horse one day and to be the first girl was special for me. When I broke my collarbone in the January of that season and was out for about five and a half weeks I thought my chance had gone. It proved very tight in the last few weeks, so to win was a great relief.'

Another highlight for Lucy came at Kelso. 'I did enjoy winning my grandad Cyril Alexander's memorial race on a horse called Jet Master with all my family there. He had proved quite a difficult ride and was winning his first novice chase after struggling to get round over fences.'

Obviously living where they do the Alexanders spend a great deal of time on the road, but Lucy has a positive attitude saying that the traffic is far less congested in the north so riding out and schooling for James Ewart in Dumfriesshire, for example, is not a problem. She and her brother Kit both fill that role at home too albeit they leave all the major training decisions to their father.

The professional consensus is that Lucy Alexander has what it takes to make a Flat jockey with the far greater remuneration involved, not to mention the much reduced risk factor. In fact she did ride six Flat winners from about a hundred rides one summer, but concedes that with a current minimum riding weight of 9st 10lb, she would not be light enough to commit to the Flat full time.

'Of course it would be more sensible injury wise,' she admits and she has endured more than her fair share of broken bones, but as with all jump riders that is accepted as par for the course. As there is not a lot to recommend the debilitating alternative of wasting, perhaps maintaining the status quo is the lesser of two evils.

Certainly the increasing number of outside rides that Lucy Alexander attracts is evidence of the high regard in which she is held by the racing community. There is no doubt she has brought a new dimension to the sport in her native Scotland and she and her very supportive family must derive enormous satisfaction from her success in what is the most demanding occupation imaginable.

34

ANOTHER DALGLEISH FOR CELTIC
SUPPORTERS

Racing in Scotland has certainly taken a giant step forward in the second decade of the 21st century. At the same time that Lucy Alexander was breaking records so too was Keith Dalgleish. He took over with a dual training licence (Flat and jumping) in February 2011 as the new incumbent of Belstane Racing Stables at Carluke in the picturesque Lanarkshire hills, about twenty minutes south of Glasgow where Kenny Dalglish started out with Celtic all those years ago.

Neither Sir Gordon Richards nor Lester Piggott, two of the great champion jockeys of the 20th century, ever enjoyed the same degree of success when they turned their attention to training, and the same could be said of their National Hunt counterparts, Tim Molony and John Francome. It is extraordinary how Clive Cox, a journeyman jump jockey, has surpassed his landlord John Francome when it comes to training.

While Clive Cox concentrates on the Flat, one of his riding colleagues has excelled with training jumpers. For the most part Paul Nicholls rode for relatively small trainers in the West Country where he embarked upon his new career and he has been champion National Hunt trainer an extraordinary eleven times from 2005–6 to 2015–16.

Paul has always had the inestimable benefit of a unique supply of young horses in the pipeline orchestrated by his neighbour Richard Barber. Keith Dalgleish's baptism into the training ranks was altogether different. The stables were owned by Gordon McDowall and within a few years, the businessman with pharmaceutical interests in Glasgow had dispensed with the services of two trainers, Linda Perratt and Ian Semple. Keith only took up the challenge when, at the last moment, Yorkshire based Noel Wilson decided to relocate elsewhere.

A native of Hawick, Keith Dalgleish had experience of pony racing in the Borders and rode a few winners. As he showed an aptitude for riding, during one school holidays his father sent him to Mark Johnston at Middleham where he mucked out, rode out and learnt how to dress the horses over. And when he left school aged sixteen he went right back to Kingsley House to start full-time employment.

Reflecting on those days Keith admits that he owes everything to the Middleham maestro. He says he was in the right place at the right time and was given every opportunity to advance his riding career. Standing 6 feet, his weight was always going to be a problem. With rigorous wasting he could go to scale at 8st 10lbs – nowadays 15st is nearer the mark. Indeed the struggle proved insurmountable and he retired from race riding aged just twenty-one.

From 285 races won, his favourite horse would be the stable stalwart Yavana's Pace. On Sunday 11 August 2002, the combination triumphed at Cologne when the ten-year-old gelding became the oldest winner of a Group 1 contest – his partner was just nineteen. That season he also recorded the first of two Royal Ascot successes, on Helm Bank in the Chesham Stakes, while at the following year's Royal Meeting he prevailed in another photo finish on Fantastic Love in the King George V Handicap. That July he also scored on Lucky Story in the Vintage Stakes at Goodwood.

From the time Keith ceased race riding to when he took up permanent residence at Belstane as a salaried trainer, Keith remained at Kingsley House for a few years riding out, before assisting Ann Duffield and her husband George, the former top jockey, at their stables in Leyburn. And then came a spell breaking in yearlings and doing some pre training, all of which encouraged him to take the plunge as a trainer.

Keith Dalgleish's relentless progress up the training ladder has been spectacular and his modus operandi is very much akin to Mark Johnston. Both know the importance of their horses being happy and relaxed in their work, and one of the keys is to keep it simple by following a strict routine. And like his fellow Scot, he is prepared to criss-cross the UK in search of the best opportunities. Indeed they are constantly in direct competition.

To ensure that travelling expenses are kept to a minimum, Keith invariably takes three or four horses together in the horsebox on long journeys south. Like Lucy Alexander he looks at the positives when contemplating his Scottish base saying that he is ideally situated so far as the motorway network is concerned and with only a handful of other Flat trainers in Scotland he has far less competition on the doorstep than all his many colleagues based in Yorkshire.

One of the more meaningful indications of his rise to the top is that in 2012 he was able to buy Belstane Racing Stables from Gordon McDowall. In that short space of time he had already bettered George Boyd's seasonal record for a Scottish-based trainer of fifty-nine Flat races won in 1957 – admittedly there was far less racing then, but conversely the competition nowadays is that much greater.

His switch from being a salaried trainer to carrying the can himself has certainly been vindicated as the statistics for races won during the last three seasons clearly indicate: in 2014 (67 races for £416,000), 2015 (75 for £672,000) and 2016 (81 for £742,000). After a couple of seasons his string doubled in size to about forty horses when he envisaged that it might grow to between sixty or seventy at the most.

The Carluke trainer, who is assisted by his brother Kevin, is on record as saying, 'We'll never be a one hundred horse yard', but by the beginning of the 2017 season the number of horses registered with Weatherbys had escalated to one hundred and thirteen. No fewer than thirty of them were juveniles, mostly purchased as yearlings in partnership with Irish bloodstock agent Bobby O'Ryan.

Amongst the horses that Keith inherited when he took over at Belstane from Valentine Donoghue (he held the licence temporarily when Ian Semple departed) was the seven-year-old gelding Chookie Hamilton and he was joined by his three-year-old half-brother Chookie Royale. To the close of 2016 this pair had won thirty-two races between them. Homebred by the owners of the Glasgow-based Raeburn Brick company, their dam Lady of Windsor boards at Gordon Thom's New Hall Stud at Pettochside, near Ayr, which provides a base for so many breeders in Scotland.

Like the two 'Chookies', the majority of the Dalgleish horses are handicappers. Royal Ascot might seem a step too far, but the stable has been knocking at the door at this the most competitive of meetings. In the young trainer's initial season (2011), Stonefield Flyer finished runner-up in the Windsor Castle Stakes. In 2015 Tommy Docc finished second in the Queen's Vase, and in 2016 Clem Fandango was third in the Queen Mary Stakes – and in 2017 Lady of Windsor's latest juvenile Chookie Dunedin took his chance in the Coventry Stakes.

When one considers that Tommy Docc cost just £10,000 as a yearling and Clem Fandango €11,000, these Royal Ascot placings are remarkable. And their performances were no flash in the pan as Tommy Docc was also third in the Group 3 Bahrain Trophy at the Newmarket July Meeting and Clem Fandango won the Harry Rosebery Stakes (Listed) at Ayr before returning to Ascot to finish second in the Group 3 Cornwallis Stakes.

With the preponderance of large fashionable stables in the south bolstered by seemingly unlimited Arab funds, the possibility of any of Belstane's new recruits emulating George Boyd's classic victory with Rockavon in the Two Thousand Guineas is non existent, but then no one could have envisaged the enormous success that Keith has already made of his fledgling career as a trainer (in July 2017 he saddled no fewer than fifteen winners, which is thought to be a monthly record for a Scotland-based trainer). At the end of the day Mark Johnston managed to get the Maktoum family on board, so one never knows!

Neither Johnston nor Dalgleish overemphasise their dependency on jockeys and it seems that the latter has no one specifically nominated as the stable retainer. However, one senior jockey who seems to be getting an ever-increasing number of rides for the Carluke trainer is Graham Lee. When the partner of the 2004 Grand National hero Amberleigh House made the unorthodox decision to switch from jumps to the Flat, his initial success was very much owed to Jim Goldie, another Scottish trainer close to Glasgow. Connor Beasley also rides regularly for the stable.

A number of Keith Dalgleish's Scottish colleagues have also emerged from relative obscurity in the last few seasons, albeit the emphasis has been on the winter game. A former permit holder Sandy Thomson, who is based at Greenlaw, near Duns in Berwickshire, has fielded two very popular Saturday chasers in Seeyouatmidnight and Harry The Viking. His stepdaughter, the artist and designer Annie Galbraith, is the partner of Grand National winning jockey, Ryan Mania.

Prior to Lucinda Russell, the leading jumps trainer in Scotland was Len Lungo and after he retired his well-appointed stables in Dumfriesshire were taken over by Iain Jardine. He trains a sizeable string under both Rules. Unusually his stable star is better known for defeat rather than victory. In 2016 the gelded Nakeeta was touched off in valuable handicaps in England (Chester Cup) and Ireland.

In the heart of the Cotswolds, to the south of Cheltenham, is a coterie of leading National Hunt trainers and one of the rising stars is Graeme McPherson who has gradually been increasing his tally of winners with a score of twenty-eight races won during 2016–17. Although based at Stow on the Wold, his origins are not too difficult to fathom. Somehow he manages to combine training with practising as a QC so he is a bit of a law unto himself.

Most of Scotland's foremost trainers have a dual licence (Flat and jumping) and they produce their share of winners. In jumping terms Lucinda Russell led the pack for the 2016-17 season with the winners of forty-three races, then came Nick Alexander from Glenrothes (20); Sandy Thomson from Duns (19); Stuart Coltherd from Selkirk (18); James Ewart from Langholm (18); Iain Jardine from Carrutherstown (17); and Alistair Whillans from Hawick (11).

Realistically, One For Arthur's Grand National victory can be classified as a one-off occurrence, but the increasing number of trainers who are making a worthwhile contribution to racing on both sides of the border must be indicative of the well being of Scottish involvement in general. The country has an illustrious turf history and fights well above its weight when it comes to prize money. With talents like Lucinda Russell, Lucy Alexander and Keith Dalgleish, there seems every prospect that the Scottish influence will continue to flourish.

APPENDIX

The following are additional personalities with strong Scottish connections, who have not featured, at least to any marked extent, in the main text of the book. Some have made their mark when resident in Scotland, others whilst based south of the border. The emphasis is on the era after the Second World War, but a few outstanding historical figures have also been included, as have a handful of expatriate Scots in the Republic of Ireland. The list is not intended to be comprehensive, but it includes a cross-section of people, famous and not so famous, who have contributed to the Turf in various spheres over a period of time.

NEIL ADAM

Neil Adam, MRCVS, whose family hails from Edinburgh, had been expected to follow his parents into the medical profession, but instead he qualified as a veterinary surgeon aged thirty after National Service in the Royal Army Veterinary Corps. He worked briefly as a pathologist at the Equine Research Station at Newmarket before setting up in practice at Melton Mowbray, when he was also associated with the Newmarket Bloodstock Agency.

For six years (1975–80) he trained with considerable success from Racecourse Farm, Bescaby, Melton Mowbray, the site of the Duke of Rutland's old Melton racecourse which was ploughed up during the First World War. In only his second season he recorded a Royal Ascot double with Gentilhombre in the Cork & Orrery Stakes (now Golden Jubilee Stakes), and Cawston's Clown in the Coventry Stakes.

Gentilhombre, who cost just 1,000 guineas as a yearling, proceeded to win the Prix de l'Abbaye de Longchamp in both 1976 (dead-heat) and 1977, when his stable companion Haveroid finished third. Gentilhombre also won the July Cup and Haveroid won the equivalent of the Nunthorpe Stakes.

307

Another smart sprinter was Hei'land Jamie, winner of the Portland Handicap at Doncaster.

By the 1980s Racecourse Farm had a dual role as a training stable and a stud. Neil Adam bought Aislabie Stud at Stetchworth on the outskirts of Newmarket when Cawston's Clown was one of two stallions to make the move. As Collin Stud (the name of his first wife), it became one of the first specialising in boarding walking-in mares to outside stallions, which is now standard practice.

For a number of years Neil Adam, an early exponent of interval training, suffered from MS and became totally dependent on his stud manager, to whom he left the stud on his death in 2002. However, Adam's two daughters contested the will in a high-profile case at the High Court which ruled in their favour.

Collin Stud has now reverted to its original name of Aislabie having been bought in August 2007 by Fawzi Nass, a trainer based in Bahrain. The resident manager is bloodstock agent, Oliver Gaisford-St Lawrence.

PETER ADAMS

Most amateur riders are remembered for feats in hunter chases and point-to-points, but Peter Adams has a unique claim to fame as the owner, trainer and rider of Blue Venom, who triumphed in the 1966 Scottish Champion Hurdle.

Belonging to a farming family, Peter trained Blue Venom under permit at his Torhousekie Farm, near Wigtown, where the gelding was stabled at one end of the cow-byre and his daily rations included a gallon of milk.

The son of Le Dieu d'Or had been procured by Peter and his brother, Sandy, for only £250 from Hawick trainer Harry Bell, who, at that time, also trained three of his siblings. When he scored his great Ayr victory, Blue Venom was one of only two horses that Peter Adams had in training.

In the run-up to Ayr, Blue Venom had gained three consecutive victories and there was no fluke in the result of the Scottish Champion Hurdle. In establishing a new course record he defeated Kirriemuir and Spartan General, who had finished first and second in the 1965 Champion Hurdle at Cheltenham.

As someone who did not take up race riding until he was in his late twenties, Peter Adams had a short career in the saddle, retiring to concentrate on his farm (he was a noted breeder of blue-faced Leicester sheep) and his family. He died in Dumfries Infirmary aged seventy-two in 2009.

EARL OF AIRLIE

The 12th Earl of Airlie (1893–1968), one of whose sons, Angus Ogilvy, married Princess Alexandra, had the extraordinary good fortune to be part-owner of the 1924 Grand National hero, Master Robert. This horse's romantic background was very much in keeping with National heroes, as he had once pulled a plough.

A former stable companion on the Curragh to the brilliant 1920 National hero, Troytown, Master Robert was regarded as extremely moderate in his native Ireland and he came into David Airlie's ownership after winning a point-to-point in England. He was bought specifically for his new owner to ride in a military race at Perth and he duly scored under a welter 13st 13lb – 37lb overweight!

A fourth Grand National winner for Wroughton trainer Aubrey Hastings (one of them a wartime affair at Gatwick), Master Robert was ridden by Bob Trudgill, who collapsed on dismounting – a leg injury incurred the previous afternoon had required extensive stitches and these had burst. Always a thick-winded individual, who became increasingly lame due to navicular disease, Master Robert was promptly retired.

The family seat, Airlie Castle, is in Angus at Kirriemuir, the name of the 1965 Champion Hurdle winner. It was also the birthplace of J.M. Barrie, the author of *Peter Pan*, and mountaineer Sir Hugh Munro, who gave his name to all those hills in Scotland exceeding 3,000ft.

RAYMOND ANDERSON GREEN

Raymond Anderson Green and his wife Anita realised their ultimate goal when Merigo triumphed in the Scottish Grand National in 2010 so imagine their delight when he brought off the double in 2012 – he was ridden on both occasions by their son-in-law, Timmy Murphy.

Born in Thurso, Caithness, Ray was brought up on a family farm at Castletown, not far from the Queen Mother's Castle of Mey, before spending his working life in London as a banker and property developer.

Ray's first love is amateur soccer and in March 2010 he reached a personal target of 700 goals under AFA rules, many of them scored for his home team of Haddington in East Lothian. Much of Anita's time has been devoted to her role as deputy chairman of the NSPCC and their green and yellow racing colours carry the organisation's logo.

He started with horses on the Flat with Michael Jarvis, his first winner being the juvenile, Green Spirit, at Lingfield Park in September 1984. Since then the Anderson Greens have won over 350 races, the great majority of them under NH Rules. The first was Brandy Hambro at Carlisle in March 1987 and their mare, Life Is Life, won the 2001 Queen Alexandra Stakes at Royal Ascot.

Brandy Hambro was trained by Colin Parker at Lockerbie in Dumfriesshire and he saddled 118 winners for the Anderson Greens, amongst them the brilliant novice, Sparky Gale, whose dozen wins included the Cathcart Chase at the 1997 Cheltenham Festival. Following Colin's death in September 2000, his son Andrew added another fifty or so winners of whom Merigo, a yearling purchase in his native France, was outstanding.

Another to make his mark was Arctic Sandy. The only bumper winner ever trained by Ken Oliver, he was also the very last winner for the Hawick trainer, and the first winner for his widow, Rhona, when she took over the licence. Before Merigo, Ken Oliver's Cockle Strand in 1982 was the last winner of the Scottish Grand National to be trained in Scotland.

The Anderson Greens have also been patrons of Pauline Robson's stable at Capheaton, outside Newcastle, and her partner (in the modern sense) and assistant is Andrew Parker's brother, David. Whereas Andrew rode as an amateur, David was a professional jockey. Colin Parker was born in Cumbria, Andrew was born in Hexham, and David was born in Hawick.

DAVID ARBUTHNOT

Educated at Wellington College, David has also spent much of his career as a trainer in Berkshire. Following seven years in neighbouring Oxfordshire as assistant to Fulke Johnson Houghton at Blewbury, he set up his stall at the beginning of 1981 in the hamlet of Eastbury just down the valley road from Lambourn.

He then moved to Compton, where he occupied Uplands Stables, Yew Tree Stables and Hamilton Stables in turn, returning to Uplands for the 2007 season after an interim period at Saxon Gate, Upper Lambourn. Uplands was owned by George Ward of Bonusprint (which became one of racing's biggest sponsors) for whom David saddled Oscar Park to win the 2007 Pertemps Final at the Cheltenham Festival.

It was George Ward's smart juvenile, Padre Pio, who helped to get his young trainer off the mark, as did the former Johnston Houghton-trained Tizzy. In the long term David has excelled with older horses, none more so than the mare, Ringmoor Down, who recorded Group victories as a five-year-old in the 2004 King George Stakes at Goodwood and The Flying Five at the Curragh.

There have been some particularly notable handicap successes at Doncaster. In 1990 Love Legend won the Portland Handicap; in 2002 Zucchero was successful in the Lincoln; and in 2008 Tropical Strait won the November Handicap. The latter was bred by George Ward and carried the colours of his two sons, Francis and Anthony. Two more stable stars were Rinja (Bessborough Handicap, Royal Ascot) and Monkston Point. Successful in three Listed races as a two-year-old, Monkston Point was subsequently placed in numerous Group sprints.

For the last few years David has been based at the Wates family's Henfold House, near Dorking in Surrey, where their 1996 Grand National winner Rough Quest was trained.

David's wife, Diane, is director of operations for the charity Retraining of Racehorses, an organisation devoted to the care and welfare of ex-racehorses. Her husband is the younger brother of Sir Keith Arbuthnot, the 8th Baronet, who lives in Peeblesshire. The family traces back to the Lairds of Arbuthnott, landowners in Kincardineshire from about 1160.

GEORGE ALEXANDER BAIRD

One of the most colourful Turf characters of the Victorian era, George Alexander Baird (1861–93) was known to the racing public as Mr Abington, his *nom de course*, and to his close associates as 'The Squire'.

Only eleven when his father (also George) died, this only son was reputed to have inherited £3m-worth of shares in Scottish railways and estates in Scotland with rents of £100,000 per annum on coming of age. Part of that vast fortune was bequeathed by an uncle who had also donated £200,000 to the Church of Scotland, a gift described as the highest premium against fire ever paid!

George Snr had his business roots in Glasgow and made a fortune as an ironmaster. By the middle of the nineteenth century William Baird & Company owned Gartsherrie, the largest iron works in the world with production running at 300,000 tons per annum, yielding a £1m profit. Upwards of 30,000 people depended on the Bairds, who built houses, schools and churches for their employees. The richest industrialists in Scotland, they invested their money in land and country estates.

Born at Stitchill near Kelso in 1861, George Baird Jnr was educated at Eton and Cambridge. He had much in common with the notorious James Merry, as both loved cockfighting and prizefighting and surrounded themselves with many of the more unsavoury characters attracted by such pursuits.

When it came to race riding, George Baird had two mentors, the great Fred Archer to whom he bore a striking resemblance, and the celebrated Scottish amateur, Charlie Cunningham. However, that did not prevent him from being warned off by the Jockey Club for two years aged twenty-one for alleged foul riding when finishing first on his own horse, Billy Banks, in a seller at Four Oaks Park (Birmingham). He would have been disqualified anyway, having failed to draw the correct weight on weighing in.

A competent amateur jockey in the 1880s, he obtained far more satisfaction from riding a modest winner than from owning a more prestigious one ridden by a professional. In 1889 he was champion gentleman rider with sixty-one winners.

As an owner he won the 1884 One Thousand Guineas and Oaks with Busybody and the 1887 Derby with the maiden, Merry Hampton. Busybody had cost top price of 8,800 guineas as a two-year-old from the dispersal of Lord Falmouth's bloodstock.

One of his loves was the actress Lillie Langtry (mistress of the Prince of Wales, later King Edward VII). It was from him that she procured two of her first good winners, Milford (Coventry Stakes, July Stakes) and Lady Rosebery (Jockey Club Cup).

In 1893 George Baird and some of his dubious cronies went to America. By then in poor health, he died that March in New Orleans aged thirty-two. His body was repatriated aboard the *Majestic* sailing from New York, to be buried in the family vault at Stitchill.

His name lives on in Newmarket through Abington Place stables, where that great jockey Harry Wragg was succeeded by his son, Geoff, who retired at the end of the 2008 season. Geoff Wragg was educated at Fettes in Edinburgh.

SANDY BARCLAY

Sandy Barclay was selected by Noel Murless to succeed his long-term predecessors, Gordon Richards and Lester Piggott, as his future stable jockey, an amazing vote of confidence considering that the teenager was still an apprentice.

Belonging to a famous sporting family from Belston in Ayrshire, one of Sandy's forebears was the famous Captain Barclay of Ury. In 1809 he won a £1,000 wager that he could walk 1,000 miles in 1,000 hours, a feat emulated by Richard Dunwoody in 2009 over the self-same repetitive route in Newmarket from Bedford Lodge to the Bury Road. Another of the captain's accomplishments was to drive the London to Aberdeen mail coach through all its stages.

Both Sandy's father, James, and grandfather, Hugh, trained and rode as amateurs and like them Sandy learnt to ride out hunting. The champion apprentice of 1966, his indentures were transferred from Harry Whiteman at Ayr to Noel Murless at Newmarket for the 1967 season, when he rode the lightweights.

The following year he was appointed stable jockey at Warren Place, when Lester Piggott's temporary replacement, George Moore, returned to his native Australia after just one glorious season. During the ensuing three years that he was retained by Noel Murless, Sandy rode the winners of 273 races, 131 of them for the home side. In 1968 he was runner-up to Lester Piggott for the jockeys' championship with 116 winners.

He made a brilliant start, winning the King George VI and Queen Elizabeth Stakes, Eclipse Stakes and Coronation Cup on the previous year's Derby hero, Royal Palace. He also partnered two classic winning fillies with Celina (Irish Guinness Oaks) and Caergwrle (One Thousand Guineas) – she was homebred by Noel's wife who also came from Ayrshire. In 1970 he won the Eclipse Stakes on Connaught, the Oaks on Lupe, and the Coronation Cup on Caliban.

However, by then the cracks were beginning to show in the relationship between trainer and jockey, and they decided to go their separate ways. It was a particularly disappointing and premature end to an already proven partnership which had seemed destined for greatness. Thereafter the jockey's long-term career went into terminal decline.

Following an interim period in France with François Boutin, the Scot returned to England and achieved a degree of success riding in the north for Sam Hall and Denys Smith. One of his more notable wins came on Guy Reed's Dakota in the Ebor Handicap. However, a serious knee injury sustained while riding work at Newmarket marked the virtual end of his riding career.

Sandy and his wife, Miranda, who is a sister to Lady Lloyd Webber, live at Woodbridge in Suffolk. The Lloyd Webbers own the famous Watership Down Stud on the Hampshire/Berkshire border, where they produced their star homebred fillies, Dar Re Mi and The Fugue.

One of Sandy's brothers, Jim, trains near Kinross and another, Hugh, began as a starter in 1980 – his big moment used to come when dispatching the Grand National field. Their father, James, was one of four sons who were apprenticed to their grandfather, Hugh Barclay of Shillahill, Lochmaben, in Dumfriesshire, immediately after the Second World War.

At Perth in 1949 Hugh achieved a remarkable treble when saddling three winners partnered by three different sons.

HENRY BEEBY

In 2017 Henry Beeby announced that he was applying for Irish citizenship. However, he was born, bred and raised in Hawick and as managing director of Doncaster Bloodstock Sales (with father Harry as chairman), which has always had its administrative headquarters in this Borders town, he has been the key to its ever expanding business.

Obviously the political situation has had a strong bearing on Henry's decision to forsake his Scottish roots as he has been based in Ireland since the historic merger between DBS and Goffs (now Goffs UK), when he became the new group chief executive. He and his American wife and their two children all live in Kilcullen, about fifteen minutes away from Goffs' sales complex.

Henry's great-grandfather was a Leicestershire horse dealer and his grandfather, George, trained the Cheltenham Gold Cup winners Brendan's Cottage (1939) and Silver Fame (1951). His most noted Flat horse was the top sprinter and sire, Grey Sovereign.

Leaving school at sixteen, Henry was always destined to join DBS. Following brief spells at Furnace Mill Stud in the Midlands and Coolmore in Ireland and with the American auctioneering house, Fasig-Tipton, in the USA, he made his debut as an auctioneer after a selling race at Kelso in December 1985. He sold at Doncaster for the first time in June 1986.

Henry's working life has revolved around the promotion of DBS and Goffs UK, which has grown out of all recognition since he took over the helm. He nominates the brilliant juvenile filly, Lyric Fantasy, as one of the best he has sold over a quarter of a century. His all-time favourite is probably Red Rum. Appropriately both were sold as youngsters by Doncaster and Goffs.

Equally enthusiastic about the Flat as he is about jumping, his favourite meetings are Royal Ascot and the Cheltenham Festival in England, and the Punchestown Festival in Ireland.

Actually Henry Beeby does have Scottish genes in his blood. His mother was born on the Mull of Kintyre and, as a member of the Addis family, he is entitled to wear the Hunting Stuart tartan, which he does when the occasion arises.

HARRY BELL

Harry Bell was based at Midshiels, near Hawick. The records show that he was an extremely skilful trainer with no fewer than three Scottish Grand Nationals to his credit: Quick Reply (1972), Sebastian V (1977) and Astral Charmer (1981).

Victory in the Grand National proper came agonisingly close. In 1978 Sebastian was runner-up to the Scottish-owned Lucius and the following year Rubstic, whom Bell had saddled to finish second at Ayr, actually won the Grand National, trained by John Leadbetter just down the road. It was Bell who had originally bought Rubstic for his owner.

The Bell family was also involved with the luckless Wyndburgh as they stood his sire, Maquis, at Midshiels. Bred by Sir Victor Sassoon, Maquis was acquired for 450 guineas out of John Goldsmith's Aston Tirrold stable when one of the last lots at the 1947 Newmarket July Sales. The stallion had to be put down during only his fourth covering season in Scotland as the result of a kick.

Ten years old when his parents moved across the border from Northumberland, Harry Bell was hunting with the Buccleuch and Jedforest and proved a proficient amateur rider before taking out a licence to train in 1958. He quickly made his mark. Amongst his early flag-bearers were Welsh Admiral, winner of thirteen consecutive races, Too Slow, successful in more than twenty races, and homebred Bridge of Orchy, who invariably won easily, albeit he was very prone to fall.

Harry Bell was a great judge of a horse and equally expert at placing them. Many of his owners liked a bet and he was not averse to accommodating them. Consequently his runners came under the close scrutiny of the stewards. Not for the first time, he was summonsed to the Jockey Club's Portman Square headquarters in 1964 regarding an across-the-card double at Kelso and Wetherby. Not satisfied with his explanation, the stewards administered a five-year ban.

It says much for Harry Bell's resilience that he returned to the fray and successfully rebuilt his stable from scratch. It was during this latter period that all three of his Scottish Grand National winners accrued. Sebastian, the second of them, was the best horse he ever trained and a versatile one who was proficient over a variety of distances.

The Hawick trainer's number one priority when it came to training was 'natural' feed, so his final fall from grace was ironic. In November 1984, he was found guilty at Jedburgh Sheriff Court of causing unnecessary cruelty to a filly and sentenced to six months' imprisonment. La Gavina had been reported by the RSPCA 'as emaciated and suffering from malnutrition'.

There is an ongoing training connection in the family, as Harry Bell's daughter, Mary, is married to trainer John Mackie, a Scotsman based at Church Broughton in Derbyshire. He was formerly assistant to Ken Oliver and Ian Balding.

SIR ALEC BLACK

At the beginning of the First World War, Alec Black placed his fleet of Grimsby-based trawlers at the disposal of the British government to be used as minesweepers, a patriotic gesture that earned him his title.

Alec's father, William, a marine engineer who died when his son was only three years old, had migrated to Grimsby from Scotland. His father, also William, was a flax mill manager from Dundee. On leaving school Alec became a clerk in a local fish merchant's office, but within ten years he was the registered owner of the Earl Steam Fishing Company.

Always more interested in breeding than racing, he made his first notable acquisition in 1917, when he paid 3,600 guineas for one of the first yearlings bred by the newly formed National Stud, which was then based in Ireland. Named The Panther, he gained a hard-fought victory in the Two Thousand Guineas, but proved a disappointing favourite in the Derby; he was duly sold to the Argentine.

The Panther had enjoyed a successful two-year-old career, whereupon Sir Alec submitted him to the Newmarket Sales in October, but no one was prepared to offer the disclosed reserve of £40,000. His owner only raced from 1918 to 1921, later turning his attention to breeding. From about 1926 he kept his mares at Compton Stud at Sandley in Dorset, which in due course became the new National Stud.

Soon afterwards, Sir Alec transferred his breeding operation to Newmarket, where he created Compton Park Stud, on a substantial block of arable land between Duchess Drive and Woodditton Road, which now constitutes the principal part of Sheikh Mohammed's Dalham Hall complex. There he adopted the idea of ranching his bloodstock with shelters in every paddock so that they could lie out winter and summer, a concept that never really caught on.

Alec Black bred three classic winners with Singapore (1930 St Leger), Brown Betty (1933 One Thousand Guineas) and Colombo (1934 Two Thousand Guineas). All three were sold as yearlings, both Singapore (12,500 guineas) and Colombo (510 guineas) being acquired for Lord Glanely and trained for him by Scotsman Tommy Hogg. Due to ill health, Alec Black offered all his breeding stock at the 1931 Newmarket December Sales; Colombo, who also finished third in the Derby, was then a foal.

Not only did Black and Glanely make their fortune from the sea (Glanely was involved with shipping), but they both died on the same day, Sunday, 28 June 1942. By a remarkable coincidence Tommy Hogg died two months later.

Benevolent to his employees, Alec set up a generous trust when he died. This was to provide 'the finest bedlinen and down pillows' for hospitals in England and Scotland, and to help the hard-working Grimsby fishermen and dock-workers to whom he owned his considerable fortune.

DICKY BLACK

Dicky Black, who was born at Ayr in 1915, proved a highly competent amateur jockey before the Second World War and a proficient professional afterwards, riding some 500 winners altogether. The first of them was his mother's Gossamer in a selling chase at Market Rasen in 1933.

Joining up in the army on the outbreak of war, he escaped twice from German prison camps. A fellow internee was John de Moraville, who subsequently set up as a trainer at Childrey, near Wantage (his son of the same name became a BHA handicapper) and, as his retained jockey, Dicky Black partnered the stable's first winners, not only over hurdles and fences, but also on the Flat.

Cheltenham provided Dicky Black with two major triumphs. In 1939 he won the National Hunt Chase on Litigant for the Furlong family synonymous with dual Grand National hero, Reynoldstown, and in 1947 he won the Gold Cup on the six-year-old Fortina, to become only the second amateur to do so – the first was Hugh Grosvenor.

The solitary entire to win the Gold Cup, Fortina became a celebrated sire of jumpers. This French-bred was trained in Lambourn by Hector Christie, who had actually embarked upon his career as private trainer for Countess Lindsay in Fife. Although he served in the Gordon Highlanders in the war when he too was a prisoner of war of the Germans, he was not a Scot.

In 1947 Fortina also won the Lancashire Chase at Manchester, one of four winners for Dicky Black that afternoon from as many rides. Another memorable occasion that year occurred back in his native Scotland when he triumphed in the Scottish National at Bogside on the Fulke Walwyn-trained Rowland Boy. That season he finished runner-up to Lord Mildmay in the amateur riders' championship and promptly turned professional.

A fine horseman and a fearless rider, Dicky Black was a popular figure. He died of cancer in 1988 aged seventy-two.

BRADBURNE FAMILY

Now retired, Susan Bradburne, from Cupar in Fife, embarked on her training career in August 1988 and the majority of her 200-plus jumping winners were in the north. In 1999 she came close to a sensational success in the Grand National when Blue Charm finished runner-up to the Irish invader, Bobbyjo, after jumping the last fence in the lead.

Sue was assisted by her husband, John, with the family business, Bradburne & Co. (chartered surveyors), as sponsors of this mixed stable which usually had fewer than twenty inmates. Their two children Mark and Lorna both rode for the yard. The former missed riding Blue Charm in the National having broken his collarbone in the Foxhunters' the day before.

Mark registered his first ever winner at the Fife point-to-point in May 1992 and rode on a regular basis for Henry Daly. Three of his best mounts were Behrajan, Hand Inn Hand and Lord Atterbury. In July 2007 he suffered a double vertebrae fracture in a fall at Uttoxeter from which he made an amazing recovery. Since retiring he has acted as a jockey coach.

His wife and brother-in-law also distinguished themselves in the saddle. Gee Armytage was one of the first ladies to excel as a professional jump jockey, and her brother, Marcus Armytage, who gained a famous victory in the 1990 Grand National on Mr Frisk, is the last amateur to prevail in the great Aintree steeplechase.

Gee was personal assistant to Sir Tony McCoy, while her brother is an author and racing correspondent with the *Daily Telegraph*. Ironically McCoy denied Mark Bradburne a memorable victory in the dying strides when winning the 2009 Bet365 Gold Cup at Sandown Park.

In 2008, Sue Bradburne saddled Lochiel to record his handler's first ever Flat success when scoring at Hamilton in May, prior to winning the historic Cumberland Plate at Carlisle.

BRUCE FAMILY

The 1953 Cheltenham Foxhunters' produced a never-to-be-forgotten duel with Dunboy II and Merry dead-heating for first place.

Dunboy, who was qualified with the Jedforest, was owned by the Bruce family, hill farmers from Mervinslaw, near Jedburgh in Roxburghshire, and ridden by another local farmer, Charlie Scott. Both families made an inordinate contribution to the world of hunter-chasing and point-to-points – Charlie Scott owned the dual Foxhunters' hero, The Callant, an iconic grey, trained by Stewart Wight.

Likewise a prolific scorer between the flags, Dunboy carried Pat Bruce's colours at Cheltenham and she and her twin sisters, Jackie and Jill, were all highly competent riders in their day. Jackie married Tommy Dun and Jill married Bobby Brewis and these two extended families enjoyed another memorable National Hunt Meeting at Cheltenham in 1958.

That year Spud Tamson, ridden by Jackie's brother-in-law, Robin Dun, triumphed in the National Hunt Chase by ten lengths in a snowstorm. The next day Whinstone Hill – owned, trained and ridden by Bobby Brewis from Belford in Northumberland – triumphed in the Foxhunters', a victory they repeated two years later.

Jackie Dun, the mother of leading jockeys Geordie and Peter Dun, had been given Spud Tamson as a wedding present by her father. Spud Tamson looked as bright a National prospect for the 1959 renewal as any horse trained in Scotland during the post-war period, only to suffer a fatal haemorrhage while exercising at home.

SIR GEORGE BULLOUGH

Belonging to a wealthy family of Scottish ironmasters, John Bullough of Glen Lyon in Perthshire owned two castles, Meggernie in Perthshire, and Kinloch on the Isle of Rum.

His son, Sir George Bullough, 1st Baronet, preferred to live in Newmarket, where he built an impressive house, on the top of Warren Hill opposite Warren Place and styled on a French château near Le Touquet.

Subsequently both Warren Hill Stud and the adjoining Ashley Heath Stud were acquired by Greek shipping tycoon Marcos Lemos, the breeder of Pebbles. In 1999 the imposing house was pulled down and replaced with another grand mansion when David and Patricia Thompson bought the two studs as an extension to their Cheveley Park complex.

In 1917 Bullough's Ballymacad won a substitute Grand National (designated the War National Steeplechase) at Gatwick, the third of four National winners trained by Aubrey Hastings at Wroughton, whereupon the owner donated his winnings to St Dunstan's Home for Blinded Soldiers.

Turning to the Flat, Bullough became a patron of Jack Jarvis's Newmarket stable. Their best representative proved to be Golden Myth – in 1922 he completed the Gold Cup and Gold Vase double at Royal Ascot, in addition to winning the Eclipse Stakes.

Whereas Golden Myth failed to come up to expectations at stud, Campanula, who was Bullough's solitary classic winner in the 1934 One Thousand Guineas, became rather a distinguished foundation mare. She was homebred at Longholes Stud, which backed on to his Warren Hill establishment and was managed on his behalf by Jack Jarvis.

That year's Oaks was won by Light Brocade, who had finished runner-up to Campanula in the Guineas. The former was homebred by George Bullough's son-in-law, the 5th Earl of Durham (a relative of the great trainer, George Lambton). Remarkably, both classic winning fillies were reared at Ashley Heath Stud where they proved inseparable paddock companions.

Following George Bullough's death in 1939, Longholes passed to Lord Durham. Duly inherited by John Lambton, he used to stand stallions there. The owner of a good filly in Wake Up Maggie, he then sold the property in August 2013 to Sheikh Fahad Al Thani from Qatar. Providing an essential foothold in Newmarket for the new big investors in bloodstock worldwide, Longholes has since been transformed into a state of the art training yard and rehabilitation centre.

A tall man, well over six feet in height, George Bullough was a member of the Jockey Club and of the National Hunt Committee. He was a familiar sight around Newmarket, driving round rather comically in a baby Austin car.

BURNS FAMILY

Known in his adopted country as 'The Scotchman', Tommy Burns had accompanied his father, James, to Ireland in 1914 when the latter went to train for William Hall Walker, later Lord Wavertree. His racing manager was Jock Fergusson, a leading Scottish amateur rider in his day.

Subsequently, James Burns returned to his native Ayr, winning the Ayrshire Handicap with Wildwood and Beech Hill, and the Ayr Gold Cup with Forest Guard, all entire horses. He retired from training in 1932, by which time Tommy (who rode Forest Guard) was established as one of the most brilliant jockeys based in Ireland.

Twice Irish champion, Tommy rode twenty-two classic winners in Ireland, six of them in the Irish St Leger, before retiring in 1953. His sons, James and Thomas (T.P.), also became leading jockeys, but the former was killed in action during the Second World War. As trainer and jockey respectively, father and younger son teamed up to gain a memorable victory with Vimadee in the 1961 Irish St Leger.

T.P. Burns, who was fourteen when riding his first winner in June 1938 at the Curragh, headed the list of jockeys in Ireland three times. In 1957 he rode the great Ballymoss in all his races as a three-year-old. Vincent O'Brien's colt provided him with his only success in an English classic in the St Leger, and the first of six Irish classics in the Derby.

Because of increasing weight, T.P. Burns turned increasingly to jumping, and he rode an amazing eight winners of the Gloucestershire Hurdle (now Supreme Novices' Hurdle) for the Ballydoyle stable. However, serious spinal injuries incurred in a fall in 1952 obliged him to stop competing over fences, albeit he continued riding until 1975, when he was fifty.

As assistant to Vincent O'Brien, T.P. Burns' expertise as a work rider at Ballydoyle proved incalculable.

CALDER FAMILY

Duns, the county town of Berwickshire, is famous for one flying Scotsman in Jim Clark, but there was another one in the appropriately named Flying Ace.

A typical sporting farmer from the Borders, Adam Calder rode successfully as an amateur under Rules as well as in point-to-points. He first took out a permit to train from his home, Marigold Farm, near Duns, in 1958. He trained a good horse in Toffee Apple, successful in the Rothbury Cup at the now defunct Northumbrian course.

However, he will always be associated with the homebred Flying Ace. The son of champion hurdler, Saucy Kit, gained a fiftieth victory (thirty point-to-points, twenty hunter chases), when scoring at Perth in May 1988, an astonishing record considering that the twelve-year-old did not run until he was seven, having been operated on for a wind problem.

In all but one of those victories Flying Ace had been partnered by Adam's daughter, Doreen Calder. She had missed one ride due to a dislocated shoulder, when Charlie Macmillan had been substituted at the Dumfriesshire fixture. However, just twelve days after the hunter chase at Perth, Doreen notched up her own half-century with Flying Ace at Hexham.

Bred, owned and trained by Adam Calder, the gelding raced almost exclusively in the north. He never ran in either the Cheltenham or Liverpool Foxhunters', but he competed regularly in the Horse and Hound Cup at Stratford-upon-Avon, winning this prestigious event in 1985. Astonishingly he won seventeen consecutive starts in his first two seasons, sixteen between the flags and a hunter chase.

This popular campaigner was out of a little mare called Flying Eye, who was purchased from Ken Oliver – the Hawick trainer considered that the daughter of Vulgan was on the small side to jump fences, but would make an ideal broodmare. First she won thirteen point-to-points and two hunter chases.

Doreen Calder was born on Christmas Day and Flying Ace was certainly the best present she ever received!

PETER CALVER

Born in Edinburgh, where he went to school, Peter Calver qualified as a veterinary surgeon in Glasgow. The son of Sir Robert Calver QC, he enjoyed the remarkable distinction of having two future Grand National winners through his hands with Highland Wedding (1969) and Rubstic (1979), the latter being the only National winner trained in Scotland until One For Arthur in 2017.

Originally based at Park House, Cholderton, near Salisbury – the yard from which Jim Ford dispatched the 1955 Cheltenham Gold Cup winner Gay Donald – Peter had a unique involvement with Highland Wedding. An enthusiastic owner-rider as well as a permit-holder and practising vet (he started off in general practice in Gloucestershire), he partnered Highland Wedding to victory in point-to-points despite the horse's tendency to break blood vessels.

Highland Wedding, whom Peter had originally acquired privately as a four-year-old for just £185, was then sold on for £5,000 to join Toby Balding. At the time Peter was Toby's stable vet and also worked at the sales on behalf of Richard Galpin (Newmarket Bloodstock Agency) and David Minton.

Rubstic proved another bargain – Peter had bought him as a yearling for 500 guineas and sold him as an unraced three-year-old for 1,050 guineas to Harry Bell, then training for the gelding's Grand National-winning owner, John Douglas.

A permit holder from 1956 until taking out a full licence in 1975, Peter always shod his own horses. During the 1970s, he was based at Hockley House Stud, near Alresford in Hampshire (then owned by Lord Chetwode), until moving to Lord Zetland's Whitcliffe Grange Farm, near Ripon in North Yorkshire.

In 1975 Peter saddled his wife's Cabar Feidh to win the Aurelius Hurdle at Ascot. Later he concentrated on the Flat and was involved with a number of useful sprint handicappers, amongst them the 1987 Stewards' Cup winner, Madraco. Perryston View was his final runner when scoring at Doncaster in November 1999. Other good winners included Relatively Sharp, Eradicate and Norgabie.

Latterly Peter gave freely of his time to racing – he was on the committee of the National Trainers' Federation, a trustee of the Northern Racing College and veterinary advisor to the Racehorse Owners' Association. It was following a council meeting of the ROA in May 2002 that he collapsed and died at York railway station aged sixty-eight.

ATTY CORBETT

The second son of the 2nd Lord Rowallan, the former Chief Scout and Governor of Tasmania, Atty Corbett, a highly proficient NH jockey turned trainer, belonged to a family with strong racing connections.

His much younger sister Fiona married David Cecil (twin brother of Henry Cecil) who trained at one time in Lambourn. His sister-in-law, Catherine Corbett, who has a predilection for grey fillies, is a sister to Robert Acton, formerly manager to Sheikh Mohammed at Dalham Hall Stud, Newmarket, and to the late Klaus Jacobs at Newsells Park Stud in Hertfordshire.

The 1st Lord Rowallan, Cameron Corbett, had been Liberal MP for Tradeston in Glasgow. He lived at Rowallan Castle, near Kilmarnock (famous for Johnnie Walker whisky), with views of the coast and Ailsa Craig in the distance. An Arts and Crafts creation by the Scottish architect, Sir Robert Lorimer, the castle, built in the Scottish baronial style, bears the family coat of arms and the motto 'Deus Pascit Corvos' – God feeds the ravens (or corbies), a pun on the Corbett family name.

After Eton and wartime service with the Grenadier Guards – for which he was awarded the MC – Atty Corbett started riding as an amateur before turning professional. Altogether he partnered about 100 winners, amongst them Ellesmere in the National Hunt Chase and Domata in the Mildmay Memorial Chase.

In 1958 he embarked upon his training career at Yew Tree House, Compton, enjoying conspicuous success with that particularly handsome chaser, Blessington Esquire.

Soon Atty was concentrating on the Flat with Lord Carnarvon as one of his principal owners. In 1963 he had forty-two winners, placing him fourth on the leading trainers' list. The two major contributors were Queen's Hussar, winner of the Lockinge Stakes and Sussex Stakes, and the unbeaten champion two-year-old Talahasse, successful in the Gimcrack Stakes and Champagne Stakes. Queen's Hussar retired to Carnarvon's local Highclere Stud, where he became champion sire of 1972 thanks to the great Brigadier Gerard.

At the end of 1967 Atty Corbett moved to Newmarket's Lagrange Stables (now occupied by Edward Dunlop), where he trained Sweet Revenge to win the Prix de l'Abbaye de Longchamp and King's Stand Stakes.

In 1976, aged fifty-five, the rather shy and retiring Scotsman met with a fatal car accident while walking with his horses on the road. Perhaps his inherent deafness was a contributory factor.

CRAWFORD BROTHERS

Jock Crawford and his younger brother, James, were sons of a much-respected blacksmith from Beith in Ayrshire.

Both qualified as veterinary surgeons at Glasgow University, then went to India, where they gained tremendous experience with remounts for the army. They then came home to earn their livelihood though racing, Jock as a bloodstock agent, and Jimmy as a trainer and stud manager.

Following an interim period of wartime service in the Royal Army Veterinary Corps, Jimmy Crawford returned from India to train in Wiltshire for the Bombay cotton-mill owner, Mathradas Goculdas, for whom Parth finished third to Papyrus in the 1923 Derby, prior to winning that season's Prix de l'Arc de Triomphe.

Parth carried different colours at Longchamp as Goculdas ran out of funds. His considerable bloodstock interests, including the Bungalow Stud on the outskirts of Newmarket, were taken over by Sir Victor Sassoon, who also raced extensively in India. Destined to become the biggest and most successful owner-breeder in the UK, he installed Jimmy Crawford as his private trainer at Newmarket's Fitzroy House.

In 1929, two years after saddling Hot Night to finish runner-up in the Derby and St Leger, Jimmy died from pneumonia aged just forty-two. Only the previous year he had procured the four-year-old filly, Lady Wembley, at

Goffs in Ireland for 750 guineas and in due course she produced Sir Victor Sassoon's homebred Exhibitionist, winner of the 1937 One Thousand Guineas and Oaks.

The following year Jock Crawford, who had served in the RAVC during the Boer War, was killed in a motoring accident in South Africa, while on one of his overseas excursions as a director of the British Bloodstock Agency. He had joined the firm (then based in London's Charing Cross Road) in 1924, buying the shares of one of two founder members.

As someone who had not only established a thriving veterinary practice in Bombay, but had also set up a successful public stud in India, Jock Crawford was a tremendous asset to the BBA. There was no more respected figure in the business and he had no equal as an ambassador for British bloodstock.

His input was crucial at the BBA, which came to be regarded as the world's premier bloodstock agency, a reputation that it maintained until the status quo was changed for ever by the Arab involvement over the last four decades.

CHARLIE CUNNINGHAM

Born at Morebattle Tofts, Kelso, Charlie Cunningham (1849–1906) was an outstanding amateur rider of the late nineteenth century.

Belonging to an old Ayrshire family, he attended the Edinburgh Academy and would have gone into the army but for the death of his father, from whom he took over the running of the family estate. Standing over 6ft, he was hardly built to be a jockey and fought a constant battle with his weight, but he was a very hard man to beat across country. Though quick-tempered and outspoken, he was also extremely popular and entertaining.

Early on in his career he was fortunate to own three half-brothers, Percy, Merryglass and Douglas, who between them won more than fifty races. In a vintage era for corinthian riders, he was the leading amateur in 1882–3 with forty-seven winners. He won the Scottish Grand National at Bogside four times in nine years with Bellman (1881), Wild Meadow (1885), Orcadian (1887) and Deloraine (1889).

However, he never achieved his ultimate ambition of winning the Grand National, although he was runner-up in 1889 on Why Not, on whom he had won the National Hunt Chase three years earlier. That was the first of seven appearances by Why Not in the National and he won in 1894 ridden by Arthur Nightingall.

Charles's record in the saddle was quite exceptional as he rode the winners of 417 races from a total of 952 rides, albeit many of them were UBH (United Border Hunt) events confined to amateurs.

His career was effectively ended when he had a crashing fall out with the Buccleuch Hunt at Softlaw in 1902, damaging his spine, an injury which necessitated an operation in Edinburgh a couple of years later. He died from cancer at Muirhouselaw, near St Boswells, in his mid-fifties.

HARRY DOBSON

Co. Carlow trainer, Jim Bolger, has struck up a rewarding partnership with Harry Dobson, who was born in Scotland some sixty-eight years ago but is now resident in Monte Carlo.

Harry hails from the Borders and still owns the farm, Lycestane, at Lauder in Berwickshire, where he spent his childhood. This property marches with Thirlestane Castle, owned by Gerald Maitland-Carew, a well-known steward in Scotland and at Newmarket – Thirlestane stages a major horse trials. Harry has a real farming background as his father farmed in Lauderdale and so too did his mother's father.

Mining and prospecting for minerals have been his stock in trade and nowadays he is chairman and a prime investor in two major exploration companies, one backing plans to construct a £2 billion oil refinery in Newfoundland, and the other searching for oil in the South Falklands' basin. A major stakeholder in Manchester United Football Club, he is also involved in commercial property.

Just recently two own-sisters trained by Jim Bolger and owned in partnership by Harry Dobson and Jim's wife, Jacqueline, have been placed in the One Thousand Guineas – in 2009 Cuis Ghaire finished runner-up to Ghanaati and in 2010 Gile Na Greine was third in a blanket finish behind Special Duty and Jacqueline Quest. Gile Na Greine was also second in the Coronation Stakes.

Previously the Dobson colours were carried into third place in the 2005 Irish Two Thousand Guineas by Democratic Deficit, who also won the Craven Stakes, Railway Stakes and Ballycorus Stakes. Other colts to have made their mark include Project Manager (Gallinule Stakes), and Irish Memory (Tetrarch Stakes).

Harry also owns a number of broodmares in partnership with Jim Bolger, who keeps all his breeding stock and runs all his bloodstock affairs which he has done for more than two decades.

NORMAN DONALDSON

Owner of the 1949 One Thousand Guineas and Oaks winner, Musidora – whose name is commemorated by the important Oaks Trial run at the York May Meeting – Norman Donaldson (1878–1955) died in his native Glasgow.

Educated at Kelvinside Academy and Loretto (in Musselburgh), he became a prominent figure in the world of shipping, particularly on the Clyde. Chairman of the Donaldson Line, the family shipping business founded by his father, he had many other commitments in Scottish maritime circles – he was also a director of Lloyd's *Register of Shipping*. Having served in the Boer War, he was awarded a CBE for his contribution to anti-submarine warfare in the First World War.

He embarked on ownership with some jumpers trained by Stewart Wight at Grantshouse, his very first winner being Acre Valley at Carlisle in 1946, partnered by his son-in-law, Ewen Cameron. Thereafter he concentrated on the Flat with some expensive yearling purchases made by the leading Malton-based trainer, Charles Elsey.

The first good horse to carry his 'black and pink stripes, black sleeves, white cap', was Hope Street, who was beaten a short head for the 1948 Jersey Stakes at Royal Ascot. Hope Street had run unplaced in the Derby, but classic success was just round the corner as it was in the following year that Musidora prevailed in the two fillies' classics.

Musidora was one of three daughters of Nasrullah that Norman Donaldson acquired as yearlings in successive years. She cost 4,700 guineas in 1947, followed by Catchit (6,300 guineas) and Cassydora (2,000 guineas). All three fillies scored at Ayr as juveniles, Catchit going on to dead-heat for second place in the 1950 One Thousand Guineas.

Musidora retired to her owner's Balfron Stud, near Bletchley, in Buckinghamshire; her female line has persisted down to the twenty-first century and she features as the third dam of the 1990 St Leger hero, Snurge.

Just before his death, Norman Donaldson attended a jump meeting at Ayr where his grandson, Sam Cameron, rode one winner and his own colours were successful with the Stewart Wight-trained Scarlet Flower.

A keen farmer and breeder of Aberdeen Angus cattle, he also enjoyed sailing and fishing. He and his brother, W. Betts Donaldson, were prominent figures in the world of yacht racing.

DUDGEON FAMILY

A farmer and MFH from Kirkliston, West Lothian, who also acted as a steward at Perth, Edinburgh and Hamilton, John Dudgeon trained under permit. His son, Sandy, a chartered accountant turned banker, proved a very capable amateur rider for the stable.

Between them they shared many successes during the 1980s with that good hunter-chaser, Gayle Warning. Procured as an unbroken four-year-old, Gayle Warning progressed from point-to-points to provide Sandy Dudgeon with a first ever success under Rules, at Kelso in 1980. Altogether he rode over sixty winners under Rules and in point-to-points.

Although they had little luck in the Cheltenham Foxhunters', the combination of Gayle Warning and Sandy Dudgeon did commendably well in the Liverpool equivalent on three successive occasions. After finishing second in 1982 and third in 1983, it proved third time lucky in 1984.

Sandy was associated with another distinguished Scottish-trained campaigner in Helen Hamilton's Peaty Sandy. The partnership came about because the horse's regular rider, Geordie Dun, had increasing commitments as stable jockey to Ken Oliver. Together Peaty Sandy and Sandy Dudgeon shared ten victories.

In 1989 Sandy Dudgeon was elected to the Jockey Club and in 2009, at the age of fifty-one, he was appointed a steward of the Jockey Club, joining fellow Scot the Duke of Roxburghe. He has acted as a racecourse steward at Aintree, Ayr, Hamilton and Perth.

GEORDIE DUN

Geordie Dun was only twenty years of age when he won the Bollinger Trophy as the leading amateur for the 1978–9 season, with twenty-eight winners. It was an amazing achievement considering that he had gained his very first winner under Rules at Perth on 18 May 1977.

At that early stage of his career, he was based with Arthur Stephenson at Bishop Auckland, where his younger brother, Peter, also went after leaving school – both boys attended George Watson's in Edinburgh. Peter made an equally brilliant start to his riding career until a horrendous life-threatening fall in a chase at Hexham in May 1985.

Geordie Dun gained his first major victory in the 1981 Welsh National on Peaty Sandy, owned by Scottish-based Helen Hamilton, when still an amateur. By the time he won the 1983 Waterford Crystal Stayers' Hurdle (forerunner to the World Hurdle) on A Kinsman, he had turned professional and the pair gained another Cheltenham Festival success in the 1984 Sun Alliance Novices' Chase.

A Kinsman was trained by John Brockbank, from Wigton in Cumbria, who had plenty of riding experience himself as a master of foxhounds and in point-to-points. It was a very sad day when A Kinsman broke a leg in the 1985 Whitbread Gold Cup. That December, Geordie Dun had an altogether happier experience when finishing third on the popular Scottish-based Earls Brig in the King George VI Chase.

Peaty Sandy and A Kinsman were Geordie Dun's two favourites, although he rode plenty of winners when retained by Michael Dickinson and Ken Oliver, before moving on to John Wilson, who had not long taken out a dual licence, operating from the famous Cree Lodge stable at Ayr.

When he married, Geordie, whose mother is Jackie Bruce (see above), made his home at Nether Brotherstone, near Heriot, high in the Moorfoot Hills – about halfway between Edinburgh and Helen Hamilton's base at Innerleithen. He retired from the saddle at the close of the 1986–7 season.

EARL OF ELLESMERE

Like his kinsmen the Dukes of Sutherland, the 4th Earl of Ellesmere (1872–1944), who was both senior steward of the Jockey Club and president of the MCC, was a substantial landowner. The family farms on the Cambridgeshire/Suffolk border around Newmarket used to include Stetchworth Park, which his father had bought. Nowadays the property is owned by Bill Gredley, the owner-breeder of User Friendly and Big Orange.

Two outstanding fillies by Tetratema, trained by Fred Darling at Beckhampton, carried John Ellesmere's 'red, white sleeves, black cap'.

Unbeaten Tiffin headed the Free Handicap at two years when winning the Cheveley Park Stakes, while at three she won the Fern Hill Stakes (then a Royal Ascot feature), July Cup and King George Stakes. The Newmarket sprint provided a memorable duel with Royal Minstrel.

Tiffin's racing career was terminated by a knee injury to add to her previous woes – she had been badly affected by worms as a foal (when bought for 1,100 guineas) and a near-fatal illness had prevented her from competing in the One Thousand Guineas. She died from peritonitis after producing her first foal, Merenda, a juvenile scorer at Royal Ascot.

Four Course succumbed to tetanus at the outset of her stud innings. Purchased by John Ellesmere as a yearling from her trainer for 3,000 guineas, she won the July Stakes, Richmond Stakes and Gimcrack Stakes as a juvenile. She stayed surprisingly well for a daughter of Tetratema, winning the 1931 One Thousand Guineas and finishing runner-up in the Oaks.

Homebred Lemnarchus (King's Stand Stakes) was a prolific winning sprinter. He was also responsible for breeding the unbeaten champion hurdler, Trespasser, winner of the Imperial Cup on three occasions. At the time the Sandown Park race was the most important event staged over hurdles.

John Ellesmere inherited his title upon the death of his father, the 3rd Earl, in 1914 – his main contribution to the Turf was as the owner of Hampton (1872). Resident at Stetchworth Park Stud, he established one of the most important male lines in *The General Stud Book*, from which Hyperion descended. A lock from Hampton's tail was preserved for posterity and kept in the stud office.

ROBERT FAIRBAIRN

During his training career, Robert Fairbairn was based at various establishments in the Borders: Glenside, St Boswells; Sunderland Hall, Galashiels; and Over Whitlaw, Selkirk. Previously he had run a livery and breaking yard at Glenside and it was his reputation as a first-rate nagsman that encouraged him to take out a licence to train.

The most famous horse he broke in was almost certainly Rhona Wilkinson's Grand National stalwart, Wyndburgh. When he proved too strong for his owner to handle, she sent him to Glenside as a three-year-old, where he remained to be trained for the 1954–5 season, when finishing unplaced in all six of his outings over hurdles.

However, with the able assistance of his wife Ethel and daughter Barbara, Bobby Fairbairn enjoyed conspicuous success. His two principal patrons were the Robertson sisters. Members of the Cutty Sark whisky family, they always returned home from a meeting in their chauffeur-driven car immediately after the race in which they had a runner – hanging idly about a racecourse was not their idea of amusement!

Two of the Robertsons' most memorable victories were at Ayr – with African Patrol in the 1966 Scottish Grand National and with Easter Pirate in the 1970 Scottish Champion Hurdle. While African Patrol won the first Scottish National to be run at Ayr, their trainer also saddled Painted Warrior, the very last winner at the race's previous home, Bogside.

Not surprisingly, Ayr was Bobby Fairbairn's favourite course, but his runners also did notably well at Liverpool, winning the Mildmay Chase, Christmas Cracker Chase and Coronation Hurdle. Additional successes included the Great Yorkshire Chase, Doncaster, and Bob Wigney Hurdle, Cheltenham. The trainer died in 2012.

JIM FAIRGRIEVE

As head lad to Peter Cazalet's Fairlawne stable outside Tonbridge in Kent, from the end of the Second World War until the death of this eminent trainer in 1973, Jim Fairgrieve was the linchpin of that important establishment.

Born in Linlithgow, he had been brought up at Mellerstain, near Kelso, where his father looked after the horses owned by Lord Haddington's agent. After working in various hunting establishments, Jim's career was interrupted by the war, in which he served with the Royal Army Veterinary Corps. Invalided out of the army, he spent a few years looking after the stallions at Scaltback Stud, Newmarket.

The well-known pharmaceutical manufacturer, Burroughs & Welcome, had leased part of Fairlawne for testing vaccines. To enable them to perform the requisite experiments they maintained a handful of mares and stallions. In response to an advertisement, Jim Fairgrieve was engaged to look after them.

When Peter Cazalet returned home from the war he asked Jim to come and work for him and what started out on a strictly trial basis became an enormously successful association lasting twenty-seven years.

Jim also became an invaluable scout for suitable young store horses in the north – most of them emanated from around the Borders. Amongst his protégés were the Aintree specialist Cupid's Charge and that fine staying chaser, Kapeno (acquired from John Barclay of Lockerbie), as well as the Queen Mother's stalwarts, Escalus and Greystoke Pillar.

Two more stable stars for whom he was responsible were Lord Kybo and Choice Exit. They achieved their success after Jim had perfected the electronic healing methods pioneered by Sir Charles Strong for treating injuries, a technique much favoured by the Fairlawne trainer.

GEORGE FORBES

A world-renowned bloodstock agent based at Epsom, George Forbes, MRCVS, died from cancer at the age of fifty-eight in November 1969.

The old Etonian veterinary surgeon, a graduate of the Dublin Veterinary College, started off in general practice, but soon began specialising in horses. He set up the Veterinary Bloodstock Agency in 1947, which apart from buying Thoroughbreds of every description, did all its own shipping and insurance.

An extraordinarily hard worker, he also established Epsom Veterinary Remedies, as well as standing a number of modest stallions, and would spend two months every year travelling abroad promoting British bloodstock in general and his own agency in particular.

But it was at the sales that he is best remembered. He invariably stood at the entrance to the ring looking intently over his half-moon spectacles. Up to the time of his death, Botterills' monthly Ascot Bloodstock Sales were flourishing and it seemed that George Forbes would buy every other lot, mostly for export to some far-flung frontier.

He operated at all levels of the market; indeed, only the month before his death, his widow, Joan, a partner in the business, bought an own-sister to Fleet for 51,000 guineas at the Newmarket Houghton Sales, a British auction record for a yearling.

Three of the most notable acquisitions were Amerigo, who excelled as a racehorse in the USA, Prince Royal (Prix de l'Arc de Triomphe), whom he bought as a foal, and the Derby third Pipe of Peace, who became a top sire in Australia.

Once he had the novel idea of syndicating horses to working men's clubs, but the Jockey Club was less enthusiastic! Although only a handful of horses ever carried his Forbes tartan colours, one of them, Fair Hearing, provided top jump jockey, Bill Rees, who later became a starter, with his first success over fences when scoring at defunct Hurst Park.

George Forbes's flair for bloodstock was inherited by the eldest of his six daughters, Fiona Marner, who created a new stud, Windmill Farm Lambourn, just below her former one, Kingwood Stud. Previously married to former trainer, Nicky Vigors, Fiona also became an accomplished horse photographer. Like her father, she has a decided predilection for the Forbes tartan and her son Charlie Vigors wore these colours successfully in point-to-points – he now runs Hillwood Stud, close to Lambourn.

George Forbes's annual Derby Day luncheon at his Epsom home, Burley Lodge, was always a major event for the racing fraternity and he was also a staunch supporter of the Mid-Surrey Farmers' Draghounds.

The family home is Forbes Castle, Strathdon in Aberdeenshire, which made national headlines in the media over the rights of ramblers to cross its land.

DR ANNE GILLESPIE

Relatively few medics have proved significant bloodstock breeders, although Dr Frank Smorfitt, a GP from Warwickshire, was responsible for the 1964 Derby winner, Santa Claus.

With the Scottish predilection for medicine, there just had to be some other member of the profession to have made his or her mark in the realms of Flat breeding. One to qualify is Dr Anne Gillespie, who commutes from her home at Balfron to Glasgow where she specialises in corporate medicine – 'looking after companies', as she describes it.

Anne Gillespie is a graduate of Glasgow University as is her original mentor, Mark Johnston, and he trained her first winner, Lifewatch Vision, a useful two-year-old of 1989. He also bought her Oh So Well, a daughter of the phenomenally fast multiple scorer, Soba, who has proved the cornerstone of her small breeding operation.

Oh So Well (by Sadler's Wells), who cost 25,000 guineas as a yearling, was unraced due to injury, so she was retired to Lennie Peacock's historic Manor

House Stud, Middleham – an introduction effected by Mark Johnston, one of Lennie's neighbours. Manor House is where the 1945 wartime Derby winner, Dante, was bred for Sir Eric Ohlson, who traded as Friar Ings Stud.

In 1995 Oh So Well produced the Anshan colt, Dark Moondancer, who was sold as a three-year-old after winning the St Simon Stakes to race in France. He excelled the following season, winning the Prix Ganay and Gran Premio di Milano, both Group 1, and the Group 2 Prix d'Harcourt.

These performances earned his breeder the Thoroughbred Breeders' Association's Langham Cup which is presented annually to a deserving small breeder. At about this time Anne Gillespie declared that breeding was more important to her than racing *per se*, but it has not all been plain sailing since then.

JIM GOLDIE

Jim Goldie's training operation, which is based just south-west of Glasgow at Libo Hill Farm, Uplawmoor, is very much a family affair. His wife Davina is in charge of the office and their two sons, James and George, act as assistants. Another indispensable member of the team is Ben Holohan, an equine chiropractor and dentist.

Jim, who was in the garden fencing business, used to ride for his father, Thomas, a permit-holder from Kilwinning in Ayrshire, before taking out a full training licence in March 1992. Initially the operation was geared towards jumpers – with a good percentage of animals by Destroyer, who stood at Coylton, near Ayr – but the emphasis soon shifted to the Flat.

The flagship horse proved to be the game entire, Orientor. A Group-winner at Sandown Park and Newcastle with a preference for some cut in the ground, this durable sprinter cost Jim Goldie 12,000 guineas at the 1999 Doncaster St Leger Yearling Sales. Orientor retired to stud in 2008.

Jim Goldie has the reputation for improving horses from other trainers, 'retreads' as he refers to them, and the best known is Hawkeyethenoo. He proved the stable's most consistently high profile representative winning both the Stewards' Cup at Goodwood (the only Scottish trained horse to do so) and the Victoria Cup at Ascot. Another stalwart was the grey Nanton – placed three times in the Cambridgeshire, he remained in training as a 13-year-old.

One of the all time favourites at Libo Hill Farm has been Jack Dexter. Both his sire Orientor and dam Glenhurich were homebred and he was named after Goldie's two grandsons. Probably a superior sprinter to his sire, Jack Dexter has made many sorties south. Placed in numerous Group sprints, he finished third in the British Champions Sprint and fourth in the King's Stand Stakes, both at Ascot.

July 2017 proved quite a landmark month for the Scottish stable – Hawkeyethenoo was retired aged eleven; Jack Dexter won a valuable handicap at Ascot's 'King George' meeting on his fourteenth visit to the Berkshire course; and Cheeni, a mare by Orientor, headed a remarkable 'first four home' for the stable in a handicap at Ayr.

Graham Lee enjoyed a successful partnership with Jack Dexter, Jim Goldie being a great supporter when the Grand National-winning jockey decided to switch from jumping to the Flat. Indeed he provided Graham's first winner on switching codes with Northern Fling at Musselburgh in May 2012. Gary Bartley did well for the stable as an apprentice and his amateur wife, Carol, won the prestigious ladies' race on the stable's Middlemarch on King George Day at Ascot.

There have been some notable jumping successes. In 2007 and 2008 Lampion du Bost and Endless Power both won the historic Grand Sefton Chase at Aintree over the Grand National fences. Lampion du Bost scored at 66–1. This French-bred also won a novice chase over the Mildmay fences at the Grand National meeting, but Endless Power died tragically after breaking his pelvis in the 2009 Racing Post Chase.

It was another feather in Jim Goldie's cap when the four-year-old, La Vecchia Scuola, scored over hurdles on successive afternoons at the 2008 Scottish Grand National Meeting at Ayr. Early in 2010 the stable won another prestige event in Scotland with Hillview Boy in the Listed Braveheart Stakes at Hamilton.

TOMMY GOSLING

Tommy Gosling will always be associated with Sir Winston Churchill's Colonist II. This popular French-bred grey was a singularly appropriate winner of the Winston Churchill Stakes at Hurst Park in 1951 when beating King George VI's Above Board. Afterwards Tommy spent a convivial time drinking champagne with the two owners.

That season, Colonist finished runner-up in the Ascot Gold Cup and fourth in the inaugural King George VI and Queen Elizabeth (Festival of Britain) Stakes. Tommy also partnered the former prime minister's High Hat to win the Winston Churchill Stakes; he was also third on Vienna, another of his owner's homebreds, in the St Leger. The nearest he came to classic success was on Arabian Night, runner-up in the 1954 Derby to Never Say Die, ridden by a young Lester Piggott.

Tommy was born in New Lanark in July 1926 and died at his home outside Paris in November 2008 aged eighty-two. The fourth of five children, he left school aged fourteen to work as a messenger boy in Lanark for Lipton's, the grocers, and as a petrol pump attendant, before deciding to go south and embark on a career in racing.

Apprenticed to Ossie Bell in Lambourn, he was joint-champion apprentice with Frankie Durr in 1945 with ten winners, one of them on Happy Grace in a substitute Stewards' Cup at Windsor. It was for the Australian trainer that he won the 1947 Victoria Cup and Cambridgeshire on Fairey Fulmar. That winter he was riding in India when Mahatma Gandhi was assassinated and spent six days hiding in a basement as riots escalated outside.

Moving to Epsom, he soon caught the eye of Colonist's trainer, Walter Nightingall, who became known as the 'Saturday Specialist'. In 1953 he rode Paddy Prendergast's champion juvenile colt, The Pie King, and champion juvenile filly, Sixpence, to win at Royal Ascot (Coventry Stakes) and Chester respectively. The best sprinter he rode was Arcandy, successful in the Stewards' Cup, Stanley Ford Stakes (Birmingham) and Diadem Stakes in 1957.

Other good winners during that decade included HVC (Horris Hill Stakes), Westinform (Oxfordshire Stakes – now Geoffrey Freer Stakes), Tudor Castle (Knight's Royal Stakes – now Queen Elizabeth II Stakes), Double Bore (Goodwood Cup) and Hindu Festival (Ormonde Stakes). In 1961 he won the Irish One Thousand Guineas on Lady Senator.

Tommy suffered his share of falls, the most serious of which occurred after riding a winner at Leicester in 1956. While he was endeavouring to pull up, the saddle slipped and in the ensuing fall he was kicked on the head, causing a blood clot to the brain. This galvanised the Jockey Club into making reinforced crash helmets obligatory for all Flat jockeys.

However, it was weight problems that forced Tommy Gosling's retirement, whereupon he started training at Priam Lodge, Epsom. His place as retained jockey to Walter Nightingall was filled in due course by Duncan Keith, another Scottish jockey to suffer from serious weight problems.

Tommy Gosling trained at Epsom from 1964 to 1982. He won the 1965 Irish One Thousand Guineas with Ardent Dancer owned by Pat McAllister, whose husband's family came from Stirling. Others to make their mark included Excel (Greenham Stakes), Quartette (Yorkshire Cup, Vaux Gold Tankard), L'Apache (Classic Trial) and Sol Argent (Extel Handicap, Geoffrey Freer Stakes).

Tommy's first wife was Gill Leach, whose father, Jack, was a well-known jockey, trainer and racing correspondent. His second wife, Valerie, was the daughter of Herbert Vickery, who kept horses at Priam Lodge, but had others with Ryan Price at Findon. One of them, Levanter, was temporarily ante-post favourite for the 1971 Derby.

Initially Tommy Gosling retired to live near Dorking where he and Val ran a livery yard. In 2000 they moved to Normandy where they bred and showed Percherons. It was a proud moment when they won the €100 prize at the local show. Another hobby in later life was sailing.

Tommy Gosling was an ardent football fan and as a young man he had had a trial for Airdrie. In 1949 he not only captained a jockeys' side versus a boxers' eleven at Arsenal's Highbury ground, but he also scored a hat-trick to secure a 5–3 victory. There were 41,000 spectators that evening at what was reputed to be the first football match to be played under floodlights.

DUKES OF HAMILTON

The premier peers of Scotland and Hereditary Keepers of the Palace of Holyroodhouse in Edinburgh, the Dukes of Hamilton, whose seat is just outside Haddington, have not involved themselves in racing for many a long day, but time was when they were enormous supporters of the Turf.

Archibald Hamilton (1740–1819), the 9th Duke, holds a unique record and one that can assuredly never be surpassed as horses carrying his colours won the St Leger on seven occasions from 1786 to 1814. This septet comprised Paragon, Spadille, Young Flora, Tartar, Petronius, Ashton and William. All were homebred with the exception of Tartar whose breeder was the Duke of Cumberland, the butcher of Culloden.

While the 12th Duke, William Douglas-Hamilton (1845–95), could not aspire to quite such a record, he also won the St Leger with Ossian in 1883, and three years later he won the One Thousand Guineas and Oaks with Miss Jummy. Both homebreds were trained at Newmarket by the royal trainer, Richard Marsh.

Their owner came into racing at a young age and he was only twenty-two when winning the 1867 Grand National with Cortolvin, whose previous owner had discarded him for lacking courage and stamina. That year at Bogside he also won the inaugural West of Scotland Grand National as it was called with The Elk, who gave his name to a race at Ayr. A heavy gambler, he was reputed to have won £10,000 in bets on both occasions.

Like some of his horses, the duke had two ways of running. As a young man he was something of a corinthian figure, proficient at riding to hounds, shooting, yachting and boxing. However, his conviviality had a disturbing habit of being replaced at a moment's notice by an altogether less friendly demeanour – perhaps this could be attributed to gout, which got progressively worse as he grew older.

William Douglas-Hamilton had two other bugbears in life: a shortage of available funds due to betting on such a colossal scale which caused him to be blackballed by the Jockey Club, only to be reinstated; and his weight which varied between eighteen and twenty stones. He was endeavouring to slim down when he died at a comparatively early age.

LORD HAMILTON OF DALZELL

Scotland has produced its share of racing administrators, but few have been more influential than the 2nd Lord Hamilton of Dalzell (1872–1952). Formerly a regular in the Scots Guards, he was largely instrumental in the innovation of Totalisator betting in Great Britain, during his tenure as senior steward of the Jockey Club.

Chairman of the committee established to ascertain the viability of Tote betting, he remained the Jockey Club's representative on the Racecourse Betting Control Board (later the Horserace Totalisator Boad) for the next two decades.

Introduced to Parliament as a private member's bill, the Racecourse Betting Act became law in 1928, despite strong opposition from two unlikely allies, the bookmakers and the Church. Tote betting became a reality on British racecourses in July of the following year.

In 1928 Lord Dewar's homebred The Black Abbot had justified favouritism in the Gimcrack Stakes and as the guest of honour at the annual Gimcrack dinner he paid the most generous of tributes to his fellow Scot. In his speech Tom Dewar said, 'His name will go down in history written large in letters of indelible ink across the annals of racing.'

From 1934 to 1945 Gavin Hamilton was His Majesty's Representative at Ascot. He was succeeded by Bernard Fitzalan Howard, 16th Duke of Norfolk. He also made a significant contribution as chairman to two racecourses closer to his Motherwell home – Lanark, which closed in 1977, and Hamilton Park. In conjunction with Sir Loftus Bates, he was responsible in 1926 for the revival of racing at Hamilton, now the only dedicated Flat racing venue in Scotland.

BILLY HAMILTON

Billy Hamilton, from Bonchester Bridge, near Hawick, was a farmer, point-to-point rider and permit holder. It was on Naughty Tara, who was not the most reliable of conveyances, that he won the Heart of All England at Hexham, a much-coveted hunter chase in the north-east.

Mated with Scotland's star National Hunt stallion, New Brig, who began and ended his stud career in Roxburghshire with an interim period in East Lothian, this Black Tarquin mare produced the amazing Earls Brig as her first foal – initially he excelled between the flags, winning eleven consecutive point-to-points.

Appropriately, homebred Earls Brig made the transition to racing under Rules by winning the Hamilton Memorial Chase at Kelso (see below). Later he won the Greenall Whitley Chase at Haydock Park prior to finishing third in the 1985 Cheltenham Gold Cup behind Forgive'N Forget and Righthandman, despite some indifferent jumping. That year he also finished third in the King George VI Chase.

Not many permit-holders aspire to a placed runner in the Blue Riband of steeplechasing, but the fact that 'Briggs' started second favourite shows that he had more than earned his place in the field. Twelve months earlier he had looked the likely winner of the Foxhunters' when falling six fences from home.

HELEN HAMILTON

When Helen Hamilton's father died, the family stables at Brigend, near Melrose, were taken over by Susan Chesmore, who trained Peaty Sandy to win three times over hurdles.

After the yard was afflicted by the virus, Miss Hamilton decided to take Peaty Sandy (named after a bay in Caithness) home to Whitehope. She trained the son of Spartan General on her hill farm near the mill town of Innerleithen – just down the road is Traquair House, the oldest inhabited house in Scotland.

Adept at herding the sheep on the steep Peeblesshire slopes, Peaty Sandy developed into one of the best staying chasers in the country, gaining his most memorable victory as favourite for the 1981 Welsh National, at a time when most of Britain was virtually snowbound. He was ridden by leading Scottish amateur, Geordie Dun. Later one of his colleagues, Sandy Dudgeon, became his regular partner.

The first Scottish-trained horse to win the Welsh National, Peaty Sandy gained all his other triumphs in the north. Half his twenty victories were recorded at Newcastle, the last of them in the marathon Eider Chase as a thirteen-year-old. The reason for his parochial record was due to an allergy problem – he always had to be bedded on newspaper with no hay in sight and feed was always washed. So overnight stays in a racecourse stable were to be avoided.

Peaty Sandy was also successful at Ayr six times and at Kelso three times. It was at Kelso that Helen initiated the Hamilton Memorial Chase in memory of her mother, Constance, in whose colours their homebred star used to race.

LADY HAY

Married to Sir Bache Hay, the 11th Baronet who died in 1966, Lady Hay started owning horses with Neville Crump just after the Second World War, at which time she was an enthusiastic rider to hounds.

She had a succession of top staying chasers trained at Middleham, the first being Goosander. Bought privately from his breeder, the father of top northern jump jockey, Dick Curran, Goosander started a warm favourite at 5–1 for the 1957 Grand National, following three consecutive victories at Haydock Park, only to finish sixth behind Sundew.

Another top performer in her white colours with a Hay tartan crossbelt was Arcturus, winner of the 1968 Scottish Grand National, beating that season's Grand National hero, Red Alligator. Her last notable representative, Even Melody, won the 1977 Massey Ferguson Gold Cup just a month before his octogenarian owner died at her Peeblesshire home, Haystoun.

Just like Lady Beaverbrook with her Flat performers, Judy Hay always went to extreme lengths to ensure that her horses were well cared for in their retirement. On leaving Middleham, both Goosander and Arcturus ended their days in Scotland and were seen out hunting regularly with the Buccleuch.

TOMMY HOGG

One of the youngest ever graduates of the Royal (Dick) Veterinary College in Edinburgh, where he qualified aged twenty-one, Tommy Hogg MRCVS came from Berwickshire. He served in the Royal Army Veterinary Corps in both the Boer War and the First World War. It was in South Africa that he became great friends with fellow Scottish vet, Jock Crawford (see above).

For an intermediate period, Tommy Hogg acted as veterinary surgeon to the Turf Club in Johannesburg as well as training before returning to England to supervise a small string at Epsom. After the First World War he based himself in Wiltshire, first at Ogbourne and then at Russley Park. It was at the latter establishment, close to Lambourn, that he trained Happy Man, whom he had acquired for just thirty guineas as a yearling to win the 1923 Ascot Gold Cup.

Tommy Hogg's ability with mostly moderate horses was recognised by Lord Glanely, one of the country's foremost owners, and in 1928 Tommy was appointed his private trainer at Lagrange Stables in Newmarket. From 1930 to 1937 they were rewarded with four classic winners, Rose of England (Oaks), Singapore (St Leger), Colombo (Two Thousand Guineas) and Chulmleigh (St Leger). Chulmleigh was by Singapore out of Rose of England.

Having relinquished his training licence in 1938 due to ill health, Tommy Hogg subsequently trained a small string at Heath House. Altogether he had saddled around 600 winners by the time of his death in August 1942 aged sixty-three. He also provided Sir Gordon Richards with many of his early winners when this great jockey was associated with Russley Park.

JARDINE FAMILY

Three successive Jardine baronets were involved in racing and breeding, from Victorian times through to the period running up to the Second World War – Sir Robert Snr; his son, Sir Robert Jnr; and the latter's son, Sir John Buchanan Jardine.

In business circles, the name Jardine is synonymous with the Far East trading company, Jardine Matheson, which was founded by two Scotsmen, William Jardine from Dumfriesshire, and James Matheson from Sutherland. Their fortune accrued initially from importing tea from China and trading opium from India into China via Hong Kong. This led to the Opium Wars of the 1840s which resulted in Hong Kong being ceded to Great Britain until 1997.

Despite the considerable wealth that they had accrued in Asia, the returns that members of the Jardine family from Lockerbie, Dumfriesshire, gained from investing in top-quality bloodstock was hardly commensurate with the money they spent. While they were tremendously successful entrepreneurs when it came to business, luck seemed to desert them on the Turf.

However, Sir Robert Snr did come close to hitting the jackpot. In 1888 he and his then trainer, John Porter, bought a yearling colt from the Royal Studs at Hampton Court for 500 guineas. As joint owners they sold Sainfoin to Sir James Miller as a three-year-old for £6,000, prior to the Derby, for which the John Porter-trained Surefoot started a long odds-on favourite. Sainfoin won with Surefoot unplaced. It was small consolation that a contingency entitled the former partners to share half the winning prize money.

Sir Robert's son of the same name did manage to win a classic, his homebred filly, Cinna, winning the 1920 One Thousand Guineas and Coronation Stakes, Royal Ascot. In the interim she had been expected to win the Oaks but was beaten a neck – later her son, Beau Pere, became a stallion sensation in Australasia.

Robert's first love was coursing and long before Cinna came along he had won the Waterloo Cup twice, with Long Span (1907) and Jabberwock (1911).

When Robert Jnr died in 1927, his New England Stud at Newmarket passed to his son and heir, John. Two smart handicappers carried his dark blue and silver braid colours in Obliterate (1925 Northumberland Plate) and Nothing Venture (1928 Ayr Gold Cup). For a time they stood alongside each other at New England, homebred Obliterate siring the 1935 Oaks heroine, Quashed.

One of the greatest racemares of all time, Quashed won a memorable renewal of the Ascot Gold Cup.

In 1939 Sir John Buchanan Jardine sold New England Stud to the flour miller, James V. Rank, a great supporter of racing under both Rules and another coursing enthusiast. Following Rank's death in 1952 the stud was bought by Richard Stanley. The current owner is his nephew, Peter Stanley, the present Lord Derby's younger brother.

ANDREW JOHNSTONE FAMILY

Before the computerised age, *Dams of Winners* was one of the most essential works of reference in pedigree research. It was compiled by Professor Keylock, whose son-in-law, Andrew Johnstone, duly took over the publication. He also owned Brickfields Stud, Exning, on the outskirts of Newmarket, which used to stand such top stallions as Darius and Worden II.

Andrew Johnstone, who served in the Royal Scots Greys during the Second World War, belonged to a well-known Dumfriesshire family from Lochmaben, whose relations included the Jardines, the great Scottish business entrepreneurs associated with the Hong Kong trading company, Jardine Matheson. It was through the Johnstone family, owners of the Halleaths Estate at Lochmaben in Dumfriesshire, that the Jardines became involved in the Turf.

In 1869 John Johnstone (Andrew's great-grandfather) won the Two Thousand Guineas and Derby with Pretender. He had bought the colt as a yearling as he stood the sire, Adventurer. Pretender was trained in Yorkshire by Tom Dawson, the eldest son of George Dawson of Stamford Hall, Gullane in Scotland (see Chapter 4), and he was the last Epsom Derby winner to be trained in the north. Dante won a substitute affair on the July Course at Newmarket in 1945.

Pretender was ridden at Epsom by John Osborne, the most popular and successful jockey in the north during the second half of the nineteenth century – John Johnstone Snr and Robert Jardine Snr had a retainer on his services.

In 1902 John Johnstone's grandson of the same name went out to the Far East and, by the time he returned permanently to the family home in Scotland in 1923, he was the head of Jardine Matheson. In the interim he had ridden nearly 1,000 winners as an amateur in China and Hong Kong, including fourteen runnings of the China Grand National. At one Hong Kong meeting in 1915 he scored on sixteen of his thirty mounts. He was a steward of the Hong Kong Jockey Club and the Shanghai Race Club.

John Johnstone Jnr, who also rode with success at home, maintained a small stud and racing stable at Halleaths and became a prominent figure on northern racecourses. He died in 1935 aged fifty-three while attending the National Hunt Meeting at Cheltenham.

SIR FREDERIC JOHNSTONE

In Victorian times a racing partnership was frequently referred to as a 'confederacy' and one of the most successful existed between Lord Alington and Sir Frederic Johnstone. It was always referred to as 'The Old Firm'.

Both were members of the Jockey Club (Johnstone became a member at the tender age of twenty-two) and had a reputation as shrewd gamblers. From an old Scottish family, Johnstone, the 8th Baronet (1841–1913) of Westerhall, Dumfriesshire, was the elder of twin boys and like their father and grandfather, Sir Frederic was MP for Weymouth over a long period.

Although Johnstone was sixteen years junior to Alington, the horses invariably ran in the former's name – his colours were chocolate with yellow sleeves. The partnership started in 1868 and survived until Alington's death in 1904. During that period they were rewarded with six classic victories.

Indeed, the very first horse they owned, Brigantine, trained by William Day at Woodyates in Wiltshire, brought off a sensational double by winning the 1869 Oaks and Ascot Gold Cup. Brigantine had been bought for just 150 guineas, but The Old Firm's three subsequent classic winners were all homebred by Alington at his Crichel Stud, near Wimborne, in Dorset.

This trio comprised the 1883 Derby winner, St Blaise, the 1891 Triple Crown hero, Common, and the 1894 St Leger winner, Throstle. Common and Throstle were half-brothers. All were trained by John Porter at Kingsclere, to whom the partners had transferred their horses in 1881. Between them they recorded over 100 victories worth in excess of £100,000.

St Blaise became champion sire in North America in 1890, but tragically was killed in a fire at the advanced age of twenty-nine. Common was sold for £15,000, then a vast sum, to furniture magnate Sir Blundell Maple, and retired to his Childwick Bury Stud in Hertfordshire.

DUNCAN KEITH

As first jockey to Walter Nightingall (1961–7) and then Peter Walwyn (1968–72), Duncan Keith held retainers with two of the country's most powerful stables. In the close season he also rode extensively in India, where he earned a considerable reputation by winning all the classics in Calcutta.

Born and brought up in the Gorbals district of Glasgow, the Scot learned the rudiments of stable-craft grooming Clydesdales as a youngster. He also had the opportunity to ride show ponies for a local farmer. Obviously he had a thorough grounding, as within a few weeks of joining Ted Smyth at Epsom he was given a ride in public and his first winner soon followed – Zator at Folkestone in 1954.

On completing his apprenticeship, he became stable jockey to Walter Nightingall. His runners were renowned for making the running and these tactics provided one of the biggest upsets of the 1961 season when Sir Winston Churchill's High Hat defeated Petite Etoile at Kempton Park. Duncan Keith became adept at riding a waiting race from the front and never more so than when partnering Tacitus around Sandown Park.

In 1965 the same trainer-jockey combination won the Two Thousand Guineas with Niksar and the following year's Coronation Cup with I Say. The latter was owned by Louis Freedman who transferred his horses to Peter Walwyn following Walter Nightingall's death in 1968, by which time Duncan Keith had become the Lambourn trainer's new stable jockey.

Consequently Duncan became associated with Louis Freedman's brilliant filly, Lucyrowe. In the year that they won the Coronation Stakes, he also won the Cheveley Park Stakes on her stable companion, Humble Duty. The ensuing season they notched up some top-class victories, but weight problems prevented him from riding this exceptional grey to victory in the One Thousand Guineas.

During the course of his riding career with over 650 winners, Duncan Keith survived two particularly bad falls which put him out of action for the remainder of the season. Ironically he was riding Walter Nightingall's London Melody on both occasions, first at Newbury in May 1964 and then a year later at Lingfield Park. As a result, the Jockey Club took the unprecedented step of barring London Melody from future competition.

The jockey was also involved in another unfortunate double. In 1971 and

1972 he finished first on the Peter Walwyn-trained Rock Roi in the Ascot Gold Cup, only for the horse to be disqualified on both occasions. The first time a routine dope test proved positive and on the second occasion Rock Roi was deemed to have caused interference to the runner-up.

Only weeks later, increasing weight forced Duncan Keith to retire and he started training from Red House, Littleton, near Winchester, where Les Hall masterminded so many spectacular coups. Unfortunately his new career did not prove a comparable success. He died aged seventy-six in 2014.

LORD KILMANY

Sir William Anstruther-Gray of Cupar in Fife became Lord Kilmany in 1966, though the title is now extinct. He was one of the best-known figures on northern racecourses, both before and after the Second World War. A long-serving MP in Scotland and a prominent figure at Westminster, he was involved in just about every aspect of racing so far as jumping was concerned and was much involved with the campaign to save the Grand National in the 1970s.

He was a member of both the Jockey Club and the National Hunt Committee (then two separate entities), as well as the Horserace Betting Levy Board. He also served as a steward at Ayr, Perth, Newcastle and Hexham for jumping and at Hamilton for the Flat.

Bill Kilmany rode as an amateur from 1929 to 1935, when his most successful mount was a black gelding named Our Empire. During the Second World War he served in the Coldstream Guards and became the recipient of an MC. He was also one of the very first people to be granted a permit to train and as Bill Anstruther-Gray he saddled Bruno II to win the 1948 National Hunt Chase in his light blue and chocolate colours, ridden by Guy Cunard.

He only ever had a handful of horses at his home in Fife. Amongst the more notable were Mischievous Monk (Champion Novice Chase, Ayr), Scarfell (Totalisator Handicap Hurdle, dead-heat) and The Engineer (George Graham Memorial Chase, Ayr).

Any success at Ayr had a particular relevance, as he was patron there as well as at Perth and Hexham. One of just a handful of broodmares he owned was Sage Warbler, the dam of Mischievous Monk and The Engineer. Lord Kilmany continued to train until his death in 1985.

Lord Kilmany's wife Monica – also a Jockey Club member and a relative of that great trainer George Lambton – was the first woman to be appointed a steward, acting at Edinburgh and Hamilton. The family tradition is maintained by their daughter, Jane Gillies, a prominent figure on Scottish racecourses as a former steward and now a director of Perth.

The Kilmany Cups staged at Perth and Musselburgh are both chases, but their identity is somewhat obscured by sponsorship.

LEN LUNGO

Len Lungo eclipsed the Scottish record set by Ken Oliver when sending out the winners of fifty-nine races under NH Rules in 2000–1, and reached sixty-three on two subsequent occasions. He decided to retire in the summer of 2009 when his overall tally of winners stood at 646.

Born and brought up in Motherwell, Len Lungo became keen on riding thanks to a childhood pony and in his early teenage years he was sufficiently competent to school horses for local trainer, Jimmy Barrett. Leaving school at sixteen, he rode a few winners for Linlithgow trainer, Craig Brown.

For an interim period he was based in the West Country, where he rode mostly for Gerald Cottrell, for whom he was stable jockey, and Les Kennard. He also partnered Martin Pipe's first winner, Hit Parade, in 1975. Altogether he rode around 100 winners before being forced to retire through injury.

Returning north of the border to run three public houses and a snooker club, he bought Hetland Hill Farm, Carrutherstown, just a few miles north of Gretna Green overlooking the Solway Firth. Originally a 400-acre farm, part arable and part hill, it was transformed into a purpose-built training establishment with all modern facilities, the indispensable indoor school being the size of an aircraft hangar.

He took out a licence to train in 1990, and his first winner was Cumbrian Ceilidh, who scored over hurdles at Edinburgh (now Musselburgh) the following year. The stable's first big success was with Celtic Giant in the 1999 Kim Muir Chase and a second Cheltenham Festival winner came with Freetown in the 2002 Pertemps Hurdle Final.

Other high-profile winners included The Bajan Bandit (Champion Bumper) and Crazy Horse (Oddbins Hurdle) at the Aintree Grand National Meeting; Direct Access (EBF Novice Hurdle Final, Sandown Park); and Mirjan (Swinton

Hurdle, Haydock Park). Mirjan also won the Northumberland Plate and Silvertown won the Cumberland Plate, another historic northern handicap.

In 2008 Against The Grain won the Ayr Silver Cup, having previously scored at Doncaster after an absence of 610 days. Len Lungo did even better with Laouen on 1 April 2007. The former invalid, who had been treated with stem-cell implants, scored over hurdles at Hexham after a lay-off of nearly four years – 1,410 days to be precise.

Training is a team effort and a key figure in this particular success story was head lad Roy Barrett (no relation to the trainer mentioned above), who used to be with Wilfrid Crawford at Haddington, before joining Rose Dobbin outside Alnwick.

Len Lungo, who became the only Scottish-based trainer on the council of the National Trainers' Federation, was never frightened to express his opinion. Two of his major concerns were the need for jumping stores to be more precocious and the high rate of injuries to jumpers. In his opinion too many racecourses have 'bad ground, unacceptable road crossings and badly filled hurdles'.

In retirement, the former Dumfriesshire trainer, whose stables are now occupied by Iain Jardine, planned to spend more time at his holiday homes in Spain and Portugal. His youngest daughter, Lucinda, is married to Newmarket trainer, James Tate, MRCVS.

GRAHAM MACMILLAN

Graham Macmillan from Lockerbie, Dumfriesshire, was runner-up for the amateur riders' championship for three seasons: to Chris Collins in 1965–6; to Michael Dickinson in 1969–70; and to John Lawrence in 1970–1.

It has always been a thorn in Graham's side that the future Lord Oaksey only won the third of those titles by purloining a ride off Terry Biddlecombe in the very last race of the season. In the circumstances many observers thought that a dead-heat would have been much the most sporting outcome.

Graham, who hunted with the Dumfriesshire Foxhounds from the age of four, started off race riding in flapping events. He partnered ninety point-to-point winners, the first of them aged just fifteen, and was still riding in his fifties. As one of few amateurs who could hold his own against the professionals, the NH authorities subsequently restricted him to fifty rides per season.

Three of his more memorable successes came on Roe Gemmel in the Mildmay Memorial Chase, Liverpool, for Bobby Fairbairn; on Credit Call in the Horse and Hound Cup, Stratford-on-Avon, for Arthur Stephenson; and on Tee Cee Bee in the Whitbread Trial Chase, Newcastle, for Tom Bell. His best season was 1970–1, when he rode sixteen winners.

Although attached to Arthur Stephenson's stable for a period, Graham relied throughout his career upon the support of permit-holders, one of the first being John Nixon, from Wigton in Cumbria. As well as Tee Cee Bee, Graham rode another smart chaser for Tom Bell from Carluke, near Glasgow, in the ill-fated Angus M. Another favourite trained in Scotland was Harry Bell's Union Pacific.

While Graham favoured jump-racing proper, his brother Charlie concentrated on point-to-points. During the 1967–8 season they rode fourteen hunter chase winners between them, amongst Charlie's successes being the Cheltenham Foxhunters' on Robin Dun's mare, Bright Beach. Charlie was also instrumental in the early education of the 1986 Scottish Grand National winner, Hardy Lad.

On one memorable occasion, Graham beat the great Freddie at Friars Haugh, Kelso, riding his own horse, Baie Noir, whom he had acquired out of Peter Cazalet's stable through Jim Fairgrieve. However, he always rated Queensberry Lad as the best horse he owned, the son of New Brig scoring twelve times over fences and seven times between the flags.

Graham Macmillan rode his first winner under National Hunt Rules in May 1955 at Hexham. By the time he hung up his boots over thirty-five years later he had partnered more than 170 winners. By then he was already acting as a steward at Ayr, Carlisle and Hexham.

ALAN MACTAGGART

As contemporaries, Alan Mactaggart and Graham Macmillan proved two of the most proficient amateur riders over jumps that Scotland has ever produced. They excelled during a golden period for Scottish jumpers, particularly in the field of outstanding hunter-chasers.

Alan, whose base at Denholm, outside Hawick, is just across the water from the Olivers' Hassendean Bank establishment, rode over sixty winners under Rules. It was his good fortune to be associated with Freddie, one of the most popular horses ever trained in Scotland. In 1964 he partnered him to victory in the Cheltenham Foxhunters' (by six lengths at 3–1 on) and the Vaux Hunter Chase (Catterick), then an even more valuable prize for hunters.

In the same year (1964) Alan got married and took out a permit to train, in which sphere he also excelled. Amongst his more notable winners have been Ted Broon, Knock Twice, Norbor and Run'n Fly. The latter is the dam of homebred Running Moss whom he saddled to win the 2002 Scottish Borders National at Kelso, where he acts as a steward.

Alan Mactaggart was involved for many years with the stallions standing at Mary Young's Woodside Stud, Greenlaw, Berwickshire, and as a regional representative for the Thoroughbred Breeders' Association, embraced an area covering not only the whole of Scotland, but also Northern Ireland and the north of England.

A noted breeder, Alan brought off a tremendous double during the 1990–1 season, winning two of the TBA's annual awards thanks to the success of Docklands Express in the Whitbread Gold Cup and Racing Post Chase, and Blitzkrieg in the Captain Morgan Aintree Chase and Victor Chandler Chase.

The Mactaggart clan is certainly a force to be reckoned with around Hawick. Alan has two sons, David, an amateur rider, and Jeremy, a director of Goffs UK (formerly Doncaster Bloodstock Sales). They also have two cousins – Stuart, also a director of the firm, and Bruce, who trains.

McALLISTER FAMILY

One of the first mares Jim McAllister bought to start a small stud at his home, Lyndsay Hall, Ingatestone, Essex, was Snow Blossom. In October 1970 he sold her at the Newmarket sales, covered by Firestreak, for just 940 guineas. The foal she was carrying was Snow Knight, winner of the 1974 Derby!

A native of Stirling, Jim had been encouraged to start breeding when Ardent Dancer, a yearling bargain at just 1,000 guineas in 1963, carried his wife's colours to victory in the Irish One Thousand Guineas, saddled by Tommy Gosling, the Epsom trainer who was born near Lanark. However, it was a less talented filly, Western Air, who was to prove the stud's foundation mare.

Western Air was transferred from Ingatestone to Chippenham Lodge Stud when the McAllisters bought this property on the Ely side of Newmarket (later run by Jim's son Bruce), from Michael Wyatt of Dunchurch Lodge Stud. She is the dam of Western Jewel and Mr Fluorocarbon; the second dam of Redback; and the third dam of Barathea Guest, all Group winners bred by the McAllisters.

Both Redback and Barathea Guest finished third in the Two Thousand Guineas. Two classic placed fillies associated with Chippenham Lodge are Wannabe Grand (Cheveley Park Stakes, Cherry Hinton Stakes), who was runner-up in the 1999 One Thousand Guineas, and homebred Summitville – she finished third in the 2003 Oaks. In 2006 Summitville's half-brother by Galileo realised 300,000 guineas, the top price the stud received for a yearling.

The reason that Bruce McAllister gave for selling the majority of his breeding stock at Tattersalls' Newmarket December Sales in 2009 was the escalating overheads in running a top commercial yearling stud in the modern age.

McHARG FAMILY

No family has been more closely involved with the administration of racing in Scotland over the years than the McHargs from Ayr – father Alec, son Bill and grandson David. Indeed, to many followers of the sport Bill McHarg OBE was regarded as 'Mr Racing' in Scotland.

Bill was clerk of the course at four of the remaining five courses in Scotland. His father had been clerk of the course at Bogside where young Bill was brought up, and Bill's son David succeeded his father at Edinburgh (now Musselburgh) in 1980. It was here that Bill had taken up his first appointment back in 1949.

The war interrupted Bill McHarg's university education at Glasgow. Joining up as a trooper in the Ayrshire Yeomanry, he came out as a major in the Gunners, with an MC. Although he returned to university to finish his law degree, his workplace became the racecourse rather than a solicitor's office. And when his father, Alec, died in 1956, Bill was ready to succeed him.

The 1960s provided major challenges to racecourse administration. The most revolutionary was the introduction of off-course betting and high-street betting shops, which necessitated a whole new concept of racecourse funding. To compensate for the deficit caused by falling attendances, Bill McHarg mastered an entirely different financial structure, based on subsidy, grants and loans and a vastly increased fixture list.

At one time during the 1980s, David McHarg was clerk of the course at all five Scottish tracks. A noted innovator, he presided over the introduction of Musselburgh's successful jumping course. However, he had an altercation with the influential Western Meeting Club at Ayr in 1991, whereupon he left Scotland to become racing manager for the Singapore Turf Club.

Subsequently he returned to Britain to run the popular jumping courses, Fontwell Park and Plumpton in Sussex, where he died in March 2007, aged fifty-four.

McINTYRE FAMILY

Andrew McIntyre is the fourth member of his family in father-to-son sequence to have managed their Theakston Stud. It is situated near Bedale, in a picturesque part of North Yorkshire, with the Hambleton Hills to the east and the Pennines to the west.

The first of them was Archibald McIntyre from Glen Etine, Argyll. A prominent Thoroughbred breeder in the middle of the nineteenth century, he was consigning stock to Tattersalls' sales back in 1865. He also bred Aberdeen Angus cattle and the herd which he started in 1889 is still going strong – it is the oldest established Angus herd in England.

Archie bought Theakston Hall, together with 600 acres, in 1893. He had previously been based at Neasham Hall Stud, near Darlington, where James Cookson had bred Kettledrum and Dundee, first and second in the 1861 Derby. While living in Co. Durham, Archie also bred some good horses in partnership with his father-in-law, Thomas Hewett of Gibside Park.

After the Second World War two horses became indelibly linked with Theakston. In 1945 Sir Eric Ohlson's homebred Dante became the last Derby winner to have been trained in Yorkshire, albeit he won a substitute race run on the July Course at Newmarket, and he spent the duration of his stud innings at Theakston. Dante, who suffered from moon blindness, died in September 1956 aged only fourteen.

That April Theakston-bred Sovereign Path was foaled. Sold as a yearling for 700 guineas, this grey was a leading miler, albeit a very highly strung one, who became a noted sire of sires worldwide. His dam, Mountain Path, had been procured for Theakston for 480 guineas and was responsible for Grischuna, one of the foundation mares of Gerry Oldham's Citadel Stud and the granddam of his triple Ascot Gold Cup hero, Sagaro.

Both Dante and Mountain Path, who lived to the ripe old age of thirty-one, are buried at Theakston. During their lifetime the stud was managed first by John McIntyre, who succeeded his father of the same name – John Jnr is Archie's grandson and Andrew's father.

Amongst the stallions to have stood at Theakston are the Scottish-trained Rockavon, who deprived Theakston-bred Prince Tudor of victory in the 1961 Two Thousand Guineas. It was a sensational result as both colts started at 66–1. In 1977 the One Thousand Guineas was won by Yorkshire-bred Mrs McArdy out of Theakston-bred Hanina, who was sold as a yearling for just 820 guineas.

For many years Andrew's aunt, Susan McIntyre, managed Copgrove Hall Stud, also in North Yorkshire, for owner-breeder Guy Reed. His breeding operation revolved around Sovereign Path's grey son, Warpath. In 2005 Guy Reed's homebred filly La Cucaracha won the Group 1 Nunthorpe Stakes and Theakston-bred Gift Horse won the Stewards' Cup. This represented a notable sprint double as Gift Horse was a half-brother to the dam of La Cucaracha, both of them bred by Theakston.

John McIntyre Jnr and Guy Reed both died in 2013 and John's sister Susan died in 2015.

JIMMY McLEAN

Sixty years a bookmaker in his native Glasgow, Jimmy McLean was readily identifiable from his flowing white hair and the cape he wore. He founded McLeans (The Bookmakers) Ltd of Glasgow and over that extended period his clients included such infamous Turf characters as Edgar Wallace, Horatio Bottomley and Bob Sievier.

At the time of his death aged eighty-six in December 1964, he was Honorary President of the Scottish Bookmakers' Protection Association. He had been assisted in the family business by his three sons – George, who predeceased him in 1953, had been seriously wounded as an officer in the Black Watch during the Second World War.

Jimmy was a much-respected figure in bookmaking circles and he was also very persuasive. He led a deputation to lobby the then Chancellor of the Exchequer, Winston Churchill, about the imposition of a betting tax, which was withdrawn shortly afterwards. And when not attending to the family business, he was actively engaged in charity work.

He was also an owner, his best-known horse being the entire, Flush Royal, whom he bought in France in 1948 as a three-year-old for about £35,000, a colossal sum in those days. The purchase was only sanctioned after protracted negotiations with the Treasury. It seems almost inconceivable that the powers that be did not have better things to do at the time.

Having finished third in the Prix du Jockey Club (French Derby), Flush Royal was beaten a head on his British debut in the Lanark Silver Bell by former compatriot, Tsaoko. Because his jockey, Rae Johnstone (flown over specially from France to Prestwick for the day), predicted the reversal, the colt's owner reduced his proposed wager from £10,000 to £2,000. Not many jockeys receive a present of £500 for losing on a fancied runner!

A versatile and consistent horse, Flush Royal won five of his ten races at six years, and six of his twelve races at seven years. In the interim he had been acquired at Tattersalls' 1951 December Sales for 2,200 guineas by the two bookmaker brothers, George and James McLean. For them he gained his crowning achievement by winning the following year's Cesarewitch, trained by Jack Fawcus at Middleham.

Retired to Highfield Stud, Oakham, Rutland, Flush Royal was put down in 1963 aged eighteen. His progeny made quite an impact under National Hunt Rules. One breeder who did particularly well with the stallion was Jack Fawcus's patron, Katherine Pitman from Lauder.

CHARLIE MANN

Charlie Mann is a maverick in the training ranks. A highly competent jump jockey, he became an even more successful trainer, based at his Whitcoombe House Stables, Upper Lambourn. He also has a number of successful business ventures to his credit.

Charlie Mann was born in Dumfries and brought up near St Boswells in the Buccleuch country, where he hunted as a boy with his training contemporary, David Arbuthnot. His father was a regular soldier in the King's Own Scottish

Borderers who served throughout the Second World War. His mother, a niece of Cuddy Stirling-Stuart (see Chapter 12), was an accomplished horsewoman in her day, representing the Scottish show-jumping team at White City; later she became a successful dealer in ponies.

Charlie left Sedbergh aged fifteen to pursue a career in racing. Following a brief spell with Peter Poston in Newmarket, he went to Yorkshire when he rode for Tony Gillam and David Chapman. In 1978 he became a conditional jockey for Nicky Henderson, who was then in his first season training, an arrangement that lasted for six years. He has remained in Lambourn ever since.

His first winner was Tony Gillam's La Valse over hurdles at Southwell in 1977. Much to his dismay, he was forced to hand in his licence after breaking his neck in a fall at Warwick in 1989. At the time he had 149 winners to his credit.

After a spell as assistant to Cath Walwyn in Lambourn, he trained and rode It's A Snip to win the awesome Velka Pardubicka in Czechoslovakia in October 1995, and his mother was there to watch him. 'Snippy' also finished second and third in the Pardubicka, which helped to bring his trainer's name to the fore, but the real flag-bearer proved to be multiple scorer, Celibate. His handler's all-time favourite, he pent his retirement at Whitcoombe.

Celibate provided his trainer with a first Grade 1 success when winning the BMW Chase at the Punchestown Festival in May 1999. Other top winners have included General Rusty (Charisma Gold Cup, Kempton Park), Keltic Bard (Scottish Champion Novices' Chase, Ayr), and Moral Support (Rehearsal Chase, Chepstow). Two more stars are Air Force One (Champion Novice Chase, Punchestown) and Moon Over Miami (November Novices' Chase, Cheltenham).

Two top flight professional jockeys to have been closely associated with the stable are champion Richard Dunwoody and champion conditional Noel Fehily, as well as former champion amateur, Dave Crosse. The day-to-day policy is to use the best available.

Charlie Mann recorded his best seasonal tally numerically in 2008–9 with sixty-three victories. Since then he has moved from Whitcombe House Stables to his present base at Neardown on the other side of the village.

Harvey Smith, husband of Sue Smith, and Nick Skelton, father of Dan and Harry, have shown that showjumping and jump racing are not necessarily poles apart but Charlie may think otherwise. In 2017 he was asked to prepare an enormously valuable showjumper for the Hickstead Derby in June, only for the grey to suffer a fatal heart attack.

TOM MASSON

Tom Masson took up training in England after working alongside his father, a Perthshire farmer. With a natural flair as a horseman, he gained considerable experience by schooling horses for Bertram Mills' Circus, prior to setting up his stall training at Lewes on the south coast.

In the 1930s he cured two equine miscreants for the celebrated trainer, George Lambton. Big Ben had been bought as a potential point-to-pointer for his son, Teddy, to ride but had proved an erratic jumper; and Damascus had a decidedly suspect temperament. Duly impressed, Lambton encouraged Masson to take out a licence to train in 1939.

Tom was also a good instructor. Three of his protégés were the top amateurs: John Hislop (see Chapter 24), Teddy Underdown and the leading Flat jockey Jimmy Lindley. In 1947 Tom dispatched John Hislop and Kami to finish third to Caughoo in the Grand National and he would very likely have saddled the winner at Aintree three years later had Cloncarrig not fallen at the penultimate fence. Cloncarrig was the best chaser he ever trained.

Equally adept at handling Flat horses, Tom had two very good performers who were both Astor cast-offs. The first was Shatter, winner of the Ascot Stakes and Brown Jack Stakes. The other was Persian War – he was sold on at a very handsome profit and duly won the Champion Hurdle in 1968, 1969 and 1970 to emulate Hatton's Grace and Sir Ken.

Few small trainers have horses of sufficient class to run in the Derby, but in 1962 the Lewes stable fielded not one but two runners, having never previously been represented in the premier classic. Unbelievably both Pindaric (Lingfield Derby Trial Stakes) and Persian Fantasy were brought down, along with the favourite, Hethersett, in the mêlée which occurred on the downhill approach to Tattenham Corner.

Tom Masson died in 1969 aged seventy-one following a car accident, whereupon his stable at Lewes was taken over by his son, Michael. He trained a mixed string until the mid-1980s but died young. One of his best winners was the top juvenile hurdler Varma (National Spirit Challenge Trophy, Fontwell Park), an appropriate winner of the Wyld Court and Tom Masson Trophy at Newbury.

However, Tom Masson's biggest legacy is human rather than equine. One of his stable men was Harry Hannon, who set up as a trainer in his own right at Collingbourne Ducis in Wiltshire. He is the father of Richard Hannon Snr, three times champion trainer, and his son Richard Hannon Jnr was champion trainer in 2014, the year he took over from his father.

JAMES MERRY

As the MP for Falkirk Burghs, James Merry (1805–77) was once summoned back to his native Scotland from his London home in Eaton Square to explain to members of his constituency in Falkirk why he had run a horse in France on the Sabbath. When it was explained that he would be spending the winnings north of the border all was forgiven.

Such was James Merry's involvement in racing that the then prime minister, Benjamin Disraeli, used to refer to him in the House of Commons as 'The Member for Thormanby'. His colt Thormanby triumphed in the 1860 Derby, a feat repeated by James Merry's Doncaster in 1873. Both horses went on to win the Gold Cup.

In the interim, his yellow colours were successful in two more Gold Cups with Buckstone (1863) and Scottish Chief (1864). The latter was a son of his owner's first classic winner, Lord of The Isles (Two Thousand Guineas), who sired another good colt in the same ownership in Dundee. He finished runner-up as favourite for the 1861 Derby, despite breaking down irrevocably in running.

A heavy gambler, James Merry had a mean and suspicious nature and trusted no one, least of all his many trainers. Two of them were Scotsmen, Mat Dawson, who trained Thormanby, and James Waugh, who trained Merry's second Two Thousand Guineas winner, Macgregor. Both men were to hand in their resignation as Merry's private trainer at Russley Park, outside Lambourn.

The highlight of Merry's racing career came in 1873 when Doncaster's Derby victory was augmented by Marie Stuart's classic double in the Oaks and St Leger. Due to poor health their owner decided to sell all his horses in 1875 – he sold Doncaster privately to his trainer, Robert Peck, for 10,000 guineas, and Marie Stuart to William Stirling-Crawfurd for 3,500 guineas.

James Merry had inherited a fortune from his father, an itinerant pedlar who had become a prosperous ironmaster. With a penchant for betting, be it on cockfighting or racing, his colours had a popular following as he ran his horses in a straightforward manner. The fact that he frequently blamed his jockeys for injudicious riding when they lost was another matter.

PETER MONTEITH

Although he trained a Cheltenham Festival winner in Dizzy – who landed the County Hurdle in 1994, only to break her neck in the Scottish Champion Hurdle a few weeks later – Peter Monteith regarded Musselburgh, Ayr and Kelso as his favourite courses. Based at Rosewell, just outside Edinburgh, he had Musselburgh on his doorstep.

A chartered surveyor by profession, he took out a licence to train in 1982 and after twenty-five years he recorded his first ever treble in March 2007 at Ayr. That was over jumps, but the stable, which was sponsored by Lithoprint, was equally adept at producing winners on the Flat. Four of the more notable ones were Moment of Truth, Rossel, Valdictory and Citaverde.

It was after doing well with some of David Johnson's cast-offs, bought at the sales, that this leading jumps owner from the south became Peter Monteith's number one patron. Two of his multiple winners, Standin Obligation and Marcel, were switched from David Pipe in the hope that the bracing Scottish air might help them to regain their form. And the ploy worked on other occasions too. Peter died in 2010.

PAT MULDOON

From Bo'ness on the southern shores of the Firth of Forth, Pat Muldoon, a wine importer and wholesale spirit merchant, will always be associated with Sea Pigeon. Originally bought out of Jeremy Tree's Beckhampton stable, he proved one of the most versatile racehorses of his or any other generation.

Sea Pigeon was sent first to Gordon Richards and then to Peter Easterby. An exceptionally versatile performer, the American-bred won sixteen Flat races and twenty-one over hurdles, highlighted by the 1980 and 1981

Champion Hurdles, as well as the Scottish and Welsh equivalents. He also won consecutive Chester Cups and the Ebor Handicap under a record weight of 10st. Sea Pigeon lived until he was thirty years of age and is buried at Habton Grange where Peter Easterby trained.

Pat Muldoon, who died in 2014, used to have a considerable number of horses in training, both Flat and jumping. His colours, 'McIntyre tartan, red sleeves and cap', were also successful with Sonnen Gold in the 1979 Gimcrack Stakes.

After a long absence these colours were successful on the Flat again when the syndicate-owned Embra scored at Ayr in July 2008.

JIM MULLION

Born in Scotland and educated at Calder Academy in Glasgow, James Robertson Mullion was a leading owner-breeder during the 1960s, together with his wife, Margaret. At one time they had homes in Hong Kong, Paris and Ireland.

A prominent figure in the international shipbroking world, Jim Mullion originally left Scotland for London. During the Second World War he became a member of a special committee set up by the British government which acquired ships from neutral countries to assist the Allied cause. In 1950 he moved to Hong Kong where he extended his own fleet to twenty-six vessels. His support and expertise were paramount in laying the foundations of Gibraltar as an international financial centre.

Jim Mullion's first horse was the two-year-old gelding, Stem, who was given to him in 1951 as a birthday present. Trained by Derrick Candy outside Lambourn, he scored twice that season and like so many of the Mullion runners carried the colours of his wife, Meg. Each had predominantly white colours incorporating the Robertson tartan.

Subsequently the Mullions based their bloodstock principally in Ireland and in 1956 they bought Ardenode Stud, Co. Kildare. The majority of their horses were trained by Paddy Prendergast, close by on the Curragh.

As owner-breeders, the Mullions were rewarded with five Irish classic winners in Ballymore (Two Thousand Guineas), Princess Pati (Oaks) together with Gazpacho, Wenduyne and Sarah Siddons, all of whom won the local One Thousand Guineas. The victories of Princess Pati and Ukraine Girl (French

One Thousand Guineas) came after Paddy Prendergast's death in 1980.

Their outstanding horse was Ragusa. Rejected by his American owner-breeder's trainer, Cecil Boyd-Rochfort, for being too small, this 3,800 guineas yearling won the Irish Derby, St Leger and King George VI and Queen Elizabeth Stakes to make Jim Mullion the leading owner of 1963. The following year Ragusa won the Eclipse Stakes. The son of Ribot retired to stand at Ballymore Eustace, where the Mullions built a separate stallion stud named after their champion.

Another yearling acquisition was Court Harwell. Trained by Sir Gordon Richards and racing in Jim's colours rather than those of his wife, he had the rare distinction of becoming a champion sire both at home and in the Argentine. Interim attempts to reacquire him for stud duties in Great Britain failed.

Other trainers to handle the Mullion horses were Robert Armstrong and John Dunlop in England, Robert Collet and Francois Boutin in France, and Irish-based Con Collins, Dessie Hughes, Jim Bolger and John Oxx.

ALAN MUNRO

A jockey of international standing, Alan Munro may have been born in York and brought up in Stevenage, but his roots are firmly in Scotland. His father, Angus, who was an electrical engineer with BAC (British Aircraft Corporation) and worked as a designer for Kodak, then moved to Rosyth. The family came from Paisley where his grandfather owned a jeweller's shop.

Angus's son, who served his apprenticeship with Barry Hills in Lambourn, is as well known in the Far East as he is in Great Britain. He first sprang to prominence when replacing Paul Cole's stable jockey, Richard Quinn, on the horses trained at Whatcombe for Prince Fahd Salman of Saudi Arabia. Only weeks later the new triumvirate won the 1991 Derby with Generous.

Before the summer was out, Generous had also won the Irish Derby and King George VI and Queen Elizabeth Diamond Stakes, to become the first to complete this high-profile treble in the same season. In the interim, owner, trainer and jockey achieved a remarkable juvenile treble at Royal Ascot with Dilum (Coventry Stakes), Magic Ring (Norfolk Stakes) and Fair Cop (Chesham Stakes).

Dilum proceeded to win the Richmond Stakes and over the next couple of seasons the new Whatcombe team had more juvenile success with Velvet

Moon (Lowther Stakes) and Splendent (Gimcrack Stakes), not to mention some major victories overseas.

For ten years from 1994, Alan Munro was based abroad, mostly in Hong Kong, under contract to the HK Jockey Club. He also rode regularly in Japan, South Africa and latterly in New Zealand. During that time he took a lengthy sabbatical from racing, achieving a black belt in karate and becoming a convert to Taoism, an age-old Chinese philosophy.

Back home for the 2005 season, he enjoyed the support of Peter Chapple-Hyam, for whom he had ridden in Hong Kong, and Rod Millman. It was for the West Country trainer that he won the 2005 Northumberland Plate, Ebor Handicap and Cesarewitch on Sergeant Cecil. The first horse to complete the treble in the same season, most unusually for a handicapper, he was voted 'Horse of the Year'.

In 2006 Alan Munro won the Irish Two Thousand Guineas and St James's Palace Stakes on Araafa. At Royal Ascot he also gained another success in the Norfolk Stakes, this time on Dutch Art, trained by Peter Chapple-Hyam. It was while en route to Deauville in a light aircraft to partner the colt in the Prix Morny (which the colt duly won) that he suffered a seizure, caused not from epilepsy as was first thought, but from a combination of low blood pressure and dehydration.

Not only did ill health jeopardise his riding career; it also almost certainly deprived him of a second Derby winner. Authorized was a stable companion and exact contemporary of Dutch Art, and then there were all the subsequent Group victories achieved by the ever-popular Sergeant Cecil.

For their erstwhile jockey, whose crouched style and whip technique used to be much more American than European, it was an unfortunate scenario. However, he was back in the saddle for the start of the 2008 Turf season and the winners soon rolled in, with Langs Lash (Queen Mary Stakes) augmenting his formidable record with two-year-olds at Royal Ascot.

LADY MURLESS

As the wife of Sir Noel Murless, the greatest trainer of his generation, Lady Murless played a pivotal role in her husband's success. Their daughter, Julie, was married to Henry Cecil, her father's successor at Warren Place.

Born and brought up in Ayrshire, Gwen Murless (née Carlow) enjoyed hunting and racing from an early age. However, both her parents came from business families in Glasgow: the Carlows were coal exporters and the Stevensons owned a stone quarry. Gwen's brother, Charles Carlow, was also an enthusiastic owner whose red colours with Cambridge blue cross-belts were well known on the Scottish circuit.

Noel and Gwen first met in their twenties after a memorable day's racing at Kelso in May 1935, when each owned a winner, Gwen with Golden Crown, whom she also trained, and Noel with Eagle Hill. Although that was the very year that Noel embarked upon his training career at Hambleton, Eagle Hill was actually trained by a friend, Roddy Fenwick-Palmer.

Amongst Noel's first winners in the pre-war years was his wife's Limace. This seven-year-old mare, who scored at Stockton in April 1939, had been given to Gwen by Sir Victor Sassoon as the mare had failed to breed – quite a coincidence, in view of Noel's future involvement with Sassoon's enormous bloodstock empire.

Early during his career, Noel took a lease on Cliff Stud at Helmsley, high on the North Yorkshire Moors near Thirsk, from local landowner, Lord Feversham. This arrangement endured until the lease was taken over by Henry Cecil. Two of the original mares were purchased at Newmarket in 1942, Congo for 130 guineas in September, and Cuddlededee for forty-five guineas in December.

It was Cuddlededee's son, Closeburn, who provided Noel Murless with one of his first major successes in the 1947 Stewards' Cup. Congo, whose half-brother, Nimbus, went on to triumph in the 1949 Two Thousand Guineas and Derby, was barren when Gwen bought her, but became a notable foundation mare with numerous stakes winners to her credit, all bred in Gwen's name and trained by her husband.

However, classic success for Gwen Murless came via a homebred mare who produced just one foal before being resold. Cheetah scored as a three-year-old after being sold by her breeder, the Queen, at the previous year's Newmarket July Sales for 460 guineas. She duly became the dam of Caerphilly and the latter bred Caergwrle (pronounced 'Caer-girlie') who was cleverly named after a village on the Welsh border.

This filly carried Gwen's distinctive colours of royal blue with lemon cross-belts to victory in the 1968 One Thousand Guineas, ridden by the Warren Place stable jockey, Sandy Barclay, also from Ayrshire. The preceding year her half-brother, St Chad, had proved a top miler. Both were sired by homebred Sassoon Derby winners trained by Noel Murless, Crepello and St Paddy, respectively. One of Caergwrle's descendants (Rajasinghe) won at Royal Ascot in 2017.

PETER NIVEN

With over 1,000 winners to his credit, Peter Niven is the top professional jump jockey to emerge from Scotland since the Second World War. At the close of the twentieth century he lay fifth behind Ulsterman Richard Dunwoody as the winning most rider.

Peter Niven was brought up in Angus, between Carnoustie (world famous for golf) and Arbroath (world famous for kippers). He was encouraged to ride from an early age by his mother Joan, who was district commissioner for the local Pony Club. However, he was to struggle with his weight throughout a distinguished race-riding career.

A pupil assistant to David Nicholson in Gloucestershire and then to Jimmy Fitzgerald at Malton, he subsequently became assistant trainer to Mary Reveley at Saltburn, and the great majority of his winners were saddled by the Cleveland trainer from the 1980s until his retirement in 2001.

Overall the Reveley stable was noted more for the quantity than the quality of its winners. Nonetheless, Peter rates one of them, Cab On Target, as the best he ever rode – he loved fast ground and had a great turn of foot. Additional Reveley winners included Marello, Firm Price and Batabanoo.

Cab On Target and Marello both won the Long Distance Hurdle, Ascot, and the West Yorkshire Hurdle, Wetherby. In fact the former won the Yorkshire race twice, as well as providing his regular partner with victories in the Mildmay Novice Chase, Liverpool, and the Champion Novice Chase, Ayr.

Peter Niven's solitary Cheltenham Festival winner was Monsieur Le Cure, trained by John Edwards, in the 1994 Royal & SunAlliance Novices' Chase. Another major victory over fences was recorded aboard Sybillin, trained by Jimmy Fitzgerald, in the Tingle Creek Chase at Sandown Park. There was also success in the 1997 Midlands Grand National on Seven Towers at the expense of Lord Gyllene, who triumphed at Aintree just three weeks later.

The popular Scotsman enjoyed his best ever season in 1992–3 with 108 winners – the previous season he recorded 105 wins from 420 mounts, a staggering ratio of one winner in every four rides. His very first winner was

Loch Brandy at Sedgefield in May 1984. It was at Mary Reveley's local course that he suffered the worst injury of his career, a broken neck.

Virtually all of Peter Niven's small string at Barton-le-Street, near Malton, are jumpers, but ironically the stable star Clever Cookie has proved an extremely good stayer on the Flat. Bred by his octogenarian mother from Carnoustie on Tayside, the winner of the Yorkshire Cup and Ormonde Stakes was still in training in 2017 at the age of nine. He was reared on the family farm in Angus.

KATHERINE PITMAN

Katherine Pitman – or more formally Mrs Ian Pitman of Allanbank at Lauder – had horses in training at Middleham, first with Jack Fawcus, who was born in Northumberland, and then with his erstwhile stable jockey, Jumbo Wilkinson.

The best-known horse to carry Kit Pitman's Graham tartan colours with a white cap was Quelle Chance. Bred by Jack Fawcus, he won sixteen races and finished second in the 1962 Champion Hurdle to the grey Anzio, and third the following year to the one-eyed Winning Fair, the mount of amateur Alan Lillingston.

Quelle Chance and Ruddy Alf, another multiple Pitman winner, were own-brothers by the French-bred Flush Royal, whom Jack Fawcus had saddled as a seven-year-old to win the 1952 Cesarewitch for the McLean brothers, the long-established Glasgow bookmakers. One week Quelle Chance and Ruddy Alf completed a splendid double at Doncaster and Newcastle.

Two more winners for Kit Pitman were Sand Link, an own-brother to Lady Hay's grand chaser, Goosander, and Thirsktown, who cost just twenty pounds – they won seven races apiece.

Of her homebreds, the most notable was the smart hurdler, Murgatroyd, whom Jumbo Wilkinson took over from Jack Fawcus when the latter died as the result of a motoring accident in 1967. Murgatroyd was the one and only foal that Mrs Pitman bred from her seventeen-year-old mare, Prejudice.

RICHARD QUINN

It is remarkable that two such outstanding Scottish Flat jockeys as Willie Carson and Richard Quinn should both hail from the historic town of Stirling.

Richard announced his retirement from the saddle aged forty-four after riding the 2,163rd winner of his career at Royal Ascot in 2006, but he was back in the winner's enclosure there twelve months later riding as a freelance. In the interim he had been treated for two slipped discs in his back.

He was champion apprentice in 1984, whilst serving his time with Paul Cole – they shared a highly rewarding seventeen years. Together they won a host of top races at home and abroad, many of the horses owned by Prince Fahd Salman, the principal patron of the Whatcombe stable at that time.

However, these excluded the 1991 Derby winner, Generous, the outstanding horse to be trained by Cole, as his owner chose to have Alan Munro (see above) to ride him. Richard Quinn had partnered the colt to win the Dewhurst Stakes, so this must have been a bitter blow, but one which he took philosophically.

Richard's English classic winners comprised Love Divine (2000 Oaks), in the first of four seasons as Henry Cecil's retained jockey, and two winners of the St Leger: Snurge (1990) for Paul Cole, and Millenary (2000) for John Dunlop.

He rode regularly for David Elsworth and teamed up on occasions with his great stayer, Persian Punch. He partnered three Irish classic winners, Knight's Baroness (1990 Oaks), and the St Leger duo, Ibn Bey (1990) and Strategic Choice (1995). His classic winners overseas include Paul Cole's Italian Derby victors, Zaizoom (1987) and Time Star (1994).

Three times runner-up in the domestic jockeys' table and fourth on the all-time list of jockeys never to be champion, Richard Quinn was held in the highest possible regard. On his premature and temporary retirement (having ridden in over twenty different countries) he became a 'horse whisperer' in the Monty Roberts tradition.

As a jockey, Richard has never been seriously injured, but ironically he then broke a leg out hunting with the Old Berks when qualifying the useful chaser, Scots Grey, for hunter chases. The grey proceeded to win that season's Fox Hunters' Chase at Aintree. Astonishingly Scots Grey was bred by Willie Carson!

ELSPETH RILEY-SMITH

During the 1960s and 1970s the Henderson tartan colours of Elspeth Riley-Smith were much to the fore in England and France.

The great majority were homebred by Elspeth and her husband, Douglas, at their Brewhurst Stud, near Billingshurst, in the Weald of Sussex. Virtually all of them were descended from the mare, Lemonade, whom her father-in-law had purchased for 920 guineas from King George V at the 1921 Newmarket December Sales, carrying her first foal.

Drink featured prominently as the Riley-Smith family fortune was owed to the Yorkshire brewery, John Smith's of Tadcaster, whose magnanimous sponsorship of racing used to include the Grand National.

Elspeth Riley-Smith owned some outstanding fillies including two winners of the Yorkshire Oaks in Tenacity and Parthian Glance, the One Thousand Guineas runner-up Hecuba, and the Oaks third Pouponne, all descendants of Lemonade. Two more relatives were the colts Knight Templar (Prix Gladiateur) and King Log (Gordon Stakes).

She also owned Roi Soleil (Queen Anne Stakes), who finished third to Nijinsky in the Two Thousand Guineas. The latter is the grandsire of the last top horse to carry her tartan colours, Sergeyevich, winner of the 1987 Goodwood Cup and Italian St Leger, and runner-up in the Ascot Gold Cup. He had a useful own-sister in Princess Sobieska (named after Bonnie Prince Charlie's mother).

In later years, Elspeth had horses trained in Sussex by John Dunlop, Ryan Price and Josh Gifford and she also boarded a few mares locally at the Macdonald-Buchanans' Lavington Stud, near Petworth. Another of her interests was breeding and showing goats.

Her father, Sir John Craik-Henderson, was a solicitor from Glasgow and he was MP for Leeds North during the 1940s. Chairman of the Scottish Conservative Party, he was knighted by the Queen after the war at the very first investiture ceremony over which Her Majesty presided.

EARL OF ROSSLYN

Francis Robert St Clair-Erskine, the 4th Earl of Rosslyn (1833–90) belonged to a leading Roman Catholic family in Scotland long ensconced at Dysart, an estate in Fife overlooking the northern shores of the Firth of Forth.

Rosslyn Chapel in Midlothian featured prominently in the best-selling novel, *The Da Vinci Code*. It was at the nearby Roslin Institute that Dolly the Sheep, the first living clone, was created – an experiment that could have catastrophic repercussions for Thoroughbred breeding.

Autocratic and charming in equal measure, Francis Rosslyn's standing in society was enhanced amongst the louche Marlborough House set as the stepfather of Daisy Warwick, one of the favourite paramours of the Prince of Wales (later King Edward VII). He was also reputed to employ the best cook in London.

Something of an expert when it came to bloodstock, Lord Rosslyn established a stud, Burleigh Paddocks at Brook End on part of the Countess of Warwick's Easton Estate, near Great Dunmow in Essex, where he acted as her agent. Unlike most Victorians, his involvement in bloodstock centred on breeding to sell rather than breeding to race, and he proved singularly successful.

Much the best horse he bred was Tristan, whom he sold as a yearling to a French patron of Tom Jennings' Newmarket stable. An extremely versatile performer, who proved himself over a wide variety of distances, Tristan won twenty-nine races, highlighted by the Gold Cup and July Cup. This horse with an uncontrollable temper was finally exported to Austria–Hungary, where he killed himself by banging his head against the wall of his stallion box.

Tristan's lasting testimonial was to sire that great matriarch, Canterbury Pilgrim, and another celebrity bred by Lord Rosslyn made his name as a broodmare sire – St Serf (1887), winner of the Epsom Grand Prize and Rous Memorial Stakes, Royal Ascot. Another of St Simon's progeny bred by Rosslyn and raced by the Duke of Portland was the 1893 Oaks heroine, Mrs Butterwick – she also made her mark at stud.

The present Lord Rosslyn (the 7th Earl) is better known as Commander Peter Loughborough, head of the Royalty Protection Squad and holder of the Queen's Police Medal. Another surprise is that the Rosslyns are related to the Scudamores, that family of eminent National Hunt jockeys from Herefordshire.

CHARLIE SCOTT

Charlie Scott's name is synonymous with The Callant, one of the top hunter-chasers of all time.

The Borders farmer from Mossburn Ford, near Jedburgh, owned and bred this iconic grey, who won sixteen chases and seventeen point-to-points,

APPENDIX

highlighted by the 1956 and 1957 Cheltenham Foxhunters'. He was ridden on both occasions by Jimmy Scott-Aiton, who farmed at Legerwood, near Lauder.

A great local favourite sired by St Michael, a premium stallion for the Buccleuch Hunt, The Callant was qualified with the Jedforest and early on he had the distinction of winning two major hunter chases in the same season, the Heart of All England at Hexham, and the Buccleuch Cup at Kelso.

The Callant's first and last victories were at the local Lauderdale fixture at Mosshouses. As Charlie Scott was more interested in hunting than racing, The Callant only went to be trained professionally by Stewart Wight after inadvertently kicking his owner when having a tail bandage applied – an incident that required Scott to spend a spell in hospital.

A top rider over jumps himself, Charlie Scott knew all about close finishes in the Cheltenham Foxhunters'. In 1953 he had dead-heated on Dunboy and in 1970 his nephew, Peter Elliot, a farmer high up in the Cheviots, was beaten a short head on homebred Jedheads, whose dam was an own-sister to The Callant.

Ironically Charlie had had to pull up Merryman, the best horse he ever rode, in the 1959 Cheltenham Foxhunters' before winning the equivalent Liverpool version a few weeks later. The following year Merryman triumphed in the Grand National, ridden by the Middleham-based professional Gerry Scott (no relation).

IAN SEMPLE

Ian Semple managed to transform a bleak hilltop farm at Carluke, near Hamilton, in what is now designated South Lanarkshire, into the most successful Flat yard north of the border – Gordon McDowall's Belstane Racing Stables, which has certainly had its share of ups and downs in recent times.

At the age of fifteen, having never ridden before, Ian left his native Glasgow to become an apprentice with Dick Hern in Berkshire. Serious injury prevented him pursuing a career as a jockey, but anxious to remain in racing he became a key member of staff first for John Dunlop and then for John Gosden.

Assistant to Gosden at Newmarket when Benny The Dip won the 1997

369

Derby, he returned to Scotland to start up on his own as a salaried trainer. Having been associated with three of the most powerful stables in the land, his fledgling operation must have been in stark contrast. As he recalls, it proved a long, hard struggle: 'It took us three years to fill ten boxes and nearly ten years to fill forty.'

In 2006 the expanding Semple stable recorded a first Group success with the gelded Big Timer winning the recently elevated Acomb Stakes at the York Ebor Meeting, while Appalachian Trail won a Listed race at Newmarket. Of course bread and butter winners were more commonplace, like Chookie Heiton, dual winner of the Beverley Bullet, and Kelburne.

Latterly Ian Semple, whose best season was in 2006 when he saddled forty-nine winners, had a worrying time, incurred by litigation over a serious injury that Chris Kinane received in the paddock at Wolverhampton in April 2005 when kicked in the head by one of Semple's runners – the dispute was eventually settled out of court.

Meanwhile, the future for Belstane Racing Stables looked in jeopardy. Briefly they were taken over by Linda Perratt to whom Semple remained an assistant, and he was then reinstated before it was announced that Yorkshire trainer Noel Wilson would be taking up residence. However, Wilson was to move to Co. Durham instead and eventually Beltane embarked upon a new era of prosperity under Keith Dalgleish (see Chapter 34).

ARCHIE SMITH-MAXWELL

A very experienced stockman who died in 2013, Archie Smith-Maxwell, was equally *au fait* with livestock as bloodstock. One of the saviours of Irish Draught horses in Britain, he won prizes with his pedigree sheep and cattle at the Royal Show on numerous occasions.

Home for the Smith-Maxwells was Craigend Castle, Milngavie, outside Glasgow (home also to the well-known Scottish owner Sandy Struthers), but Archie himself was brought up in Cheshire – he was born at Tarvin near Chester, but spent most of his childhood at Bunbury on the other side of Tarporley.

One of Archie's grandfathers had served in the Boer War, the other grandfather and an uncle had both been killed on the Somme, and his father had seen action in the Second World War. Archie also joined the army as a young man – he served in the Royal Dragoons until 1949, buying his home,

Welland Lodge Farm, Upton-on-Severn, in Worcestershire, soon afterwards.

Archie has bred Group winners at home and abroad with never more than two or three broodmares. His entrée into breeding Thoroughbreds came when the smart race mare, Last Case, was given to him as a present and her first two foals for him were Final Call and On Stage.

A top sprinter, On Stage won ten races including the Palace House Stakes and Group 1 Natal Flying Championship in South Africa, where he was a successful sire. A minor juvenile winner herself, Final Call became a worthy foundation mare with a dozen winners to her credit.

By comparison, Happy Lady cost a substantial 50,000 guineas at the 2001 Tattersalls' December Sales. She is the dam of the smart Penny's Gift, winner of the 2009 German One Thousand Guineas as well as the Bosra Sham Stakes, Newmarket, and Watership Down Stud Sales Race, Newbury.

JOHN SORRIE

John Park Sorrie, who left school aged fourteen, reckoned that his Middlefield stables, outside Inverurie in Aberdeenshire, made him not only the most northerly trainer in Great Britain, but probably in the world. Nowadays Jackie Stephen trains there.

For John Sorrie training was a wonderful relaxation from his business as a turkey farmer and he was amazingly successful with horses whom he not only owned but also bred. From 1950, when first taking out a licence, he saddled a host of winners in Scotland carrying his 'white, scarlet diamonds, quartered cap'. It was only because of pressure of business that he relinquished his licence in 1965.

His most noted performer was the entire, Windyedge, whose ten victories included the Royal Burgh of Ayr Handicap at the prestigious Western Meeting. Glenythan also won fourteen races and bred a smart juvenile in Fair Scot. Another prolific winner was Abernicky – bought at Newmarket for just 110 guineas as a two-year-old, he proceeded to score ten times.

Remarkably Windyedge and Glenythan were not only homebred, but were also sired by John Sorrie's own stallion Rocket, who stood initially with Archibald Macdonald, first at Lossiemouth in Morayshire, before moving next door to John Sorrie. An unraced grey by Felicitation, Rocket died in 1969 at the advanced age of twenty-eight.

In his final season John Sorrie saddled The Spaniard, a three-year-old, to score a hat-trick of victories in Scotland prior to being sold at the Doncaster Sales in August for 1,900 guineas, en route to Ken Oliver's stable. One of the most prolific winners ever trained at Hassendean Bank, his nineteen victories for the stable included the 1970 Scottish Grand National.

DAVID SPENCE

A retired hotelier from Newton of Forbes, near Alford, Aberdeenshire, beside the River Don (the best brown-trout river in Scotland), David Spence and his father Charles shared ownership of that outstanding sprinter Lochnager.

Lochnager was called after a mountain on the Balmoral Estate in Aberdeenshire, but unfortunately the name was registered incorrectly with Weatherbys – the spelling should have been Lochnagar. Evidently it was Lord Byron's poem 'Dark Lochnagar' that first inspired Queen Victoria's love affair with Deeside and the Highlands.

Lochnager's trainer, Mick Easterby, sold the colt privately to David Spence as a foal, with the toss of a coin determining that the price was 1,800 guineas rather than 1,600 guineas. However, David got the best of the deal in the long term as this unfashionably bred colt was duly syndicated for £260,000 to stand at the Easterby family's Easthorpe Hall Stud at Malton in Yorkshire for the 1977 covering season.

The previous year, Lochnager had become the champion sprinter of Europe. Indeed, he became the first horse to win the King's Stand Stakes, July Cup and Nunthorpe Stakes (all these races now rank as Group 1) in the same season since the mighty Abernant back in 1949. Lochnager, who enjoyed only limited success at stud, died in 1994 aged twenty-two.

Like that other Aberdeenshire breeder, the late John Sorrie, David Spence was used to having stallions as well as mares at his Forbes Arms Stud. Breeding stock for both Flat racing and jumping, one of the best was Stearsby, winner of the 1986 Welsh National.

DAVID STEVENSON

In corporate terms, David Stevenson has been one of the leading Scottish-based owners of National Hunt horses in Great Britain, with as many as fifty horses in a single season divided between Len Lungo, Nicky Richards, Venetia Williams, Paul Nicholls, Malcolm Jefferson and Bruce Mactaggart. Nowadays he has horses in the name of Ashleybank Investments Limited, which he runs from his home at Langholm in Dumfriesshire.

A former Olympic and Commonwealth Games pole vaulter, David was founder of the Edinburgh Woollen Mill Limited, formerly a dye company owned by his father. Specialising in the manufacture and sale of Scottish knitwear from its Waverley Mills at Langholm, the business at one time had 280 retail outlets throughout the country with a flagship store on Edinburgh's Princes Street. In addition there was a large mail order business.

As the executive responsible for the firm's involvement in racing, David became one of the most familiar faces on northern jump courses, and the well-known Edinburgh Woollen Mill's colours of 'beige, brown hooped sleeves, orange cap' were carried by such prolific scorers as Tartan Tailor, The Langholm Dyer and Randolph Place.

All were trained by Gordon Richards at Penrith and invariably ridden by stable jockey Phil Tuck. Sponsored by the Edinburgh Woollen Mill (which also used to sponsor the Scottish National), Phil Tuck once equalled the record of ten straight wins under NH Rules. It was another memorable occasion when connections gained an initial Cheltenham Festival victory with Tartan Tailor in the 1987 Supreme Novices' Hurdle.

In 1996–7 the Stevenson family sold the Edinburgh Woollen Mill and transferred the racing interests to its parent company, Ashleybank Investments, with most of the horses joining Len Lungo's local stable. That combination was rewarded by many multiple scorers, amongst them the evergreen The Bajan Bandit, Direct Access and Crazy Horse. And Gordon Richards' son, Nicky, has saddled another prolific scorer in Telemoss.

ALEC STEWART

The premature death from cancer in 2004 of Alec Stewart, aged forty-nine, deprived the Newmarket training ranks of an extremely capable and popular figure.

Alec was the eldest son of Robert Stewart from Dollar, a territorial colonel in the Argyll and Sutherland Highlanders and a one-time

Lord Lieutenant for Kinross-shire. His family had no connections with racing, and he was not the first young man to leave the City of London for a training career – or indeed to have attended the Royal Agricultural College, Cirencester.

A chance meeting with Gavin Hunter resulted in Alec becoming his pupil assistant at East Ilsley in Berkshire, before moving onto Newmarket to assist Harry Thomson Jones. Remaining in Newmarket, he took out a licence to train on his own account at Moulton Paddocks (later a base for Godolphin horses) in 1983, going to Clarehaven three years later.

One of the horses that made the short journey between the two stables was Sheikh Ahmed Al Maktoum's backward three-year-old, Mtoto, whom Alec had selected as a yearling for 110,000 guineas. He was at the zenith of his powers as a five-year-old in 1988 winning the 'King George' and the Eclipse Stakes (which he had won the previous season). An unlucky runner-up in the Prix de l'Arc de Triomphe, his only reversal that season, he was voted 'Horse of the Year'.

Mtoto's handler also did well with Opale (Irish St Leger), another son of Busted. Three of his leading horses won the September Stakes: Mutamam (whose dam was a half-sister to Mtoto) twice, Wagon Master and Mtoto's son, Maylane. Amongst the top fillies he trained was Dubian, destined to become the dam of champion filly, Sayyedati.

Following a period in the wilderness for Godolphin as a four-year-old, Mutamam returned to Alec Stewart only to prove better than ever over the next two seasons, culminating in a magnificent victory as a six-year-old entire in the Grade 1 Canadian International at Woodbine. This was a nostalgic occasion for Alec as he had worked with horses in Alberta when he was younger.

One of Alec's undoubted strengths was his patience and willingness to give horses plenty of time. Fortunately that met with the approval of his principal patron, Sheikh Ahmed, owner of the Aston Upthorpe Stud in Oxfordshire, where Mtoto went to stud. Retired from stallion duties at the advanced age of twenty-four in 2007, he sired a Derby winner (Shaamit) and a Gold Cup winner (Celeric).

The former master of Clarehaven, who was a close personal friend of his Newmarket colleague, Luca Cumani, is commemorated by the Alec Stewart Nursery at Newmarket's Cesarewitch Meeting in the autumn.

BILL STIRLING

Bill Stirling chose to spend most of his life in the West End of London (he lived in Mayfair) and was a much more frequent visitor to his clubs, White's, Guards and Buck's, than to his native Scotland. He had migrated south from Ochtertyre in Stirlingshire via school at Ampleforth in North Yorkshire, and Trinity College, Cambridge.

Bill and his brother David volunteered for the Commandos during the Second World War, as did a number of other members of White's, who readily forsook their creature comforts in St James's for the rigours of training on some bleak Scottish moor.

The Stirling brothers gained almost legendary status in the desert with a reputation for dispatching German sentries with the same finesse that they had applied in their youth to strangling rabbits. David Stirling was the founder of the SAS.

As an owner-breeder, Bill enjoyed a particular connection with Sussex. Not only were a number of his horses trained latterly by John Dunlop at Arundel, but he also boarded his mares at Yarbrook Stud, near Chichester, with Sandy Scratchley, who acted as his stud and racing manager – he was also manager to the Duke and Duchess of Norfolk at their Angmering Park Stud, close to Arundel.

No horse carried Bill's black and blue halved colours with more distinction than Sing Sing. Trained by Jack Watts at Newmarket, this homebred Tudor Minstrel colt was unbeaten in six juvenile starts, culminating with the Cornwallis Stakes, and became an outstanding stallion based at the Macdonald-Buchanans' Lavington Stud, also in Sussex. With the likes of Mummy's Pet and Song, his sons were noted sires of sprinters.

When she was twenty years of age, Agin The Law, the homebred dam of Sing Sing, produced his very close relative, Burglar. Bill Stirling sent him to John Dunlop and he excelled at Newmarket, winning the July Stakes and the Challenge Stakes. The latter victory was a splendid bonus for David Wills who had bought him as a potential stallion, in which role he proved rather disappointing.

FERGUS SUTHERLAND

Fergie Sutherland, who died in 2012, enjoyed the greatest day of his racing life when Imperial Call beat Rough Quest to win the 1996 Cheltenham

Gold Cup. The following month Rough Quest proceeded to win the Grand National.

Imperial Call was just one of half a dozen horses that Fergie trained at his home in Ireland, Aghinagh House, Killinardrish, Co. Cork. It was a triumph for a small stable and a good old-fashioned stamp of chaser, who also won three Grade 1 chases in Ireland, the Hennessy Cognac Gold Cup at Leopardstown and a couple at Punchestown. Nowadays there is an Imperial Call Chase staged over three miles at Cork.

Ireland had become Fergie's adopted home following the death of his father, a retired colonel in the Black Watch, in 1962, when the family home at Cringletie in Peeblesshire was sold. Here Fergie was born and brought up until leaving Eton for the Royal Military College, Sandhurst, before joining the 5th Royal Inniskilling Dragoon Guards.

He saw active service in Korea, where he had the misfortune to lose a leg in action (despite which he still managed to win the Melton Hunt Club cross-country race), and in Egypt during the Suez crisis. In the mid-1950s he went as a pupil assistant to Geoffrey Brooke at Newmarket's Clarehaven Lodge. It was during those four seasons that the latter saddled Our Babu to win the Two Thousand Guineas.

In 1958 Fergie took out a licence to train on his own account at Carlburg Stables, which like Clarehaven Lodge is on the Bury Road. His predecessor there was the great Joe Lawson, who helped him enormously. Previously based at Manton, where he trained a succession of classic winners, Lawson had dispatched Never Say Die from Carlburg to triumph in the 1954 Derby and St Leger.

The new man in charge at Carlburg made a fairytale start when A.20 justified favouritism in the 1958 Queen Mary Stakes at Royal Ascot. It was significant that this juvenile filly should have provided her trainer with the most prestigious victory of his short Flat training career as his mentor, Geoffrey Brooke, was recognised as the master trainer of two-year-olds at that time.

Fergie Sutherland trained another good filly in Tournella, winner of the 1962 Falmouth Stakes during his final season at Newmarket. He also enjoyed conspicuous success at Manchester, where Erinite made a handsome contribution to his tally of winners on the now defunct Castle Irwell course.

DAVID THOM

Dave Thom, whose training career in Newmarket spanned forty years from 1960 to 2000, died aged seventy-nine in February 2005. Originally from Pollokshields, a suburb of Glasgow, he served as a Royal Marine Commando during the Second World War and participated in the Normandy landings on D-Day.

In the 1950s, following experience travelling premium stallions around the country, he and his first wife, Beryl, ran a livery yard near Saffron Walden for point-to-pointers, many of whom he rode himself. In 1960 he took out a licence to train from a farm near Newport in Essex, but the following season he moved to Newmarket.

Initially he operated from stables close to the town centre, but he then switched to Harraton Court Stables, at Exning. For the last couple of seasons he was at neighbouring Exeter Stables, by which time Hugh Collingridge had succeeded him at Harraton Court, where Dave would have the occasional horse in training.

Small of stature with a moustache and invariably attired in a sheepskin coat during the winter months, Dave Thom proved a highly proficient trainer against all the odds. (When Barney Curley first arrived in Newmarket from Ireland, he was the assistant trainer.) In those bygone days Newmarket had a distinct hierarchy and it would not have been easy for an outsider to get established, but get established he did, in double-quick time.

The mare Narratus helped to get him noticed by winning the 1962 Great Metropolitan Handicap, Epsom, and the 1963 Chester Cup. Two years later he won the Bessborough Stakes, Royal Ascot, Moet & Chandon Silver Magnum, Epsom and Doncaster Cup with Prince Hansel, who excelled on soft ground and became a jumping sire in Ireland.

Later he trained two speedy juveniles in Forty Winks – runner-up to subsequent Two Thousand Guineas winner, Nebbiolo, in the Gimcrack Stakes – and the grey Absent Chimes, winner of the Molecomb Stakes. Another grey was that good sprint handicapper, Touch of Grey (Wokingham Stakes, Royal Ascot).

One of just a handful of trainers in Newmarket to have jumpers, Dave Thom had an exceptional young chaser in the mid-1960s with Master Mascus. A top novice, he won the Compton Chase, Newbury, and Tote

Investors' Chase, Ascot. He was pulled up after starting favourite for the Totalisator Champion Chase (later Royal & SunAlliance) at the National Hunt Meeting at Cheltenham. A post-race examination revealed that the gelding had been doped.

LORD AND LADY WEIR

Chairman and chief executive of the Weir Group and a member of the Royal Company of Archers (the Queen's Bodyguard for Scotland), the 3rd Lord Weir from Kilwinning, near Ayr, had horses in training locally with Harry Whiteman, as well as with Ryan Price at Findon in Sussex.

The Weirs enjoyed a sensational year in 1969 and seldom can a husband and wife have experienced such a contrasting run of good fortune, the former with a brilliant unbeaten two-year-old and the latter with a top-class staying chaser. The success of these two very different horses certainly demonstrated the consummate skill of their trainer, Ryan Price.

Ironically, Quarryknowe, who gained his most important success in the National Stakes, Sandown Park, made the first and the last of his five juvenile starts at Ayr, in May and September (Ladykirk Stakes). Unfortunately this grey, who had cost a bargain 1,900 guineas as a yearling, failed to train on and was eventually exported to Australia.

Just two months before Quarryknowe made his first public appearance, Lady Weir's What A Myth bid a sensational farewell to the racecourse. Encountering the soft ground that he relished, the twelve-year-old triumphed in the Cheltenham Gold Cup to become the joint oldest horse (with Silver Fame) ever to win the Blue Riband of steeplechasing. He was retired immediately afterwards.

Lucy Weir had become the outright owner of What A Myth, who was bred by Fawley Stud (see Chapter 25), when paying 4,200 guineas at the Ascot Sales in November 1964 to buy out her partner in the seven-year-old gelding, Sir Archibald James. A veteran of the Royal Flying Corps, he lived near Ryan Price in Sussex and introduced the Weirs to him.

In 1967 the Findon trainer found himself in deep water when Hill House finished first in the Schweppes Gold Trophy at Newbury, only to record a positive dope test for cortisone afterwards. Appalled at the treatment meted out to their trainer, the Weirs offered financial assistance for any legal expenses. Furthermore Lucy Weir acquired expert evidence confirming that such high levels of cortisone could be produced naturally; Ryan Price was duly exonerated.

The Weirs' involvement in racing was maintained by their son, George, and his wife, Jane, daughter of Lord Kilmany. George owned some useful performers under both Rules, notably Crimson Silk, dual winner of the Canada Dry Shield at Ayr. Other notable successes came with the half-brothers Clued Up and The Engineer. They were homebred out of Sage Warbler, from whom Lord Kilmany bred Mischievous Monk.

Now deceased, George Weir was a member of the Jockey Club and a steward at various racecourses including Newmarket and Ayr.

LADY WESTBROOK

Lady Westbrook, who died in 2004, was the only daughter of the 1st Lord Strathalmond, who was born William Fraser. His family came from Glasgow and he was chairman of British Petroleum during and after the Second World War. A man of sporting tastes, he chose to have a stag, a pheasant and a grouse on his coat of arms.

Joan Westbrook of Pumpherston, West Lothian, and her husband, Sir Neil Westbrook (knighted in 1988, died in 2014), a one-time mayor of Manchester, shared a love of racing and breeding and all their bloodstock activities were indelibly linked with the Easterby family from Yorkshire.

The Westbrooks started breeding in the 1960s, boarding their animals at Stockwell Stud, Tadcaster, first with Walter Easterby and then with his son, Henry. Subsequently the mares were transferred to Easthorpe Hall Stud, Malton, owned by Peter Easterby – he trained their horses until succeeded by his son, Tim.

The Westbrook horses invariably had the first name Bollin, taken from the river flowing through their Cheshire home, Castle Hill, Prestbury. The second name of their horses was usually that of some relative. While most of their winners stem from Bollin Charlotte, who was acquired back in 1965, Bollin Zola, a yearling purchase in 1987, proved even more significant as a broodmare.

Bollin Zola has played a leading role in Tim Easterby's training career as the dam of Bollin Joanne (Duke of York Stakes), his first stakes winner as well as his first Group winner, while the latter's half-brother, Bollin Eric (2002 St Leger), was his first classic winner.

Named after a cousin, Bollin Eric, who became the first northern-trained winner of the St Leger since Peleid in 1973, retired to stand at the National Stud where his sire, Shaamit, had also embarked upon his stud career. Bollin Eric was later transferred to Norton Grove Stud outside Malton, where he was trained.

Not only was Joan Westbrook an enthusiastic and successful breeder of racehorses on a strictly limited budget, but in her younger days she also owned a prize herd of pedigree Aberdeen Angus cattle. Never keen for her horses to run in any sort of appendages, she had an abhorrence of any superfluous nosebands, blinkers, tongue-straps or cheek-pieces.

This popular lady is commemorated by the Joan Westbrook Lecture Theatre at the National Stud, as well as a race at her favourite course, Haydock Park.

LADY WHENT

Although Lady Whent does not consider herself to be Scottish, she recalls that her father most certainly did – as a member of the Macdonald clan he never forgave the Campbells of Glen Lyon, acting on the instructions of King William III, for the Glencoe massacre of 1692!

More relevant to the present day is that her father, Teddy Donaldson, whose family hailed from Haddington, was an air commodore in the RAF. Like him, two of his three brothers were highly decorated Battle of Britain pilots during the Second World War. Subsequently, Teddy Donaldson had the added distinction of establishing a new world air speed record, flying a Meteor jet.

The success which his daughter, Sarah, has enjoyed as an owner-breeder is owed to a filly whom she procured privately for just £600 from Lord McAlpine (see Chapter 23) of Dobson's Stud, near Henley-on-Thames, where Sarah and her husband, Sir Gerry Whent, the founder of long-time Derby sponsor, Vodafone, were then living.

From Daring Ditty, Sarah Whent bred the very speedy Bold Edge (Prix Maurice de Gheest, Cork & Orrery Stakes, Diadem Stakes). He retired to her Raffin Stud, near Lambourn. Despite fertility problems, he sired another good homebred sprinter in Assertive, winner of the 2008 Duke of York Stakes, who succeeded his own sire at Throckmorton Court Stud in Worcestershire following the latter's death. Both Bold Edge and Assertive were trained by Richard Hannon Snr.

Lady Whent's right-hand man at Raffin Stud was her long-standing stud groom, Robert Irvine, who came with her to Raffin from her Horris Vale Stud, south of Newbury. Originally from Galashiels, Rob has a racing background, having previously worked for Scotland's two greatest NH trainers, Stewart Wight at Grantshouse, before becoming head lad to Ken Oliver at Hawick.

Lady Whent sold her stud in December 2016 whereupon it was renamed Carisbrooke Stud. The new manager there and joint partner in the business is Charlie Oakshott (see Chapter 2), who had previously been running Hungerford Park Stud just down the road.